EDGAR ALLAN POE: THE CRITICAL HERITAGE

THE CRITICAL HERITAGE SERIES

General Editor: B. C. Southam

The Critical Heritage series collects together a large body of criticism on major figures in literature. Each volume presents the contemporary responses to a particular writer, enabling the student to follow the formation of critical attitudes to the writer's work and its place within a literary tradition.

The carefully selected sources range from landmark essays in the history of criticism to fragments of contemporary opinion and little published documentary material, such as letters and diaries.

Significant pieces of criticism from later periods are also included in order to demonstrate fluctuations in reputation following the writer's death.

EDGAR ALLAN POE

THE CRITICAL HERITAGE

Edited by

IAN WALKER

London and New York

First published in 1986
Reprinted in 1997 by Routledge

11 New Fetter Lane
London EC4P 4EE
&
29 West 35th Street
New York, NY 10001

Compilation, introduction, notes and index © 1986 Ian Walker

Printed in Great Britain by
TJ Press, Padstow, Cornwall

Printed on acid-free paper

British Library Cataloguing in Publication Data

ISBN 0-415-15929-6

General Editor's Preface

The reception given to a writer by his contemporaries and near-contemporaries is evidence of considerable value to the student of literature. On one side we learn a great deal about the state of criticism at large and in particular about the development of critical attitudes towards a single writer; at the same time, through private comments in letters, journals or marginalia, we gain an insight upon the tastes and literary thought of individual readers of the period. Evidence of this kind helps us to understand the writer's historical situation, the nature of his immediate reading-public, and his response to these pressures.

The separate volumes in the *Critical Heritage Series* present a record of this early criticism. Clearly, for many of the highly productive and lengthily reviewed nineteenth- and twentieth-century writers, there exists an enormous body of material; and in these cases the volume editors have made a selection of the most important views, significant for their intrinsic critical worth or for their representative quality – perhaps even registering incomprehension!

For earlier writers, notably pre-eighteenth century, the materials are much scarcer and the historical period has been extended, sometimes far beyond the writer's lifetime, in order to show the inception and growth of critical views which were initially slow to appear.

In each volume the documents are headed by an introduction, discussing the material assembled and relating the early stages of the author's reception to what we have come to identify as the critical tradition. The volumes will make available much material which would otherwise be difficult of access and it is hoped that the modern reader will be thereby helped towards an informed understanding of the ways in which literature has been read and judged.

B.C.S.

In lieu of the rest I venture to place in your hands the published opinions of many of my contemporaries. I will not deny that I have been careful to collect & preserve them. They include, as you will see, the warm commendations of a great number of very eminent men, and of these commendations, I should be at a loss to understand why I have not a right to be proud.

(Poe to Charles Anthon, late October 1844)

Poe was sensitive to opinion. He sought, at least, as I often witnessed, with an intense eagerness the smallest paragraph in a newspaper touching himself or his writings. What if he had lived a little longer to enjoy the European fame which his works were on the eve of receiving when he died. A few months longer and 'Fame that the clear spirit doth raise' might have proved the beacon and incentive to a better and higher life.

(MS. Diary of E.A. Duyckinck, 1 November 1875)

Contents

CONTENTS

ix

CONTENTS

CONTENTS

CONTENTS

Preface and Acknowledgments

The materials gathered together in this book constitute the primary record of Poe's literary reputation in America and Europe between the publication of his first volume of poetry, *Tamerlane and Other Poems* (1827), and Griswold's edition of *The Works of the Late Edgar Allan Poe* (1850). I have included in the collection all the significant reviews and critiques of Poe and his work that I have been able to locate, together with many minor and even desultory notices, and I have endeavoured wherever possible to identify the reviewer. I have also included such items as letters, publicity devices, biographical accounts, obituary notices and Poe's own prefaces – in short, anything that could be helpful in shedding light on Poe's contemporaneous reputation as a writer and literary personality, or on the chaotic literary milieu in which he created his art. It should be borne in mind, while consulting this collection, that the literary environment in which Poe wrote and published was anything but conducive to fair or constructive reviewing, and many of the reviews and notices he received derived from public and private allegiances and antagonisms.

In writing this book I have sustained many obligations both to individuals and to libraries and institutions which I am now pleased to acknowledge. The following libraries provided me with many courtesies and much assistance: Amherst College Library, the British Library, the Library of Congress, the Free Library of Philadelphia, The Historical Society of Pennsylvania, the John Rylands University Library of Manchester, Manchester Central Library, New York Historical Society, New York Public Library, University of North Carolina Library, Ohio Historical Society, Virginia Historical Society, Virginia State Library, and the Alderman Library, University of Virginia. I am also grateful to the New York Public Library, Astor, Lenox and Tilden Foundations, for permission to quote from the MS. Diary of

E.A. Duyckinck. A grant from the University of Manchester Staff Travel Fund enabled me to consult library resources. Liselotte Marshall provided invaluable help with the translation of E.D. Forgues' essay (No. 66); but of all the many individuals who have helped me with advice and assistance over the years, my greatest debt is to Burton Pollin: his generosity and patience never failed, and this book owes much to his willingness to allow me to ransack his encyclopaedic knowledge of Poe and his world.

Abbreviations

The following abbreviations have been used throughout:

(*Works*) *The Complete Works of Edgar Allan Poe*, ed. James A. Harrison, 17 vols (New York, 1902).

(*Poems*) *The Collected Works of Edgar Allan Poe*, Vol. 1, *Poems*, ed. Thomas O. Mabbott (Cambridge, Mass., 1969).

(*Letters*) *The Letters of Edgar Allan Poe*, ed. John Ostrom, 2 vols (New York, 1966).

Introduction

FRUSTRATIONS OF AUTHORSHIP

Writing in October 1844 to Charles Anthon, the eminent classical scholar, Poe related a pitiful, though not entirely trustworthy, account of the privations and disadvantages he bravely endured in his career as a magazinist in America:

... Thus I have written no books and have been so far essentially a Magazinist – bearing not only willingly but cheerfully sad poverty & the thousand consequent ills and contumelies which the condition of the mere Magazinist entails upon him in America – where more than any other region upon the face of the globe to be poor is to be despised.

The one great difficulty resulting from this course, is that unless the journalist collects his various articles he is liable to be grossly misconceived and misjudged by men of whose good opinion he would be proud – but who see, perhaps, only a paper here and there, by accident – often only one of his mere extravaganzas, written to supply a particular demand. He loses, too, whatever merit may be his due on the score of *versatility* – a point which can only be estimated by collection of his various articles in volume form and altogether. ...

Setting aside, for the present, my criticisms poems & miscellanies (sufficiently numerous) my tales a great number of which might be termed Phantasy Pieces, are in number sixty-six. They would make, perhaps, 5 of the ordinary novel volumes. I have them prepared in every respect for the press; but, alas, I have no money, nor that influence which would enable me to get a publisher – although I seek *no* pecuniary remuneration. (*Letters*, 1, 270–1)

He closed with an appeal for Anthon to intercede with the publishers Harper & Brothers and persuade them to bring out a new collection of his tales. Although he was not personally acquainted with Poe, Anthon graciously acceded to his plea, and on 2 November he reported the discouraging results of his enquiry:

I have called upon the Harpers, as you requested, and have cheerfully exerted with them what influence I possess, but without accomplishing anything of importance. They have *complaints* against you, grounded on certain movements of yours, when they acted as your publishers some years ago; and appear very little inclined at present to enter upon the matter which you have so much at heart. (*Works*, 17, 193)

The exact nature of these *'complaints'* and *'movements'* is unclear. Harpers may have been irritated by some aspect of their publication of *The Narrative of Arthur Gordon Pym* in 1838; but it is also likely that they were not well pleased by Poe's involvement with Thomas Wyatt and his textbooks on conchology. Wyatt published his *Manual of Conchology* with Harpers in 1838; it was an expensive book which sold badly, and Harpers refused to issue a cheaper version. So Wyatt devised a rival volume entitled *The Conchologist's First Book,* published in Philadelphia in 1839, and Poe was associated in the scheme at least to the extent of allowing his name to appear on the title page, for which he was paid fifty dollars. The general sense of Anthon's reply, however, is clear enough, and must have sounded familiar to Poe: most of his previous approaches to publishers had met with similar discouraging responses, and the difficulties of authorship evident in this exchange of letters – poor financial rewards for writing, inadequate publishing opportunities, the lack of an established audience, and the consequent dispersal of effort among the multitude of magazines and newspapers – these were the routine experiences of his literary life. Poe's confession to Anthon that he had 'written no books' was, of course, a fabrication: he had by then produced three books of verse, two collections of tales, and a novel; but his unwillingness to acknowledge his publications to a man whose discrimination he respected is a clear indication of his dissatisfaction with their achievement.

From the start of his career Poe was sensitive to the importance of public opinion; in 1829 he explained to John Allan: 'At my time of life there is much in being *before the eye of the world* – if once noticed I can easily cut out a path to reputation ... ' But his poems did not bring him 'before the eye of the world', so in 1831 he turned to fiction and the magazines. His earliest tales were submitted for the hundred dollar prize offered by the Philadelphia *Saturday Courier,* and although he was unsuccessful, the *Courier* was sufficiently interested in him to publish five of his contributions anonymously in 1832. But Poe may not have known about these printings, and it is unlikely that he was paid for them, since literary competitions of this kind invariably claimed publication rights on all entries. The first press comment came in the same year from Baltimore: Lambert Wilmer, editor of the *Saturday Visiter,* complimented Poe's style, though his promise to publish his tales in the *Visiter* was not fulfilled (see No. 8). Poe was more successful, however, in the *Visiter* competition of 1833, for which he entered his poem 'The Coliseum', along with six stories from his 'Tales of the Folio Club'. He won the story contest and fifty dollars with 'MS. Found in a Bottle', and believed that he would have won the poetry prize too, had it not been for the unfair entry of John Hill Hewitt, who had succeeded Wilmer as editor of the *Visiter*. The competition judges, who included the influential novelist John Pendleton Kennedy, issued a report praising Poe's tales for their inventiveness and variety, and recommending their publication in book form (No. 9).

For Poe, the most important outcome of the *Saturday Visiter* contest was the friendship and patronage of Kennedy. Poe initially intended to publish his 'Tales of the Folio Club' by public subscription in Baltimore (see No. 8); but this scheme, which would have stood little chance of success, was quickly abandoned when Kennedy introduced him to his own publishers, Carey, Lea & Blanchard of Philadelphia, in November 1833. Henry Carey, the senior partner in the firm, evidently agreed in principle to take Poe's collection, but publication was set aside when it became apparent that the national financial crisis was seriously harming the publishing and bookselling business. In November 1834, Poe, desperate for money as usual, applied via Kennedy for an advance from Carey; a month later Kennedy passed on the publisher's discouraging reply: 'His answer let me know that he would go on to publish, but the expectation of any profit from the undertaking he considered doubtful, – not from any want of merit in the production but because small books of

detached tales however well written seldom yield a sum
sufficient to enable the bookseller to purchase a copyright'
(*Works*, 17, 3). Carey further suggested that Poe should sell
his tales to the magazines and annuals in the first instance,
and so bring his name to public attention, though he confided
to Kennedy that, '*that is not often done by short stories*'.[1] Since
Carey did not 'go on to publish' as he had indicated he
would, Poe had little alternative but to accept his advice and
try to build a reputation in the journals.

Although Kennedy was unable to secure the publication of
'Tales of the Folio Club', he encouraged Poe through a
period of depression and uncertainty, and introduced him to
Thomas White, owner of the recently established *Southern
Literary Messenger* of Richmond: 'I told him to write
something for every number of your magazine, and that you
might find it to your advantage to give him some permanent
employ. He has a volume of very bizarre tales in the hands of
Carey and Lea, in Philadelphia, who for a year past have been
promising to publish them. This young fellow is highly
imaginative, and a little given to the *terrific*.'[2] Poe's first
contribution to the *Messenger* was 'Berenice' (March 1835); it
was in the '*terrific*' style, and James E. Heath, the editor,
considered it too sensational (No. 10). Poe defended himself
to White on the grounds that 'Berenice' was arresting
magazine material: 'But whether the articles of which I speak
[popular British tales of terror] are, or are not in bad taste is
little to the purpose. To be appreciated you must be *read,* and
these things are invariably sought after with avidity' (*Letters*,
1, 58). Nevertheless, he was not unresponsive to the
sensibilities of his readers; he assured White that he would
not 'sin quite so egregiously again', and his next horror
story, 'Morella' (April 1835), was less gruesome and violent.
Poe also agreed to write a tale each month for the *Messenger*,
and promised that 'no two of these Tales will have the
slightest resemblance one to the other in matter or manner ...' Over the following months he published in the
Messenger tales from his Folio Club collection, as well as
newly written pieces – 'Hans Phaall' being particularly well
received (Nos 10, 11) – adding to the variety of his styles and
types, with the hope of book publication always in mind.

By September 1835, Poe had thought up a new plan to put his tales on the market, and once again he approached J.P. Kennedy for assistance: 'Mr White is willing to publish my *Tales of the Folio Club* – that is *print* them. Would you oblige me by ascertaining from Carey & Lea whether they would, in that case, appear nominally as the publishers ...' (*Letters*, 1, 74). Kennedy was hesitant about the scheme, but with his usual kindness he agreed to pass on Poe's request to the publishers. Carey replied on 4 October: he was dismayed by Poe's casual indifference to publishing ethics, questioned if he were sane, and dismissed the proposal out of hand: 'I do not know what to say respecting Poe. Is he not deranged? I should care nothing about aiding him as you propose, but I should like to be sure that he was sane; let me hear from you.'[3] Doubtless realizing that he could not succeed without Carey's support and co-operation, White decided not to undertake the printing himself, though he still tried to promote his unstable young editor's literary ambitions. Early in 1836, he asked the prominent satirist and novelist James Kirke Paulding to interest Harpers in Poe's work, and Paulding courteously agreed. Harpers predictably declined the collection, but they did eventually write to Poe explaining their reasons: these centred on the magazine origins of the stories (they were literally 'twice-told tales'), their intellectual sophistication, and hence their limited public appeal:

The reasons we declined publishing them were threefold. First, because the greater portion of them had already appeared in print – Secondly, because they consisted of detached tales and pieces; and our long experience has taught us that both these are very serious objections to the success of any publication. Readers in this country have a decided and strong preference for works (especially fiction) in which a single and connected story occupies the whole volume, or number of volumes, as the case may be; and we have always found that republications of magazine articles, known to be such, are the most unsaleable of all literary performances. The third objection was equally cogent. The papers are too learned and mystical. They would be understood and relished by only a very few – not by the multitude. The numbers of readers in this country capable of appreciating and enjoying such writings as those you submitted to us is very small indeed. We were therefore inclined to believe that it was for your own interest not to publish them. It is all important to an author that his *first* work should be popular. Nothing is more difficult, in regard to literary reputation, than to overcome the injurious effect of a first failure.[4]

It is ironic that Carey's well-meant advice to Poe to first sell his tales to the magazines, far from furthering his career, should have proved a positive hindrance, at least in his dealings with Harpers. Yet it was probably Harpers' authoritative analysis of the tastes and priorities of literary publishing that prompted Poe to write what he must have hoped would be a novel for the 'multitude': *The Narrative of Arthur Gordon Pym* began as a serial in the *Southern Literary Messenger* in January 1837, and was published in book form by Harpers in July 1838. Unfortunately, neither party was satisfied with the work: Poe seems to have thought little of his performance and ignored its existence later in his life; moreover, it sold badly, and Harpers informed Poe in February 1839 that less than a hundred copies had been disposed of in America.[5]

Meanwhile, Poe made at least two further attempts in 1836 to market his tales. The English firm of Saunders & Otley, who had recently established an agency in New York, expressed some interest in his collection, but nothing came of it, so in September he offered it to Harrison Hall, a Philadelphia printer, 'or to any bookseller of your acquaintance', adding, 'In regard to remuneration, as ¾ of the book will have been published before, I shall expect nothing beyond a few copies of the work' (*Letters*, 1, 104). Poe even offered a small inducement, promising to review 'fully' any books Hall might care to send him, but no reply has been located.

Surprisingly, in view of the financial uncertainties of publishing at that time, Poe's collection, now entitled *Tales of the Grotesque and Arabesque,* was accepted by Lea & Blanchard in September 1839. The firm had, of course, a commendable record of publishing American authors, and since Henry Carey had retired perhaps they felt some responsibility towards a young author they had misled and disappointed over the past five years. Nevertheless, at the last moment Lea

& Blanchard attempted to escape from their commitment, and Poe received no payment for the small edition of 750, merely a few copies for distribution. Two years later, when Poe asked the firm to print a new edition on similar ungenerous terms to himself, he met with a dusty reply: 'As yet we have not got through the edition of the other work and up to this time it has not returned to us the expense of its publication' (*Works*, 17, 102).

By 1842, Poe had ready a new and enlarged edition of his tales which he provisionally entitled 'Phantasy-Pieces', but once again he was unable to find a publisher. Instead, in 1843, the first number of a projected 'Uniform Serial Edition' of *The Prose Romances of Edgar A. Poe* appeared in pamphlet form in Philadelphia. The publisher, William H. Graham, brother of George Graham the magazine entrepreneur, clearly intended his production for the cheapest end of the book market: it was flimsy, poorly printed, contained only two stories ('The Murders in the Rue Morgue' and 'The Man that was Used Up'), and sold for 12½ cents. However, since no further issues of the edition were forthcoming, a lack of public interest may be assumed; at any rate, Poe did not mention the pamphlet in his correspondence, and it quickly passed into obscurity.

The only work by Poe to approach commercial respectability was *Tales* of 1845, which was issued as the second number in Wiley & Putnam's 'Library of American Books'. The publication owed its existence to Poe's friendship with and press support of Evert Duyckinck, Wiley & Putnam's reader, who not only negotiated Poe's contract, but also selected the tales for publication, much to Poe's annoyance. No records covering the early years of Wiley & Putnam are extant, so it is impossible to determine exactly how many copies of *Tales* were printed, though four months after publication Poe claimed that 1,500 copies had been sold, which on a royalty of eight cents per copy meant that he had earned $120. The modest success of *Tales*, together with widespread newspaper interest in 'The Raven', encouraged the publishers to bring out *The Raven and Other Poems* as No. VIII in their 'Library of American Books'. Poe was evidently given $75 for this project, but there is no evidence to show that the publishers were particularly pleased with him or he with them; on the contrary, there was no response when he attempted to dispose of the copyright on a further collection of stories for $50 in January 1846. Later in that year, he wrote with some bitterness to George Eveleth: 'It may be some years before I publish the rest of my Tales, essays etc. The publishers cheat – and I must wait till I can be my own publisher' (*Letters*, 2, 332). Yet from the publisher's viewpoint, Poe was not a sound commercial property, and Wiley & Putnam could hardly have been expected to print a new edition when they could not readily move their 1845 printing; indeed, there were enough unsold copies of *Tales* in stock in 1849 to justify John Wiley's investing in a remainder issue.

Poe's last book, *Eureka,* was published in 1848 by George Putnam, Wiley's erstwhile partner, in a small edition of 500 copies. Poe begged, and was reluctantly given, an advance of $14 on a work which he believed would revolutionize thinking on God and the Cosmos; but Putnam also made him sign a humiliating contract in which he promised not to ask for further loans or advances.

It would seem that Poe's total income from all his books over a period of more than twenty years amounted to a little under $300. But his case was not unique or even very unusual. Publishing conditions during the 1830s and 40s were not conducive to originality, and William Charvat, the historian of literary publishing in America, has pointed out that 'Not a single literary work of genuine originality published in book form before 1850 had any commercial value to speak of until much later, and most of our classics were financial failures ...[6] Moreover, the short story, which absorbed so much of Poe's artistic energy, was essentially a magazine form, and one in which book publishers showed little interest. Henry Carey merely stated a commonplace fact of publishing life when he reminded John Pendleton Kennedy in 1834 that 'writing is a very poor business unless a man can find a way of taking the public attention, and that is not often done by short stories. People want something larger and longer'.[7] Nathaniel Hawthorne fared little better than Poe in his struggles to find a publisher for his magazine tales: plans for three collections were frustrated, and it was necessary for his friend Horatio Bridge to put up $250 in 1837 to subsidize the publication of *Twice-Told Tales* by the American Stationers Company. Oberon, the disillusioned young author in Hawthorne's 'The Devil in Manuscript', reflected the unhappy experiences of many American authors when he confessed that he had approached no less than seventeen publishers before being honestly told 'that no American publisher will meddle with an American work, – seldom if by a known writer, and never by a new one – unless at the author's risk'.

Along with many of his literary contemporaries, Poe believed that the depressed condition of American authorship was in large part due to the absence of an international copyright agreement – in 1842 he told F. W. Thomas: 'Literature is at a sad discount. There is really nothing to be done in this way. Without an international copyright law, American authors may as well cut their throats' (*Letters*, 1, 210). The copyright issue sent shivers of insecurity through the hierarchy of American letters, from writers with widely established reputations, notably James Fenimore Cooper and Washington Irving, to magazinists of local and temporary fame. Surveying the literary scene from the *Southern Literary Messenger* in 1835, George Watterston was merely representative when he reported gloomily:

Literature does not receive that encouragement and patronage under the Republic, which are calculated to give it a vigorous growth or a permanent and healthy existence. There is not much individual wealth, and few can afford ... to purchase the productions of American authors. There is ... another cause which operates to the disadvantage of American literature ... it is the cheapness and facility with which the productions of the British press can be republished in this country .... Few can afford to write for mere fame, and no great inducement is offered to write for anything else.[8]

Ten years later, in one of his 'Marginalia' pieces, Poe argued that American reluctance to grant copyright facilities to foreign authors was short-sighted expediency ('more reading for less money'), which in the long term demoralized American literature:

First, we have the injury to our national literature by repressing the efforts of our men of genius; for genius, as a general rule, is poor in worldly goods and cannot write for nothing. Our genius being thus repressed, we are written *at* only by our 'gentlemen of elegant leisure', and mere gentlemen of elegant leisure have been noted, time out of mind, for the insipidity of their productions. In general, too, they are obstinately conservative, and this feeling leads them into imitation of foreign, more especially of British models. This is one main source of the imitativeness with which, as a people, we have been justly charged, although the first cause is to be found in our position as a colony. Colonies have always naturally aped the mother land. (*Works*, 16, 78–9)

In spite of persistent and impassioned agitation in England and America on behalf of international copyright legislation, the publishers responded in the main to commercial rather than patriotic pressures, and justified their activities by proclaiming their unselfish interest in the 'free' transmission of knowledge. In practice, however, they preferred to print known British authors whom they were under no legal obligation to pay, rather than risk capital on untried and possibly inferior American products.[9]

Poe's opportunities as an author were inevitably damaged by the depression of 1837–43, which seriously dislocated the book trade: publishers were forced to cut costs and output, and retrenchments invariably began in the most unstable area of the market, 'light' literature. In the wake of the depression came a flood of cheap, pirated literature; newspapers proliferated, and the mass-circulation market was dominated for a while by 'mammoth' weeklies such as *Brother Jonathan* and its near relative, the *New World*, whose giant pages offered vast quantities of reading fodder for a few cents. In addition, these papers published supplements or 'Extras' with a complete book in each number. In 1843 the *New World* put out thirty-six 'Extras'; they were ephemeral and hard to read because of their tight printing, but they were much cheaper than regular books – each number generally cost 12½ cents on the streets, but less to regular subscribers to the paper. Sales were briefly spectacular: printings of 20,000 and more were commonplace, and figures of 50,000 were claimed for titles by Bulwer Lytton and Dickens. Faced with this unprecedented onslaught upon their territory, the older publishing houses took refuge behind safe religious, technical, and educational projects, though Harpers, the largest publishers in America, went into fierce competition with the 'mammoths' and issued their own cheap editions of popular authors.[10] In this hostile and disordered environment new or unusual American authors stood little chance of finding a market, and Poe's *Prose Romances* containing but two tales for 12½ cents could not compete with Harpers' edition of *Martin Chuzzlewit* 'with fourteen well executed plates, for forty-four cents'.[11] Indeed, even well-known American writers who had recently commanded good sales, found conditions in the early 1840s disheartening. In 1841 Isaac Lea warned William Gilmore Simms, one of his firm's best-selling names, that the prospects ahead were dismal: 'We do not see much hope in the future for the American writer in light literature – as a matter of profit it might be abandoned. The channel seems to be glutted with periodical literature particularly the mammoth Weeklies – besides which we go into market for $1.50 a copy agt. English reprints at 90c.'[12]

One result of these inhospitable book publishing conditions was that American writers turned for visibility and support to the rapidly multiplying and voracious magazines – it has been estimated that between 1825 and 1850 the number of periodicals other than newspapers increased from a little under one hundred to around six hundred.[13] Writing in the *Broadway Journal* of 15 February 1845, Poe argued that 'The want of an International Copy-Right Law, by rendering it nearly impossible to obtain anything from the booksellers in the way of remuneration for literary labour, has had the effect of forcing many of our best writers into the service of the Magazines and Reviews...'; and in a notice of 'The Magazines' in the same issue he continued: 'Magazine literature is the only literature that can flourish among us until we have an international copyright law... A book, by itself, is getting every day rarer and rarer in our literature, and there being no other channel than the Magazine for our thoughts to flow in, the Magazine should be cherished until a better day dawn upon us.'[14] In the meantime, Poe was, as he confessed to Charles Anthon, 'essentially a Magazinist':

from 1835 onwards he made an often precarious living by editing and contributing to the magazines and newspapers – he wrote for more than thirty journals and had editorial connections with at least five; all but one of his tales first appeared in the periodicals, as did all his poetry after 1831.

In his letter to Anthon, Poe represented himself as a victim of the magazine business; a few months later he elaborated this pitiful self-image into a sketch for the *Broadway Journal* entitled 'Some Secrets of the Magazine Prison-House'. In this mock-melodrama the 'poor devil' author, unable to find a publisher to take his books, is driven into magazines, where he is humiliated, cheated, and literally starved to death by the prosperous and unfeeling 'editor and proprietor'. Although Poe ironically maintained that he did not write from personal experience, and that he had no 'proprietor now living' in mind, the contemporary targets of the satire were, of course, recognized by his readers, and there was an immediate press rejoinder from Philadelphia in defence of the influential magazine owners George Graham and Louis Godey, both of whom boasted of their generosity towards American authors. This in turn provoked a cutting editorial from Poe in the *Broadway Journal*: 'We are extremely happy to learn that GRAHAM paid COOPER fifteen hundred dollars in seventeen months, and that GODEY keeps almost as many ladies in his pay as the Grand Turk; but we have have heard of writers, whose articles are certainly equal to anything of COOPER's that we have seen in *Graham*, to whom that munificent publisher pays nothing.'[15] The following week, however, Poe's discretion overcame his valour, and the *Broadway Journal* carried a flattering notice of the latest *Graham's*, together with an apology for any 'injustice' done to the proprietor. Yet in spite of this diplomatic retreat, Poe had good reason to be sceptical of the self-proclaimed altruism of the publishers; and, like Hawthorne, he might have protested that writing for the periodicals was 'the most unprofitable business in the world'.

In his authoritative study of American magazines, Frank Luther Mott concluded that most journals prior to 1842 did not possess either the means or the security to treat contributors fairly;[16] and even after the rise of *Graham's*

Magazine and its neighbour and rival, *Godey's Lady's Book*, with their sustained high circulations (*Graham's* claimed 40,000 in 1842) and 'liberal' rates of pay, decent rewards were available in few magazines, and then only to authors of 'caste', whose names might be expected to attract readers and revenue. W.G. Simms commented sourly on the situation in 1845, and Poe eagerly reprinted his editorial:

Nor is the pay derived from periodical writing of a better character. It should be better, for no species of literary labour is more utterly exhausting, as its habitual exercise demands constant transition of subject, and as constant transitions of the mind from thought to thought. But, of all American periodicals, there is not one which pays all its contributors. Among the best of them, but one in a score receives any compensation, and this is usually an amount so small, as to discourage the industry of writers who set much value upon their performances.... In the matter of magazine and periodical writing, we may add, that the author is constantly the victim of lying editors and publishers, who beguile him of his writings and abuse him, from their chair of criticism, if he ventures to complain. There is not a professional literary man of the country, who has not a long story to relate, of the arts by which he has been swindled of his contributions by that class of insects of literature, whom Moore compares with the maggot who is said to feed and fatten upon the brains of the elk, – the noble animal perishing finally, the prey of the miserable insect which has fed upon his life.[17]

Magazine payments were determined largely by an author's public reputation; and Poe, whose name frequently appeared in the papers associated with undignified quarrels and scandals, did not have the prestige necessary to command good rates of pay – hence his disgruntled reply to Philip Pendleton Cooke's enquiry: 'you ask me for information about the usual pay of the Magazines. A definite answer is impossible. They graduate their pay by mere whim – apparent popularity – or *their own* opinion of merit. Real merit is rather *no* recommendation' (*Letters*, 2, 313–14). Poe received little financial encouragement from the magazine business. Early in his career, he seems to have been promised 80 cents per column by the *Southern Literary Messenger* (a journal dedicated to the advancement of Southern letters); even so, when he was sent $20 in July 1835, he had to remind Thomas White that the money due to him had been 'miscalculated': 'There are 34 columns in all. "Hans Phaall" cost me nearly a fortnights hard labour and was written especially for the *Messenger*' (*Letters*, 1, 66). Poe's economic status as a magazine writer was slow to improve: in 1838 he sold 'Ligeia', which he sometimes spoke of as his finest story, for $10, or a paltry 80 cents a page; and by his own reckoning, *Graham's Magazine* did not value his work very highly – he was given only $4 a page for features such as 'The Murders in the Rue Morgue' and 'The Masque of the Red Death', whereas in 1842 Hawthorne expected $5 per '*Graham* page', and Willis asked for and got at least $10 for his sentimental sketches. Poe boasted that Graham paid him $8 a page for 'The Philosophy of Composition' in 1846; and although his claim seems exaggerated, Graham may have been tempted into generosity by the prospect of cashing in on the success of 'The Raven'. However this may be, a few months later Poe was willing to write for *Graham's* at the 'old price' of $4 a page. Only rarely was he able to get more than *Graham's* rate, and then usually from what he considered to be inferior publications: he told Cooke that *Arthur's Magazine* had given him $10 a page for his two-page story 'The Sphynx', but added, that 'the pay is no pay for the degradation'; and in 1849 he sold several articles for $5 a page to the Boston weekly *Flag of Our Union*, which he condescendingly described as 'not a *very* respectable journal, perhaps, in a literary point of view, but one that pays as high prices as most of the Magazines' (*Letters*, 2, 425). In January 1849 he confided to Annie Richmond that he had made 'permanent engagements' with every periodical in America (save one), and the '*least* price' he got was $5 a page – a fantasy sadly belied in letters to less impressionable correspondents. A week earlier, he told John R. Thompson that he was willing to write 'Marginalia' for the *Southern Literary Messenger* for a mere $2 a page.

Although Poe enjoyed occasional journalistic triumphs – notably the 'Autography', 'Secret Writing' and 'Literati' papers; the 'Balloon' and 'Valdemar' hoaxes; the story of 'The Gold-Bug'; and 'The Raven' – his tales and poems were not in continual demand by the magazines; nor were they, with the exception of 'The Raven', widely 'clipped' and copied from paper to paper, as happened with genuinely popular authors like N.P. Willis, Longfellow, and the omnipresent Mrs Lydia H. Sigourney. Moreover, Poe did not always find it easy to place his work to his best advantage, as his experience with 'The Mystery of Marie Rogêt' illustrates. This story was written in the summer of 1842 as a sequel to 'The Murders in the Rue Morgue'; but perhaps because of its length (it ran to 20,000 words), and its unsavoury subject matter (it was based upon the recent murder of Mary Rogers, 'the beautiful segar girl', in the vicinity of Weehawken, New Jersey), it was not taken by *Graham's Magazine*, which was then edited by Rufus W. Griswold. Poe was doubtless anxious to dispose of his story before public interest in the murder waned; so on 4 June he tried to persuade George Roberts of the 'mammoth' Boston *Notion* to buy it for $50: 'From the nature of the subject, I feel convinced that the article will excite attention...'(*Letters*, 1, 200). Poe maintained that 'Marie Rogêt' was worth double his asking price (though in fact it would have only brought about $78 from *Graham's*), but he could not have been confident of interesting Roberts, since on the same day he offered the story to his old friend J.E. Snodgrass of the Baltimore *Saturday Visiter*, for $40, and he may have written in a similar vein to the *Messenger* in Richmond. None of these journals took the story, however, and it eventually ended up in William Snowden's 'namby-pamby' *Ladies' Companion* – a magazine Poe professed to despise as 'the *ne plus ultra* of ill-taste and vulgar humbuggery'.[18]

Poe generally lived a hand-to-mouth existence in wretchedly poor circumstances, so it is not surprising that he should at times have despaired of making a living from literature. In 1838 he unsuccessfully applied to James Kirke Paulding (who had been appointed Van Buren's secretary of the navy) for 'the most unimportant Clerkship in your gift – *any thing by sea or land* – to relieve me from the miserable life of literary drudgery to which I, with a breaking heart submit, and for which neither my temper nor my abilities have fitted me, I would never again repine at any dispensation of god. I feel I could then (having something beyond mere literature as a profession) quickly elevate myself to the station in society which is my due'.[19] Insecurity rather than political ambition motivated him to seek a minor government post in the Philadelphia Custom House in 1843; but his negotiations were naive, confused, and futile. So too were his chimerical schemes to establish a superior literary journal of his own, which he imagined would attract a secret 'aristocracy of talent', build up a circulation of 100,000, and make him into a wealthy and powerful arbiter of taste. But his dreams of preferment and wealth were as unrealistic as his social pretensions, and in reality, the only profession he ever knew or cared about was 'mere literature' – as he told F. W. Thomas in 1849: 'Depend upon it, after all, Thomas, Literature is the most noble of professions. In fact, it is about the only one fit for a man' (*Letters*, 2, 427).

Margaret Fuller observed in 1846 that 'The magazines' object is primarily to cater to the amusement of vacant hours . . .';[20] Poe's contributions, however, rarely seemed designed to satisfy such casual needs. His fiction was too idiosyncratic, ironic, and disturbing in its implications; his poetry too private and elusive, to have the sustained support of large circulation magazines like *Graham's* and *Godey's* and their imitators, dominated by female sensibilities (Hawthorne's 'damned mob of scribbling women'), writing for a conservative home- and family-centred audience. He was unable to accommodate the prevailing interest in sentimental romance, or write, as he was advised to by Philip Pendleton Cooke, 'a book full of homely doings, of successful toils, of ingenious shifts and contrivances, of ruddy firesides – a book healthy and happy throughout, and with no poetry in it at all anywhere, except a good old English "poetic justice" in the end. Such a book, such as Mr Poe could make it, would be a book for the million, and if it did nothing to exalt him with the few, yet would certainly *endear* him to them' (No. 83). But Poe did little to 'endear' himself to the multitude: he openly declared his contempt for democratic opinion, and to many he appeared a quarrelsome, arrogant, unstable person, while his poverty and drunkenness made him an easy target for his enemies. Rufus Griswold could not have assassinated

Poe's character with such righteous vindictiveness so soon after his death (No. 92) had not Poe prepared the way and established his notoriety in his lifetime.

Responding to the question 'Why did he [Poe] not work and thrive?', George Graham, in 1850, blamed the 'precarious tenure' of the literary artist in America (a situation which, ironically, Poe had charged him with contributing to), and then went on to suggest that 'The character of Poe's mind was of such an order as not to be very widely in demand. The class of educated mind which he could readily and profitably address was small – the channels through which he could do so at all were few ...' (No. 107). The view that Poe did not possess a secure popular base is supported by commentators who knew the man and his literary environment well. E.A. Duyckinck, for example, spoke of him as an 'ideologist', remote from the commonplace concerns of life, and hence 'a greater favorite with scholars than with the people' (No. 104); Willis, too, observed that Poe wrote with 'fastidious difficulty' in a style 'much above the popular level' (No. 96); while J.M. Daniel argued that had Poe possessed mere talent rather than genius 'even with his unfortunate moral constitution, he might have been a popular and money-making author' (No. 106). In his *Fable for Critics* (1848), James Russell Lowell also presented Poe as an oddity, an outsider, and he sensed that it was the dominance of 'mind' over 'heart' in his work that limited his appeal and significance to his contemporaries:

> There comes Poe, with his raven, like Barnaby Rudge,
> Three-fifths of him genius and two-fifths sheer fudge,
> Who talks like a book of iambs and pentameters,
> In a way to make people of common sense damn meters,
> Who has written some things quite the best of their kind,
> But the heart somehow seems all squeezed out by the mind.

II

THE EARLY POETRY

(a) TAMERLANE AND OTHER POEMS (1827)

Poe left his home in Richmond in mid-March 1827, following bitter quarrels with his foster-father, John Allan.

He probably went initially to relatives in Baltimore; but little has been discovered about his activities until he joined the United States army in Boston on 26 May, under the name of 'Edgar A. Perry'. Within the next two months he made arrangements to have his poems printed in Boston by Calvin F.S. Thomas, who advertised 'Book & Job Printing' 'On the Most Reasonable Terms'. Nothing is known of the contract between Poe and the young printer, though in view of Poe's lack of funds the edition would have been very small – at the most two hundred copies costing between $10 and $20. *Tamerlane and Other Poems* 'By a Bostonian' is now one of the rarest and most valuable works of American literature,[21] but in 1827 this cheaply produced forty-page pamphlet was on sale for a few cents, and since neither the author nor the printer had the means to promote and distribute their publication, it created no public interest. No reviews of it have been located, though it was listed as having been received by two Boston magazines with offices close by Thomas's printing shop: the *United States Review and Literary Gazette* (August 1827), and the *North American Review* (October 1827). The only contemporary comment came from Poe himself in his 'Preface' (No. 1) – a brief, conventional apology for the unworthy compositions of his boyhood, together with a declaration of undiminished poetic ardour.

Tamerlane and Other Poems did little to satisfy Poe's literary ambitions, and he later seems to have been reluctant to accurately recall its existence. In his 'Advertisement' to the 1829 printing of 'Tamerlane' he explained that the poem had been 'suppressed through circumstances of a private nature', while in 1831 he advertised *Poems* as a 'Second Edition', thus ignoring the Boston printing entirely. In 1843 he resorted to further mystification: in his *Saturday Museum* biography he let it be known that his first collection of verse entitled 'Al Aaraaf, Tamerlane, and Minor Poems. By a Virginian' had been published 'before he had completed his fifteenth year'. This claim was, of course, a fabrication; though Poe was less fanciful when he went on to admit that both this apocryphal printing and the edition of 1827 'attracted but little attention, on account of their slovenly printing and their modes of publication'.[22]

(b) AL AARAAF, TAMERLANE, AND MINOR POEMS (1829)

Soon after his release from the army in April 1829, Poe submitted 'Al Aaraaf' to Isaac Lea, partner in the prestigious house of Carey & Lea of Philadelphia. Realizing that American publishers would not entertain the work of unknown poets on commercial terms, Poe appealed to his estranged foster-father for $100 to subsidize his collection. John Allan's scribbled note on Poe's letter leaves no doubt as to his response: 'replied to Monday 8 June 1829/strongly censuring his conduct & refusing any aid' (*Letters*, 1, 21). Poe's negotiations with Carey & Lea came to nothing; but he continued to circulate his poems, and sent a copy of 'Fairy-land' (then entitled 'Heaven') to the controversial novelist and critic John Neal, who printed extracts in the *Yankee and Boston Literary Gazette*. Although Neal dismissed 'Heaven' as 'rather exquisite nonsense', he did discern evidence of poetic flair (No. 2a), and this modest praise produced an excited letter from Poe thanking Neal for 'the very first words of encouragement I ever remember to have heard', and enclosing further poems. Neal again responded favourably, praising Poe's poetic promise, but advising him to acquire determination and strength of mind (No. 2b). Poe also sent a copy of 'Heaven' to N.P. Willis, the bright young editor of the *American Monthly Magazine*; but he treated the poem with contempt, and reported to his readers that he had burned the unsolicited manuscript.[23]

By November, however, Poe had made arrangements to have his poems published in Baltimore: he told John Allan that 'The poems will be printed by Hatch & Dunning of this city upon terms advantageous to me they printing it and giving me 250 copies of the book' (*Letters*, 1, 34). What exactly these 'advantageous' terms were is not clear; but Hatch & Dunning, who were only a small concern, may have printed 250 copies at relatively low cost, all of which were then given over to the author for distribution.[24] How Poe paid for even a modest printing is also obscure, though it is not inconceivable that John Allan relented and provided assistance – Poe certainly kept him informed about the book's progress.

Al Aaraaf, Tamerlane, and Minor Poems was in print by December, and Poe at once sent a copy to John Neal, to whom he now dedicated 'Tamerlane'. On 29 December he wrote to Neal: 'I await anxiously for your notice of the book', adding tactfully, 'You will do me justice' (*Letters*, 1, 35). But when Neal's notice did appear it was brief and ambiguous (No. 3) and scarcely justified Poe's high expectations, or those of his cousin Neilson Poe, who was moved to write to his future wife by the prospect: 'Edgar Poe has published a volume of Poems one of which is dedicated to John Neal the great autocrat of critics – Neal has accordingly published Edgar as a Poet of great genius etc. – Our name will be a great one *yet*.'[25] Only two additional reviews have been traced, both in Baltimore papers: one was kindly but not very perceptive (No. 4), the other, by John Hill Hewitt, was both unperceptive and hostile (No. 5).

(c) POEMS (1831)

Poems 'By Edgar A. Poe' was published in New York in April 1831, shortly after the termination of the author's brief spell at West Point Military Academy. How Poe paid for the edition of perhaps five hundred copies is not known, though a long-established tradition has it that his fellow cadets at West Point subsidized the publication by contributing 75 cents each. Although *Poems* was issued by Elam Bliss, an established publisher with an interest in American poetry, it was hardly noticed by the reviewers. Only two reviews have been located, and both are brief and uncertain in their judgments. Once again Poe turned to john Neal for recognition: he sent Neal a presentation copy of *Poems*, and Neal duly responded with a review in the *Morning Courier and New York Enquirer* warning against mistaking 'oddity' for 'exellence' (No. 7). Neal was puzzled by Poe's poems which he considered a confusion of 'genius' and 'nonsense', and his feelings were shared by the reviewer in the *New-York Mirror* (probably the editor, George P. Morris), who complained of 'numerous obscurities' (No. 6).

Poems, like Poe's two earlier collections, stirred little interest, and found only minimal circulation. James Russell Lowell, a devoted reader of poetry, does not seem to have been aware of their existence until Poe brought them to his attention in 1843; then he wrote to Poe: 'Your early poems display a maturity which astonished me & I recollect no individual (and I believe I have all the poetry that was ever written) whose early poems were anything like as good. Shelley is nearest, perhaps.'[26] In his critical biography of Poe commissioned for *Graham's Magazine* (No. 50) Lowell publicly reiterated his admiration for Poe's youthful verses, but such interest was unusual. Anthologies are often useful guides to current tastes, and American compilations from the 1830s and '40s indicate that Poe's verse was not held in high regard by the editors, even if it was known to them: he was not, for instance, among the sixty or so poets represented in George Cheever's *American Commonplace Book of Poetry* (1831); nor does he appear in John Keese's *Poets of America* (1838), or William Cullen Bryant's *Selections From the American Poets* (1840) – all of which Poe argued had made prejudiced and incompetent selections.[27] Only three poems by Poe were included in the first edition of Rufus Griswold's popular and wide-ranging anthology *The Poets and Poetry of America* (1842); by the tenth edition of 1849, however, Poe's quota had risen to fourteen poems. This increase may be partly explained by Griswold's decision to exclude 'Female Poets' from this anthology; but the increased representation also suggests that it was not until Poe self-consciously turned to writing magazine verse, beginning with 'The Raven' in 1845, that he became read or acknowledged as a poet.

III

IN SEARCH OF AN AUDIENCE

(a) THE NARRATIVE OF ARTHUR GORDON PYM (1838)

Poe was encouraged to write what he must have hoped would prove a popular and money-spinning novel by the advice he received from Harper & Brothers. In March 1836 they informed him via James Kirke Paulding and Thomas White that they were unwilling to publish his 'Tales of the Folio Club' on the grounds that they had 'a degree of obscurity in their application, which will prevent ordinary readers from comprehending their drift'; they did, however, suggest that if Poe would modify his elitist pretensions and 'lower himself a little to the ordinary comprehension of the generality of readers', they would be pleased to consider his work; indeed, they would 'make arrangements with him as will be liberal and satisfactory'.[28] In June Harpers wrote directly to Poe advising him that 'Readers in this country have a decided and strong preference for works (especially fiction) in which a single and connected story occupies the whole volume, or number of volumes, as the case may be ...'[29] Paulding, too, advised him to 'undertake a Tale in a couple of volumes, for that is the magical number', and promised that 'a work of yours would at least bring you a handsome remuneration, though it may not repay your labours, or meet its merits'.[30] In their letter, Harpers had warned Poe that they would not be interested in reprinting stories from the magazines, but his urgent need for cash and copy tempted him to commence *The Narrative of Arthur Gordon Pym* as a serial in the *Southern Literary Messenger*: two instalments appeared in January and February 1837, but then with Poe's departure from the *Messenger* the story lapsed. Harpers took out copyright on *Pym* in June 1837, but the printing was delayed for over a year, probably because of financial uncertainties in the publishing business following the suspension of specie payments by the banks in May 1837.[31]

The publishers impressed on Poe that it was in an aspiring author's best interests (and by implication their own) to aim for the popular market, so Poe contrived his novel of nautical wonders and terrors with this end in view. Arthur Gordon Pym's narrative of bizarre adventures amidst uncharted regions might have been expected to attract those eager for sensational revelations; and Poe also intended to exploit current fascination with the Antarctic, evidenced by the widespread interest aroused by the United States Exploring

Expedition which sailed in 1838. However, despite the provocative nature of the fiction, and the business expertise of the publisher, the sales of *Pym* were poor, and Harpers were dissatisfied with the venture. Poe himself seems to have thought little of his book, which did not, of course, carry his name on the title page: in 1840 he admitted to William Burton that *Pym* was 'a very silly book' (*Letters*, 1, 130), and E.A. Duyckinck recalled that Poe, 'who was generally anything but indifferent to the reception of his writings, did not appear in his conversation to pride himself much upon it'.[32]

No publication from the firm of Harpers could be ignored by the reviewers, and research by Burton R. Pollin has revealed that *Pym* was quite widely noticed by journals in New York and Philadephia – though many of the twenty or so American notices are perfunctory, and some are scarcely more than announcements of publication.[33] The reviewers were not taken in by Poe's pretence that Pym's narrative was true: the New York *Evening Post*, for example, described the book as a 'fictitious journal' and a 'tale of wonders'; the *Sunday Morning News* recommended it as pleasant reading for 'the lovers of the marvellous'; while *Alexander's Weekly Messenger* of Philadelphia called it 'a very clever extravaganza' (No. 18). The notices in the *New-York Mirror* and the *Knickerbocker Magazine* were surprisingly mild in view of Poe's attacks on them during the furor that followed his slashing review of Theodore Fay's *Norman Leslie*. The *Knickerbocker* found Poe's style 'slip-shod', but admitted that 'The work is one of much interest' (No. 16), whereas the *Mirror* admired Poe's 'fine mastery over language, and powers of description rarely excelled', but regretted his inability to master '*vraisemblance*' (No. 15). The only really hostile review came from *Burton's Gentleman's Magazine,* which condemned the novel as being badly written, unoriginal, and foolishly unrealistic; in short, 'a mass of ignorance and effrontery' (No. 19).

It would appear that *The Narrative of Arthur Gordon Pym* was more widely read in Britain than in America. In February 1839 Harpers wrote to Poe: 'We are inclined to think that *Pym* has not succeeded or been received so well in this country as it has in England. When we published the work, we sent 100 copies of it to London – And we presume they have been sold.'[34] In addition, Wiley & Putnam in association with Whittaker & Co., and Charles Tilt published a London edition in October 1838, with Harpers' synoptic title page slightly abbreviated, and Pym's final diary entry unaccountably omitted. This edition, which was almost certainly unauthorized, was itself pirated by John Cunningham's cheap format *Novel Newspaper* in 1841.[35] The English reviewers were surprisingly tolerant of this romance from the pen of an unidentified American author: the influential *Spectator* praised it as 'a fiction of no mean skill; displaying much power, much nautical knowledge, and a DEFOE-like appearance of reality' (No 23); while the *Monthly Review* singled it out from recent American fiction on account of its 'originality, boldness, and skill' (No. 25). The symposium in the *New Monthly Magazine* regarded Pym as a fantasy and responded in like humour (No. 24); while the reviewer in the *Atlas* found Pym's adventures of such interest that he took three folio columns to retell them (No. 22). Even the reviewer in the *Metropolitan Magazine* who claimed to be outraged by the author's hoaxes – 'a bungling business – an impudent attempt at imposing on the credulity of the ignorant' – had to admit that he found parts of the novel 'sufficiently amusing and exciting'.[36] The reviews so far discovered do not support the persistent myth (it was recorded in Griswold's 'Memoir', and may have been started by Poe himself) that in England *Pym* was read as a factual narrative; on the contrary, it was read and appreciated as an extravagant romance with a readily discernible element of hoax and humour about it.

(b) TALES OF THE GROTESQUE AND ARABESQUE (1839)

In the summer of 1838, Lambert Wilmer, Poe's friend from his Baltimore days, welcomed him to Philadelphia with an ode in the *Saturday Evening Post:*

> But the same wind whose angry tones
> Sends small dull craft to Davy Jones,

Is but an impulse to convey
The nobler vessel o'er the sea; –
So thou dear friend, shalt haply ride
Triumphant through the swelling tide
With fame thy cynosure and guide.[37]

In reality, though, Poe's situation in Philadelphia was quite obscure, and his prospects of fame remote. Soon after his arrival in the city, he unsuccessfully pleaded with J.K. Paulding to rescue him from his 'miserable life of literary drudgery'; but during the early part of 1839, he helped Thomas Wyatt with the preparation of textbooks on conchology and natural history; then, in May, he accepted William Burton's offer of $10 a week to assist in the editing of his *Gentleman's Magazine*.

It was during this period of uncertainty that Poe wrote some of his finest and best-known stories: 'Ligeia', 'The Fall of the House of Usher', and 'William Wilson' have long been recognized as masterpieces of their genre, and they were not without their critics and admirers when they first appeared in the magazines. Philip Pendleton Cooke, the young Virginian poet, was particularly fascinated by 'Ligeia', and he wrote to Poe explaining his understanding of the tale and suggesting that the 'ghostly proprieties' had not been managed as well as they might have been (No. 27). Poe was clearly delighted by Cooke's enthusiasm, though his reply contains a hint of irony: he declared that the praise he received from Washington Irving was 'but dust in the balance when compared with those discriminating opinions of your own, which teach me that you feel and perceive' (*Letters*, 1, 118). Doubtless with the intention of eliciting further publishable compliments, Poe also sent Cooke a print of 'The Fall of the House of Usher' and drew his attention to the forthcoming 'William Wilson', but he may have been disappointed by Cooke's rather confused response (he confessed that he was unable to 'clearly comprehend' the meaning of 'William Wilson'), and the letter was not included among the carefully edited 'Personal Opinions' published in support of the collected tales (No. 29).

Of the stories Poe wrote for *Burton's Gentleman's Magazine*, 'The Fall of the House of Usher' attracted most attention. It was quickly pirated in England by *Bentley's Miscellany,* from where it was repirated by the American press – a procedure which Poe observed with ironic amusement.[38] The reviewers classified 'Usher' simply as a 'powerful', 'singular', and 'graphic' tale of terror: for example, Joseph C. Neal of the *Pennsylvanian* supposed that it would 'possess many attractions for those who love to dwell upon the terrible'; while the critic in the New York *Evening Star* claimed that it 'would have been considered a *chef d'oeuvre* if it had appeared in the pages of *Blackwood'* (No. 29). On the other hand, James E. Heath, the conservative editor of the *Southern Literary Messenger*, rejected the story on the grounds that 'German' fiction of this kind did nothing to 'improve the heart' – a view which he reiterated publicly in an editorial warning Poe away from the pitfalls of 'gloomy German mysticism' (No. 26). Poe was clearly irritated by these charges, and although he anticipated that Washington Irving's endorsement of his skills would enable him to 'triumph over those little critics who would endeavor to put me down by raising the hue and cry of *Exaggeration* in style, of *Germanism* & such twaddle' (*Letters*, 1, 121), he considered it necessary to defend the integrity and complexity of his art in the 'Preface' to his collected *Tales of the Grotesque and Arabesque* (No. 28).

In September 1839, Lea & Blanchard unexpectedly decided that they were willing to print 'at our own risque & expense a Small Ed. say 1750 copies' of Poe's tales. The publishers, however, soon realized that the market for such a collection was likely to be negligible, so in November they asked to be released from their earlier promise: 'If the offer to publish was now before us we should certainly decline it, and would feel obliged if you knew and would urge some one to relieve us from the publication at cost, or even at a small abatement.'[39] Of course, Lea & Blanchard found no one to take the book off their hands, so they reluctantly issued their two-volume edition in December (the title page was dated 1840), but only 750 copies were printed. Poe was left to promote his work as best he could: he collected what he termed 'encomiums of a most unusual nature' and had them bound in as advertisements (No. 29) – he pointed out to Dr

J.E. Snodgrass that he could not afford to neglect such publicity through a 'false sense of modesty' (*Letters*, 1, 121). He also distributed the few copies given to him by the publisher for review purposes. On 19 December, about two weeks after publication, Poe told Snodgrass that 'the edition is already very nearly exhausted'; but this news would probably have surprised Lea & Blanchard, who still had unsold copies on hand in 1841 when they refused to consider a new edition.

The publisher's lack of confidence in *Tales of the Grotesque and Arabesque* was matched by a general lack of understanding among the reviewers. In Philadelphia, several papers carried brief, laudatory notices praising the author's learning and imagination (Nos 30, 31, 33); but the review in *Godey's* was perfunctory (No. 36), while the *North American* reprimanded Poe in a schoolmasterly report: 'These tales betoken ability on the part of the author to do better. Let him give up his imitation of German mysticism, throw away his extravagance, think and write in good sound sober English, and leave all touches of profanity to the bar room, and he will employ his talents to much better advantage.'[40] The few notices that have been discovered do not lend unqualified support to Poe's claim that 'The Philadelphians have given me the *very highest possible* praise ...' (*Letters*, 1, 125). He must also have expected that his tales would provoke some comment in Baltimore, and he asked Snodgrass to scan the papers, but only one minor item has come to light. In Richmond, Heath continued to complain about Poe's lack of 'beneficial tendency', while the Boston press was downright hostile: the *Notion* dismissed the stories as the products of a disordered mind ('they fall below the average of newspaper trash'),[41] while the *Boston Post* was equally contemptuous (No. 32). The New York papers were more friendly, but the reviewers seem to have been baffled by the collection and, with one notable exception, at a loss for words. The only substantial and discerning notice appeared in the *New-York Mirror*: on 21 December *Tales of the Grotesque and Arabesque* was recommended as 'one of the most extraordinary and original works of the day'; a week later this was followed by a thoughtful review by F.L. Tasistro, who argued that Poe's skilful studies of inner states signified 'the advanced state of our literature' (No. 35).

(c) PROSE ROMANCES (1843)

In April 1841, *Graham's Magazine* announced a new editorial appointment:

It is with pleasure the Proprietor announces, that he has made arrangements with EDGAR A. POE, Esq., commencing with the present number, by which he secures his valuable pen, as one of the editors of the Magazine. Mr POE is too well known in the literary world to require a word of commendation. As a critic he is surpassed by no man in the country; and as in this Magazine his critical abilities shall have free scope, the rod will be very generously, and at the same time, justly administered.

With this additional editorial strength, the Magazine may be expected to take a high position in literary merit, among the periodicals of the day.

Poe's status as a critic and story writer benefited considerably from his association with George Graham's ambitious enterprise. When he joined the magazine, the circulation stood at around 5,500; a year later a readership of 40,000 was boasted of; and although there were a variety of factors to be taken into account in the rise of *Graham's*, Poe naturally emphasized his own part in the success story. In a letter to F. W. Thomas he declared: 'Now that man [Graham] knows that I have rendered him the most important services; he cannot help knowing it, for it is rung in his ears by every second person who visits the office, and comments made by the press are too obvious to be misunderstood' (*Letters*, 1, 192).

Of Poe's fictional contributions to *Graham's*, 'The Murders in the Rue Morgue' (April 1841) aroused the greatest interest, and it was chosen to initiate the *Prose Romances* project. F.W. Thomas (the novelist and politician who encouraged Poe to apply for a post with the Tyler administration) thought it 'the most ingenious thing of the kind on record. It is managed with a tact, ability, and subtlety that are absolutely marvellous'; while Park Benjamin reckoned it to be of 'extraordinary interest', adding, 'We regard this gentleman [Poe] as one of the best writers of the English language now living. His style is singularly pure and idiomatic. He never condescends to affectations but writes with a nervous clearness that inspires the reader with perpetual confidence in his powers.'[42] Longfellow, too, probably had this story in mind when he assured Poe of his belief in him as a writer: 'You are mistaken in supposing that you are not "favourably known to me". On the contrary, all that I have read from your pen has inspired me with a high idea of your power; and I think you are destined to stand among the first romance writers of the country, if such be your aim.'[43] The 'Secret Writing' and 'Autography' papers further advanced Poe's already considerable reputation for ingenuity; Jesse E. Dow of the Washington *Index* said of him: 'Mr Poe is a wonderful man. He can read the hieroglyphics of the Pharaohs, tell you what you are thinking about while he walks beside you, and criticise you into shape without giving offence.'[44]

Poe's offerings in other periodicals were also generally well received at this time. For example, when the morbidly sentimental 'Eleonora' appeared in *The Gift* for 1842 (actually on sale the previous September), it was quickly copied by at least five magazines and papers. Early in 1843, 'The Tell-Tale Heart' was singled out by Willis from the first issue of Lowell's *Pioneer* as 'the only thing in the number that most people will read and remember'; then later in the year the editors of the *Saturday Evening Post* introduced their readers to 'The Black Cat':

'The Black Cat', by Mr Poe, is written in that vein of his which no other American writer can imitate, or has, successfully. The accompaniment of probable events with improbable circumstances, so blended with the real that all seems plausible; and the investiture of the whole with a shadowy mythic atmosphere, leaving a strong and ineffaceable impression upon the reader's mind, is an effort of imagination to which few are equal. For our own part, we are bound to give the *pas* to all black cats, henceforth and forever; and to treat them with most obsequious consideration.[45]

In June, 'The Gold-Bug' won the $100 prize given by the Philadelphia *Dollar Newspaper*, and soon became remarkably popular. Less than a year later, Poe boasted to Lowell that more than 300,000 copies had been circulated – a claim which may not be wildly exaggerated since the story was published four times by the *Dollar Newspaper* and reprinted by several other journals. 'The Gold-Bug' also caused a stir in the local press, where Poe was accused of plagiarism and of collusion with the awarding committee; it was dramatized briefly at the Walnut Street theatre, Philadelphia, and it was the first of Poe's tales to be translated into a foreign language – a French version appeared in the *Revue britannique* in November 1845.

Yet despite Poe's growing reputation in the magazines, and his proven willingness to adapt his fictional style and materials to popular expectations, he was unable to persuade a publisher to risk a new edition of his collected tales; so instead, he came to an arrangement in 1843 with William H. Graham of Philadelphia to produce 'Phantasy-Pieces' in serial form. The first number containing two stories of deception and illusion – 'The Murders in the Rue Morgue' and 'The Man that was Used Up' – was ready in July; but to judge by its present extreme rarity, the printing must have been small and the distribution poor.[46] Only a handful of reviews of *Prose Romances* have come to light, and several of these are merely polite notices of publication in the local papers. However, of the more extensive and considered reviews in the Philadelphia press (Nos 38–41), all were unanimous in their praise of Poe's originality, ingenuity, and literary skill; though the observation by the reviewer in the *Saturday Courier* (No. 40) that the stories would not have much appeal to the 'extended multitude' seems to have been accurate, as no further numbers of the series were issued.

IV

WIDENING HORIZONS

(a) TALES (1845)

The immediate reason for Poe's sudden move from Philadelphia to New York in April 1844 is obscure, but it was undoubtedly largely connected with his plans to establish a high-quality literary magazine of his own, and his need to extend his reputation. The magazine world of Philadelphia was dominated by businessmen like Graham, Godey, and Peterson, and by ladies' magazines and family miscellanies 'so nearly alike, that if the covers were changed, it would not be easy to distinguish one from the other'.[47] Poe had failed to persuade George Graham to provide financial backing for his 'Stylus' project; moreover, he had also been unable to find a publisher in Philadelphia willing to take a new edition of his collected tales. But New York was now the book and newspaper publishing centre of the country, and with a rapidly growing population already four times that of Philadelphia, the cosmopolitan metropolis offered more varied opportunities to the literary entrepreneur than its rather staid rival. At any rate, it was with schemes for the 'Stylus' and a collection of his stories in mind that Poe began manoeuvres to secure the patronage of Evert A. Duyckinck, leader of the nationalistic 'Young America' group, and an influential figure in New York literary circles. Indeed, before leaving Philadelphia, Poe had sent an ingratiating letter to Cornelius Mathews, a spokesman for 'Young America', and a close personal friend of Duyckinck, apologizing for 'a certain impudent and flippant critique' he had written of Mathews's poem 'Wakondah' (*Letters*, 1,245). In the past, Poe had been anything but a champion of literary national-ism, which he had denounced as wrong-headed and paroc-hial; but during 1844 and 1845 he became an unexpected ally of 'Young America' – notably in elaborate though uneasy puffs of R.H. Horne and Elizabeth Barrett Browning, whose poetry had been promoted in the United States by Mathews and Duyckinck. In return, Duyckinck arranged for the publication in June 1845 of a small selection of Poe's tales in Wiley and Putnam's 'Library of American Books', of which he was the editor, though by no stretch of the imagination could Poe's stories have been regarded as concerned specifically with American life or issues.

The selection of *Tales* was made by Duyckinck; and although Poe tactfully praised his patron's foresight and generosity, declaring that he 'afforded unwonted encourage-ment to native authors by publishing their books, in good style and in good company, without trouble or risk to the authors themselves, and in the very teeth of the disadvantages arising from the want of an international copyright law',[48] he clearly resented a selection which he considered did scant justice to his versatility as a short story writer. In a letter to Philip P. Cooke, he explained his discontent in detail:

Should you undertake the work for me [the continuation of Lowell's biography of him], there is one topic – there is one particular in which I have had wrong done me – and it may not be indecorous in me to call your attention to it. The last selection of my Tales was made from about 70, by Wiley & Putnam's reader, Duyckinck. He has what he thinks a taste for ratiocination, and has accordingly made up the book mostly of analytic stories. But this is not *representing* my mind in its various phases – it is not giving me fair play. In writing these Tales one by one, at long intervals, I have kept the book-unity always in mind – that is, each has been composed with reference to its effect as part of a *whole*. In this view, one of my chief aims has been the widest diversity of subject, thought, & especially *tone* & manner of handling. Were all my tales now before me in a large volume and as the composition of another – the merit which would principally arrest my attention would be the wide *diversity* and variety. (*Letters*, 2, 328–9)

Poe also complained about Duyckinck's restrictive selection in a brief, anonymous notice in the *Broadway Journal*: 'No particular arrangement has been made in the selection. The stories published in the volume before us, are neither better nor worse, in general, than the remainder of the seventy. In the composition of the whole series, variety of subject and matter, especially diversity of invention, were the objects held in view. Of course these objects are lost sight of, and must necessarily be sacrificed, in any mere selection of twelve tales from seventy';[49] and the same theme was taken up in a preliminary notice in the *Aristidean*: 'Mr P. should never have consented to so brief a selection – unless, indeed, he proposes to continue it in a series of similar volumes.'[50]

Yet despite Poe's dissatisfaction with Duyckinck's selection, *Tales* turned out to be the most commercially successful of his books, and one that attracted the interest of reviewers in Europe as well as America. Predictably, in view of Poe's continuing literary quarrels, there were a number of hostile comments in the American press – Charles Dana in the Brook Farm *Harbinger* scoffed at his 'intensities' (No. 55); Clark in the *Knickerbocker* sneered that the volume was 'so little noteworthy as to demand no remark';[51] and the *North American Review* briefly and contemptuously dismissed it as belonging to 'the forcible-feeble and the shallow-profound school'[52] – but these were outweighed by the generally favourable, though in some cases scarcely impartial, reviews. Rufus Griswold praised Poe's 'consummate art' (No. 58), as did Margaret Fuller in the *Tribune*: 'His narrative proceeds with vigor, his colors are applied with discrimination, and where the effects are fantastic they are not unmeaningly so' (No. 54). Miss Fuller was also struck by his psychological realism, his 'penetration into the causes of things', and advised him to abandon the short story ('so terribly degenerated among us'), and turn his attention to the 'metaphysical novel'. William Gilmore Simms, an ally of 'Young America', emphasized the originality of Poe's stories: 'Certainly nothing more original, of their kind, has ever been given to the American reader' (No. 64), and was supported in this by *Graham's* (No. 61), while the brief notice in *Godey's* proclaimed: 'We are tired of being merely *satisfied*; and like occasionally to be *astonished*. Talent and learning can satisfy. It takes genius to astonish. This Poe possesses, and he has exhibited some of its most decisive proofs in the volume before us.'[53] Writing anonymously in his friend Colton's *American Review*, Duyckinck described the volume as 'one of the most original and peculiar ever published in the United States', and looked forward to its 'extensive circulation' and 'cordial recognition' (No. 60). Duyckinck's Poe possessed 'a quickness of apprehension, an intensity of feeling, a vigor of imagination, a power of analysis' which set him apart from his mundane literary contemporaries; and while he will not discuss 'debatable questions in ethics or metaphysics' arising from Poe's tales, he does attempt to reply to the charge that they lacked 'utility'. The review in the *Aristidean* (No. 62) is of considerable interest, because it seems to have been written largely by Poe himself: there are intimate insights into how individual stories were written, together with sharp digs at Poe's rivals and enemies; there is a preoccupation with sins of plagiarism; a sly, hoaxing humour, and an emphasis on those qualities of intelligence Poe most admired – originality, ingenuity, and versatility.

Wiley and Putnam also issued a small English edition of *Tales*, consisting of the American sheets with a London title page. The volume had a mixed reception from British reviewers: while there was some awareness of Poe's skills as a writer, there were doubts expressed concerning the moral and aesthetic value of his stories. For example, the reviewer in *Tait's Edinburgh Magazine* declared: 'We take for granted that Edgar A. Poe is an American. His tales are of a peculiar, we had almost said, of an original character; and though monstrosities, often revolting, nay, disgusting, and chargeable with all kinds of bad taste, there is a rude power and subtlety about them which is not without a fascination of the hideous or disagreeable sort.'[54] The belated review in *Blackwood's* was also ambiguous: the stories were described as 'strange – powerful – more strange than pleasing', and while it was granted that they were written with 'marvellous skill', the reader would not return to them with pleasurable anticipation – 'In fine one is not sorry to have read these tales; one has no desire to read them twice' (No. 67). Martin Tupper in the *Literary Gazette* praised Poe's 'microscopic power of analysis'; but four of the stories he condemned out of hand, including 'The Black Cat' which was 'impossible and revolting', and 'The Fall of the House of Usher' which was 'juvenile' (No. 65). The notices in the *Atlas* and the *Spectator* were superficial and patronizing; and the influential *Critic* refused to recommend the collection to the libraries on the grounds that the contents had little or no 'utility' and dwelt too much on horror and cruelty – 'They do not anticipate the wants of the future, and the future will take no cognizance of them' (No. 59). Poe distorted facts when he boasted in the *Aristidean* that 'The British *Critic*, and other English literary journals laud it [*Tales*] most handsomely.'

It was also through *Tales* that Poe's name began to be known in France. In 1846, two loose translations of 'The Murders in the Rue Morgue' appeared in Parisian papers, though in neither case was credit given to Poe: in June, *La*

Quotidienne printed 'Un Meurtre sans exemple dans les fastes de la Justice' signed G.B. (Gustave Brunet); then in October, E.D. Forgues published 'Une sanglante énigme' in *Le Commerce* under his pen name O.N. (Old Nick). At the same time Forgues published a long, sympathetic review of *Tales* in *La Revue des deux mondes*, in which he argued that Poe's greatness was evident in the way reason triumphs over chaos in his imagination (No. 66). However, a rival paper, *La Presse*, soon recognized that the two translations were versions of the same story, and charged Forgues with plagiarism. Forgues's ensuing libel suit was unsuccessful, but during the proceedings he revealed that 'La source de l'article en question n'est pas celle qu'indique *La Presse* ... Ainsi donc ce n'est pas dans *La Quotidienne*, mais dans les Contes d'E. Poe, littérateur américain ... ' The *Gazette des Tribunaux* remarked: 'Grâce à M. Forgues, tout le monde va savoir que M.E. Poe fait des contes en Amérique...'[55] When Poe learned of this affair from Duyckinck, he asked his friend to 'make a paragraph or two for some one of the city papers' (*Letters*, 2, 336): two weeks later, the *Spirit of the Times* carried a report of the case taken from the Parisian theatrical paper, *L'Entre-Acte*, together with a note in which Poe may have had a hand, giving a misleading account of the publication history of 'The Murders in the Rue Morgue'.[56]

(b) THE RAVEN AND OTHER POEMS (1845)

In the 'Preface' to *The Raven and Other Poems*, Poe claimed that he was by choice a poet; yet his output in over twenty years was surprisingly meagre. His first three collections created little interest, and although he continued to publish occasional poems in the magazines, and some times introduced them into his stories, he was not widely recognized as a poet prior to 1845. Early in that year, however, his poetic fortunes underwent a sudden and dramatic change. First, Lowell's influential critical essay in *Graham's* drew attention to Poe's neglected achievements as a poet: 'Mr Poe's productions show that he could see through the verse to the spirit beneath, and that he already had a feeling that all the life and grace of the one must depend on and be modulated by the will of the other. We call them the most remarkable boyish poems that we have ever read' (No. 50). Then, at the end of January, came 'The Raven', which made an impact unsurpassed by any previous American poem; in 1849 John Daniel of the *Richmond Examiner* declared: '"The Raven" has taken rank over the whole world of literature, as the very first poem yet produced on the American continent' (No. 48).

After *Graham's* had turned it down, 'The Raven' was sold to Colton's *American Review*, probably for $15, and it was published there in the first week of February, along with a note on prosody in which Poe is thought to have had a hand (No. 45). But by then 'The Raven' had already been 'clipped' by the *Evening Mirror*, where it was introduced by Willis as 'the most effective example of "fugitive poetry" ever published in this country' (No. 44). Poe also sent his poem to the *Southern Literary Messenger*, where it was printed with supporting comment from the New York *Morning Express* claiming that Tennyson had now been 'excelled out of measure' (No. 46). Even the *Knickerbocker* did not remain silent, though Clark's recommendation of this 'unique, singularly effective, and most musical effusion' was tempered by an ironic aside: 'We have never, before, to our knowledge, met the author, Mr Edgar A. Poe, as a poet; but if the poem to which we allude be a specimen of his powers in this kind, we shall always be glad to welcome him in his new department.'[57] 'The Raven' was extensively copied in American papers, and provoked a rash of parodies and imitations – fifteen contemporary examples have been located.[58] In 'The Philosophy of Composition' Poe declared that his intention had been to compose a poem 'that would suit at once the popular and the critical taste', and he had reason to be pleased with his achievement; he boasted to F. W. Thomas: '"The Raven" has had a great "run" Thomas – but I wrote it for the express purpose of running – just as I did the "Gold-Bug", you know. The bird beat the bug, though, all hollow' (*Letters*, 1, 287).

In the *Broadway Journal* (13 December 1845), Poe recalled that he read the proofs of *The Raven and other Poems* (published by Wiley & Putnam in mid-November) on the

evening preceding his appearance before the Boston Lyceum.
It was through the friendly agency of Lowell that Poe
received an invitation to read a poem to the Lyceum on 16
October for a fee of $50; but his conduct in Boston plunged
him into scandal and controversy. The situation arose
because Poe was either unable or unwilling to write a new
poem for the occasion; instead, he read 'Al Aaraaf',
temporarily renamed 'The Messenger Star of Tycho Brahe',
to an audience that had already sat through a long-winded
oration by Caleb Cushing. A tactful report of the event in the
Boston *Courier* of 18 October described Poe's performance as
'an elegant and classic production', but also observed that it
was not 'appreciated by the audience', who restlessly made
'continual exits in numbers at a time'. Other Boston papers
were less charitable, notably the *Transcript,* whose editor,
Cornelia W. Walter, already had a grievance against Poe
because of his treatment of Boston's favourite poet, Longfellow. Under the heading 'A Failure', Miss Walter gave her
account of the affair:

... The poet immediately arose; but, if he uttered poesy in the first
instance, it was certainly of a most prosaic order. The audience
listened in amazement to a singularly didactic exordium, and finally
commenced the noisy expedient of removing from the hall, and
this long before they had discovered the style of the measure, or
whether it was rhythm or blank verse. We believe, however, it was
a prose introductory to a poem on the 'Star discovered by Tycho
Brahe', considered figuratively as the 'Messenger of the Deity', out
of which idea Edgar A. Poe had constructed a sentimental and
imaginative poem. The audience now thinned so rapidly and made
so much commotion in their departure that we lost the beauties of the
composition...[59]

Poe replied with a bad-tempered editorial in the *Broadway
Journal*, admitting that he had deliberately hoaxed and
insulted his Boston audience. The poem he delivered had, he
claimed, been written when he was ten years old, and he
continued: 'We do not, ourselves, think the poem a
remarkably good one: – it is not sufficiently transcendental.
Still it did well enough for the Boston audience – who
evinced characteristic discrimination in understanding, and
especially applauding, all those knotty passages which we

ourselves have not yet been able to understand.'[60] But despite his bravado, Poe's weak Lyceum performance, and subsequent undignified behaviour, left his character open to assassination, and seriously damaged the reception of *The Raven and Other Poems*. The success of 'The Raven' in the papers could not sustain Poe's wider reputation as a poet.

Reviewing the collection in the New York *Daily Tribune*, Margaret Fuller pointed out that the many victims of Poe's 'weapons of criticism' would now be lying in wait, ready to 'rend and slash in turn, and hoping to see his own Raven left alone to prey upon the slaughter of which it is the herald' (No. 69). While Miss Fuller was not displeased by this prospect, she did not join in the blood-letting herself, but primly restricted herself to declaring that all Poe's poems, apart from 'The Raven', were 'fragments'. Others, however, were quite prepared to 'rend and slash'. The *Boston Post* described the volume as 'a parcel of current trash' made up of verse ranging from 'mediocrity to absolute nonsense' (No. 71); yet only in July the same paper had spoken with enthusiasm about *Tales*: 'There is not one uninteresting or *mediocre* tale in the volume.'[61] Thomas Dunn English in the *Aristidean* praised 'The Raven', but found little else of value in the collection; indeed, he was troubled by Poe's lack of healthy normality: 'He has nothing to do with every day life' (No. 70). John S. Dwight in the *Harbinger* was also hostile: he imputed Poe's behaviour in Boston to insanity, and though he admired his skill as a versifier, he too was dismayed to discover that 'Edgar Poe does not write for humanity' (No. 72). The reviewer in a Cincinnati magazine went so far as to identify Poe with the mad, terror-stricken narrator of 'The Raven' (No. 75). Clark, who had ignored *Tales*, eagerly joined in the attack: his *Knickerbocker* review has nothing sensible to say about Poe's poems, but takes the opportunity to mock and vilify his character and literary pretensions. Duyckinck, under whose auspices the volume appeared, does not seem to have been active in its promotion, and some of the periodicals that might have been expected to take an interest remained silent, notably the *American Review*, *Graham's*, and the *Southern Literary Messenger*. Perhaps some of the reviewers were influenced by Poe's odd, self-deprecating

'Preface' in which he said: 'In defence of my own taste, nevertheless, it is incumbent upon me to say, that I think nothing in this volume of much value to the public, or very creditable to myself.' Certainly some of the notices were perfunctory and unenlightened. The New York *Illustrated Magazine* confessed: 'It bothers us how to rate the author...'; the *Anglo-American* volunteered the opinion that Poe's early poems should not have been published; while the *Golden Rule* found that 'Some of them are of rare beauty, and some of them are puerile.'[62] The New York *Evangelist* also did not know quite what to make of the book:

There is great diversity of opinion respecting Mr Poe's poetry – more so than respecting his talents as a prose writer, or temper as a critic. But the reader of 'The Raven' will never deny him originality and great power, both of thought and versification. It is an extraordinary performance and of itself is enough to establish the author's reputation as a poet. The other poems are various in subject and merit; but usually evince great skill in versification, and if obscurity is the test, uncommon originality.[63]

The strongest support for Poe's poetry at this time came from his Southern ally William Gilmore Simms. In his defence of Poe's Lyceum performance in the Charleston *Southern Patriot*, Simms declared that Poe was 'one of the most remarkable, in many respects, among our men of letters', being an 'admirable critic', and a poet 'too intensely spiritual for the ordinary reader' (No. 52). Simms argued that Poe had miscalculated by agreeing to the Lyceum engagement; his poems were too imaginative for an audience given to listening to 'moral or patriotic commonplaces in rhyming heroics' while at the same time 'munching peanuts'. Later, Simms wrote a more specific review of *The Raven and Other Poems,* in which he identified one of the causes of the book's indifferent reception: 'The wild, fanciful and utterly abstract character of these poems, will prove incomprehensible to him who requires that poetry shall embody an axiom in morals, or a maxim in philosophy or society ...' (No. 77). An English edition of *The Raven and Other Poems*, consisting of the American sheets with a cancel title page, was published by the London office of Wiley & Putnam in mid-January 1846. The British critics were unimpressed. Thomas Kibble Hervey, writing in the influential *Athenaeum*, complained that 'we have waited in vain for American poetry'; Poe neglects the American scene, and borrows his obscurities from English models (No. 76). The *Critic* and the *Literary Gazette* also found Poe's poetry 'essentially imitative': the *Critic* detected the influence of Coleridge and Tennyson (No. 79), while the *Literary Gazette* saw Elizabeth Barrett as Poe's inspiration. There is no evidence to suggest that the English reviewers found *The Raven and Other Poems* to be anything more than yet another American imitation of English poetic forms and themes.

(c) EUREKA (1848)

On 13 November 1845, a month after the Boston Lyceum fiasco, Poe wrote to Evert Duyckinck: 'I seem to have just awakened from some horrible dream, in which all was confusion, and suffering – relieved only the constant sense of your kindness, and that of one or two other considerate friends. I really believe that I have been mad – but indeed I have had abundant reason to be so' (*Letters*, 1, 300). Unfortunately, the 'horrible dream' was far from over, and the Lyceum episode, which dragged on in the Boston papers well into 1846, proved to be only the prelude to a two-year period of scandal and controversy in Poe's life, which seriously injured his health and reputation, and left him vulnerable to the attacks of his enemies.

Following the triumph of 'The Raven', Poe was, for a short time, quite a celebrity in the New York literary salons; but his image as a chivalrous Southern gentleman was badly tarnished through his involvement with two amorous literary ladies – Frances Osgood and Elizabeth Ellet. Mrs Osgood met Poe in March 1845, and shortly afterwards she initiated a sentimental, poetic flirtation with him in the pages of the *Broadway Journal*. But what started as a stylized magazine romance was soon inflated by gossip into a full-blown scandal, replete with a jealous rival for Poe's affections (the vindictive Mrs Ellet, whose 'loathsome love' Poe later claimed to have repelled 'with scorn');[64] allegations of indiscreet letters from both ladies to Poe; and a cast of outraged friends and relations of the supposed victims. In this drama, Poe found himself playing the role of the villain, the 'wretch ... steeped in infamy',[65] and he evidently had to plead insanity to escape the vengeance of Mrs Ellet's bellicose brother.

The publication of 'The Literati of New York City' in *Godey's Lady's Book* (May–October 1846), in which Poe threatened to reveal that 'The most "popular", the most "successful" writers among us, (for a brief period, at least,) are, ninety-nine times out of a hundred, persons of mere address, perseverance, effrontery – in a word, busy-bodies, toadies, quacks' (*Works*, 15, 2), provoked his enemies into a ruthless campaign to discredit him.[66] Most of the sketches turned out to be less severe than might have been expected, but his savage lampoon of Thomas Dunn English, with whom he had quarrelled over the Ellet letters, brought a coarse and libellous response from English, which in turn roused Poe into instituting legal proceedings against Hiram Fuller and the New York *Mirror*, the publishers of the offending article. Although Poe won his case against the *Mirror* in February 1847, and was cleared of English's charge of forgery, he was unable to defend himself adequately against the sustained barrage of innuendo and abuse put out by Fuller and his allies in the *Knickerbocker* clique – he was pilloried as a charlatan, a madman, a drunkard and moral reprobate. And these calumnies had their effect on Poe's health and standing. He confided to Willis: 'Of the facts, that I myself have been long and dangerously ill, and that my illness has been a well understood thing among my brethren of the press, the best evidence is afforded by the innumerable paragraphs of personal and literary abuse with which I have been latterly assailed' (*Letters*, 2, 338). Poe and his friends were almost silenced; though in a brief, anonymous item in the *Home Journal* (introduced at Poe's request), Duyckinck noted the irony that at the time Poe was beginning to win acclaim in Europe, he was persecuted and starved of employment in America (No. 82).

Yet despite his griefs and calamities, by early 1848 Poe's health and spirits seemed to be on their way to recovery, and he was looking forward to re-establishing his literary career through his 'Stylus' project; he told George Eveleth: 'My ambition is great. If I succeed, I put myself (within 2 years) in possession of a fortune & infinitely more' (*Letters*, 2, 356). In January, Philip Pendleton Cooke's revision of Lowell's essay on Poe appeared in the *Southern Literary Messenger* (No. 83). Cooke discussed Poe's distinctive merits as a poet and story writer, but significantly made no mention of his activities as a critic. It is evident that Poe too wished to avoid any new controversy that might damage his plans for the 'Stylus'. On 22 January, he wrote to Willis announcing his intention to visit the South and West to gather funds and subscribers for the 'Stylus'. As a first step he proposed to lecture at the Society Library in New York on 3 February, 'and, that there be no cause for *squabbling*, my subject shall *not be literary* at all. I have chosen a broad text – "The Universe"' (*Letters*, 2, 359). When Poe booked the Society Library though his friend H. D. Chapin, he anticipated an audience of between three and four hundred; but the lecture was poorly advertised (Willis did not print the publicity notice in the *Home Journal* until after the event), and on the night, which was cold and stormy, only about sixty people attended.[67] Poe was dissatisfied with the quality of the press coverage of 'The Universe' – he complained to Eveleth: 'You could have gleaned, however, no idea of what the lecture was, from what the papers said it was. All praised it – as far I have yet seen – and all absurdly misrepresented it' (*Letters*, 2, 361) – but at least most of the notices were favourable. The reviewer in the New York *Weekly Universe* said that those among the 'select audience' who could follow the scope and reasoning of the long lecture (it took upwards of two hours) found it 'profoundly interesting';[68] as did 'Gothamite' of the Philadelphia *Saturday Evening Post:* 'the discourse upon the whole, was one of the most unique and well digested, that I have ever heard'; while the New York *Courier and Enquirer* declared: 'The lecture was a nobler effort than any other Mr Poe has yet given to the world.'[69] Even the reviewer in the *New World*, whom Poe considered 'grossly incompetent to the task which he undertook' (*Letters*, 2, 363), though he admitted his inability to give an adequate account of the

lecture, was clearly fascinated by Poe's histrionic performance as the inspired philosopher.[70] The only report Poe
exempted from his general criticism was that written by John
Henry Hopkins for the New York *Evening Express* (No. 84).
Hopkins praised 'The Universe' as 'beyond all question the
most elaborate and profound effort we ever listened to in the
shape of a lecture'; he also recognized Poe's artistry – 'The
work has all the completeness and oneness of plot required in
a poem...' – and urged that 'it should be published as
delivered in order to present it fairly to the mind of the
reader'. The notices in the *Weekly Universe* and the *Literary
World* also recommended publication of the lecture.

According to George Putnam, a few days after the lecture
Poe came to his office in a state of frenzied excitement, and
insisted that at least fifty thousand copies of his revolutionary
enquiry into the nature of the cosmos should be immediately
printed.[71] But Putnam's stories about Poe are usually
fanciful, and it is unlikely that *Eureka* was ready for
publication before the early part of May, when J.H. Hopkins
saw the manuscript in Putnam's office. However, *Eureka* was
in print by the second week of July, though only in an edition
of 500–750 copies, a third of which, Putnam claimed, were
unsold a year later. The reviews of the book were sparse and
disappointing, especially after the relatively encouraging
response to 'The Universe': the major monthlies ignored it; it
was scarcely noticed outside New York; and almost half the
press reports were mere notices of publication, with little or
no informed comment. The reviewer in the *Evening Express*
came close to absurdity when he likened Poe's hurried and
second-hand speculations to the discoveries of Newton (No.
85); other commentators, though, were more skeptical.
Although there is nothing in Poe's correspondence to
indicate that he was other than completely serious in his high
claims for *Eureka*, several reviewers suspected a hoax. Epes
Sargent of the Boston *Transcript* accused Poe of a lack of
'sincerity', and continued, 'The mocking smile of the hoaxer
is seen behind the grave mask. He is more anxious to mystify
and confound than to persuade, or even to instruct ... (No.
86). Perhaps Sargent still had in mind Poe's Lyceum reading
and its aftermath. Between hearing 'The Universe' lecture

and reading the finished text, J.H. Hopkins developed doubts concerning the orthodoxy of Poe's ideas, and these doubts are reflected in his *Literary World* review (No. 87). Hopkins, too, suspected that this 'very strange work' might be a hoax, 'an elaborate quiz upon some of the wild speculations of the day – a scientific hoax of the highest order', and it is known that Hopkins visited Poe and discussed *Eureka* with him at his request. More important, however, from Hopkins's Christian standpoint, was Poe's dangerous flirtation with pantheism, a tendency also detected and regretted by George Bush in his Swedenborgian magazine (No. 90).

V

DEATH AND AFTERMATH

Poe died in the Washington College Hospital in Baltimore on the morning of 7 October 1849, from what a news report in the *Clipper* referred to as 'congestion of the brain',[72] probably brought on by a bout of heavy drinking. It is hardly surprising that such a life, marked as it was by notoriety and controversy, should have given rise to a good deal of comment and speculation. Two days after Poe's death, a writer in the New York *Journal of Commerce* remarked: 'His life has been an eventful and stormy one, and if anyone shall be found to write its history, we venture to say that its simple truths will be of more thrilling interest than most romances' (No. 93). It turned out that there was no shortage of people prepared to write Poe's 'history', though the 'simple truths' were sometimes hard to detect, and were often obscured or distorted by particular viewpoints.

Stories about Poe's drunkenness had been rife for years; now the moralistic press, deeply imbued with temperance sentiments, eagerly seized upon his tragic end as a 'horrible example' of a life, and possibly a great literary talent, ruined by alcohol. This is the message behind the brief obituary printed in the Boston *Evening Transcript* of 9 October:

He had talents, with which he might have done great things, had he united to them stable principles, earnest purposes and self-denying habits. Some of his poems are marked with flashes of genius and

originality ... As a critic he was intolerably conceited, undiscrimi-
nating and prejudiced. But his literary abilities were unquestionable; and had they been properly chastened and exerted under the
guidance of a clear heart and head, he might have left a name
among the first upon the list of those who have enriched American
literature with productions of lasting interest and value.

In papers formally pledged to the temperance cause, the
moral of Poe's life and death was unequivocally stated; for
example, the *Journal of the American Temperance Union*
declared: 'Edgar A. Poe, author of the "Raven" and other
poetical writings, recently died of a melancholy attack in a
hospital in Baltimore – alas! for brandy and poetry',[73] and the
readers of the New York *Organ* were given an 'awful
warning': 'Think of Poe's miserable end, and then resolve to
touch not, taste not the cup that poisoned him. When
tempted to break your pledge, point to that grave and
answer, No, never!' (No. 95).

More damaging to Poe's reputation than these crude
sermonizings was the widely circulated and seemingly
knowledgeable obituary written by Rufus Griswold, under
the pseudonym 'Ludwig', for the New York *Daily Tribune*
(No. 92). Griswold's survey of Poe's life prior to 1841 was
taken directly from Poe's romanticized account of himself;
but the damning character sketch that followed was Griswold's own work. He depicted Poe as a friendless, alienated
person for whom few would grieve; a 'dreamer – dwelling in
ideal realms – in heaven or hell', a lost soul who 'walked the
streets, in madness or melancholy, with lips moving in
indistinct curses', whose 'harsh experience had deprived him
of all faith in man or woman'. Griswold completed his
caricature of Poe by likening him to Francis Vivian, the
Byronic reprobate in Bulwer Lytton's novel *The Caxtons*. Of
Poe's writings, Griswold had little to say – his tales and
poems were briefly praised for their ingenuity, but as a critic,
'*He was little better than a carping grammarian.*' Griswold's
'Ludwig' article has often been condemned as a vicious
fabrication; but despite its distortions and self-conscious
striving after effect, it does reflect an important aspect of
contemporary opinion of Poe. Moreover, Griswold's primary intention may have been dramatic rather than malicious:

the character study gives only a general impression of Poe, and makes no mention of the particular scandals associated with his name – his drinking, his instability, and his literary quarrels. In a mild rebuke to Griswold sent in December 1849, Sarah Helen Whitman said: 'I was much interested by your eloquent sketch of his life published in the *Tribune* – I cannot doubt the justice of your remarks, although my personal experience would lead me to think his disposition more gentle and more gracious than you esteem it to be'; to which Griswold replied: 'I wrote – as you suppose – the notice of Poe in the *Tribune* – but very hastily. I was not his friend, nor was I his, as I remember to have told you; but I endeavored always to do him justice; and though the sketch has been deemed harsh, I did not mean that it should be so.'[74]

However this may be, Griswold's calumnies did not go unchallenged. In a Richmond paper, Susan Archer Talley protested against 'so unjust and distorted a view as to be almost unrecognizable to those who best knew him', and spoke of Poe's 'warm and affectionate' nature.[75] From Philadelphia, George Lippard and Lambert Wilmer made angry replies. Lippard stoutly defended Poe's character: 'But he was a man of genius – a man of high honor – a man of good heart. He was not an intemperate man', and predicted that 'As an author, his name will live, while three-fourths of the bastard critics and mongrel authors of the present day go down to nothingness and night' (No. 98). Wilmer attacked Griswold's notice as a 'hypocritical canting document', the work of a 'slanderous and malicious miscreant', though he later admitted: 'I do not know that this *vindication* was copied by a single paper; whereas the whole press of the country seemed desirous of giving circulation and authenticity to the slanders.'[76] Henry Hirst, who claimed to have known Poe 'perhaps better than any other man living', saw him through a romantic haze as a 'Gulliver ... in the hands of the Lilliputians', a genius destroyed by 'carping muck worms' (No. 97). But the most effective reply to Griswold at this time came from Willis in the *Home Journal*, who created an alternative but socially acceptable image of Poe. Writing from his personal experience of the time Poe worked on the *Mirror,* Willis described him as a 'quiet, patient, industrious, and most gentlemanly person, commanding the utmost respect and good feeling by his unvarying deportment and ability' (No. 96). Willis maintained that it was only by rumour that he knew of Poe's 'lamentable irregularities', and went on to tell the rather unlikely story of how with a *single glass of wine*' Poe became a 'reversed character', casting off his meek habits for a 'temporary and almost irresponsible insanity'. Clearly, if this was the case, then it would be possible to see Poe as the victim of an unfortunate constitution, rather than the pitiful slave of alcohol. Willis also exploited the sentimentality of his readers when he pictured Poe's idealized home life blessed by the selfless maternal devotion of Mrs Clemm, 'one of those angels upon earth that women in adversity can be'.

Griswold was not, as he admitted to Mrs Whitman and Lowell, a friend of Poe's; but he was highly thought of as an editor, and had many contacts among publishers and reviewers; so despite the 'Ludwig' article, he was invited to be Poe's literary executor. In her letter 'To the Reader' printed in the first volume of Poe's *Works*, Mrs Clemm stated that before leaving on his last trip to Richmond, Poe, 'under an impression that he might be called suddenly from the world, wrote ... requests that the Rev. Rufus W. Griswold should act as his literary Executor, and superintend the publication of his works ...' It is unlikely that Poe made such definite arrangements; but whatever the truth of the matter, the responsibility for editing Poe's writings was given to Griswold by Mrs Clemm with the support of the Lewis family, with whom she went to live after Poe's death. Griswold had some difficulty finding a publisher; but when he eventually persuaded his friend J.S. Redfield to undertake the project, it was rapidly put to press: in January 1850, two volumes of Poe's *Works* were on the market. The first volume contained thirty-one tales, plus Willis's 'Death of Edgar A. Poe' and a revised version of Lowell's essay of 1845; the second volume collected the remaining stories, *Eureka,* and the poems and essays on poetry.

The responses to Griswold's edition were often factional, and showed evidences of old prejudices and quarrels. C.F Briggs, whom Poe had mocked in the 'Literati' as being 'grossly uneducated' (*Works*, 15, 22), retaliated by claiming that Poe was 'altogether a strange and fearful being, and a true history of his life would be more startling than any of the grotesque romances which he was so fond of inventing' (No. 102); his poetry was dismissed as 'mere machine work', while 'His merits as a critic were very slender, he was a minute detector of slips of the pen...' Clark in the *Knickerbocker* admitted that 'few of our American authors have possessed more of the creative energy or the constructive faculty', but also maintained that Poe was 'destitute of moral or religious principle'.[77] George Ripley also could not avoid the personality of Poe: since he had 'no earnestness of character, no sincerity of conviction, no faith in human excellence', his tales must have an unhealthy effect on the reader – 'like breathing the air of a charnel house' (No. 103). Ripley also repeated what was by now a commonplace complaint of the critics – that Poe's poems were lacking in 'the gushing spontaneity, the inspired, ecstatic burst of soul, which are essential to an immortal song'. John Daniel wrote a long tirade in the *Southern Literary Messenger* denouncing the 'dirty little fleas and flies' (Griswold, Lowell and Willis) who sponged off Poe's genius – 'No other American has half the chance of remembrance in the history of literature' (No. 16). But although Daniel was aware of Poe's genius, he did not like what he had heard and seen of his 'Ishmaelite' character: he was horrified by his bad drinking habits ('He did drink most barbarously'), and repeated a nasty piece of Richmond gossip implying that Poe had behaved improperly towards John Allan's second wife. Along with Duyckinck, Daniel recognized Poe as an 'ideologist', a man of ideas and abstractions, whose greatest defect was 'his want of sympathy with, and indeed likeness to, the human kind'. Even an appreciative reader like G.W. Peck found it difficult to imagine Poe in terms of normal human experience; for Peck, Poe seemed a kind of refugee from the Valley of the Many-Colored Grass: 'Poor Poe! It was a sad day for him when he was forced from dreams like these into the real world, where there were many "far wiser" than he. No wonder he sometimes lost his heart and temper, and soon died!' (No. 105).

Two notices – those by John Neal and George Graham – caused Griswold particular annoyance. In a rambling and disjointed article in the *Portland Daily Advertiser*, Neal not only repudiated Griswold's characterization of Poe, but also questioned his integrity (No. 108). George Graham also indignantly rejected Griswold's Poe as an 'immortal infamy', a 'fancy sketch of a perverted, jaundiced vision', the product of a 'warped and uncongenial' imagination (No. 107). Writing, he claimed, from a much better knowledge of Poe than Griswold possessed, Graham elaborated Willis's domestic story; Poe appears as a 'polished gentleman, the quiet, unobtrusive, thoughtful scholar, the devoted husband, frugal in his personal expenses, punctual and unwearied in his industry, *and the soul of honor* in all his transactions'. Somewhat incongruously, perhaps, Graham also presented this decent model-citizen as an ethereal figure, a 'fine essence' who 'moved in an atmosphere of spirits', and who died a victim of 'poverty and disappointment' in a vulgar, money-grubbing society. It was this latter romantic image of Poe that so fascinated Baudelaire, and contributed to his fantasy of Poe the martyr and outcast in the 'vast prison' that was democratic America (No. 111).

In September 1850, the third volume of the *Works* appeared; it contained 'Marginalia' and the 'Literati' papers, together with Griswold's infamous 'Memoir' of Poe. (A fourth volume containing *Pym* and the 'Miscellanies' was belatedly added in 1856, but it created much less interest.) Griswold bitterly resented the attacks made on him by Neal and Graham, and in the 'Memoir' he set out to show that in his 'Ludwig' notice he had been fair, even generous, in his judgments. In the 'Memoir' Poe is presented in the worst possible light, and Griswold even went so far as to falsify documents in order to support his allegations.[78] The charges against Poe's character originally brought up in the 'Ludwig' article are repeated; but now there are also continual references to his unreliability, drunkenness and general moral weakness. Moreover, Griswold argued (and it was an argument that would be widely circulated in America and Britain over the next fifty years or so) that Poe's moral deficiencies are reflected in his writings: thus his tales possessed 'analytical subtlety' but no profundity; his poems revealed 'little genuine feeling', while his criticisms were merely a jumble of 'unsupported assertions and opinions'. In addition, Poe, the great detector of plagiarisms, was himself marked by Griswold as a plagiarist of the first order: 'Indeed some of his plagiarisms are scarcely paralleled for their audacity in all literary history...'[79]

There were those who protested against Griswold's vilification of the man whose works he had been entrusted to edit: C.J. Peterson spoke of a flagrant 'breach of trust' (No. 109), while Duyckinck, besides asking pertinent questions about Griswold's editorial policy, and noting the absence of any 'unhandsome references' to the editor in the volume, warned that he had 'lent himself to an enterprise where no honor can be acquired' (No. 14). C. Chauncey Burr, the Universalist minister and editor of the *Nineteenth Century*, who had helped Poe in Philadelphia in 1849, now wrote in defence of his character and of his artistic skill and detachment:

Poe was undoubtedly the greatest *artist* among modern authors; and it is his consummate skill as an artist, that has led to these mistakes about the properties of his own heart. That perfection of horror that abounds in his writings, has been unjustly attributed to some moral defect in the man. But I perceive not why the competent critic should fall into this error. Of all authors, ancient or modern, Poe has given us the least of himself in his works. *He wrote as an artist.* He intuitively saw what Schiller has so well expressed, that it is an universal phenomenon of our nature that the mournful, the fearful, even the horrible, allures with irresistible enchantment. He probed the general psychological law, in its subtle windings through the mystic chambers of our being, as it was never probed before, until he stood in the very abyss of its centre, the sole master of its effects.[80]

Nevertheless, Griswold's 'Memoir', coming as it did from Poe's authorized editor, was generally regarded as an authentic account of a wilfully ruined life. In Britain, too, Griswold's calumnies were circulated, accepted, and even exaggerated: in 1852, in an unsigned article on 'Contemporary Literature of America' written for the *Westminster Review*, Griswold himself slyly repeated his charges;[81] two years later, the Rev. George Gilfillan, a popular critic in the moralistic vein, said of Poe (though, ironically, from a modern perspective his description seems more applicable to Griswold): 'He was no more a gentleman than he was a saint. His heart was as rotten as his conduct was infamous. He knew not what the terms honour and honourable meant... He showed himself, in many instances, a cool, calculating, deliberate blackguard';[82] while in 1858, the *Edinburgh Review* declared that 'Edgar Allan Poe was incontestably one of the most worthless persons of whom we have any record in the world of letters.... He outraged his benefactor, he deceived his friends, he sacrificed his love, he became a beggar, a vagabond, the slanderer of a woman, the delirious drunken pauper of a common hospital, hated by some, despised by others, and avoided by all respectable men.'[83] Griswold did his dishonourable work well; and despite the efforts of some of Poe's friends to vindicate him (most importantly George Graham and Sarah Helen Whitman),[84] it was Griswold's caricature – part fiend and degenerate, part wasted genius – that prevailed in the English-speaking world for two decades and more.

VI

CHANGING FORTUNES: 1870 ONWARDS

Judging by the number and variety of printings and reprintings, Poe's tales and poems (especially the poems, which were frequently embellished with sentimental illustrations, and issued in elaborate 'gift' bindings) were quite widely read in both America and Britain during the period 1870–1910. In France, Poe had a significant influence on Mallarmé and the Symbolist movement; in Britain, too, his work was admired by writers and artists including Swinburne, the Rossettis, William Allingham, Robert Louis Stevenson, Conan Doyle, Kipling and Aubrey Beardsley. In America, however, Poe's status was far from secure, and most critical estimates of him from this period now seem vague and superficial. Commentators often found it difficult to separate what they had read of his life and personality from his literary achievement, and there was a feeling, particularly in those areas dominated by the high seriousness of the New England Brahmin outlook, that his writings lacked the moral earnestness and commitment required of great, or even of good, literature. Writing on Baudelaire in 1876, Henry James expressed something of this feeling:

For American readers, furthermore, Baudelaire is compromised by his having made himself the apostle of our own Edgar Poe. He translated, very carefully and exactly, all of Poe's prose writings, and, we believe, some of his very valueless verses. With all due respect to the very original genius of the author of the 'Tales of Mystery', it seems to us that to take him with more than a certain degree of seriousness is to lack seriousness one's self. An enthusiasm for Poe is the mark of a decidedly primitive stage of reflection.[85]

The only writer of eminence to attend the sadly parochial ceremonies to mark the dedication of the Poe Memorial in Baltimore in 1875 was Walt Whitman, but his brief essay on 'Edgar Poe's Significance' (1880) reveals his basic lack of sympathy for Poe's poetry:

Almost without the first sign of moral principle, or of the concrete or its heroisms, or the simpler affections of the heart, Poe's verses illustrate an intense faculty for technical and abstract beauty, with the rhyming art to excess, an incorrigible propensity toward nocturnal themes, a demoniac undertone behind every page – and – by final judgement, probably belong among the electric lights of imaginative literature, brilliant and dazzling, but with no heat.[86]

In 1893, the New York *Critic* promoted a poll to discover the ten 'best' books produced in America: the voters placed Emerson's essays first, followed by *The Scarlet Letter*; Poe's tales and poems came nowhere – a result which provoked the English man of letters Edmund Gosse to write to the *Critic* expressing his astonishment at this neglect of 'the most perfect, the most original, the most exquisite of the American poets'.[87] Of the articles occasioned by the centenary of Poe's birth in 1909, one of the most weighty and widely circulated was by the influential American scholar W. C. Brownell, who argued that it was 'idle to endeavor to make a great writer of Poe because... his writings lack the elements not only of great, but of real, literature', and concluded: 'The cult of Poe, is not in the interests of literature, since as literature his writings are essentially valueless.'[88] Such an opinion would have seemed absurd to George Bernard Shaw, who saw Poe, together with Whitman, as the 'only two men born since the Declaration of Independence whose plea for mercy could avert a prompt sentence of damnation on the entire nation'. To Shaw, Poe was 'the greatest journalistic critic of his time ... His poetry is so exquisitely refined that posterity will refuse to believe it belongs to the same civilization as the glory of Mrs Julia Ward Howe's lilies or the honest doggerel of Whittier.... In his stories of mystery and imagination Poe created a world-record for the English language; perhaps for all languages...'[89]

That Poe was better understood in Britain than in America during the later years of the nineteenth century was due, in no small part, to the pioneer work of John Henry Ingram. In the early 1870s, Ingram, an English civil servant, began his mission to redeem Poe from Griswold's calumnies and misrepresentations. He wrote tirelessly to those who had known Poe (notably Annie Richmond and Mrs Whitman), or who possessed, or thought they possessed, information about him, and from the resulting flood of letters and documents,[90] he constructed the first authentic biography of Poe: it originally appeared in 1874, and in its complete form in two volumes in 1880. In addition, he prepared a four-volume edition of Poe's *Works* (1874–5) containing important new material, wrote almost fifty articles on Poe, and even located the first copy of *Tamerlane and Other Poems* – in the British Museum Library. Ingram devoted much intellectual and emotional energy to rescuing Poe from his detractors, and he bitterly resented the attempts of rival American biographers – William Gill, R.H. Stoddard and Eugene Didier – to intrude into what he thought of as his private domain, or in any way to take credit away from him. But Ingram's presentation of Poe as a literary gentleman and misunderstood idealist was naive and partisan, and by the centenary year his labours had been largely overtaken by George E. Woodberry's more realistic and impartial, as well as more complete, biographical studies: his *Edgar Allan Poe* appeared in the American Men of Letters series in 1885, and was later revised and expanded into *The Life of Edgar Allan Poe, Personal and Literary* (2 Vols, 1909). Several multi-volume 'complete' editions of Poe were published around the turn of the century, though only two possess any scholarly significance: Woodberry produced a ten-volume collection in 1894–5, but this was superseded in 1902 by the Virginia Edition, edited by James A. Harrison in seventeen volumes. Although the Virginia Edition is by now outdated, it is still the most complete scholarly collection of Poe's writings that we have, and will probably remain so until the edition begun by the late Thomas O. Mabbott, and presently being continued under the supervision of Burton Pollin, is brought to completion.[91]

In the earlier decades of this century, Poe scholarship was primarily concerned with basic biographical, historical and textual matters: Margaret Alterton's *Origins of Poe's Critical Theory* (1925) was a pioneering study of his intellectual backgrounds; so too were Killis Campbell's papers on Poe's sources, canon, cultural interests and contemporaneous reputation, collected in *The Mind of Poe and Other Studies* (1933). During the 1920s and '30s, a number of new studies of Poe appeared, some of which were characterized by their single-minded devotion to Freudian interpretations. Joseph Wood Krutch's *Edgar Allan Poe, A Study in Genius* (1926) advanced unprovable notions about Poe's sexuality (or rather his lack of it) to account for the patterns of his life and art; so did Marie Bonaparte, whose *Edgar Poe, étude psychoanalytique* (1933, translated into English by John Rodker in 1949) is a fascinating but ultimately rather bizarre Freudian analysis, based on the supposition that Poe's fiction and poetry were compulsive revelations of his own infantile sexual phobias and fixations. More important, from a biographical view-point, were two studies published in 1926: Hervey Allen's romantic and popular *Israfel: The Life and Times of Edgar Allan Poe* drew attention to new information about Poe's early life; while Mary Phillips's *Edgar Allan Poe: The Man*, despite poor organization and eccentric lapses of style and insight, contains valuable documentary and photographic records of Poe's life and associations. The biographical researches of this period culminated in Arthur Hobson Quinn's *Edgar Allan Poe: A Critical Biography* (1941), which provides a sober, full and systematic account of Poe's life and career, but is too defensive about his character, and is dull and sometimes critically inept on his imaginative writings. During the forty years that have elapsed since Quinn's painstaking study, a considerable number of 'new' biographies of Poe have appeared: without exception they tell and retell the established facts of Poe's life, (three such volumes were published in 1979)[92] and some then go on to advance theories concerning his mental or physical infirmities, but they have added little to our understanding of the man, his environment, or his literary aims and achievements.

Poe has long been a subject of interest to other writers , so it is not surprising that some of the most influential, as well as the most controversial, estimates of Poe's literary and cultural significance should have been made by people who were themselves distinguished creative artists. D.H. Lawrence, writing on 'The Fall of the House of Usher' and 'Ligeia' in *Studies in Classic American Literature* (1923), presented Poe as an early explorer of the modern neurosis of love:

He was an adventurer into vaults and cellars and horrible underground passages of the human soul. He sounded the horror and the warning of his own doom.

Doomed he was. He died wanting more love, and love killed him. A ghastly disease, love. Poe telling us of his disease: trying even to make his disease fair and attractive. Even succeeding.[93]

In his *In the American Grain* (1925), William Carlos Williams repudiated the still widespread notion of Poe as 'the bizarre, isolate writer, the curious literary figure. On the contrary, in him American literature is anchored, in him alone, on solid ground.' For Williams, Poe was a revolutionary figure in American culture: 'Poe gives the sense for the first time in America, that literature is *serious*, not a matter of courtesy but of truth.'[94] Allen Tate also insisted upon Poe's seminal importance, and in his essay on 'The Angelic Imagination' (1952) he declared: 'Poe is the transitional figure in modern literature because he discovered our great subject, the disintegration of personality, but kept it in a language that had developed in a tradition of unity and order.' At the other extreme, Aldous Huxley could find little to admire in Poe's writings, which he dismissed as 'vulgar' – a view enthusiastically supported and elaborated by the poet and critic Yvor Winters, who wrote in 'Edgar Allan Poe: A Crisis in the History of American Obscurantism' (1937):

To illustrate the weakness in detail of his poems and stories is no easy matter; to illustrate the extent of that weakness is impossible, for his work is composed of it....

We are met on every page of his poetry with resounding puerilities such as 'the pallid bust of Pallas', and 'the viol, the violet, and the vine.'...This is an art to delight the soul of a servant girl; it is a matter of astonishment that mature men can be found to take this kind of thing seriously.

...It is unlikely, on the other hand, that the course of romantic literature would have been very different except (perhaps) in America, had Poe never been born; in any event, his influence could only have been a bad one, and to assert that he exerted an influence is not to praise him.

T.S. Eliot was never quite able to make up his mind about Poe. In 'From Poe to Valéry' (1948), he discussed the 'enigma' of Poe's influence on the French Symbolist tradition, and admitted that 'by trying to look at Poe through the eyes of Baudelaire, Mallarmé, and most of all Valéry, I became thoroughly convinced of his importance, of the importance of his *work* as a whole'. Nevertheless, like Henry James and Walt Whitman, he remained unconvinced of Poe's seriousness:

That Poe had a powerful intellect is undeniable: but it seems to me the intellect of a highly gifted young person before puberty. The forms which his lively curiosity takes are those in which a pre-adolescent mentality delights: wonders of nature and of mechanics and of the supernatural, cryptograms and cyphers, puzzles and labyrinths, mechanical chess-players and wild flights of speculation. The variety and ardour of his curiosity delight and dazzle; yet in the end the eccentricity and lack of coherence of his interests tire.

During the last thirty years or so, a vast number of books and academic articles of widely varying interest and quality

have been written about Poe, not only in English, but in all
the major European languages. The sheer quantity, as well as
the miscellaneous nature of these studies, precludes the
possibility of anything like an adequate survey of modern
Poe scholarship in this book;[95] all that can be indicated here
are a few of what seem to be the more important pathways
through a very congested field. In 1957, two influential
monographs appeared: in *Poe: A Critical Study*, Edward H.
Davidson examined Poe's aesthetic and symbolism within the
general framework of Western romantic idealism; while
Patrick F. Quinn in *The French Face of Edgar Poe* approached
Poe's writings through the insights of his French critics and
admirers: he argued that 'To read Poe properly we should
realize that the experience which his stories uniquely offer us
is that of participating in the life of a great ontological
imagination. It is an experience of exploration and discovery
that is offered us, a voyage of the mind.'[96] Although *The
Narrative of Arthur Gordon Pym* has always had its supporters
(including Prince Amerigo in Henry James's *The Golden
Bowl*, and W.H. Auden who described it as 'one on the finest
adventure stories ever written'),[97] it was probably Quinn's
revelation of *Pym*'s ontological mysteries that started a wave
of interest in the novel, which in turn has produced a flood of
views and theories and one outstanding work of
scholarship – Burton R. Pollin's critical edition of the text
published in 1981. Poe's shorter fiction, and not only the
classic tales of terror and detection, but also the comedies,
satires, fantasies and science fiction pieces, including *Eureka*,
have come in for a great deal of close critical scrutiny during
the last thirty years, but one outstanding monograph has
emerged from the mass of variegated criticism: G.R.
Thompson in *Poe's Fiction: Romantic Irony in the Gothic Tales*
(1973) has suggested that 'The view of art informing both the
tales and poems, and to an extent the criticism, is that of
skeptical dissembler and hoaxer who complexly, ambivalent-
ly, and ironically explored the fads of the Romantic Age.'[98]
Source and influence studies continue to proliferate, and
while not many of them are particularly illuminating, there
are, of course, exceptions, notably Burton R. Pollin's
Discoveries in Poe (1970), which offers fascinating glimpses

into the quirky and intricate patterns of Poe's reading and thinking. Previously neglected aspects of Poe's literary career have also received attention: Sidney P. Moss in *Poe's Literary Battles* (1963) and *Poe's Major Crisis* (1970) has revealed the devastating effect Poe's assaults on the literary cliques of his day had upon his career and reputation; while Robert D. Jacobs in *Poe: Journalist and Critic* (1969) and Claude Richard in *Edgar Allan Poe, journaliste et critique* (1978) have made comprehensive surveys of Poe's work as a literary reviewer and critic. Poe's poetry, however, does not seem to be so highly regarded now as it once was, though there have been some valuable contributions. Richard Wilbur's influential introduction to *Poe* in the Laurel Poetry Series (1959), drew attention to an underlying mythology in Poe's poetry, in which the poet seeks to transcend through dream and vision the 'dull realities' of this Fallen World; and Floyd Stovall in the introduction to his edition of *The Poems of Edgar Allan Poe* (1965), and in his essays on *Poe the Poet* (1969), affirmed the once widely held belief that Poe is at his best and most enduring as a poet: 'I have long believed, contrary to the opinions of my younger contemporaries, not only that Poe was a poet by temperament and inclination but that, directly or indirectly, he made his greatest contribution to literature in his poems and his theory of poetic art.'[99]

The impression of Poe that we now have available to us is of a complex, many-sided, and highly inventive writer who evades our attempts to categorize him; a writer who also possessed greater artistic skill and detachment than some of the earlier students of his life and art made allowance for. But this is only part of the story; for Poe has a vast readership and an unshakeable reputation as a creator of weird tales of mystery and terror, and his popularity does not depend upon academic support or approval. Poe's significance for our times cannot be easily analysed (his influence has been felt not only in literature, but also in music, art and film); but T.S. Eliot recognized that it goes beyond the merits of the individual tales and poems, and Allen Tate in 'Our Cousin, Mr Poe' (1949) suggested that his appeal derives from our almost subliminal recognition of our affinity with him:

It is not too harsh, I think, to say that it is stupid to suppose that by 'evaluating' this forlorn demon in the glass, we dispose of him. For Americans, perhaps for most modern men, he is with us like a dejected cousin: we may 'place' him but we may not exclude him from our board. This is a recognition of a relationship, almost of the blood, which we must in honor acknowledge: what destroyed him is potentially destructive of us.[100]

NOTES

1 Cited in Killis Campbell, 'The Kennedy Papers', *Sewanee Review*, 25 (April 1917), p. 197.

2 See George E. Woodberry, *The Life of Edgar Allan Poe* (New York, 1909), I, 109–10.

3 See Campbell, 'The Kennedy Papers', p. 198.

4 See Arthur Hobson Quinn, *Edgar Allan Poe: A Critical Biography* (New York, 1941), 250–1 – hereafter cited as Quinn. See also Paulding's letters to White and Poe – *Works*, 17, 31–2; 377–8.

5 MS. in the Griswold collection, Boston Public Library.

6 William Charvat, *Literary Publishing in America, 1790–1850* (Philadelphia, 1959), p. 23.

7 Campbell, 'The Kennedy Papers', 197–8.

8 *Southern Literary Messenger*, 1 (May 1835), 482–3.

9 See David Kaser, *Messrs. Carey & Lea of Philadelphia* (Philadelphia, 1957), 91–116; also Eugene Exman, *The Brothers Harper* (New York, 1965), 48–59.

10 See Exman, *The Brothers Harper*, 158–83.

11 See James L. Barnes, *Authors, Publishers and Politicians: The Quest for an Anglo-American Copyright Agreement 1815–54* (London, 1974), 13–14.

12 Cited in Earl L. Bradsher, *Mathew Carey, Editor, Author, Publisher* (New York, 1912), p. 93.

13 Frank Luther Mott, *A History of American Magazines, 1741–1850* (Cambridge, Mass., 1930), 340–3.

14 *Broadway Journal*, 1 (15 February 1845), p. 109.

15 *Broadway Journal*, 1 (22 February 1845), p. 127.

16 Frank Luther Mott, *A History of American Magazines*, 504–12.

17 *Broadway Journal*, 2 (6 December 1845), p. 341; Poe copied Simms's editorial from the *Southern and Western Magazine*, 2 (November 1845).

18 *Doings of Gotham: Poe's Contributions to the Columbia Spy*, collected by Jacob E. Spannuth, with a Preface, Introduction,

and Comments by Thomas O. Mabbott (Pottsville, Pa., 1929), p. 42.

19 'Fourth Supplement to *The Letters of Poe*', ed. John Ostrom, *American Literature*, 45 (January 1974), 517–18.

20 Cited in Mott, *A History of American Magazines*, p. 495.

21 Estimates of the number of copies (not all complete) of *Tamerlane and Other Poems* vary between eleven and fourteen. The copy in the Stockhausen collection was sold in November 1974 for $123,000.

22 Philadelphia *Saturday Museum*, 1 (4 March 1843). Henry Hirst is the nominal author of this biography, but Poe supplied the data, and probably had a hand in the writing of it.

23 *American Monthly Magazine*, 1 (November 1829), 586–7.

24 Only about fifteen copies of *Al Aaraaf, Tamerlane, and Minor Poems* seem to have survived; the copy in the Stockhausen sale brought $40,000.

25 Cited in Quinn, p. 165.

26 *Letters of James Russell Lowell*, ed. Charles Eliot Norton (Cambridge, Mass., 1904), 1, 108.

27 *See Works*, 11, 150.

28 Cited in Woodberry, *Life of Edgar Allan Poe*, 1, 157–8.

29 See Quinn, 250–1.

30 Woodberry, *Life of Edgar Allan Poe*, 1, 160.

31 See Alexander Hammond, 'The Composition of *The Narrative of Arthur Gordon Pym*: Notes Toward a Re-Examination', *American Transcendental Quarterly* (Winter 1978), 8–20.

32 Evert A. and George L. Duyckinck, *Cyclopaedia of American Literature* (New York, 1855), 1, 538.

33 The notices are conveniently listed in Burton R. Pollin, 'Poe "Viewed and Reviewed": An Annotated Checklist of Contemporaneous Notices', *Poe Studies*, 13 (December 1980), 21–3.

34 MS. in the Boston Public Library.

35 Francis B. Dedmond, 'A Check-list of Edgar Allan Poe's Works in Book Form Published in the British Isles', *Bulletin of Bibliography*, 21 (May–August 1953), 16–20, lists an illustrated edition of *Pym* published in 1841 by J. Chapman – but I am unable to locate it. Nor can I find the 'obviously pirated' London printing of 1844 noted by Harold Beaver in his edition of *The Narrative of Arthur Gordon Pym* (Penguin Books, 1975), p. 32.

36 *Metropolitan Magazine*, 23 (November, 1838), p. 81.

37 See Caroll D. Laverty, 'A Note on Poe in 1838', *Modern Language Notes*, 64 (March 1949), 174–6.

38 *Broadway Journal*, 1 (30 August 1845), p. 125.

39 Cited in Woodberry, *Life of Edgar Allan Poe*, 1, p. 225.

40 Cited in Dwight Thomas, 'Poe in Philadelphia, 1838–44: A Documentary Record', unpublished dissertation (Pennsylvania, 1978), p. 95.

41 Burton R. Pollin, 'Poe and the Boston *Notion*', *English Language Notes*, 8 (September 1970), 23–8.

42 *New World* (4 June 1842).

43 *The Letters of Henry Wadsworth Longfellow*, ed. Andrew Hilen (Cambridge, Mass., 1966), 2, 302.

44 Washington *Index* (2 November 1841), p. 3.

45 *Saturday Evening Post* (19 August 1843), p. 2.

46 According to T.O. Mabbott, only five complete copies of *Prose Romances* are known – see the facsimile edition of *Prose Romances*, ed. T.O. Mabbott and G. Hatvary (New York, 1968), p. vi.

47 *Broadway Journal*, 1 (25 January 1845), p. 61.

48 *Godey's Lady's Book*, 33 (July 1846), 15–16.

49 *Broadway Journal*, 2 (12 July 1845), p. 10.

50 *Aristidean*, 1 (September 1845), p. 238.

51 *Knickerbocker Magazine*, 28 (July 1845), p. 94.

52 *North American Review*, 63 (October 1846), p. 359.

53 *Godey's Lady's Book*, 31 (June 1845), p. 271.

54 *Tait's Edinburgh Magazine*, 12 (September 1845), p. 612.

55 Cited in Celestin Pierre Cambiaire, *The Influence of Edgar Allan Poe in France* (New York, 1927), p. 32.

56 *Spirit of the Times*, 16 (16 January 1847).

57 *Knickerbocker Magazine*, 25 (March 1845), p. 282.

58 *Collected Works of Edgar Allan Poe*, ed. T.O. Mabbott (Cambridge, Mass., 1969), 1, p. 252; also J.H. Ingram's edition of *The Raven* (London, 1885), 94–123.

59 Cited in Quinn, p. 489.

60 *Broadway Journal*, 2 (1 November 1845), p. 262.

61 *Boston Post* (8 July 1845).

62 *Illustrated Magazine* (15 November 1845); *Anglo-American*, 6 (22 November 1845); *Golden Rule*, 4 (13 December 1845).

63 *Evangelist*, 16 (27 November 1845).

64 See *Letters*, 2, 393.

65 The words are Mrs Ellet's in a letter to Mrs Osgood; the letter is cited in full in Joy Bayless, *Rufus Wilmot Griswold: Poe's Literary Executor* (Nashville, 1943), 141–2.

66 The best studies of this campaign are to be found in Sidney P. Moss, *Poe's Literary Battles* (Durham, N.C., 1963), and *Poe's Major Crisis* (Durham, N.C., 1970).

67 There may have been other reasons for the poor turnout – see

Burton R. Pollin, 'Contemporary Reviews of *Eureka*: A Checklist', *American Transcendental Quarterly* (Spring 1975), 26–30.

68 Copies of the *Weekly Universe* for this date seem to have vanished; G. E. Woodberry, however, printed an extract in his edition of *The Works of Edgar Allan Poe* (Chicago, 1896), 9, 314

69 *Saturday Evening Post* (12 February 1848); *Courier and Enquirer* (11 February 1848).

70 *New World* (12 February 1848).

71 See George Haven Putnam, *George Palmer Putnam, a Memoir* (New York, 1912), 133–7; 395–7.

72 Cited in Quinn, p. 644.

73 See Burton R. Pollin, 'The Temperance Movement and its Friends Look at Poe', *Costerus*, 2 (Amsterdam, 1972), 120–44.

74 Cited in Joy Bayless, *Rufus Wilmot Griswold: Poe's Literary Executor* (Nashville, 1943), p. 173.

75 See Quinn, 651–2.

76 See Lambert Wilmer, *Merlin; Together with Recollections of Edgar A. Poe*, ed. Thomas O. Mabbott (New York, 1941), p. 26.

77 *Knickerbocker Magazine*, 35 (February 1850), 163–4.

78 On this see Quinn, 642–95; also Killis Campbell, *The Mind of Poe and Other Studies* (Cambridge, Mass., 1933), 63–99.

79 *The Works of Edgar Allan Poe* (New York, 1861), 1, p. 48. The 'Memoir' was moved into the first volume in later editions.

80 Chauncey C. Burr, 'The Character of Edgar Allan Poe', *Nineteenth Century*, 5 (February 1852), 19–33.

81 'Contemporary Literature of America', *Westminster Review*, 57 (January 1852), 305–8.

82 Gilfillan's essay first appeared in the London *Critic*, 13 (1 March 1854), 119–21; it was reprinted in *Third Gallery of Portraits* (London, 1855), and copied in America into *Littell's Living Age*, 41 (22 April 1854), 166–71, and in an abbreviated form in the *Southern Literary Messenger*, 20 (April 1854), 249–53.

83 'Edgar Allan Poe', *Edinburgh Review*, 211 (April 1858), 419–42.

84 George Graham's essay on 'The Genius and Characteristics of the Late Edgar Allan Poe' appeared in *Graham's Magazine*, 44 (February 1854), 216–25; Mrs Whitman's short study, *Edgar Poe and his Critics* was published in 1860.

85 Henry James's review of *Les Fleurs du Mal* first appeared in the *Nation* (27 April 1876); it was reprinted in *French Poets and Novelists* (1878), and is conveniently available in *The Recognition of Edgar Allan Poe*, ed. Eric W. Carlson (Ann Arbor, 1966),

65–7 – hereafter cited as Carlson.

86 Whitman's essay was published in *Specimen Days & Collect* (1882–3); it is reprinted in Carlson, 73–6.

87 Cited in Dudley R. Hutcherson, 'Poe's Reputation in England and America, 1850–1909', *American Literature*, 14 (November 1942), 211–33.

88 W.C. Brownell, 'Poe', *Scribner's Magazine*, 45 (January 1909), 69–84; also in *American Prose Masters* (New York, 1909).

89 George Bernard Shaw, 'Edgar Allan Poe', *Nation* (16 January 1909); reprinted in Carlson, 95–100

90 Ingram's papers relating to his work on Poe are in the Alderman Library, University of Virginia. They are being edited by John Carl Miller, and to date two volumes have appeared: *Building Poe Biography* (Baton Rouge, 1977), and *Poe's Helen Remembers* (Charlottesville, 1979).

91 Thomas O. Mabbott edited the *Poems* and *Tales and Sketches* (Cambridge, Mass. 1969–78), and Burton R. Pollin has contributed *The Imaginary Voyages* (Boston, 1981).

92 Wolf Mankowitz, *The Extraordinary Mr Poe*; David Sinclair, *Edgar Allan Poe*; Julian Symons, *The Tell-Tale Heart* – all were first published in London.

93 Lawrence's essay is reprinted in Carlson, 110–26.

94 The essays by Williams, Tate, Huxley, Winters and Eliot are all included in Carlson.

95 There are extensive listings of Poe scholarship in *Edgar Allan Poe: A Bibliography of Criticism, 1827–1967*, ed. J. Lasley Dameron and Irby B. Cauthen, Jr. (Charlottesville, 1974), and Esther F. Hyneman, *Edgar Allan Poe: An Annotated Bibliography of Books and Articles in English, 1827–1973* (Boston, 1974). For current items the 'Poe' listings in *American Literary Scholarship* and *Publications of the Modern Language Association* (PMLA) are useful; so are the current and fugitive listings in *Poe Studies* (founded in 1968).

96 Patrick F. Quinn, *The French Face of Edgar Poe* (Carbondale, 1957), p. 274.

97 Auden's essay was written as the 'Introduction' to the Rinehart edition of *Poe: Selected Prose and Poetry* (1950); it is also printed in Carlson, 220–30.

98 G.R. Thompson, *Poe's Fiction: Romantic Irony in the Gothic Tales* (Madison, 1973), 8–9.

99 Floyd Stovall, 'Preface' to *Poe the Poet* (Charlottesville, 1969).

100 Allen Tate's essay is included in *Poe: A Collection of Critical Essays*, ed. Robert Regan for the Twentieth Century Views Series (Englewood Cliffs, N.J., 1967), 38–50.

Note on the Text

The reviews and other materials in this volume follow the original texts in all important respects. It has sometimes been necessary, however, to omit the lengthy plot summaries, digressions, and extracts from the work under discussion that reviewers of the time so often resorted to; but all these omissions are indicated in the text. Obvious typographical errors have been silently corrected, but odd and variant spellings have been allowed to stand.

Original notes have been numbered *, †, ‡, etc.
Editorial notes have been numbered 1, 2, 3, etc.

TAMERLANE AND OTHER POEMS

1827

1. Poe's 'Preface'

1827

The greater part of the Poems which compose this little volume, were written in the year 1821–2, when the author had not completed his fourteenth year. They were of course not intended for publication; why they are now published concerns no one but himself. Of the smaller pieces very little need be said: they perhaps savour too much of Egotism; but they were written by one too young to have any knowledge of the world but from his own breast.

In Tamerlane, he has endeavoured to expose the folly of even *risking* the best feelings of the heart at the shrine of Ambition. He is conscious that in this there are many faults, (besides that of the general character of the poem) which he flatters himself he could, with little trouble, have corrected, but unlike many of his predecessors, he has been too fond of his early productions to amend them in his *old age*.

He will not say that he is indifferent to the success of these Poems – it might stimulate him to other attempts – but he can safely assert that failure will not at all influence him in a resolution already adopted. This is challenging criticism – let it be so. *Nos haec novimus esse nihil.*[1]

NOTE

1 'I myself know the unimportance of all this' – Martial (Book 13, Epigram 2).

AL AARAAF, TAMERLANE, AND MINOR POEMS

1829

---

2. [John Neal], pre-publication notices in the *Yankee and Boston Literary Gazette*

(a) September 1829, 1, 168; (b) December 1829, 1, 295–8

Neal (1793–1876) was a flamboyant, controversial author from Maine. His extravagant romances were considered outrageously frank, and so were his 'Carter Holmes' articles on American authors (1824–5) in *Blackwood's Edinburgh Magazine*. He edited the *Yankee* during its two-year existence. Poe acknowledged that Neal was the first to encourage his literary ambitions; and although the two men never met, Neal followed Poe's career with interest, and wrote a generous defence of him in the Portland *Daily Advertiser* (23 April 1850).

The quotations in (b) are from Poe's unrevised MS.; the complete texts are printed in the *Collected Works of Edgar Allan Poe: Poems*, ed. Thomas O. Mabbott (Cambridge, Mass., 1969, 89–142).

(a) If E.A.P. of Baltimore – whose lines about 'Heaven', though he professes to regard them as altogether superior to any thing in the whole range of American poetry, save two or three trifles referred to, are, though nonsense, rather exquisite nonsense – would but do himself justice, might make a beautiful and perhaps a magnificent poem. There is a good deal here to justify such a hope.

Dim values and shadowy floods,
And cloudy looking woods,
Whose forms we can't discover,
For the tears that – drip all over.

The moonlight

...............falls
Over hamlets, over halls,
Wherever they may be,
O'er the strange woods, o'er the sea –
O'er the spirits on the wing,
O'er every drowsy thing –
And buries them up quite,
In a labyrinth of light,
And then how deep! – *Oh deep!*
Is the passion of their sleep!

He should have signed it Bah! We have no room for others.

(b)   UNPUBLISHED POETRY

The following passages are from the manuscript-works of a young author, about to be published in Baltimore. He is entirely a stranger to us, but with all their faults, if the remainder of 'Al Aaraaf' and 'Tamerlane' are as good as the body of the extracts here given – to say nothing of the more extraordinary parts, he will deserve to stand high – very high – in the estimation of the shining brotherhood. Whether he *will* do so however, must depend, not so much upon his worth now in mere poetry, as upon his worth hereafter in something yet loftier and more generous – we allude to the stronger properties of the mind, to the magnanimous determination that enables a youth to endure the present, whatever the present may be, in the hope, or rather in the belief, the fixed, unwavering belief, that in the future he will find his reward. 'I am young,' he says in a letter to one who has laid it on our table for a good purpose, 'I am young – yet not twenty – *am* a poet – if deep worship of all beauty can make me one – and wish to be so in the more common meaning of the word. I would give the world to embody one half the ideas afloat in my imagination. (By the way, do you remember – or did you ever read the exclamation of Shelley about Shakespeare? – "What a number of ideas must have been afloat before such an author could arise!") I appeal to you as a man that loves the same beauty which I adore – the beauty of the natural blue sky and the sunshiny earth – there can be no tie more strong than that of brother for brother – it is not so much that they love one another, as that they both love the same parent – their affections are always running in the same direction – the same channel – and cannot help mingling.

I am and have been, from my childhood, an idler. It cannot therefore be said that

> "I left a calling for this idle trade,
> A duty broke – a father disobeyed" –

for I have no father – nor mother.

I am about to publish a volume of "Poems", the greater part written before I was fifteen. Speaking about "Heaven", the editor of the *Yankee* says, "He might write a beautiful, if not a magnificent poem" – (the very first words of encouragement I ever remember to have heard.) I am very certain that as yet I have not written *either* – but that I *can*, I will take oath – if they will give me time.

The poems to be published are "Al Aaraaf" – "Tamerlane" – one about four, and the other about three hundred lines, with smaller pieces. "Al Aaraaf" has some good poetry, and much extravagance, which I have not had time to throw away.

"Al Aaraaf" is a tale of another world – the star discovered by Tycho Brahe, which appeared and disappeared so suddenly – or rather, it is no tale at all. I will insert an extract, about the palace of its presiding Deity, in which you will see that I have supposed many of the lost sculptures of our world to have flown (in spirit) to the star "Al Aaraaf" – a delicate place, more suited to their divinity.'

[Quotes 'Al Aaraaf', part 2, lines 11–39; part 1, lines 126–32; 'Tamerlane', sections 3–7; and 'To——', lines 13–26.]

Having allowed our youthful writer to be heard in his own behalf. – what more can we do for the lovers of genuine poetry? Nothing. They who are judges will not need more; and they who are not – why waste words upon them? We shall not.

3. [John Neal], notice in the Boston *Ladies' Magazine*

January 1830, 3, 47

The *Ladies' Magazine* was 'conducted' by Mrs Sarah J. Hale, though this notice was written by John Neal – as Poe pointed out in his Philadelphia *Saturday Museum* biography (4 March 1843).

It is very difficult to speak of these poems as they deserve. A part are exceedingly boyish, feeble, and altogether deficient in the common characteristics of poetry; but then we have parts and parts too of considerable length, which remind us of no less a poet than Shelley. The author, who appears to be very young, is evidently a fine genius; but he wants judgment, experience, tact.

4. Review in an unidentified Baltimore paper

1830

This review is available only in the form of clippings in the Virginia State Library; it was printed by Randolph W. Church, *'Al Aaraaf* and the Unknown Critic', *Virginia Cavalcade* (Summer 1955, pp. 4–7), and is reprinted here with permission.

The question has been often propounded, 'why has not America produced a great Poet?' It has been met, and logically answered, by reference to local causes. No one has pretended to doubt, except our transatlantic brethren, that the talent exists, although unfortunately, not as yet developed. The time is anxiously expected, when some great being shall arise, who will delight his astonished and admiring countrymen by an Epic in twelve or twenty four books, or some *Course of Time*[1] in ten or twenty, or even a more ignoble effusion in a dozen or more Cantos. But having in view this high standard it is forgotten that Poetry is daily ushered forth of high and genuine worth. 'The feathered songsters,' 'the glistening dew drops,' 'the secret sigh and whisper in the dark,' 'the warbling woodlands and resounding shores, and all the pomp and garniture of fields,' 'the *flitting* shades,' 'the pearly tear,' 'the shadowless spirits,' and 'annoying Cupid,' all have been sung by the poets of our favored Country in strains truly admirable.

Our object, at present, is to offer our tribute of admiration and regard to the Author of *Al Aaraaf, Tamerlane, and Minor Poems,* which have recently been issued from the press in this city. We view the production as highly creditable to the Country. Throughout, there runs a rich vein of deep and powerful thought, clothed in language of almost inimitable beauty and harmony. His fancy is rich and of an elevated cast; his imagination powerfully creative. There is no laboured attempt at effect; no immoderate use of epithets; no

70

over-burdening the idea with words, no cant, no nonsense. We are well aware of the force of those beautiful lines of Beattie,

> Oh, who can tell how hard it is to climb,
> The steep where Fame's proud temple shines afar;

but we would bid the accomplished Author, be of good cheer. He has indeed 'waked to extacy the living lyre,' and we trust, that he will continue to sound its strings. Indeed we demand that he continue his efforts, for the Public have a lawful and irresistible claim upon the direction of his talents.

We will quote a few extracts for the purpose of convincing our readers, that what we have said, has not been the result of blinded partiality or mistaken judgment.

[Quotes 'Al Aaraaf', part 1, lines 1–17.]

Who is there who cannot admire the beauty of the whole extract? The sublimity of the figure contained in the last line would redeem a multitude of faults. But to continue:

[Quotes 'Al Aaraaf', part 2, lines 112–27; 'Tamerlane', stanza 23.]

We will quote a beautiful description of FAIRY-LAND. Its conception is truly grand, and its versification highly ingenious. We would refer particularly to the sixth line.

[Quotes 'Fairy-Land'.]

We would continue our extracts, were we not admonished that we are exceeding our proper limits. But we think that what we have presented to our readers, will satisfactorily convince them, that the work is of no ordinary nature. That it merits all the praises which we have bestowed upon it, we cannot think that there will be any hesitation, and we trust that the author will receive that pecuniary remuneration which he so richly merits, and which we are confident a public, when once it has examined the foundation of his claims, will cheerfully and amply confer.

NOTE

1 Robert Pollok's epic-length poem appeared in 1827.

5. John Hill Hewitt, review in the Baltimore *Minerva and Emerald*

1830

Hewitt (1801–90) was a musician, poet, and journalist. A good deal of animosity existed between him and Poe, possibly stemming from this review: Poe satirized him in 'A Decided Loss' (1832), and they quarrelled over the *Saturday Visiter* prize in 1833

No copy of the weekly *Minerva and Emerald* of this date is available; the present text is from Hewitt's MS. as printed in 'Recollections of Poe, by John Hill Hewitt', ed. Richard Barksdale Harwell, *Emory University Publications: Sources and Reprints,* Series 5 (1949).

There is something in these poems so original, that we cannot help introducing them to the public, as a literary curiosity, full of burning thoughts, which so charm the reader, that he forgets he is' travelling over a pile of brick-bats, for such we must compare the measure to. – The author will pardon us, if we claim his bantlings as our own – paid for, not by downright cash, but by the strength of our credit; consequently, we have a right to do what we please with them. It is said that poetry is the gift of nature; if so, we will venture to say she hesitated in imparting to the author of *Al Aaraaf* &c. that portion of inspiration essential to the formation of a poet of common order: we love to foster young budding genius, to place modest merit in the beams of the sun of glory, and to befriend the productions of those whom nature intended to be an honour to the literary character of our country. We have great reason for fearing that *Al Aaraaf* will not add a single radiant to our diadem. The author, after his dedication, which amounts to this –

Who drinks deepest? – Here's to him;

seems to liken himself to a transitory star. 'A star was
discovered by Tycho Brahe, which burst forth, in a moment,
with splendour surpassing that of Jupiter – then gradually
faded away, and became invisible to the naked eye.' In one
sense, an apt quotation, indicative of the transitory glory of
the poems which follow.

'Al Aaraaf' is the title of the leading poem – of its object we
have yet to be informed; for all our brain-cudgelling could
not *compel* us to understand it line by line or the sum
total – perchance, and we think we have hit it, it alludes to
the text quoted above, concerning the falling star. We shall
leave the plot in its obscurity, and take the *poetry* into
consideration. On page seventeen, we learn the color of a
smell in the following line:

And thy most lovely purple perfume, Zante!

Again, on page twenty, we learn that *sound* has form and
body, from its throwing a shadow:

'Flap shadowy sounds from visionary wings' –

Concerning the various hues of the atmosphere, we have
lived to learn that a decomposition of *blue* will produce
almost all the colors of the rainbow:

And the *red* winds withering in the sky;
With all the train, athwart the *moony* sky –
Uprose the maiden in the *yellow* night,
Of molten stars their pavement, such as fall
Through the *ebon* air,
A window of one circular diamond, there,
Look'd out above the *purple* air.
Witness the murmur of the *grey* twilight.

But we will allow 'Al Aaraaf' to rest, after having quoted a
stanza or two from 'the charm the maiden sung.' The author
deserves a premium from John Neal, for inventing rhymes:

Till they glance thro' the *shade*, and
Come down to your brow,
Like – eyes of the *maiden*
Who calls on you now –

73

> Ligeia! Ligeia!
> My beautiful one!
> Whose harshest idea
> Will to melody run.

'Tamerlane' – This poem is dedicated to John Neal – the author has thus wisely secured the favour of 'the mustard pot'; no danger from that quarter. Let us see – egad! it improves on acquaintance; its faults are so few and so trifling, that they may be passed over.

We now turn to the miscellaneous poems contained in the volume; which, if they cannot be called beautiful, possess, at least, a share of originality. Not liking to disjoint the verses 'To——'we present them to our readers entire:

[Quotes 'To——'.]

From the lines 'To M——', we make the following choice extracts:

[Quotes 'To M——'.]

The dead alive! Has the poet been struck with the numb palsy? We believe not: for then it might only be said, that the poor fellow had but 'one foot in the grave', where, as it appears by the above, that he has gone for the whole——, and fairly kicked the bucket, still possessing the full enjoyment of his faculties. We have done with the book; what more is to be done remains with the public.

POEMS

1831

---

6. Notice in the *New-York Mirror*

7 May 1831, 8, 349–50

The poetry of this little volume has a plausible air of imagination, inconsistent with the general indefiniteness of the ideas. Every thing in the language betokens poetic inspiration, but it rather resembles the leaves of the sybil when scattered by the wind. The annexed lines, which close a short poem, entitled the 'Doomed City', are less incomprehensible than most of the book, although the meaning is by no means perfectly clear:

[Quotes last 14 lines.]

It sometimes happens that poetry, at first sight unintelligible, is discovered, upon a repeated and more careful examination, to be fraught with the treasure of thought and fancy. The 'Rime of the Ancient Mariner' belongs to this class; but we cannot flatter Mr Poe with any similar hope respecting his own composition, although it occasionally sparkles with a true poetic expression, and sometimes a conflict of beauty and nonsense takes place, in which the latter seems to have the best of it. It is indeed encumbered by numerous obscurities, which we should be pleased to see either very much brightened or entirely expunged. What is the meaning of this?

> A heaven that God doth not contemn
> With stars is like a diadem –
> We liken our ladies' eyes to them.

Or these lines, (with which we close the article,) from 'Fairy Land'?

[Quotes lines 45–64.]

7. [John Neal], notice in the *Morning Courier and New York Enquirer*

8 July 1831, 7, 124

This is evidently a fellow of fine genius, but if one were disposed to believe to the contrary, and to sustain his belief, he need wish for nothing more than a passage or two, taken haphazard from the book – as for example:

[Quotes 'To Irene', lines 1–8.]

Sheer nonsense, undoubtedly, yet as undoubtedly the author has the gift, and betrays the presence, here and there that cannot be mistaken – for example:

[Quotes 'To Helen'.]

And again – read the following sonnet, and then marvel at the strangeness of the mixture. Pure Poetry in one page – pure absurdity in another.

[Quotes 'Sonnet – To Science'.]

But we are sick of poetry – so sick of it indeed, that we should not have meddled with this, but for a wish to prevent a young man – the author must be young, for there is the fever and the flush, and the strong delusion of youth about him, if not boyhood – from betraying himself unworthily. He has a fine genius, we repeat it, and may be distinguished, if he will not mistake oddity for excellence, or want of similitude to all others, for superiority over them. We have said as much to the confederacy of small poets around us and they don't like our candour.

THE YOUNG MAGAZINIST

8. Editorial in the Baltimore *Saturday Visiter*

4 August 1832, 2, 3

This notice was probably written by Lambert Wilmer, literary editor of the *Visiter*. Wilmer (1805–63) met Poe in Baltimore in 1827, and based his drama 'Merlin' on what he had heard of his romance with Miss Royster. His interest in Poe lasted: he defended him against Griswold's calumnies, and his recollections of him appeared in 1866 – see Lambert A. Wilmer, *Merlin, Together with Recollections of Edgar A. Poe*, ed. Thomas O. Mabbott (New York, 1941).

Mr Edgar A. Poe, has favoured us with the perusal of some manuscript tales written by him. If we were merely to say that we had *read* them, it would be a compliment, for manuscripts of this kind are very seldom read by any one but the author. But we may further say that we have read these tales every syllable, with the greatest pleasure, and for originality, richness of imagery and purity of the style, few American authors in our opinion have produced any thing superior. With Mr Poe's permission we may hereafter lay one or two of the tales before our readers.

9. From reports in the Baltimore *Saturday Visiter*

(a) 12 October 1833; (b) 26 October 1833

Report (a) was probably written by the chairman of the awarding committee, John Pendleton Kennedy (1795–1870), a distinguished lawyer, politician, and man of letters. He was a good friend to Poe, and introduced him to the *Southern Literary Messenger*. Other signatories were John H.B. Latrobe, lawyer, inventor, and patron of the arts; and John H. Miller, a Baltimore physician. Poe published an edited version of the report in the *Messenger*, August 1835, 1, 716.

Poe may well have had a hand in report (b).

(a) ... Of the tales submitted there were many of various and distinguished excellence; but the singular force and beauty of those offered by 'The Tales of the Folio Club', it may be said without disparagement to the high merit of others presented in the competition, left us no ground for doubt in making the choice of one from that collection. We have accordingly, awarded the prize in this department to the tale bearing the title of 'A MS. Found in a Bottle'. It would scarcely be doing justice to the author of this collection to say the tale we have chosen is the best of the six offered by him. We have read them all with unusual interest, and cannot refrain from the expression of the opinion that the writer owes it to his own reputation, as well as to the gratification of the community to publish the whole volume. These tales are eminently distinguished by a wild, vigorous and poetical imagination, a rich style, a fertile invention, and varied and curious learning. Our selection of 'A MS. Found in a Bottle' was rather dictated by the originality of its conception and its length, than by any superior merit in its execution over the others by the same author.

The general excellence of the whole of the compositions offered for the prizes is very creditable to the rising literature of our country.

(b)   THE FOLIO CLUB

This is the title of a volume from the pen of Edgar A. Poe, the gentleman to whom the committee appointed by the proprietors of this paper awarded the premium of $50. The work is about being put to press, and is to be published by subscription – we have a list at our office, and any person wishing to subscribe, will please call. The volume will cost but $1.

The prize tale is not the best of Mr Poe's productions; among the tales of the 'Folio Club' there are many possessing uncommon merit. They are all characterized by a raciness, originality of thought and brilliancy of conception which are rarely to be met with in the writings of our most favoured American authors. In assisting Mr. Poe in the publication of the 'Folio Club', the friends of native literature will encourage a young author whose energies have been partially damped by the opposition of the press, and, we may say, by the lukewarmness of the public in appreciating American productions. He has studied and written much – his reward rested on public approbation – let us give him something more substantial than bare praise. We ask our friends to come forward and subscribe to the work – there are many anxious to see it laid before the public.

10. Editorial notices of Poe's tales in the *Southern Literary Messenger*

(a) March 1835, 1, 387; (b) April 1835, 1, 460;
(c) June 1835, 1, 533

James E. Heath (1792–1862), a Virginian lawyer, editor, and minor man of letters, wrote the notices of 'Berenice' and 'Morella'. Poe believed a Mr Pleasants wrote the notice of 'Hans Phaall'—see *Letters*, 1, 65.

(a) 'Berenice', a tale, by Mr Edgar A. Poe, will be read with interest, especially by the patrons of the *Messenger* in this city, of which Mr P. is a native, and where he resided until he reached manhood. Whilst we confess that we think that there is too much German horror in his subject, there can be but one opinion as to the force and elegance of his style. He discovers a superior capacity and a highly cultivated taste in composition.

(b) 'Morella' will unquestionably prove that Mr Poe has great powers of imagination, and a command of language seldom surpassed. Yet we cannot but lament that he has drunk so deep at some enchanted fountain, which seems to blend in his fancy the shadows of the tomb with the clouds and sunshine of life. We doubt however, if anything in the same style can be cited, which contains more terrific beauty than this tale.

(c) Mr Poe's story of 'Hans Phaall', will add much to his reputation as an imaginative writer. In these *ballooning* days, when every 'punny whipster' is willing to risk his neck in an attempt to 'leave dull earth behind him', and when we hear so much of the benefits which science is to derive from the art of aerostation, a journey to the moon may not be considered a matter of mere moonshine. Mr Poe's scientific Dutch bellows-mender is certainly a prodigy, and the more to be admired, as he performs impossibilities, and details them with a minuteness so much like truth, that they seem quite probable. Indeed the *cause* of his great enterprise is in admirable harmony with the exploits which it encourages him to perform. There are thousands who, to escape the pertinacity of uncivil creditors, would be tempted to a flight as perilous as that of Hans Phaall. Mr Poe's story is a long one, but it will appear short to the reader, whom it bears along with irresistible interest, through a region of which, of all others, we know least, but which his fancy has invested with particular charms. We trust that a future missive from the lunar voyager will give us a narrative of his adventures in the orb that he has been the first to explore.

11. Philip Pendleton Cooke, from a letter to Thomas White in the *Southern Literary Messenger*

September 1835, 1

Cooke (1815–50) came from a well-known Virginian family with wide literary pretensions and contacts (John Pendleton Kennedy was his cousin). Poe cultivated Cooke's friendship – he professed to admire deeply his sentimental magazine verses like 'Rosalie Lee' and 'Florence Vane'. Cooke's letter was first printed in the *Richmond Compiler*; it was then reprinted by White in 'Opinions of the Press' on the covers of the *Messenger*. It is not clear what Cooke meant to indicate by his asterisks.

We have been favored by the proprietor of the *Southern Literary Messenger*, with the perusal of a letter from the writer of articles on 'English Poetry'. This writer, whose name we are not at liberty to give to the public, is unquestionably one of the most gifted and highly intellectual of Virginia's sons. He pays a deserved compliment to a fellow contributor to the *Messenger*; and we take pleasure in spreading an extract from his letter before our readers.

'In looking over your list of contributors, I see the name of Mr Poe. I have heard of some passages in his life, which have added to the interest with which I read his writings. ★★★ For God's sake, value him according to his merits, which are exceedingly great. I say this with deliberation, for I have been months in coming to the conclusion that he is the first genius, in his line, in Virginia. And when I say this, how many other States are included – certainly all South of us. The conversation in 'Morella' – the description in 'Berenice' of a mind dwelling with strained intensity upon some particular (trifling) object with which the eye meets – and the description of that Beckford of Venice, and his singular sanctum in the 'Visionary': as also the vague speculations of 'Hans Phaall' upon the scenery of the moon – with its shadow-stained lakes and sombre vegetation – are compositions of rare beauty. I am too much hurried to write good English, but you may understand from what I have scribbled above, that I admire Poe greatly.'

12. From the 'Supplement' to the *Southern Literary Messenger*

January 1836, 2, 133–40

(a) From the *Pennsylvanian*

The December number of the *Southern Literary Messenger* has been received. The contributions appear to be of an excellent kind; at least those from Mr Poe and others, whose reputations attracted our notice. The most striking feature of the number, however, is the critical department. Eschewing all species of puffery, the *Messenger* goes to work upon several of the most popular novels of the day, and hacks and hews with a remorselessness and an evident enjoyment of the business, which is as rare as it is amusing, in an indigenous periodical. Of the justice of the criticisms, we have not qualified ourselves to judge; but their severity is manifest enough; and that is such a relief to the dull monotony of praise which rolls smooth in the wake of every new book, that a roughness which savors of honesty and independence is welcome.

(b) From the *Norfolk Herald*

The first number of Vol. 2 of this Magazine has come to hand, greatly improved in outward appearance, as well as in literary merit. No Journal of this kind in the country has experienced so rapid, so extensive, and so unequivocal a success as the *Southern Literary Messenger*. It is now, whether we consider the extent of its patronage, the great beauty of its mechanical appearance, or the lustre of the names of its regular contributors, the first Monthly Magazine in America. In the variety, and more especially in the originality of its articles it has no equal; and among other things we must not forget that the author of the 'Lunar Hoax' is indebted to the 'Hans Phaall' of Mr Poe (a regular contributor to the *Messenger*) for the conception and in a great measure for the execution of his discoveries. Indeed several passages in the two are nearly identical. As regards the amount of absolute matter contained in a number of the *Messenger*, we cannot be far wrong in stating that it is equal to that of any two monthly Journals in the country – with the exception perhaps of *Littell's Museum*, which is made up altogether of selections from foreign Magazines....

The 'MS. found in a Bottle' is extracted from *The Gift*, Miss Leslie's beautiful Annual. It is from the pen of Edgar A. Poe, 'whose eccentric genius', says the *Charleston Courier*, 'delights in the creation of strange possibilities, and in investing the most intangible romances in an air of perfect verisimilitude'. We have heard the 'MS. found in a bottle', called the best of his Tales – but prefer his 'Lionizing' and 'Morella'. – The highest praise, however, and from the very highest quarters, has been awarded to *all* he has written.

(c) From the *Charlottesville Jeffersonian*

We have been favored by the politeness of Mr White, with the first number of the second volume of this interesting periodical, and take pleasure in adding our mite to the many well merited praises which his work has already received from other journals; and we agree with Mr White in his bright anticipations of the future. This periodical must be sustained for the literary credit of the Old Dominion and the honor of the South. Some of our Northern contemporaries have already declared it the *best* literary periodical in America, and we deem this praise not so high as when they say it is decidedly good. This number contains sufficient variety to gratify diversity of taste.

The 'MS. found in a Bottle'. By Edgar A. Poe, is good, – it is original and well told. Its wild impossibilities are pictured to the imagination with all the detail of circumstances, which truth and fearful reality might be supposed to present. Whilst we do not agree to the justness of the praise which has been bestowed upon *some* of Mr Poe's pieces, we concur in the general commendation which he has received as a writer of great originality, and one who promises well....

The editorial criticisms are many, and in the right vein. They are caustic but just. The Review of Mr Fay's novel

Norman Leslie, is amusing and will be read, though we think some passages in it are in bad taste. The author is flayed, or to use a term more congenial with his taste, and with the Reviewer's article – *blistered*.

(d) From the *Charleston Courier*

After an interval of several months, a species of literary interdict by the way which we did not much relish, we are able to announce the welcome reception of the December number of this excellent and eminently successful periodical, commencing its second volume and the second year of its bright and promising existence. The State of Virginia has reason to be proud of it, as a valuable exhibition of her mental prowess – it has gathered the stars of her intellectual firmament into close and brilliant constellation, and with their blended light burnished her literary fame. But while collecting into a focus the rays of Southern mind, the Aurora Borealis of genius has been no stranger to its pages, and its intellectual gems have been freely gathered from other portions of the republic of letters. Among its contributors, EDGAR A. POE, equally ripe in graphic humor and various lore, seems by common consent to have been awarded the laurel, and in the number before us fully sustaining the reputation of its predecessors, will be found proofs of his distinguished merit.

(e) From the *Richmond Whig*

The *Literary Messenger* – The high reputation of this periodical is acknowledged by others besides ourselves, and much more competent judges. The *Lynchburg Virginian* says:

'The *Messenger*, upon the whole, reflects credit upon Virginia and the entire South. Indeed, several distinguished Northern Journals place it at the head of periodical literature in the United States – a most enviable distinction when we recollect the eminent names that figure in our Monthlies, both as editors and contributors. Mr White deserves the thanks of the people of the South for his untiring perseverance and industry, and we are glad to hear that he is receiving them in the most substantial form – to wit, *paying subscribers.*'

And Mr Paulding in a letter to the proprietor says:

'P.S. – Your publication is decidedly superior to any Periodical in the United States, and Mr Poe as decidedly the best of all our young writers; I don't know but I might add all our old ones, with one or two exceptions, among which I assure you I don't include myself.'

13. From the 'Supplement' to the *Southern Literary Messenger*

April 1836, 2, 341–8

(a) From the *Norfolk Herald*
... A very slight inspection will convince any one at all conversant in these matters that the present number of the *Messenger* embraces as much reading matter (if not considerably more) than four ordinary volumes, such for example, as the volumes of *Paul Ulric* or *Norman Leslie*. Of the value of the matter, or rather of its value in comparison with such ephemera as these just mentioned, it is of course unnecessary to say much. Popular opinion has placed the *Messenger* in a very enviable position as regards the Literature of the South. We have no hesitation in saying that it has elevated it immeasurably. To use the words of a Northern contemporary 'it has done more within the last six months to refine the literary standard in this country than has been accomplished before in the space of ten years'....

'Epimenes'. By Edgar A. Poe – an historical tale in which, by imaginary incidents, the character of Antiochus Epiphanes is vividly depicted. It differs essentially from all the other tales of Mr Poe. Indeed no two of his articles bear more than a family resemblance to one another. They all differ widely in matter, and still more widely in manner. 'Epimenes' will convince all who read it that Mr P. is capable of even higher and better things.

'To Helen' – by the same author – a sonnet full of quiet grace – we quote it in full.

(b) From the *Richmond Compiler*

... That Mr Poe, the reputed editor of the *Messenger*, is a gentleman of brilliant genius and endowments, is a truth which I believe, will not be controverted by a large majority of its readers. For one, however, I confess, that there are occasionally manifested some errors of judgement – or faults in taste – or whatever they may be called, which I should be glad to see corrected. I do not think, for example, that such an article as the 'Duc De L'Omelette', in the number under consideration, ought to have appeared. That kind of writing, I know, may plead high precedents in its favour; but that it is calculated to produce effects permanently injurious to sound morals, I think will not be doubted by those who reflect seriously upon the subject. Mr Poe is too fond of the wild – unnatural and horrible! Why will he not permit his fine genius to soar into purer, brighter, and happier regions? Why will he not disenthral himself from the spells of German enchantment and supernatural imagery? There is room enough for the exercise of the highest powers, upon the multiform relations of human life, without descending into the dark mysterious and unutterable creations of licentious fancy. When Mr Poe passes from the region of shadows, into the plain practical dissecting room of criticism, he manifests great dexterity and power. He exposes the imbecility and rottenness of our *ad captandum* popular literature, with the hand of a master. The public I believe was much delighted with the admirable scalping of *Norman Leslie*, in the December number, and likewise of Mr Simms' *Partisan*, in the number for January; and it will be no less pleased at the caustic severity with which the puerile abortion of *Paul Ulric* is exposed in the present number. – These miserable attempts at fiction, will bring all fictitious writing into utter disrepute, unless indeed the stern rebukes which shall come from our chairs of criticism, shall rectify the public taste, and preserve the purity of public feeling.

(c) From the *Petersburg Constellation*

... Of the lighter contributions, of the diamonds which

sparkle beside the more sombre gems, commend us, thou spirit of eccentricity! forever and a day to our favorite Edgar A. Poe's 'Duc de L'Omelette' – the best thing of the kind we ever have or ever expect to read. The idea of 'dying of an Ortolan;' the waking up in the palace of Pluto; of that mysterious chain of 'blood red metal' hung *parmi les nues*', at the nether extremity of which was attached a 'cresset' pouring forth a light more 'intense, still and terrible' than 'Persia ever worshipped, Gheber imagined, or Mussulman dreamed of'; the paintings and statuary of that mysterious hall, whose solitary uncurtained window looked upon blazing Tartarus, and whose ceiling was lost in a mass of 'fiery-colored clouds'; the nonchalance of the Duc in challenging 'His Majesty' to a pass with the points; his imperturbable, self-confident assurance during the playing of a game of *ecarte*; his adroitness in slipping a card while his Infernal Highness 'took wine' (a trick which won the Duc his game by the by,) and finally his characteristic compliment to the Deity of the Place of 'que s'il n'était pas de L'Omelette, il n'aurait point d'objection d'être le Diable', are conceptions which for peculiar eccentricity and graphic quaintness, are perfectly inimitable. Of the criticisms, the most are good; that on Mr Morris Mattson's novel of *Paul Ulric*, like a former criticism from the same pen on Fay's *Norman Leslie* is a literal 'flying alive' a carving up into 'ten thousand atoms' a complete literary annihilation! If Mr Morris Mattson is either courageous or wise, he will turn upon his merciless assailant as Byron turned upon Jeffrey, and prove that he can not only do better things, but that he deserves more lenient treatment! Last but not by far the least in interest, is Mr Joseph A.Q.Z. Miller's 'Autography'. We copy the whole article as a literary treat which we should wrong their tastes did we suppose for a moment would not be as highly appreciated by each and all of our readers, as it is by ourself.

14. From the 'Supplement' to the *Southern Literary Messenger*

July 1836, 2, 517–24

(a) From the *Baltimore Gazette*

... The long and able article on Maelzel's Chess Player, contained in this number, does credit to the close observation and acute reasoning of its author, who, as the article is published under the editorial head, we infer is the talented editor himself. The question whether or not the chess-player is a pure machine, is, we think, completely put to rest. The nature of the game of chess is such, that no *machine*, however ingeniously arranged may be its mechanism, could of itself perform its constantly varying operations. We have never, at any time, given assent to the prevailing opinion, that human agency is not employed by Mr Maelzel. That such agency is employed cannot be questioned, unless it may be satisfactorily demonstrated that man is capable to impart intellect to matter: for *mind* is no less requisite in the operations of the game of chess, than it is in the prosecution of a chain of abstract reasoning. We recommend those, whose credulity has in this instance been taken captive by plausible appearances; and all, whether credulous or not, who admire an ingenious train of inductive reasoning, to read this article attentively: each and all must arise from its perusal convinced that a *mere machine* cannot bring into requisition the intellect which this intricate game demands, but on the contrary that every operation is the result of human agency, though so ingeniously concealed as to baffle detection, unless by long continued and close observation....

'A Tale of Jerusalem', is one of those felicitous 'hits' which are the forte of Edgar A. Poe. The point, like that of an epigram, lies in the conclusion.

The 'critical notices' in the present number, evince the

usual ability of the editor in this department; though, what is more to our taste, not quite so caustic, as hitherto. We accord with the review of the 'Culprit Fay'. The merits of this poem, despite the praise lavished upon it, when critically sifted, will be found to be like the little Ouphe himself, rather a small affair.

(b) From the *Baltimore Patriot*
... The *Southern Literary Messenger* is now under the editorial conduct of Edgar A. Poe, Esq. formerly of this city, and has been so, as we understand, since the commencement of the second volume. This gentleman has been, the while, a liberal contributor to its columns, and this thorough identification with a periodical, marked with unusual ability and attended with extraordinary success, must be satisfactory to the editor, and afford ample testimony at the same time that the conduct of the *Messenger* is in fit and competent hands.

(c) From the *New Yorker*
... In the matter of Criticism, the *Messenger* has involved itself in a difficulty with some of our Northern periodicals, either party, as is not unusual in such cases, being just about half right. The Southern Editor has quite too savage a way of pouncing upon unlucky wights who happen to have severally perpetrated any thing below par in the literary line, like the Indian, who cannot realize that an enemy is conquered till he is scalped and some of the mangled have no more policy than to betray their soreness by attempts at retaliation, under very flimsy disguises, invariably making the matter worse. We think the *Messenger* often quite too severe, as in the case of *Norman Leslie*, but still able and ingenious. The Poems of Halleck and Drake are reviewed this month – neither of them after the fashion of an ardent and awed admirer – but fairly, and with discrimination.

THE NARRATIVE OF ARTHUR GORDON PYM

1838

15. Unsigned review in the *New-York Mirror*

11 August 1838, 16, 55

For valuable comment on this and other reviews in this section, see Burton R. Pollin, 'Poe's *Narrative of Arthur Gordon Pym* and the Contemporary Reviewers', *Studies in American Fiction*, 2 (1974), 37–56.

A volume from the press of the Harpers, professing to give the 'details of a mutiny and atrocious butchery on board the American brig Grampus, on her way to the South Seas – with an account of the re-capture of the vessel by the survivers; their shipwreck and subsequent horrible sufferings from famine; their deliverance by means of the British schooner Jane Guy; the brief cruise of this latter vessel in the Antarctick Ocean; her capture, and the massacre of her crew among a group of islands in the eighty-fourth parallel of southern latitude; together with the incredible adventures and discoveries still further south, to which that distressing calamity gave rise'.[1] The author would have shown his ingenuity to more purpose, if he had preserved the *vraisemblance* of his narrative. As it is, the gross improbabilities and preternatural adventures through which his hero passes, soon destroy the interest of the reader, and revolt the imagination. We are constantly tempted to exclaim: 'Ferdinand Mendez Pinto was but a type of thee, thou liar of the first magnitude!' At the same time we must concede to the author, the merit of a fine mastery over language, and powers of description rarely excelled.

NOTE

1 Poe's descriptive title page provided the casual reviewer with a useful synopsis of Pym's adventures.

16. [Lewis Gaylord Clark], review in the *Knickerbocker Magazine*

August 1838, 12, 167

Clark (1808–73) was a central figure in New York literary life; under his editorship (1834–61), the *Knicker-bocker* became a widely read arbiter of taste. Clark and Poe were bitter enemies – their quarrels went back to Poe's hawkish review in 1835 of Theodore Fay's novel *Norman Leslie*. Clark's vituperative and vindictive assaults on Poe, especially during his troubles of 1845–6, did much to discredit Poe's character and prepared the way for Griswold's calumnies. On the Poe–Clark hostilities, see Sidney P. Moss, *Poe's Literary Battles* (Durham, N.C., 1963).

This work 'comprises the details of a mutiny and atrocious butchery on board the American ship Grampus, on her way to the South Seas, in the month of June, 1827, with an account of the recapture of the vessel by the survivors; their shipwreck and subsequent horrible sufferings from famine; their deliverance by means of the British schooner, Jane Guy; the brief cruise of this latter vessel in the Antarctic Ocean; her capture, and the massacre of her crew among a group of islands in the eighty-fourth parallel of southern latitude; together with the *incredible* adventures and discoveries still further south, to which that distressing calamity gave rise'. There are a great many tough stories in this book, told in a loose and slip-shod style, seldom chequered by any of the more common graces of composition, beyond a Robinson Crusoe-ish sort of simplicity of narration. The work is one of much interest, with all its defects, not the least of which is, that it is too liberally stuffed with 'horrid circumstance of blood and battle'. We would not be so uncourteous as to insinuate a doubt of Mr Pym's veracity, now that he *lies* 'under the sod'; but we should very much question that gentleman's word, who should affirm, after having thoroughly perused the volume before us, that he *believed* the various adventures and hair-breadth's capes therein recorded. Such a capacious maw would swallow, as indubitably veritable, a story we have recently read or heard, of a serpent killed in the East Indies, in whose body was found, neatly dressed in black, the chaplain of an adjacent military station, who had been missed for a week.

17. Notice in the New York *Albion*

18 August 1838, 6, 263

The *Albion* was a weekly conducted by Dr John S. Bartlett; its emphasis was on English culture and events.

The author of this work very gravely assures us that the details of his book are veritable facts; if so, they are a further illustration of the trite remark that 'Truth is strange, stranger than fiction', for such a tissue of wonderful adventures and escapes we have not read since we perused those of 'Sinbad the Sailor'. Let them pass, however, for what they are worth, in the belief of readers, but we cannot pass them by without remarking on the interest which the relator has thrown over the events, and the very attractive book he has succeeded in making. We are disposed to believe that the author is a second Capt. Lemuel Gulliver as regards authenticity, and think that although he does not deal in political and moral satire he has fabricated a volume which will be extensively read and very pleasing.

18. Unsigned notice in *Alexander's Weekly Messenger*

22 August 1838, p. 2

Charles W. Alexander (1796–1866) was a newspaper and magazine publisher in Philadelphia. He had business connections with William Burton, who probably introduced him to Poe; Poe contributed to the *Weekly Messenger* (December 1839–May 1840). See Burton R. Pollin, 'Three More Early Notices of *Pym* and the Snowden Connection', *Poe Studies*, 8 (December 1975), 32–5

[Poe's title page is cited.]

Think of that, Master Brook! What say you, reader to that for a title page? We assure you the book, if possible, is more marvellous still. Captain Riley's narrative[1] was a tame affair, compared with it. 'Incredible' forsooth! The author should have said *impossible*. What will our nautical friends say to the feat of running a sloop with a jib, when her mast has been carried away in a gale of wind? What will the government say to the discoveries near the south pole? Will they not recall the southern exploring expedition, which is rendered wholly unnecessary by Pym's discoveries? What will the Nantucket folks say to the miracle of a vessel being fitted out from that port, which had never been heard of there, by a mercantile house that never had an existence any where?

To be serious, this is a very clever extravaganza, after the manner of Defoe, understood to be written by Mr Poe, of Virginia. It indicates great talent and vivacity, and will be perused with amusement by every class of readers.

NOTE

1 Captain James Riley's *An Authentic Narrative of the Loss of the American Brig 'Commerce' Wrecked on the Western Coast of Africa, in the Month of August 1815, with an Account of the Sufferings of her Surviving Officers and Crew, Who Were Enslaved by the Wandering Arabs...* (1817) was characterized by its sensationalism; it was often reprinted.

19. [William Burton], review in *Burton's Gentleman's Magazine*

September 1838, 3, 210–11

Burton (1804–60) was an English actor and theatre manager who came to America in 1834. His *Gentleman's Magazine* (1837–40) was a moderately successful venture on which Poe was briefly employed (1839–40). Poe identified Burton as the author of this review – see *Letters*, 1, 130.

An Indian warrior pursuing a flying tory, seized his foe by the tail of his peruke, and drew his scalping knife for the purpose of consummating his victory, but the artificial head-covering of the British soldier came off in the struggle, and the bald-headed owner ran away unhurt, leaving the surprised

Indian in possession of the easily acquired trophy. After gazing at the singular and apparently unnatural formation, he dashed it to the ground in disdain, and quietly exclaimed 'A d——d lie!' We find ourselves in the same predicament with the volume before us; we imagined, from various discrepancies and other errors discovered in a casual glance, sufficient also to convince us of the faulty construction and poorness of style, that we had met with a proper subject for our critical scalping knife – but a steady perusal of the whole book compelled us to throw it away in contempt, with an exclamation very similar to the natural phrase of the Indian. A more impudent attempt at humbugging the public has never been exercised; the voyages of Gulliver were politically satirical, and the adventures of Munchausen, the acknowledged caricature of a celebrated traveller. 'Sinbad the Sailor', *Peter Wilkins*,[1] and More's *Utopia*, are confessedly works of imagination; but Arthur Gordon Pym puts forth a series of travels outraging possibility, and coolly requires his insulted readers to believe his *ipse dixit*, although he confesses that the early portions of his precious effusion were published in the *Southern Literary Messenger* as a story written by the editor, Mr Poe, because he believed that the public at large would pronounce his adventures to be 'an impudent fiction'. Mr Poe, if not the author of Pym's book, is at least responsible for its publication, for it is stated in the preface that Mr Poe assured the author that the shrewdness and common sense of the public would give it a chance of being received as truth. We regret to find Mr Poe's name in connexion with such a mass of ignorance and effrontery.

The title of the work serves as a full index of the contents. The '*incredible* adventures and discoveries' in the Antarctic ocean conclude somewhat abruptly; the surviving voyageurs, Pym and a half-breed Indian, are left, madly careering, in a frail bark canoe, in a strong current, running due south, in the immediate vicinity of the Pole – volcanoes bursting from the 'milky depths of the ocean', showers of white ashes covering the boat and its inmates, and a limitless cataract 'rolling *silently* into the sea from some immense rampart in the heavens, whose summit was utterly lost in the dimness and the distance'. Two or three of the final chapters are supposed to be mislaid; therefore, we have no account of the escape of Arthur Gordon Pym from the irresistible embraces of the cataract to his snuggery at New York.

There is nothing original in the description of the newly discovered islands in the Antarctic sea, unless we except the scene wherein a few ambushed savages precipitate *more than a million tons of soft rock* from the hillside, by merely pulling at a few strong cords of grape vine attached to some stakes driven in the ground. The shipwreck is unnecessarily horrible – a rapid succession of improbabilities destroys the interest of the reader, and the writer's evident ignorance in all nautical matters forbids the possibility of belief. We are told that when his boat, sloop rigged, carrying a mainsail and jib, lost her mast close off by the board, he boomed along before the wind, *under the jib*, and shipping seas over the counter! A cabin boy of a month's standing would have been ashamed of such a phrase! Then, we hear of a ship sailing over a boat in a gale of wind, and hooking one of the boatmen by a copper bolt in her bottom – the said bolt having gone through the back part of the neck, between two sinews, and out just below the right ear! The body was discovered by the mate of the ship, when the vessel gave an immense lurch *to windward*! and was evidently obtained after several ineffectual efforts, during the lurches of the ship – and, notwithstanding its long immersion and *peculiar* transfixion, was restored to life, and proved to be the hero of the tale, Arthur Gordon Pym.

The mutiny is rather a common place mutiny; but Pym's secretion in the hold is a matter of positive improbability. No Yankee captain of a whaler ever packed his oil casks in such a careless manner as described by the veracious A.G.P., who, by the way, sleeps a nap of three days and three nights duration, 'at the very least.' The annexed description of the river waters of the Antarctic isles is a fair specimen of the outrageous statements which 'the shrewdness and good sense of the public' are required to believe.

[Quotes Ch. 18, paragraph 9.]

NOTE

1 Robert Paltock's novel, published 1751.

20. Unsigned notice in the *New York Review*

3 October 1838, 3, 489

The *New York Review* was a respected 'intellectual' journal to which Poe contributed a lengthy review in October 1837.

Notwithstanding this circumstantial and veracious looking length of title, the work is all a fiction. It is written with considerable talent, and an attempt is made, by simplicity of style, minuteness of nautical descriptions, and circumstantiality of narration, to throw over it that air of reality which constitutes the charm of *Robinson Crusoe*, and *Sir Edward Seaward's Narrative*.[1] This work has, however, none of the agreeable interest of the two just named. It is not destitute of interest for the imagination, but the interest is painful; there are too many atrocities, too many strange horrors, and finally, there is no conclusion to it; it breaks off suddenly in a mysterious way, which is not only destitute of all *vraisemblance*, but is purely perplexing and vexatious. We cannot, therefore, but consider the author unfortunate in his plan.

NOTE

1 Jane Porter's novel, published in 1831, purported to be factual.

21. From an unsigned review in the *Torch*

13 October 1838, 2, 383–5

The *Torch* was a London literary weekly.

It is recorded of a certain good-natured bishop that, upon being asked his opinion of 'Gulliver's Voyages', he very naively replied, 'There were some things in the book he could not altogether bring himself to believe.'[1] Now this is very much the case with us in regard to the *Narrative of Arthur Pym, of Nantucket* – there are some things in the book that we cannot bring ourselves to believe, and we are sorry for it; for a good staunch faith, a credulity, that, like a high-mettled horse, stands not for hedge nor ditch, is a great help in such matters.

It would seem that to lie like truth is no such easy affair, albeit mere lying is amongst the most common of human accomplishments; at least we can call to mind but one author who has lied at all to the purpose, and that is Defoe; the veracious historian of *Captain Jack* and *Robinson Crusoe* had a gift of realizing his fables, that certainly has never been possessed to the same extent by any one else, either before or since, though the attempt to imitate him has been made over and over again by men of no mean talents. And whence arises this happy effect, which we seldom or never miss in Defoe's writings, though in other respects he was far from possessing any extraordinary powers? His style is loose, rambling, and incorrect; he has little or no invention; nor does he appear to have any particular skill in drawing characters. To what, then, are we to ascribe the wonderful reality that colours all his writings? We shall be told perhaps, that the cause is to be sought in his never outstripping the bounds of probability; but how would this apply to his story of Mrs Veal's ghost?

99

Nothing can in itself be more absurd than the idea of this familiar chatting spirit, who talks divinity over a cup of bohea, just as she would have done in the flesh; and yet of all the ghost stories extant, we know of none that carries with it such strong marks of conviction on the part of the narrator. Is not the solution to be sought in the minuteness and probability of the details that Defoe flings about the principal circumstance of all his fictions, and also in the fact of his never crowding together a course of events, which, however feasible, if separately considered, would not be likely to happen in close conjunction?

Whatever may be the secret, our friend, Mr Arthur Pym, of Nantucket, most assuredly has not discovered it, though he stands up sturdily for the truth of his narrative; he is determined not to pass for the shadow of a name, for a mere eidolon, if he can help it, and in a preface of some tact maintains his identity against all unbelievers, while, to give a colour to the matter, his supposed editor slily despatches him in a note at the end of the volume. This no doubt is an excellent trick to coax belief, and one not altogether unworthy of Defoe himself; for it is hard to deny that a man has existed, when we see his coffin carried decently to the grave, and buried with all the fitting solemnities. But even this sacrifice will not, we fear, in our unbelieving age, establish the reality of Mr Arthur Pym, though it must be allowed that the eidolon has strung together as wonderful a set of adventures as lounger or invalid can desire to while away an hour at breakfast or on a sofa.

[Then follows a résumé, supported by lengthy quotations, of Pym's adventures to the point in Ch. 10 where he sees the gull gorging off the dead sailor.]

The volume might not be inaptly divided here, as the adventures that follow, though not less interesting, are of a character totally distinct, being limited to an island of the South Sea, where nearly the whole of the ship's crew is murdered by the savage natives. Arthur and his strange companion, Peters, alone escape, and even the savages themselves pay an example penalty for their treachery in the explosion of the vessel, by which thousands of them are destroyed. Here, again, it might reasonably be supposed that we had got to a climax, but no such thing; the escape from the island, and the subsequent adventures, are to the full as surprising and as full of interest as any of the preceding pages. The volume now terminates in an abrupt manner, from the decease of the real or imaginary Arthur Pym. That such a man existed is probable – that he saw and suffered much is possible – but if the deceased did in reality leave such papers behind him, intending them to be taken for facts, he is, or rather was, the greatest liar since the days of Mendez Pinto.

22. From an unsigned review in the London *Atlas*

20 October 1838, 13, 666

In the lack of new publications of greater interest, we may venture to bestow upon this most incredible book a larger space than, under other circumstances, we should be disposed to afford to such a production. The reader may reasonably be surprised at the announcement of adventures and discoveries in the eighty-fourth parallel of southern latitude; but when he comes to read them his surprise will cease. We will run through the leading incidents of the story, which, however, would have been more entertaining, had the writer been a little more careful in subduing his tendency for the marvellous. He has so ridiculously overdone the recital, that the volume cannot impose upon anybody.

Mr PYM – who describes his adventures in the first person – informs us that upon his return a few months ago (his preface is dated last July) to the United States, he was urged to give to the public the particulars of his strange experiences in the South Seas, but he was restrained from doing so by a variety of reasons, one of which was the apprehension that his story would be regarded as 'an impudent and ingenious fiction'. At length a Mr Poe, the editor of a magazine, prevailed upon him to allow him to write in his own way a narrative 'under the garb of fiction.' Two numbers of this pretended fable appeared, but the readers of the magazine, contrary to all expectation, believed the whole narrative to be true, and Mr PYM, tempted by this circumstance, as he says, proceeded to complete it in the form in which it now appears. Such is the history of the book, as far as it is revealed to us, and the following are the main circumstances related by our imaginative voyager.

[Summarizes Pym's story, quoting extensively.]

This marvellous water [described in Ch. 18] is hardly marvellous enough for a downright romance, and much too marvellous for truth. But it is a sheer waste of time to pursue these particulars. The crew of the schooner land, are entrapped in a defile by the savages, who by a species of sorcery known only at the south pole contrive to hurl down upon the unsuspecting Englishmen [sic] the entire summits of the ranges of hills at each side, burying them in the ruins. The way in which these mighty masses were loosened appears to have been by cords of grape-vine attached to stakes – a mode quite as feasible as if you tried to lift a house from its foundations by a silk thread. Mr PYM and PETERS alone escape alive, and after sundry strange adventures in ravines, and cliffs, and caves, they at last make the shore, notwithstanding that there are at least ten thousand natives close at hand who have just blown up the unlucky Jane Guy of Liverpool. They seize a canoe, and make off for sea; and here the narrative ends, leaving them drifting in the 84' parallel, somewhat after the fashion of the monster in *Frankenstein*.

This sudden termination of the story is attempted to be accounted for by a statement at the end of the sudden death of Mr PYM, before he completed the last few chapters – but how or where he died, the writer sayeth not. The fact seems to be that having brought his narrative to a point of extravagant peril – a canoe drifting among the ice islands of the South Seas – he did not know how to bring himself home in safety, and so stopped all at once; although with such a fertile imagination he might have readily supplied the deficiency. Could he not get on the back of an albatross, and compel the bird to carry him back to Nantucket? DANIEL ROURKE, Esq. thus visited the moon on the back of an eagle.

It is superfluous to add that we hold the entire narrative to be a mere fiction.

23. From an unsigned review in the London *Spectator*

27 October 1838, ii, 1023

When we say that Mr PYM of Nantucket, proceeded as far as the eighty-fourth degree of Southern latitude, and abruptly breaks off his narrative whilst in full tilt for the South Pole, with a steady wind and a rapid current in his favour, carrying him through a hot and milky-looking ocean, with surrounding wonders of various kinds, the reader will see at once that the work is an American fiction. But, although without any definite purpose, it is a fiction of no mean skill; displaying much power, much nautical knowledge, and a DEFOE – like appearance of reality. Its ease, simplicity, and natural effects, remind one of MARRYAT.

Mr Arthur Gordon Pym, like Robinson Crusoe, had a liking for the sea; but his family having opposed his wishes, a friend smuggled him on board a vessel, and secreted him in the hold; and here, in consequence of a mutiny, Mr Pym was compelled to remain longer than he wished, exposed to all the horrors of hunger, thirst, darkness, and mephitic air. To this adventure succeeds the struggles of the quarrelling mutineers, a furious tempest, and suffering by famine, ending in the immolation of one of their party. Released from this state by an English South Sea whaler, whose captain has a taste for discovery, they proceed eight degrees further South than any previous navigator has yet succeeded in reaching, and discover a group of islands, where the natives are black, and the productions, mineral, animal, and vegetable, differ from those in the Temperate and Arctic circles. After an interchange of presents and professions, the crew are destroyed by the savages, with the exception of Mr Pym and another; who eventually escape in a canoe, and steer for the South Pole; in approaching which, the narrative breaks off, because, we imagine, the writer was at a loss how to go on.

The early part of the adventures is not physically impossible, and that is all; the later discoveries are clearly fable; but both the one and the other are told with great appearance of truth, and with a hearty confidence in the writer's belief, which gives them much of the air of reality. Interest is also excited in the narrative – that kind of breathless and absorbing interest with which we may suppose our ancestors listened to stories of 'men whose heads do grow beneath their shoulders,' or with which we in our youth perused fairy tales. The disgusting though fearful scene of the passing vessel of the dead, the horrors of the tempest and the following famine, and the escape of Pym and Peters from the mountain in whose bowels they are entombed, are all examples of this kind. Neither is the writer deficient in nautical or geographical knowledge, but intermingles both with his narrative; nor is he devoid of fancy. Take, as an instance of this latter quality, his account of the water of the new-discovered isle.

[Cites Ch. 18, paragraph 9; then Ch. 7, paragraphs 4, 5, and 6.]

We close with a specimen of Mr Pym in the more legitimate walk of fiction; powerful, but, we suspect, not always natural.

[Cites the drawing of lots episode, Ch. 12, paragraphs 6 and 7.]

24. Review in the London *New Monthly Magazine*

November 1838, 54, 428–9

This symposium style of review was inspired by Professor Wilson's popular 'Noctes Ambrosianae' (1822–35), in *Blackwood's Edinburgh Magazine*; the Rector and the Colonel were regular discussants.

The Rector. – *The Narrative of Arthur Gordon Pym, of Nantucket, North America.* – The history of the famous Robinson Crusoe is said to have made more sailors than any act of Parliament since the Wittenagemote. It may be added, that it has made more discoverers of anything but the truth than any treatise on the art of fiction since fabling was invented. Arthur Pym is the American Robinson Crusoe, a man all over wonders, who sees nothing but wonders, vanquishes nothing but wonders, would, indeed, evidently, scorn to have anything to do but with wonders, and who, after having been buried in a whirlpool a hundred fathom below the centre of the earth, comes home with a considerable fragment of the magnetic meridian in one pocket, and a frozen slice of the eighty-fourth degree of south latitude in the other, and sits down in Nantucket to write his Journal for the benefit of the remotest posterity.

The Colonel. – The blowing up of Arthur Pym's vessel, when it has been boarded by the savages of the Pole, is one of the most prodigious performances of gunpowder, since the wreck of the Spanish Armada. The crew of the devoted vessel having reached the shore, ten thousand savages, and not less by a man, march down to the beach, and a thousand go on board. The vessel is set on fire – the work of devastation goes on, however, as calmly, if not quite as coolly, as before. But the magazine begins to give signs that it is in existence: first comes a smart shock as a preliminary; but the savages still persevere in extracting nails, bolts, and all kinds of iron: but the catastrophe is at hand. First comes a puff of smoke, then a column of fire to a height above the strongest and longest telescope, then a chaos of every combustible, and then a crash, a concussion, a convulsion, an indescribable havoc, which leaves of the ship not a foot of plank nor a square inch of copper. The thousand savages suddenly finding their quarters too hot to hold them, are blown into ten thousand fragments, and the fish have a black jubilee for a month to come. We may defy black legs and arms, or even Nantucket fiction to go further.

25. Unsigned review in the London *Monthly Review*

December 1838, 3, 566–9

If however our readers will have an *out and out* romance, and the marvels of an unprecedented voyager, we are prepared to satisfy them; for here is one by a Yankee – the species being the most unscrupulous of any in the matter of marvellous stories. Before, however, saying anything of the nautical adventures of Mr Pym, comprising as they do the 'Details of a Mutiny, Famine, and Shipwreck, during a Voyage to the South Seas, resulting in extraordinary Adventures and Discoveries in the Eighty-fourth parallel of Southern

Latitude,' – (eighty-fourth! mark that,) we have to state that other recent Transatlantic works of an imaginary character and of the novel class might have been selected by us – such as *Cromwell*, by the author of *The Brothers, Burton*, &c.,[1] each of them, though falling far short of the objects and the portraitures aimed at, having a specific character which takes them out of any particular school formed in this country. We choose the adventures of Arthur Gordon Pym, however, because the work appears to us to be characterized by a greater degree of originality, boldness, and skill, than either of the former; while its extravagances, and mere attempt, as it would seem, at fancying next to miraculous things, rather than the inculcation of any valuable principles or refinement, put it out of the list of those fictions which are to be recommended as models or for general perusal. The simple fact that some of the most elaborate scenes, and where no mean power is exhibited, are disgustingly horrible, would of itself be a sufficient warning against imitation.

Pym like many other boys had a passion, so long as it was untried, for a seafaring life; and takes to it against the wishes of his family. He soon encounters more than a sufficiency of hardships and dangers to open his eyes to his rashness. But these and their various results we shall not recount. Take the following example of the sort of effort to which he puts his invention:–

[Quotes the paragraph on coloured water which ends Ch. 18.]

Except as a trial of strength and skill in the art of painting by means of words and analogies, we do not see any good in such descriptions. It must be confessed, however, that the use, at the author's command, that the tone of sincerity, the minuteness of detail, and the natural manner here so manifest, relieve the fancies strung together of much of that marvellousness that would otherwise be felt to be repulsively absurd.

Our last extract evinces no common power, while, without appearing to imitate, the fiction has a Robinson Crusoe reality about it:–

[Quotes most of paragraphs 7 and 8 from Ch. 12, on the lottery.]

NOTE

1 Henry William Herbert was the author of these novels.

TALES OF THE GROTESQUE AND ARABESQUE

1839

26. James E. Heath condemns Poe's 'Germanism'

September and October 1839

Document (a) is from a letter from Heath to Poe dated 12 September 1839; MS. in the Griswold Papers, Boston Public Library. Document (b) is from an editorial in the *Southern Literary Messenger*, October 1839, 5, 708.

Poe had evidently asked for 'The Fall of the House of Usher' to be printed in the *Messenger*, but Heath, who was assisting White with editorial duties, had no patience with 'Germanism', believing that literature should cheerfully promote sound morals. Poe probably wrote his 'Preface' in response to Heath's strictures.

(a) Since the receipt of yours of the 5 inst. I have been so exceedingly occupied and withal so very much indisposed, that I could not until within the last day or two, take a peep into the interesting magazine which you were good enough to send me. I have read your article 'The Fall of the House of Usher' with attention, and I think it among the best of your compositions of that class which I have seen. A man need not have a critical judgement nor a very refined taste to decide, that no one could have written the tale, without possessing great scope of imagination, vigorous thought, and a happy command of language; but I am sure you will appreciate my candor when I say that I never could feel much interest in that class of compositions. I mean that I never could experience pleasure in reading tales of horror and mystery however much the narrative should be dignified by genius. They leave a painful and melancholy impression on my mind, and I do not perceive their tendency to improve the heart....

He [Thomas White] is apprehensive however that the 'Fall of the House of Usher' would not only occupy more space than he can conveniently spare (the demands upon his columns being very great) but that the subject matter is not such as would be acceptable to a large majority of his readers. He doubts whether the readers of the *Messenger* have much relish for tales of the German school although written with great power and ability, and in this opinion I confess to you frankly, I am strongly inclined to concur. I doubt very much whether tales of the wild, improbable and terrible class, can ever be permanently popular in this country. Charles Dickens it appears to me has given the final death blow to writings of that description. Of course there is nothing I could say on that subject that can or ought to influence your own mind. There is no disputing in matters of taste, and there is no infallible standard to which men consider themselves obliged to defer and surrender their own judgements.

It gives me sincere pleasure to understand that your own good sense and the influence of high and noble motives have enabled you to overcome a seductive and dangerous treatment which too often prostrates the wisest and best by its fatal grasp. The cultivation of such high intellectual powers as you possess cannot fail to earn for you a solid reputation in the literary world. In the department of criticism especially, I know few who can claim to be your superiors in this country. Your dissecting knife, if vigorously employed, would serve to rid us of much of that silly trash and silly *sentimentality* with which puerile and conceited authors, and gain-seeking book sellers are continually poisoning our intellectual food. I hope in relation to all such you will continue to wield mace without 'fear, favor or affection.'

(b) ... We are pleased to find that our old assistant, Edgar A. Poe, is connected with Burton in the editorial management of the *Gentleman's Magazine*. Mr Poe, is favorably known to the readers of the *Messenger*, as a gentleman of fine endowments; possessing a taste classical and refined; an imagination affluent and splendid, and withall, a singular capacity for minute and mathematical detail. We always predicted that Mr Poe would reach a high grade in American literature, but we also thought and still think, that he is too much attached to the gloomy German mysticism, to be a useful and effective writer, without a total divorce from that sombre school. Take for example, the tale of 'The Fall of the House of Usher', in the September number of the Magazine, which is understood to be the production of his pen. It is written with great power, but leaves on the mind a painful and horrible impression, without any redeeming admonition of the heart. It resembles a finely sculptured statue, beautiful to the eye, but without an immortal spirit. We wish Mr Poe would stick to the department of criticism; *there*, he is an able professor, and he uses up the vermin who are continually crawling, unbidden, into the literary arena, with the skill and *nonchalance* of a practised surgeon. He cuts them up by piece-meal; and rids the republic of letters, of such nuisances, just as a good officer of police sentences to their proper destination, the night-strollers and vagabonds who infest our cities. We sincerely wish Mr Poe well, and hope that he will take our advice in good part.

27. Philip Pendleton Cooke, from letters to Poe

(a) 16 September 1839; (b) 19 December 1839

The letter from Poe to which Cooke replied on 16 September is unlocated. Poe had probably solicited support for *Burton's Gentleman's Magazine* and his forthcoming collection of tales – see *Letters*, 2, 686–8.

Cooke's letter of 19 December implies a further unlocated letter from Poe.

The MSS. of these letters are in the Griswold Papers, Boston Public Library.

(a) ... As to 'Ligeia', of which you ask my opinion, (doubtless without any intention of being guided by any person's but your own) I think it is very fine. There is nothing unintelligible to my mind in the 'sequel' (or conclusion) but I am impertinent enough to think that it (the conclusion) might be mended. I of course 'took' your 'idea' throughout. The whole piece is but a sermon from the text of Joseph Glanvill which you cap it with – and your intent is to tell a tale of the 'mighty will' contending with & finally vanquishing Death. The struggle is vigorously described – and I appreciated every sentence as I advanced, until the Lady Ligeia takes possession of the deserted *quarters* (I write like a butcher) of the Lady Rowena. There I was shocked by a violation of the ghostly proprieties – so to speak – and wondered how the Lady Ligeia – a wandering essence – could, in quickening *the body of the Lady Rowena* (such is the idea) become suddenly the visible, bodily, Ligeia. If Rowena's bodily form had been retained as a shell or case for the disembodied Lady Ligeia, and you had only become aware *gradually* that the blue Saxon eye of the 'Lady Rowena of Tremaine' grew daily darker with the peculiar, intense expression of the 'look' which had belonged to Ligeia – that a mind of grander powers, a soul of more glowing fires occupied the quickened body and gave an old familiar expression to its motions – if you had brooded and meditated upon the change until proof accumulated upon proof, making wonder certainty, and then, in the moment of some strangest of all evidence of the transition, broken out into the exclamation which ends the story – the *effect* would not have been lessened, and the 'ghostly proprieties' would, I think, have been better observed. You may have some theory of the story, or transition, however, which I have not caught.

As for your compositions of this class, generally, I consider them, as Mr Crummles would say, 'phenomenous'.

You *write* as I sometimes *dream* when asleep on a heavy supper (not heavy enough for nightmare). – The odd ignorance of the name, lineage, &c. of Ligeia – of the circumstances, place, &c. under which, & where, you first saw her – with which you begin your narrative, is usual, & not at all wondered at, in dreams. Such dimness of recollection does not *whilst we dream* excite any surprise or diminish the *vraisemblable* aspect of the strange matters that we dream of. It is only when we wake that we wonder that so material an omission in the thread of the events should have been unnoticed by the mind at a time when it could dream in other respects so plausibly – with such detailed minuteness – with such self-possession.

But I must come to a conclusion, as I tire myself with this out-of-the-way sort of writing.

I will subscribe to the *Gentlemen's Mag.* shortly & also contribute to it.

P.S. I would not say 'saith Lord Verulam' – it is out of the way. I am very impertinent.

(b) ... I have read your 'Fall of the House of Usher', your 'William Wilson' and your 'Conversation of Eiros and Charmion' and I will say something about them, as all authors like praise and compliment.

In the first place I must tell you (what I firmly believe) that your mere style is the very best amongst the first of the living writers; and I must let you know that I regard style as something more than the mere manner of communicating ideas. 'Words are used by the wise as counters; by the foolish as coin' is the aphorism of a person who never appreciated Jeremy Taylor or Sir Thomas Browne. You do not, to be sure, use your words as those fine old glowing rhetoricians did, as tints of the pencil – as the colours of a picture – you do not make your sentences pictures – but you mould them into an artful excellence – bestow a care which is pleasantly perceptible, and accomplish an effect which I can only characterise as the visible presentation of your ideas instead of the mere expression of them.

In your 'Fall of the House of Usher', unconnected with

style, I think you very happy in that part where you prolong the scene with Roderick Usher after the death of his sister, and the glare of the moon thro' the sundering house, and the electric gleam around it, I think admirably conceived.

Of 'William Wilson' I am not sure that I perceive the true idea. From the 'whispering voice' I would apprehend that you meant the second William Wilson as an embodying of the *conscience* of the first; but I am inclined to the notion that your intention was to convey the wilder idea that every mortal of us is attended with a shadow of himself – a duplicate of his own peculiar organization – differing from himself only in a certain angelic taint of the compound, derived from heaven, as our own wild humours are derived from Hell (figuratively); – I cannot make myself understood, as I am not used to the expression of a wild *half thought.* But, although I do not clearly comprehend, I certainly admire the story.

Of 'Eiros & Charmion' I will only say that I consider the whole very singular and excellent, and the skill of one small part of it unapproachable.

'Was I much mourned, my Eiros' – is one of the finest touches in the world. I read the other day, a small piece in an old *Messenger* entitled 'Shadow a Fable' which I take to be yours. Considered apart from some affectation it is very terrible. The Poetry headed 'The Haunted Palace' which I read in the *Balt. Museum* where it first appeared, and which I instantly understood as a picture of an intellect, I consider beautiful but grotesque.

By the way you have selected an excellent title for your volume of tales. 'Tales of the Grotesque and Arabesque' expresses admirably the character of your wild stories – and as tales of the grotesque & arabesque they were certainly never equalled.

28. Poe's 'Preface'

December 1839

The epithets 'Grotesque' and 'Arabesque' will be found to indicate with sufficient precision the prevalent tenor of the tales here published. But from the fact that, during a period of some two or three years, I have written five-and-twenty short stories whose general character may be so briefly defined, it cannot be fairly inferred – at all events it is not truly inferred – that I have, for this species of writing, any inordinate, or indeed any peculiar taste or prepossession. I may have written with an eye to this republication in volume form, and may, therefore, have desired to preserve, as far as a certain point, a certain unity of design. This is, indeed, the fact; and it may even happen that, in this manner, I shall never compose anything again. I speak of these things here, because I am led to think that it is this prevalence of the 'Arabesque' in my serious tales, which has induced one or two critics to tax me, in all friendliness, with what they have been pleased to term 'Germanism' and gloom. The charge is in bad taste, and the grounds of the accusation have not been sufficiently considered. Let us admit, for the moment, that the 'phantasy-pieces' now given *are* Germanic, or what not. Then Germanism is 'the vein' for the time being. Tomorrow I may be anything but German, as yesterday I was everything else. These many pieces are yet one book. My friends would be quite as wise in taxing an astronomer with too much astronomy, or an ethical author with treating too largely of morals. But the truth is that, with a single exception, there is no one of these stories in which the scholar should recognise the distinctive features of that species of pseudo-horror which we are taught to call Germanic, for no better reason than that some of the secondary names of German literature have become identified with its folly. If in many of my productions terror has been the thesis, I maintain that terror is not of Germany, but of the soul, – that I have deduced this terror only from its legitimate sources, and urged it only to its legitimate results.

There are one or two of the articles here, (conceived and executed in the purest spirit of extravaganza,) to which I expect no serious attention, and of which I shall speak no farther. But for the rest I cannot conscientiously claim indulgence on the score of hasty effort. I think it best becomes me to say, therefore, that if I have sinned, I have deliberately sinned. These brief compositions are, in chief part, the results of matured purpose and very careful elaboration.

29. 'Personal' and 'Editorial Opinions'

December 1839

These 'Opinions' (presumably collected by Poe) were inserted in the second volume of *Tales of the Grotesque and Arabesque*.

These Tales have received encomiums of a most unusual character, from a great variety of high sources. Besides a number of editorial opinions in their favor, some personal ones (*not* editorial) are here appended. As all these (with a single exception) have already found their way into the papers, or other prints, of the time, the publishers presume there can be no impropriety in their republication.

PERSONAL OPINIONS

These tales are eminently distinguished by a wild, vigorous, and poetical imagination, a rich style, a fertile invention, and various and cunning learning.... Of singular force and beauty. – John P. Kennedy.

I am much pleased with a tale called 'The House of Usher', and should think that a collection of tales, equally well written, could not fail of being favorably received.... Its graphic effect is powerful. – Washington Irving.

I have read a little tale called 'William Wilson' with much pleasure. It is managed in a highly picturesque style, and the singular and mysterious interest is ably sustained throughout. I repeat what I have said of a previous production of this author; and I cannot but think that a series of articles of like style and merit would be extremely well received by the public. – Washington Irving.

In 'Ligeia', by Mr Poe, there is a fine march of description, which has a touch of the D'Israeli quality. – N.P. Willis – *Letters from Under a Bridge*.

He puts us in mind of no less a writer than Shelley. – John Neal.

'Bon-bon', by Mr Poe, is equal to anything Theodore Hook ever wrote. – M.M. Noah.

Mr Poe's 'MS. Found in a Bottle' is one of the most singularly ingenious and imaginative things I ever remember to have read. Discovery is there analyzed and spiritualized in a strain of allegory which need not fear comparison with Coleridge's 'Ancient Mariner' – J.F. Otis.

– That powerful pen, whose versatile and brilliant creations I have so often admired. – Mrs L.H. Sigourney.

Mr Poe possesses an extraordinary faculty. He paints the palpable obscure with strange power, throwing over his pictures a sombre gloom which is appalling. The images are dim, but distinct; shadowy but well-defined. The outline indeed is all we see; but there they stand, shrouded in darkness, and fright us with the mystery which defies further scrutiny.... His genius, as well as private history, puts us in mind of that of Coleridge. – Judge Beverly Tucker (of Va.), author of *George Balcombe*.

There can be but one opinion in regard to the force and beauty of his style.... He discovers a superior capacity and a highly cultivated taste.... A gentleman of fine endowments, possessing a taste classical and refined, an imagination affluent and splendid, and withal a singular capacity for minute and mathematical detail.... We always predicted that he would reach a high grade in American literature.... 'Morella' will unquestionably prove that Mr Poe has great powers of imagination, and a command of language never surpassed. We doubt if anything in the same style can be cited which contains more terrific beauty than this tale. – James E. Heath (of Va.), author of *Edge Hill* and Editor of the *S. Lit. Messenger*.

Mr Poe is decidedly the best of all our young writers – I don't know but that I may say, of all our old ones. – J.K. Paulding.

– Facile princeps. – Professor Charles Anthon.

EDITORIAL OPINIONS

We must say that we derive no small enjoyment from a delineation like this. We like to see the evidences of study and thought, as well as inspiration, in the design, and of careful and elaborate handling in the execution, as well as of grand and striking effect in the *tout ensemble*. 'The Fall of the House of Usher' is what we denominate a stern and sombre, but at the same time a noble and imposing picture, such as can be drawn only by a master-hand. Such things are not produced by your slip-shod amateurs in composition. – *Phil. Weekly Messenger* (Professor John Frost).

'William Wilson', by Mr Poe, reminds us of Godwin and Brockden Brown. The writer is a kindred spirit of theirs in his style of art. He paints with sombre Rembrandt-like tints, and there is great force and vigor of conception in whatever he produces. – *Phil. Weekly Messenger* (Professor Frost).

There is also a sketch of much power and peculiar interest entitled 'The Fall of the House of Usher' which cannot fail to attract attention – ... a remarkable specimen of a style of writing which possesses many attractions for those who love to dwell upon the terrible. – *Phil. Pennsylvanian* (Jos. C. Neal).

Mr Poe's story of 'The House of Usher' would have been considered a *chef d'oeuvre* if it had appeared in the pages of *Blackwood*. – *N.Y. Evening Star*.

'Lionizing' by Mr Poe is an inimitable piece of wit and satire; and the man must be far gone in a melancholic humor whose risibility is not moved by this tale. – *S. Lit. Messenger* (E. Vernon Sparhawk).

Mr Poe's 'Hans Phaall' will add much to his reputation as an imaginative writer. The story is a long one, but will appear short to the reader, whom it bears along with irresistible interest through a region of which of all others we know least, but which his fancy has invested with peculiar charms. – *Idem*.

The author of the 'Lunar Hoax'[1] is indebted to the 'Hans Phaall' of Mr Poe for the conception and in a great measure for the execution of his discoveries. – *Norfolk Herald*.

The 'Duc de L'Omelette' by Edgar A. Poe, is one of those light, spirited, and fantastic inventions of which we have had specimens before in the *Messenger*, betokening a fertility of imagination and power of execution, that would, under a sustained effort, produce creations of an enduring character. – *Baltimore American* (Geo. H. Calvert).

The 'Duc de L'Omelette' is one of the best things of the kind we have ever read. Mr Poe has great powers and every line tells in all he writes. He is no spinner of long yarns, but he chooses his subject, whimsically perhaps, but originally, and treats it in a manner peculiarly his own. – *National Intelligencer* (J.F. Otis).

Of the lighter contributions – of the diamonds which sparkle beside the more sombre gems, commend us, thou spirit of eccentricity forever and a day, to the 'Duc de L'Omelette' – the best thing of the kind we ever have read or ever expect to read. – *Petersburgh (Va) Constellation* (H. Haines).

'The Tale of Jerusalem' is one of those felicitous hits which are the *forte* of Edgar A. Poe. – *Baltimore Gazette.*

We seldom meet with more boldness in the development of intellectual capacity, or more vividness in description than we find in the productions of Edgar Allan Poe. – *Brownsville (Pa.) Observer.*

– Equally ripe in graphic humor and various lore. – *Charleston Courier.*

– An uniquely original vein of imagination, and of humorous delicate satire. – *S.L. Messenger.*

The story of 'The Fall of the House of Usher' from the pen of Mr Poe, is very interesting – a well told tale. – *Phil. U.S. Gazette* (Jos. R. Chandler).

Many of these tales are of a very high order of merit. Mr Poe is no imitator in story-telling. He has a peculiarity of his own – dealing often in rather wild imaginings, and yet he always contrives to sustain his plots with so much novelty of incident, that you must read him out in spite of any sober realities that may occasionally flit across the mind. And as you read you are ever impressed with the truth that he has much fancy, great richness of description, and true poetry for his imagery and colorings. – *Phil. Sat. Courier* (E. Holden).

Poe can throw a chain of enchantment around every scene he

attempts to describe, and one of his peculiarities consists in the perfect harmony between each *locale* and the characters introduced. He has certainly written some of the most popular tales of American origin. – *Baltimore Post* (Dr J. Evans Snodgrass).

He is excellent at caricature and satire. – *Richmond Compiler.*

He is one of the very few American writers who blend philosophy, common sense, humor and poetry smoothly together.... He lays his hand upon the wild steeds of his imagination, and they plunge furiously through storm and tempest, or foam along through the rattling thunder-cloud; or, at his bidding, they glide swiftly and noiselessly along the quiet and dreamy lake, or among the whispering bowers of thought and feeling.... There are few writers in this country – take Neal, Irving, and Willis away, and we would say none – who can compete successfully in many respects with Poe. With an acuteness of observation, a vigorous and effective style and an independence that defies control, he unites a fervid fancy and a most beautiful enthusiasm. His is a high destiny. – *St Louis Commercial Bulletin.*

NOTE

1 Richard Adams Locke's successful hoax, 'Discoveries in the Moon' began to appear in the New York *Sun* three weeks after the publication of 'Hans Phaall'; Poe believed that Locke was indebted to him – see *Letters*, 1, 74.

30. [Joseph Clay Neal], notice in the *Pennsylvanian*

6 December 1839, p. 2

Neal (1807–47) was a journalist and humorist; he is best remembered for *Charcoal Sketches; or Scenes in a Metropolis* (1838). He became editor of the *Pennsylvanian* (a Philadelphia daily) in 1832. Poe identified Neal as the author of this review in his *Saturday Museum* biography.

Tales of the Grotesque and Arabesque, is the title of a work just published by Messrs. Lea and Blanchard. It consists of tales and sketches from the pen of Edgar A. Poe, Esq. formerly of the *Southern Literary Messenger*, and now one of the editors of the *Gentleman's Magazine* in the city, a writer who adds to extensive requirements, a remarkable vigor and originality of mind, the manifestations of which are strikingly displayed in the volumes of which we speak. These grotesque and arabesque delineations are full of variety, now irresistibly quaint and droll, and again marked with all the deep and painful interest of the German school, so that the reader, in whatever mood he may be, cannot fail to find something to suit his temper and absorb his attention. In every page, he will note matter unlike the productions of any other writer. Poe follows in nobody's track, – his imagination seems to have a domain of its own to revel in.

31. Notice in the Philadelphia *Saturday Courier*

14 December 1839, p. 2

The author of this notice was probably Ezra Holden (1803–46), editor and proprietor of the widely circulated weekly *Courier*. Holden wrote a friendly advance notice of *Tales of the Grotesque and Arabesque* on 2 November, from which Poe quoted in his supplement of 'Opinions'.

Two 12mo. volumes of Tales from the pen of Edgar A. Poe, are here presented to the public. There are twenty-five of them, and no one can read the volumes without coming to the conclusion that they embrace as much variety as could be given in the same compass, of the species of writing of which they are composed. They are generally wildly imaginative in plot; fanciful in description, sometimes to the full boundaries of the grotesque; but throughout indicating the polished writer, possessed of rare and varied learning. Some of them will bear good comparison with the productions of Coleridge, and it is not surprising that the author has often been compared with that author. The tale of 'William Wilson', and that of 'The House of Usher', are, to our judgment, the best in the volumes, and may be quoted as examples of the author's powers. On the whole, we think these tales highly creditable to the literature of our country, and we have no doubt they will be well received by the public.

32. Unsigned notice in the *Boston Morning Post*

17 December 1839, 16, 1

The contents of these volumes belong to that description of writing of which it is said neither gods nor men approve. A greater amount of trash within the same compass it would be difficult to find. The tales which he calls grotesque, are sufficiently so, but must give place to those which are impertinently called arabesque. There is a great affectation of learning throughout them all, and the writer has evidently studied the 'Dictionary of Quotations' with no inconsiderable success. Yet this raw pedant, 'the half-baked cake of oatmeal dough' makes Bulwer and Christopher North the objects of his satire! His satire! A penny trumpet against a full-toned bugle – a jew's harp against that of Carolan.

33. [John Frost], review in *Alexander's Weekly Messenger*

18 December 1839, p. 2

Frost (1800–59), a teacher and magazinist in Philadelphia, was described by Poe as 'a gentleman of fine taste, sound scholarship, and great general ability' (*Works*, 15, 243). Poe identified the reviewer in *Letters*, 1, 125, and in the *Saturday Museum*.

To say we have *read* this production attentively is not enough. We have *studied* it. It is every way worthy of such a distinction, and whoever shall give it a careful study and a philosophical analysis, will find in it the evidences of an original, vigorous, and independent mind, stored with rich and various learning and capable of successful application to a great variety of subjects. As a writer of fiction, Mr Poe passes 'from grave to gay, from lively to severe,' with an ease and buoyancy not less remarkable than the unfailing vigor of his style and prodigious extent of his resources for illustration and embellishment. He is capable of great things; and beautiful and interesting as the tales before us are, we deem them much less remarkable as actual performances than as evidences of ability for much more serious and sustained efforts. They seem to us the playful effusion of a remarkable and powerful intellect. We counsel the writer not to repose upon his laurels. He has placed himself in the foremost rank of American writers, as it respects ability. Let him maintain his position by untiring exertion and show that he fully deserves it by actual performance. He has raised the highest expectations. We trust he will not fail to fulfil them.

34. Unsigned notice in the New York *American*

21 December 1839, p. 5

Assuredly, no one can glance at these tales without being impressed with the wild and vivid fancy of the writer, his copious style and familiarity with much, and much curious learning – and yet the *cui bono* will intrude. Take for example, 'The Fall of the House of Usher', a tale as much elaborated, probably, as any one of them, and full of the author's striking peculiarities of sentiment and invention; it fails to interest deeply from its unnaturalness, and from the want of any link of feeling or sympathy between life, such as it is conceived of by most men, and the terrors and distresses, and moody solitude, and impossible catastrophes of the 'House of Usher'. Yet all will feel the writer's power over the terrible.

35. Notices in the *New-York Mirror*

(a) 21 December 1839, p. 207; (b) 28 December 1839, p. 215

Poe identified the author of (b) as Louis Fitzgerald Tasistro (1807–68), an actor, editor, and critic.

(a) The title of this volume faithfully characterizes the contents. To the lovers of imaginative writing, it may be commended as one of the most extraordinary and original works of the day. Mr Poe is a man of true genius. His sketch entitled 'Ligeia', in this work, is quite equal to any of the minor prose pieces of Bulwer. We have not had time to peruse the whole of the works, but that which we have read has been sufficient to convince us that the book is a good book, and one honourable to American talent. We commend it heartily to the public.

(b) The creation of modern literature – that species of invention which alone could body forth the infinite variety of modern society – the novel – requires much peculiar to its period, and all that the mind has ever possessed of original power. The legends of a barbaric age are, perhaps, all that the age had worth preserving: another, entirely military, is perfectly depicted in an heroic poem; where the character of a nation is exclusively political, its masterpiece is history: chivalry, with its banners and brands, lives in its own spirited ballads; and, as the varieties increased and shades multiplied, the drama became the lively and accurate reflection of the passing panorama. But to an age, reading, thoughtful, languid, with every excitement of former times added to its own – with its strange mixture of all that can form a character, yet repress its display – what could do justice – what give a picture so true, as may be given by the novel? The tale, although not so encumbered with plot and incidents, belongs to the same class of composition, and all that it has to depend upon for usefulness or effect, is its truth of principle, its fidelity to nature, and the tact and talent with which that truth is told and that fidelity is preserved. And herein is the value and beauty of that kind of truth displayed, in that it is visible and obvious to all, for it appeals to experience and awakens observation; it opens the character of humanity, and is at once food for the philosopher, and amusement for the child.

Had Mr Poe written nothing else but 'Morella', 'William Wilson', 'The House of Usher', and the 'MS. Found in a Bottle', he would deserve a high place among imaginative writers, for there is fine poetic feeling, much brightness of fancy, an excellent taste, a ready eye for the picturesque, much quickness of observation, and the great truth of sentiment and character in all these works. But there is scarcely one of the tales published in the two volumes before us, in which we do not find the development of great intellectual capacity, with a power for vivid description, an opulence of imagination, a fecundity of invention, and a command over the elegances of diction which have seldom been displayed, even by writers who have acquired the greatest distinction in the republic of letters. It would be, indeed, no easy matter to find another artist with ability equal to this writer for discussing the good and evil – the passions, dilemmas, and affectations – the self-sufficiency and the deplorable weakness, the light and darkness, the virtue and vice by which mankind are by turns affected. These volumes present a succession of richly-coloured pictures in the magic lantern of invention.

We have heard it objected, that Mr Poe's pictures are not always to be taken as a correct representation of human nature. What human nature actually is at this period, would be a matter of some difficulty to ascertain, modified as it is by education, controlled by circumstance, and compounded of customs and costumes. The novelist, the sketcher, and the essayist, must take, not make their materials: and in all states of society, whether one of furs, feathers, and paint; *au naturel* – or of those furs turned into muffs, those feathers waving over helmets and *barrettes*, and that paint softened into rouge and pearl-powder – the view taken by an acute observer will be valuable as philosophy. The human heart, like the human countenance, is endless in its variety; the tree, the flower, the bird, the beast, resemble each other, till the likeness is that of ideality. The oaks at Dodona were but like those in any English park; the steed of the Macedonian might be but as the racehorse of our modern turf. Not so with the face of man – the statue, the picture, come down to us, and we trace similarity, but no sameness; for where can be found two human beings whose individuality could be mistaken? And the varieties of mind are still more infinite: the routine of circumstances may and will be the same – the battle may be fought, the orator and statesman contend for the high places, the festival assemble the young, and the thousand great and little events of life be alike – but the spirit which vivifies them will be different; even as our present age bears no resembl- ance to its predecessors, so those in futurity are equally likely to differ from our own. If, therefore, Mr Poe appears now and then too sombre and fantastic, or deals in too wild imaginings, the fault, if fault it be, must be attributed to the advanced state of our literature, which – the incidents of invention being somewhat exhausted – makes an author frequently turn to sentiment and metaphysics rather than description or adventure.

In conclusion, we would just observe, that we have done but imperfect justice to this miscellaneous and agreeable work; one of the best lounging books we have perused for a very long while. It is quite impossible to dip into any part of it without having the attention riveted and the fancy pleased; so that, in truth, our only charge against it, is that it has detained us longer than was expedient from other volumes and affairs.

36. [Morton McMichael], notice in *Godey's Lady's Book*

January 1840, 20, 46

McMichael (1807–79) was active in Philadelphia politics and journalism from the early 1830s; Poe identified him as the author of this notice.

Mr Poe is a writer of rare and various abilities. He possesses a fine perception of the ludicrous, and his humorous stories are instinct with the principle of mirth. He possesses also a mind of unusual grasp – a vigorous power of analysis, and an acuteness of perception which have given to him high celebrity as a critic. These same faculties, moreover, aided by an unusually active imagination, and directed by familiar study of metaphysical writings, have led him to produce some of the most vivid scenes of the wild and wonderful which can be found in English literature. The volumes now published, contain favourable specimens of Mr Poe's powers, and cannot fail to impress all who read them, with a conviction of his genius.

37. [James E. Heath], review in the *Southern Literary Messenger*

January 1840, 6, 126

To say that we admire Mr Poe's style, abstractly considered, is more than we can say and speak truly; neither can we perceive any particular beneficial tendency that is likely to flow from his writings. This, of course, is a mere matter of opinion, and we may differ, in saying so, from many. At the same time, the possession of high powers of invention and imagination – of genius – is undoubtedly his. His productions are, many of them, in Literature, somewhat like Martin's in the Fine Arts.[1] His serious sketches all bear the marks of bold, fertile genius. There is the dark cloud hanging over all – there are the dim, misty, undefined shapes in the background. But amid all these arise huge and magnificent columns, flashing lamps, rich banqueting vessels, gleaming tiaras, and sweet, expressive faces. But the writings of Mr P. are well known to the readers of the *Messenger*.

The volumes before us, with a rather singular title, are composed of tales and sketches, which have appeared at different times before the public: many of them, in this journal. We have read but a portion of them. Of these, we like, as a specimen of the author's powers of humor, 'The Man That Was Used Up', and 'Why the Little Frenchman Wears His Hand in a Sling'. 'Siope' and the 'MS. Found in a Bottle', afford good specimens of the author's stronger and more graphic powers.

We recommend 'Hans Phaall' to every one who has not already read it – although our remembrance of it remains from a perusal some time since. The 'opinions' prefixed to the second volume, are in bad taste. We do not intend to write a critique, but merely to bring to the notice of the public, the production of a talented and powerful writer.

NOTE

1 John Martin (1789–1854), the historical/landscape painter, was widely considered a rare genius.

PROSE ROMANCES

1843

---

38. Unsigned notice in the Philadelphia *Saturday Museum*

22 July 1843, p. 2

The author of this notice was probably the *Museum's* editor and Poe's erstwhile partner in the 'Stylus' project, Thomas C. Clarke (1801–74).

Those who have a relish for the wild and wonderful – who would 'sup their full of horrors', revel in mysteries and riot in the deep, dark, recesses which an iron intellect is capable of investing with intense interest, have a full feast spread for them in the pages of the *Prose Romances*. But above all has the man of legal lore an opportunity of acquiring an insight into his profession, more thorough than his long days and studious nights could ever glean from all the records of criminal practices in the courts, or the pages of Blackstone or Coke. Mr Poe has the power, more than any other writer within our knowledge, not only of creating the most intricate mysteries, but unravelling them too; and had the Banks, in the great case of Eldrige, set the wits of Edgar A. Poe to work, they might have dispensed with the half-dozen lawyers of eminence and distinction, whose names we do not now remember. The banks, who were so awfully chiselled, to use a classical phrase, on that eventful occasion, might have dispensed with all that vast array of 'Philadelphia Lawyers', had they but placed their victim under the inquisitorial scrutiny of the author of the *Prose Romances*.

39. Unsigned review in the *Pennsylvania Inquirer*

26 July 1843, p. 2

Robert Morris (1809–74), the editor of this Philadelphia daily, may have been the reviewer.

We learn that the first number of the *Prose Romances* of Edgar A. Poe, Esq., has met with a ready sale. This was to be expected. Mr Poe has distinguished himself in every walk of literature; and it may be doubted whether the country boasts a writer of greater favor and more varied and finished accomplishments. As an editor of the *Southern Literary Messenger* he acquired and deserved a reputation, of which any living writer might be proud. In the field of romance, he has the rare merit of originality. Most of the tales of the day are copies, – a reiteration of incidents a hundred times recited, and a repetition of sentiments, which, however commendable, are as well known as the Lord's Prayer. Mr Poe's *Romances* are of a character entirely dissimilar. There is no apparent effort; no straining after sentiment; no daubing of red and white antithesis; no copied descriptions, a thousand times repeated, and weakened like circles in the water, with every repetition. In the present number, 'The Murders in the Rue Morgue' is the better of the two tales. Of itself it proves Mr Poe to be a man of genius. The inventive power exhibited is truly wonderful. At every step it whets the curiosity of the reader, until the interest is heightened to a point from which the mind shrinks with something like incredulity; when with an inventive power and skill, of which we know no parallel, he reconciles every difficulty, and with the most winning *vraisemblance* brings the mind to admit the truth of every marvel related. The reader is disposed to believe that this must be the actual observation of some experienced criminal lawyer, the chain of evidence is so wonderfully maintained through so many intricacies, and the connexion of cause and effect so irresistibly demonstrated. The story told by any ordinary man would seem improbable; as given by Mr Poe, the reader arises with a sense of mortification at having, for the time, so confidently believed that which is avowed to be fiction. 'The Murders in the Rue Morgue' is one of the most enchaining, finished, and powerful fictions that we have for a long time read. The second tale, 'The Man that was Used Up', is an excellent sketch, full of point and humour, but does not equal its predecessor. We trust that the publisher will so enlarge the edition as to meet the increasing demand.

40. Notice in the Philadelphia *Saturday Courier*

29 July 1843, p. 2

Is there a man, woman, or child, 'read up', as they phrase it in American Literature, who is unacquainted with Edgar A. Poe? We take it for granted that there is not: and consequently shall not, in the brief notice we are now to make of his productions, say a word of enlightenment in regard to him. Our purpose here is simply, to announce to the numerous readers of the *Saturday Courier*, that Mr W.H. Graham has just commenced a uniform serial edition of Mr Poe's *Prose Romances*, at the very low price of 12½ cents for each number. Besides, we learn each work may be purchased separately, should any reader wish to do so.

Had we space and time, we should delight to enter into an extended critique of Mr Poe's productions: and yet, should we do so, some might – perhaps justly – charge us with egotism, even in such an attempt. But we do not *now* say – we shall not, at some future day, forego that suspicion, notwithstanding – mayhap, in connection with notices of some singular, original, and extraordinary writers of American Literature. That Edgar A. Poe, has a peculiar mind, everybody admits. That he is original, all know. That he is learned – very learned – is equally well established. That he is one of the severest of critics, none deny – but many have felt. That he is one of the very best of the American Critics, we think only a few would undertake to deny. Yet, it is very certain that he sometimes wields a broad-axe, where a hatchet might have been equally efficacious. Besides, we have sometimes inclined to the opinion, that some of his book criticisms were infused with a little too much of worm-wood, with a sprinkling of gall, in doses far from being homoeopathic. That is a fault which mind – original mind – educated mind – in all ages of Literary and Scientific criticism – has been exceedingly liable to run into. Seeing literary grubs, occupying too often the places, which should be filled only by men of talent, ripe scholarship, and unmistaken and unmistakable genius – the real critics have sometimes lost their temper, and amused themselves by breaking gnats upon a wheel. That Mr Poe has sometimes played at this sport – we fully believe – but we doubt exceedingly whether the 'candle is worth the snuff'.

We leave this branch of the subject, however, for to-day – designing to resume it hereafter – and content ourselves at present, with remarking that whoever buys the *Prose Romances* of Poe, will find that they have been romancing to some purpose. They are peculiar – an original kind of Romances – but even in that very originality, we think men of mind will find gratification in revelling. Contrasted with that excellent and plain – yet eloquent and pathetic story teller, T.S. ARTHUR [1] – Mr Poe loses in comparison, as far as the applicability of his Tales is concerned, for the very general reading of the extended multitude. But for learning, uniqueness and originality – we unhesitatingly say that Edgar A. Poe, in his own country, stands entirely alone.

NOTE

1 Timothy Shay Arthur (1809–85) was a prolific and popular author of sentimental moral tracts and tales with a strong temperance bias.

41. Notice in the *Ladies' National Magazine*

September 1843, 4, 107

The *Ladies' National Magazine* was established in Philadelphia in 1842 by Charles J. Peterson as a rival to Godey's successful *Lady's Book*. Peterson (1819–87) was also associated with *Graham's Magazine*, and differences between him and Poe were rumoured to have provoked Poe's resignation. However, there are no signs of animosity in this notice – rather the contrary.

We need say but little of a writer so long and favorably known to the public. Mr Poe is a man of genius. His analytical powers are remarkable. His imagination is of the highest order. His choice of words is fine. His style is original. He is a scholar, a man of taste, and a rigid critic as well on his own productions as on those of others. With these qualifications his prose romances may be expected to be of superior merit: and such we find them to be. The leading story in this number, 'The Murders in the Rue Morgue', is one of the most intensely interesting tales that has appeared for years, and fully equal to the prize story which Mr Poe has lately written. His romances have found such favor abroad that an edition of them is about to appear in Paris.[1]

NOTE

1 No such edition appeared.

SOME POPULAR SUCCESSES

1843–5

(a) 'The Gold-Bug' (1843)

---

42. Discussion of 'The Gold-Bug' in the Philadelphia *Saturday Museum*

8 July 1843, p. 2

'The Gold-Bug'. This is the title of the story written by our friend Edgar A. Poe, Esq., which has been very justly designated as the most remarkable 'American work of fiction that has been published within the last fifteen years.' The period might very safely have been extended back to a period much more remote for so singular a concatenation of incongruous and improbable, nay, impossible absurdities, were never before interwoven in any single or half dozen works of fancy, fact or fiction; and never before, we venture to say, were such mysterious materials so adroitly managed, or a train of incongruities dovetailed together with such masterly ingenuity. Indeed the intense interest which the fiction awakens arises from the skillful management of the several improbabilities, which are so presented as to wear all the semblance of sober reality. It is the unique work of a singularly constituted, but indubitably great intellect, and we give, in another part of our paper, the substance of 'The Gold-Bug', omitting the abstruse and elaborate details in which the plot is involved.[1] We may add that the train of reasoning is throughout of a clear, strong, and highly ingenious character, such in fact as would do credit to the highest order of talent that ever puzzled a judge or mystified a jury.

NOTE

1 This issue of the *Museum* also offered a potted version of 'The Gold-Bug'.

(b) 'The Balloon Hoax' (1844)

43. Poe's account of the reception of 'The Balloon Hoax' in the *Columbia Spy*

25 May 1844

Poe's contributions to the *Spy* – an obscure paper from Columbia, Pa. – were collected by Jacob E. Spannuth and Thomas O. Mabbott in *Doings of Gotham* (Pottsville, Pa., 1929). Poe's hoax appeared as an 'Extra' of the New York *Sun*, 13 April 1844.

Talking of 'expresses' – the 'Balloon-Hoax' made a far more intense sensation than anything of that character since the 'Moon-Story' of Locke.[1] On the morning (Saturday) of its announcement, the whole square surrounding the *Sun* building was literally besieged, blocked up – ingress and egress being alike impossible, from a period soon after sunrise until about two o'clock P.M. In Saturday's regular issue, it was stated that the news had just been received, and that an 'Extra' was then in preparation, which would be ready at ten. It was not delivered, however, until nearly noon. In the meantime I never witnessed more intense excitement to get possession of a newspaper. As soon as the first few copies made their way into the streets, they were bought up, at almost any price, from the news-boys, who made a profitable speculation without doubt. I saw a half-dollar given, in one instance, for a single paper, and a shilling was a frequent price. I tried, in vain, during the whole day, to get possession of a copy. It was excessively amusing, however, to hear the comments of those who had read the 'Extra'. Of course there was great discrepancy of opinion as regards the authenticity of the story; but I observed that the more intelligent believed, while the rabble, for the most part, rejected the whole with disdain.

NOTE

1 Richard Adams Locke's famous hoax, 'Discoveries in the Moon', was published in the New York *Sun* in 1835; in 1844 Locke was editor of the paper.

(c) 'The Raven' (1845)

44. Nathaniel Parker Willis, introductory note in the New York *Evening Mirror*

26 January 1845

Willis (1806–67) was one of the most productive and successful magazinists of the day. He was a competent editor, poet, dramatist, and fiction writer, though his gossipy travel sketches brought him most attention. Willis was a good friend to Poe at this time, and for a few months from October 1844 he employed him as a 'mechanical paragraphist' on the *Evening Mirror*.

We are permitted to copy (in advance of publication) from the 2nd. No. of the *American Review*, the following remarkable poem by Edgar Poe. In our opinion, it is the most effective single example of 'fugitive poetry' ever published in this country; and unsurpassed in English poetry for subtle conception, masterly ingenuity of versification, and consistent, sustaining of imaginative lift and 'pokerishness'.[1] It is one of these 'dainties bred in a book' which we *feed* on. It will stick to the memory of everybody who reads it.

NOTE

1 Thomas Mabbott suggested that 'pokerish' meant 'spooky' (*Collected Works*, 1, 361); but the pun on Poe's name was probably also intended.

45. George Hooker Colton, introduction to 'The Raven' in the *American Review*

February 1845, I, 143

Colton (1818–47) was proprietor of the *American Review*, where 'The Raven' appeared under the pseudonym 'Quarles'. Although this introduction was signed by Colton, Poe may have contributed the ideas on prosody himself.

The following lines from a correspondent – besides the deep quaint strain of the sentiment, and the curious introduction of some ludicrous touches amidst the serious and impressive, as was doubtless intended by the author – appear to us one of the most felicitous specimens of unique rhyming which has for some time met our eye. The resources of English rhythm for varieties of melody, measure, and sound, producing corresponding diversities of effect, have been thoroughly studied, much more perceived, by very few poets in the language. While the classic tongues, especially the Greek, possess, by power of accent, several advantages for versification over our own, chiefly through greater abundance of spondaic feet, we have other and very great advantages of sound by the modern usage of rhyme. Alliteration is nearly the only effect of that kind which the ancients had in common with us. It will be seen that much of the melody of 'The Raven' arises from alliteration, and the studious use of similar sounds in unusual places. In regard to its measure, it may be noted that if all the verses were like the second, they might properly be placed merely in short lines, producing a not uncommon form; but the presence in all the others of one line – mostly the second in the verse – which flows continuously, with only an aspirate pause in the middle, like that before the short line in the Sapphic Adonic, while the fifth has at the middle pause no similarity of sound with any part beside, giving the versification an entirely different effect. We could wish the capacities of our noble language, in prosody, were better understood.

46. Introductory note to 'The Raven' in the *Southern Literary Messenger*

March 1845, 11, 186

The editor of the *Messenger*, to whom Poe sent 'The Raven', was Benjamin Blake Minor. The *Morning Express* was a New York daily founded and edited by James Brooks.

The following poem first appeared, we think, in the *Evening Mirror*; though intended for the *American Review*. It has since been frequently republished with the highest approbation. Still we take pleasure in presenting it to our readers, who must remember with delight many of the contributions of Mr Poe to the *Messenger*.

Mr Brooks, editor of the N.Y. *Express*, says:

'There is a poem in this book [the *American Review*], which far surpasses anything that has been done even by the best poets of the age: – indeed there are none of them who could pretend to enter into competition with it, except, perhaps, Alfred Tennyson; and he only to be excelled out of measure.[1] Nothing can be conceived more effective than the settled melancholy of the poet bordering upon sullen despair, and the personification of this despair in the Raven settling over the poet's door, to depart thence "Nevermore". In power and originality of versification the whole is no less remarkable than it is, psychologically, a *wonder*.'

NOTE

1 In a review of Rufus Griswold's *Poets and Poetry of America* in the London *Foreign Quarterly Review* (January 1844, 32, 321), Poe had been described as an imitator of Tennyson. Poe resented this article, which he was convinced had been written by Dickens – see *Letters*, 1, 246. In fact, John Forster seems to have been the author.

47. Elizabeth Barrett comments on 'The Raven' in letters to (a) Richard Hengist Horne, and (b) Poe

(a) 12 May 1845; (b) April 1846

Elizabeth Barrett (1806–61), who married Robert Browning in September 1845, was widely regarded as one of the most important English poets of the day, and Poe cultivated her attention. In January 1845, he sent to her via her friend Richard Hengist Horne (1803–84) his long *Broadway Journal* review of her collected poems, together with a copy of 'The Raven'. Poe had already puffed Horne's 'epic' poem, *Orion*, in *Graham's*, and hoped to use him as an intermediary with English publishers. Later, Poe dedicated *The Raven and Other Poems* to Miss Barrett; she received his presentation copy on 20 March 1846, and document (b) is part of her response. The present texts are from *Works*, 17, 229–30; 385–6.

(a) Your friend, Mr Poe, is a speaker of strong words 'in both kinds'. But I hope you will assure him from me that I am grateful for his reviews, and in no complaining humour at all. As to the 'Raven' tell me what you shall say about it! There is certainly a power – but does not appear to me the natural expression of a sane intellect in whatever mood; and I think that this should be specified in the title of the poem. There is a fantasticalness about the 'sir or madam', and things of the sort, which is ludicrous, unless there is a specified insanity to justify the straws. Probably he – the author – intended it to be read in the poem, and he ought to have intended it. The rhythm acts excellently upon the imagination, and the 'nevermore' has a solemn chime with it. Don't get me into a scrape. The 'pokerishness' (just gods! what Mohawk English!) might be found fatal, peradventure. Besides, – just because I have been criticised, I would not criticise. And I am of opinion that there is an uncommon force and effect in the poem.

(b) After which imperfect acknowledgement of my personal obligation may I thank you as another reader would thank you for this vivid writing, this power which is felt! Your 'Raven' has produced a sensation, a 'fit horror', here in England. Some of my friends are taken by the fear of it and some by the music. I hear of persons haunted by the 'Nevermore', and one acquaintance of mine who has the misfortune of possessing a 'bust of Pallas' never can bear to look at it in the twilight. I think you will like to be told our great poet, Mr Browning, the author of 'Paracelsus', and the 'Bells and Pomegranates' was struck much by the rhythm of that poem.

48. [John Moncure Daniel], introduction to 'The Raven' in the *Richmond Examiner*

25 September 1849

Daniel (1825–65) was the editor of the *Examiner*. He met Poe in Richmond in 1848 and apparently quarrelled with him, though in 1849 there was some talk of Poe working on the *Examiner*.

Mr Edgar A. Poe lectured again last night on the 'Poetic Principle', and concluded his lecture, as before, with his now celebrated poem of the Raven. As the attention of many in this city is now directed to this singular performance, and as Mr Poe's poems, from which only is it to be obtained in the bookstores, have long been out of print, we furnish our readers, today, with the only correct copy ever published – which we are enabled to do by the courtesy of Mr Poe himself.[1]

'The Raven' has taken rank over the whole world of literature, as the very first poem yet produced on the American continent. There is indeed but one other – the 'Humble Bee' of Ralph Waldo Emerson, which can be ranked near it. The latter is superior to it, as a work of construction and design, while the former is superior to the latter as work of *pure art*. They hold the same relation the one to the other that a masterpiece of painting holds to a splendid piece of mosaic. But while this poem maintains a rank so high among all persons of catholic and generally cultivated taste, we can conceive the wrath of many who will read it for the first time in the columns of this newspaper. Those who have formed their taste in the Pope and Dryden school, whose earliest poetical acquaintance is Milton, and whose

latest Hammond and Cowper – with a small sprinking of
Moore and Byron – will not be apt to relish on first sight a
poem tinged so deeply with the dyes of the nineteenth century. The poem will make an impression on them which they
will not be able to explain – but what will irritate them –
Criticism and explanation are useless with such. In spite of
our pleas, such will talk of the gaudiness of Keats and the
craziness of Shelley, until they see deep enough into their
claims to forget or be ashamed to talk so. Such will angrily
pronounce 'The Raven' flat nonsense. Another class will be
disgusted therewith, because they can see no purpose, no
allegory, no 'meaning', as they express it, in the poem. These
people – and they constitute the majority of our practical
race – are possessed with a false theory. – They hold that
every poem and poet should have some moral notion or
other, which it is his 'mission' to expound. That theory is all
false. To build theories, principles, religions, &c., is the
business of the argumentative, not of the poetic faculty. The
business of poetry is to minister to the sense of the beautiful
in human minds. – That sense is a simple element in our
nature – simple, not compound; and therefore the art which
ministers to it may safely be said to have an ultimate end in so
ministering. This 'The Raven' does in an eminent degree. It
has no allegory in it, no purpose – or a very slight one – but it
is a 'thing of beauty', and will be a 'joy forever', for that and
no further reason. In the last stanza is an image of settled
despair and despondency, which throws a gleam of meaning
and allegory over the entire poem – making it all a personification of that passion – but that stanza is evidently an
afterthought, and unconnected with the original poem. 'The
Raven' itself is a mere narrative of simple events. A bird
which has been taught to speak by some former master, is
lost in a stormy night, is attracted by the light of a student's
window, flies to it and flutters against it. Then against the
door. The student fancies it a visitor, opens the door, and the
chance word uttered by the bird suggests to him memories
and fancies connected with his own situation and the dead
sweetheart or wife. Such is the poem. – The last stanza is an
afterthought.[2] The worth of 'The Raven' is not in any
'Moral', nor is its charm in the construction of its story. Its

great and wonderful merits consist in the strange, beautiful and fantastic imagery and colours with which the simple subject is clothed – the grave and supernatural tone with which it rolls on the ear – the extraordinary vividness of the word painting, – and the powerful but altogether indefinable appeal which is made throughout to the organs of ideality and marvelousness. Added to these is a versification indescribably sweet and wonderfully difficult – winding and convoluted about like the mazes of some complicated overture by Beethoven. To all who have a strong perception of tune, there is a music in it which haunts the ear long after reading. These are great merits, and 'The Raven' is a gem of art. It is stamped with the image of true genius – and genius in its happiest hour. It is one of those things an author never does but once.

NOTES

1 This was the last printing of 'The Raven' to be authorized by Poe.
2 Daniel states this twice; he may have heard it from Poe.

(d) 'The Facts in the Case of M. Valdemar' (1845)

49. 'Mesmerism in America', London *Popular Record of Modern Science*

(a) 10 January 1846, No. 41, 17–20; (b) 11 April 1846, No. 54, 225–7

Poe's tales of mesmeric mystification – 'Mesmeric Revelation' and 'The Facts in the Case of M. Valdemar' – aroused considerable interest and excitement, and were widely printed. The gruesome 'Valdemar' hoax held a particular fascination for English readers; Elizabeth Barrett spoke of it as 'throwing us all into "most admired disorder", and dreadful doubts as to whether "it can be true", as the children say of ghost stories' (*Works*, 17, 229). The story appeared in the *Sunday Times* and the prestigious *Morning Post*, before being taken up by the *Popular Record*, which was interested in 'disputed doctrines' of all kinds, including mesmerism. In a belated expose of the *Popular Record's* gullibility, Poe declared: 'This work has a vast circulation, and is respected by eminent men' (*Graham's Magazine*, March 1848, 12, 178–9); but the claim seems exaggerated.

(a) The following narrative appears in a recent number of the *American Magazine*, a respectable periodical in the United States. It comes, it will be observed, from the narrator of the 'Last Conversation of a Somnambule',[1] published in the *Popular Record* of the 29th of November.

In extracting this case, the *Morning Post* of Monday last, takes what it considers to be the safe side by remarking 'For our own parts we do not believe it; and there are several statements made, more especially with regard to the disease of which the patient died, which at once prove the case to be either a fabrication or the work of one little acquainted with consumption. The story, however, is wonderful, and we therefore give it.' The editor, however, does not point out the especial statements which are inconsistent with what we know of the progress of consumption, and as few scientific persons would be willing to take their pathology any more than they would their logic from the *Morning Post*, his caution, it is to be feared, will not have much weight. The reason assigned by the *Post* for publishing the account is quaint, and would apply equally to an adventure from Baron Munchausen; 'it is wonderful and we therefore give it!'

[Prints 'The Death of M. Valdemar of New York, by Edgar A. Poe'.]

The above case is obviously one that cannot be received except on the strongest testimony, and it is equally clear that the testimony by which it is at present accompanied, is not of this kind. The most favourable circumstances in support of it, consist in the fact that credence is understood to be given to it at New York, within a few miles of which city the affair took place, and where, consequently, the most ready means must be found for its authentication or disproval. The initials of the medical men and of the young medical student must be sufficient in the immediate locality to establish their identity, especially as M. Valdemar was well known, and had been so long ill as to render it out of the question that there should be any difficulty in ascertaining the names of the physicians by whom he had been attended. In the same way the nurses and servants under whose cognizance the case must have come during the seven months which it occupied, are of course, accessible to all sorts of inquiries. It will therefore appear that there must have been too many parties concerned to render prolonged deception practicable. The angry excitement and various rumours which have at length rendered a public statement necessary, are also sufficient to show that *something* extraordinary must have taken place.

On the other hand, there is no strong point for disbelief. The circumstances are, as the *Post* says, 'wonderful', but so are all circumstances that come to our knowledge for the first time – and in mesmerism everything is new. An objection may be made that the article has rather a magazinish air, Mr Poe having evidently written with a view to effect, and so to excite rather than to subdue the vague appetite for the mysterious and the horrible which such a case under any circumstances is sure to awaken – but apart from this there is nothing to deter a philosophic mind from further inquiries regarding it. It is a matter entirely for *testimony*.

Under this view we shall take steps to procure from some of the most intelligent and influential citizens of New York all the evidence that can be had upon the subject. No steamer will leave England for America till the 3rd of February, but within a few weeks of that time we doubt not it will be possible to lay before the readers of the *Record*, information which will enable them to come to a pretty accurate conclusion. Whether it be a fact or an imposture, it is equally interesting and important to trace it out.

(b) The *Popular Record*, of the 10th January contained a case of Mesmerism, by Mr Edgar A. Poe, extracted from the *American Magazine*, a respectable periodical in the United States. It will be remembered that it described the death of a M. Valdemar, 'the well-known compiler of the *Bibliotheca Forensica*', and intimated that, for more than six months preceding his decease, the patient had remained in a state of trance caused as it was supposed by the mesmeric manipulations of Mr Poe; that upon being aroused from this condition by his mesmeriser, he uttered some incoherent exclamations that, 'he was dead'; and that upon his expiring shortly afterwards, his body became suddenly rotten and putrescent. The scene of the occurrence was Harlem, a village within a few miles of New York, in which city, according to the *Morning Post* and other papers, by whom the account was first published in this country, Mr Poe's narrative was understood to have found credence.

As no portion of the case involved anything absolutely inconsistent with the laws which govern the human organisation, so far as the knowledge of those laws extends, it was of course one that would depend entirely on the testimony by which it might be supported. All the testimony that was possessed at the time consisted, first, in the fact that Mr Poe, the narrator, was known as an American author, and as the reporter of a previous case, which had not only been also published in a respectable periodical, the *Columbian Magazine*, but which had been remarked upon as authentic by the American press; and, secondly, in the circumstances already stated that credence was given to his narrative at New York, where abundant means must have existed for ascertaining its genuineness or the reverse. This, however, although it would be regarded as strong testimony, in any ordinary case, (since, apart from the reception of the matter by Mr Poe's fellow citizens, it was extremely improbable that a person having any reputation whatever would run the risk of a fabrication, which on its detection must exclude him from society,) was, of course, in regard to so remarkable an occurrence, only sufficient to induce that amount of attention which would prevent it from being altogether dismissed until further inquiry had been instituted. With the belief that, 'whether it was a fact or an imposture, it was equally interesting and important to trace it out,' we made application to some friends at New York to furnish us with all that might have subsequently transpired respecting it, and this information (after an accidental delay) arrived a few days back.

The result is as follows. It appears that the statement actually proceeded from Mr Poe, and that it was published with his concurrence; that immediately after its appearance, 'it was republished in many papers as "truth stranger than fiction;"' that it was 'fully credited by many wise and shrewd men;' that inquiries were accordingly instituted, and that these inquiries terminated in an avowal on the part of Mr Poe, that there was not one particle of truth either in the statement in question or in that by which it had been preceded.

One of the gentlemen, whom we requested to inquire into

the matter, wrote direct to Mr Poe. The reply which he received contained the following paragraphs:

The philosophy detailed in the 'Last Conversation of a Somnambule', is my own – original, I mean, with myself, and had long impressed me. I was anxious to introduce it to the world in a manner which should insure for it attention. I thought that by representing my speculations in a garb of vraisemblance – giving them as revelations – I would secure for them a hearing, and I depended upon what the *Popular Record* very properly calls the 'Magazinish' tone of the article to correct any false impression which might arise in regard to the question of fact or fable. In the case of Valdemar, I was actuated by similar motives, but in this latter paper, I made a more pronounced effort at verisimilitude for the sake of effect. The only material difference between the two articles is, that in one I believe actual truth to be involved; in the other I have aimed at merely suggestion and speculation. I find the Valdemar case universally copied and *received as truth*, even in spite of my disclaimer.

Mr Poe is understood to profess that he had no deliberate intention to deceive. In his first statement of the 'Conversation of a Somnambule', he 'depended on a magazinish tone', to prevent its being received as genuine, but men of honour, at least in England, are not in the habit of putting forth deliberate assertions, with the expectation and hope that such assertions will be regarded by the public as lies, merely on account of some peculiarity of style. A few years back, Lord Ellenborough put forth an inflated proclamation, regarding the gates of Somnath, but he would have been very much surprised to find the facts stated in that proclamation treated as fabrications.[2] Again, a month or so ago, Sir Bulwer Lytton wrote an article, detailing certain remarkable circumstances concerning the water-cure, and which was characterized to the fullest extent by his romantic mode of composition, yet no person would ever think of expressing a doubt as to the literal truth of any one of the statements it contained, however they might differ regarding the writer's deductions.[3] Wherever, as in this country, a strong sense prevails of the irretrievable disgrace consequent upon a man's name being connected with a falsehood, writers will always manifest the greatest care not to put forth any statements, about which danger can exist of their intentions being misunderstood; and, at the same time, as a natural consequence, there will always be found a general readiness on the part of the public to receive in good faith whatever may be asserted, (provided it is not in absolute contradiction to known facts,) by those who will furnish their names as a guarantee. In England, amidst the strongest intemperance and bigotry of party, it is rarely that any attempt is made to throw doubt upon the veracity of deliberate allegations. Anything stated by a man of character, as the result of personal experience, is always conceded to be correct; it is only regarding the *inferences* to be deduced from such experience that warfare is carried on.

And even if the plea of 'peculiarity of style' could exonerate Mr Poe from wilful deceit regarding his first case, it will not apply to his second. When he published this, he had experience that the public did not necessarily associate the idea of falsehood with a fluent and dramatic style of composition, yet he deliberately made 'a greater effort at verisimilitude'. His best palliation, therefore, must consist in the fact that he must have anticipated that the imposture could not long remain undetected; but this has been felt by many men in committing offences, and, consequently, avails but little in putting the matter on a more creditable footing. Moreover, it is never possible to insure that the subsequent explanation or contradiction of a statement shall reach all the parties to whom the statement itself has made its way. A falsehood once put forth is gone beyond recall, and this consideration to a man possessing the slightest feeling of conscientiousness would always be sufficient to suggest the strictest care.

It will be seen from Mr Poe's latest averment, (which must now pass for what it is worth,) that the views expressed in the 'Last Conversation of a Somnambule', are really those which he himself entertains. Supposing this to be true, it will account, in a great measure, for the clearness, force, and apparent sincerity, with which they are developed. It may be questioned, however, if it be not highly probable that, for the most part, the views are actually such as have been put forward by a somnambule, and that they have been noted down by Mr Poe, and applied to his own purposes. It is also by no means unlikely that some of the phenomena detailed in the case of M. Valdemar were drawn from peculiar facts which had come under his observation. There is a fair amount of evidence on record to show that a prolonged state of trance may be induced by the action of mesmerism on sick persons, and some well known facts, observed in Canada, and other cold climates, regarding the rapid decomposition of animal substances under certain circumstances, may also have contributed to make up the narrative. It may seem discourteous to Mr Poe not to receive his explanation simply as he gives it, but we do not yet feel sufficiently familiar with his varieties of style, to form any positive opinion as to when he wishes it to be understood that he is speaking the truth.

The most disagreeable circumstance connected with the matter, is the confirmation it affords of the general prejudice existing in Europe, regarding the little dependence to be placed upon American veracity. When Mr Poe's statements were first re-published here, the ground of disbelief most frequently mentioned was, that 'they came from America,' – an objection which is now shown to have been a valid one. All efforts of those who feel friendship to the United States, and who wish to promote a respectful bearing, and a candid intercourse between the people of the two countries are thus constantly frustrated, and it is now become a habit to receive nothing from America, except with the largest allowance. This feeling is not one of choice, but of necessity. Men engaged in the pursuit of science, are too eager to receive new light, not to deplore the necessity for doubting it. It is vain, therefore, for the Americans to charge the prevailing distrust to any ungenerous disposition on this side. It is to the small tricks of such gentlemen as Mr Poe that they owe the origin and perpetuation of their disgrace. They may urge it to be unfair to condemn the many on account of the few, but the few compromise the many, when they show a perfect confidence that they can gratify their inclinations without jeopardy to their social standing.*

---

* It is proper, however, to mention that some of the letters we have received indicate, from their tone, a due opinion of the position in which Mr Poe has placed himself.

In conclusion, it is, at all events, satisfactory to point out, from the rapid detection of Mr Poe's fiction, the ease and certainty with which got-up cases may usually be shifted, and the inference to which we are thus led of the validity of the immense number of Mesmeric cases, (some of them quite as remarkable, though not so exciting as those of Mr Poe), in which all the names of the parties were duly stated, and in which, despite of unceasing attempts, it has been found impossible to detect error or imposition.

NOTES

1 'Mesmeric Revelation'.
2 Lord Ellenborough, Governor-General of India, captured the gates during the 1842 Afghan war, believing them to have been stolen from the ancient Hindu temple at Somnath by Muslim invaders; the gates turned out to be unauthentic.
3 Edward Bulwer Lytton, *Confessions of a Water Patient, in a Letter to W. Harrison Ainsworth* (London, 1846).

GENERAL ESTIMATES

1845

50. James Russell Lowell, 'Our Contributors – No. XVII. Edgar Allan Poe', *Graham's Magazine*

February 1845, 27, 49–53

Lowell (1819–91) was a respected poet and critic; he later became an Establishment 'Man of Letters'. Poe contributed to Lowell's short-lived magazine, the *Pioneer* (1843), and conducted a flattering correspondence with him in the hope of persuading him to take part in the 'Stylus' enterprise. Lowell wrote this essay at Poe's invitation: Poe supplied him with his 1843 *Saturday Museum* biography, but did not correct the romantic fabrications about his life that had appeared there. In 1849, Griswold asked Lowell to revise his essay for inclusion in the forthcoming edition of Poe's work: the resulting article omitted about a third of the original, and was markedly less enthusiastic about Poe's genius (the omitted passages, together with the revised ending, are printed here within brackets). Some scholars have suggested that Griswold maliciously tampered with Lowell's essay, but the revisions were probably authorized by Lowell.

The situation of American literature is anomalous. It has no center, or, if it have, it is like that of the sphere of Hermes. It is divided into many systems, each revolving round its several suns, and often presenting to the rest only the faint

glimmer of a milk-and-watery way. Our capital city, unlike
London or Paris, is not a great central heart, from which life
and vigor radiate to the extremities, but resembles more an
isolated umbilicus, stuck down as near as may be to the
center of the land, and seeming rather to tell a legend of
former usefulness than to serve any present need. Boston,
New York, Philadelphia, each has its literature almost more
distinct than those of the different dialects of Germany; and
the Young Queen of the West has also one of her own, of
which some articulate rumor barely has reached us dwellers
by the Atlantic. [Meanwhile, a great babble is kept up
concerning a national literature, and the country, having
delivered itself of the ugly likeness of a paint-bedaubed, filthy
savage, smilingly dandles the rag baby upon her maternal
knee, as if it were veritable flesh and blood, and would grow
timely to bone and sinew.]

[But, before we have an American literature, we must have
an American criticism. We have, it is true, some scores of
'American Macaulays,' the faint echoes of defunct originali-
ties, who will discourse learnedly at an hour's notice upon
matters, to be even a sciolist in which would ask the patient
study and self-denial of years – but, with a few rare exceptions, America is still to seek a profound, original, and
aesthetic criticism. Our criticism, which from its nature
might be expected to pass most erudite judgement upon the
merit of thistles, undertakes to decide upon

The plant and flower of light.

There is little life in it, little conscientiousness, little
reverence; nay, it has seldom the mere physical merit of
fearlessness. It may be best likened to an intellectual
gathering of chips to keep the critical pot of potatoes or
reputation a-boiling. Too often, indeed, with the cast
garments of some pigmy Gifford, or other foreign notoriety,
which he has picked up at the ragfair of literature, our critic
sallies forth, a self-dubbed Amadis, armed with a pen,
which, more wonderful even than the fairy-gifts in an old
ballad, becomes at will either the lance couched terribly at
defiant windmills, or the trumpet for a halfpenny paean.]

Perhaps there is no task more difficult than the just

criticism of contemporary literature. It is even more grateful to give praise where it is needed than where it is deserved, and friendship so often seduces the iron stylus of justice into a vague flourish, that she writes what seems rather like an epitaph than a criticism. Yet if praise be given as an alms, we could not drop so poisonous a one into any man's hat. The critic's ink may suffer equally from too large an infusion of nutgalls or of sugar. But it is easier to be generous than to be just [though there are some who find it equally hard to be either], and we might readily put faith in that fabulous direction to the hiding-place of truth, did we judge from the amount of water which we usually find mixed with it. [We were very naturally led into some remarks on American criticism by the subject of the present sketch. Mr Poe is at once the most discriminating, philosophical, and fearless critic upon imaginative works who has written in America. It may be that we should qualify our remark a little, and say that he *might be*, rather than that he always *is*, for he seems sometimes to mistake his phial of prussic-acid for his inkstand. If we do not always agree with him in his premises, we are, at least, satisfied that his deductions are logical, and that we are reading the thoughts of a man who thinks for himself, and says what he thinks, and knows well what he is talking about. His analytic power would furnish forth bravely some score of ordinary critics. We do not know him personally, but we suspect him for a man who has one or two pet prejudices on which he prides himself. These sometimes allure him out of the strict path of criticism, * but, where they do not interfere, we would put almost entire confidence in his judgements. Had Mr Poe had the control of a magazine of his own, in which to display his critical abilities, he would have been as autocratic, ere this, in America, as Professor Wilson has been in England; and his criticisms, we are sure, would have been far more profound and philosophical than those of the Scotsman. As it is, he has squared out blocks enough to build an enduring pyramid, but has left them lying carelessly and unclaimed in many different quarries.]

Remarkable experiences are usually confined to the inner life of imaginative men, but Mr Poe's biography displays a vicissitude and peculiarity of interest such as is rarely met with. The offspring of a romantic marriage, and left an orphan at an early age, he was adopted by Mr Allan, a wealthy Virginian, whose barren marriage bed seemed the warranty of a large estate to the young poet. Having received a classical education in England, he returned home and entered the University of Virginia, where, after an extravagant course, followed by reformation at the last extremity, he was graduated with the highest honors of his class. Then came a boyish attempt to join the fortunes of the insurgent Greeks, which ended at St Petersburg, where he got into difficulties through want of a passport, from which he was rescued by the American consul and sent home. He now entered the military academy at West Point, from which he obtained a dismissal on hearing of the birth of a son to his adopted father, by a second marriage, an event which cut off his expectations as an heir. The death of Mr Allan, in whose will his name was not mentioned, soon after relieved him of all doubt in this regard, and he committed himself at once to authorship for a support. Previously to this, however, he had published (in 1827) a small volume of poems, which soon ran through three editions, and excited high expectations of its author's future distinction in the minds of many competent judges.

That no certain augury can be drawn from a poet's earliest lispings there are instances enough to prove. Shakespeare's first poems, though brimful of vigor and youth and picturesqueness, give but a very faint promise of the directness, condensation and overflowing moral of his maturer works. Perhaps, however, Shakespeare is hardly a case in point, his *Venus and Adonis* having been published, we believe, in his twenty-sixth year. Milton's Latin verses show tenderness, a fine eye for nature, and a delicate appreciation of classic models, but give no hint of the author of a new style in poetry. Pope's youthful pieces have all the sing-song, wholly unrelieved by the glittering malignity and eloquent irreligion of his later productions. Collins' callow namby-pamby died and gave no sign of the vigorous and original genius which he afterward displayed. We have never thought that the world lost more in the 'marvelous boy,' Chatterton, than a very ingenious imitator of obscure and antiquated dullness. Where he becomes original (as it is called) the interest of ingenuity ceases and he becomes stupid. Kirke White's promises were endorsed by the respectable name of Mr Southey, but surely with no authority from Apollo. They have the merit of a traditional piety, which, to our mind, if uttered at all, had been less objectionable in the retired closet of a diary, and in the sober raiment of prose. They do not clutch hold of the memory with the drowning pertinacity of Watts'; neither have they the interest of his occasional simple, lucky beauty. Burns, having fortunately been rescued by his humble station from the contaminating society of the 'best models', wrote well and naturally from the first. Had he been unfortunate enough to have had an educated taste, we should have had a series of poems from which, as from his letters, we could sift here and there a kernel from the mass of chaff. Coleridge's youthful efforts give no promise whatever of that poetical genius which produced at once the wildest, tenderest, most original and most purely imaginative poems of modern times. Byron's *Hours of Idleness* would never find a reader except from an intrepid and indefatigable curiosity. In Wordsworth's first preludings there is but a dim foreboding of the creator of an era. From Southey's early poems, a safer augury might have been drawn. They show the patient investigator, the close student of history, and the unwearied explorer of the beauties of predecessors, but they give no assurances of a man who should add aught to [the] stock of household words, or to the rarer and more sacred delights of the fireside or the arbor. The earliest specimens of Shelley's poetic mind already, also, give tokens of that ethereal sublimation in which the spirit seems to soar above the region of words, but leaves its body, the verse, to be entombed, without hope of resurrection, in a mass of them. Cowley is generally instanced as a wonder of precocity. But his early insipidities show only a capacity for rhyming and for the metrical arrangement of certain conventional combinations of words, a capacity wholly dependent on a delicate physical organization, and an unhappy memory. An early poem is only remarkable when it displays an effort of *reason*, and the rudest verses in which we can trace some conception of the ends of poetry are worth all the miracles of smooth juvenile versification. A schoolboy, one would say, might acquire the regular seesaw of Pope merely by an association with the motion of the playground tilt.

Mr Poe's early productions show that he could see through the verse to the spirit beneath, and that he already had a feeling that all the life and grace of the one must depend on and be modulated by the will of the other. We call them the most remarkable boyish poems that we have ever read. We know of none that can compare with them for maturity of purpose, and a nice understanding of the effects of language and meter. Such pieces are only valuable when they display what we can only express by the contradictory phrase of *innate experience*. We copy one of the shorter poems written when the author was only *fourteen!* There is a little dimness in the filling up, but the grace and symmetry of the outline are such as few poets ever attain. There is a smack of ambrosia about it.

[Quotes 'To Helen'.]

It is the *tendency* of the young poet that impresses us. Here is no 'withering scorn', no heart 'blighted' ere it has safely got into its teens, none of the drawing-room sansculottism which Byron had brought into vogue. All is limpid and serene, with a pleasant dash of the Greek Helicon in it. The melody of the whole, too, is remarkable. It is not of that kind which can be demonstrated arithmetically upon the tips of the fingers. It is of that finer sort which the inner ear alone can estimate. It seems simple, like a Greek column, because of its perfection. In a poem named 'Ligeia,' under which title he intended to personify the music of nature, our boy-poet gives us the following exquisite picture:

> Ligeia! Ligeia!
>   My beautiful one,
> Whose harshest idea
>   Will to melody run,
> Say, is it thy will
>   On the breezes to toss,
> Or, capriciously still,

Like the lone albatross,
Incumbent on night,
As she on the air,
To keep watch with delight
On the harmony there?

John Neal, himself a man of genius, and whose lyre has been too long capriciously silent, appreciated the high merit of these and similar passages, and drew a proud horoscope for their author. [The extracts which we shall presently make from Mr Poe's later poems fully justify his predictions.]

Mr Poe has that indescribable something which men have agreed to call *genius*. No man could ever tell us precisely what it is, and yet there is none who is not inevitably aware of its presence and its power. Let talent writhe and contort itself as it may, it has no such magnetism. Larger of bone and sinew it may be, but the wings are wanting. Talent sticks fast to earth, and its most perfect works have still one foot of clay. Genius claims kindred with the very workings of Nature herself, so that a sunset shall seem like a quotation from Dante or Milton, and if Shakespeare be read in the very presence of the sea itself, his verses shall but seem nobler for the sublime criticism of ocean. Talent may make friends for itself, but only genius can give to its creations the divine power of winning love and veneration. Enthusiasm cannot cling to what itself is unenthusiastic, nor will he ever have disciples who has not himself impulsive zeal enough to be a disciple. Great wits are allied to madness only inasmuch as they are possessed and carried away by their demon, while talent keeps him, as Paracelsus did, securely prisoned in the pommel of its sword. To the eye of genius, the veil of the spiritual world is ever rent asunder, that it may perceive the ministers of good and evil who throng continually around it. No man of mere talent ever flung his inkstand at the devil.

When we say that Mr Poe has genius, we do not mean to say that he has produced evidence of the highest. But to say that he possesses it at all is to say that he needs only zeal, industry, and a reverence for the trust reposed in him, to achieve the proudest triumphs and the greenest laurels. If we may believe the Longinuses and Aristotles of our newspapers, we have quite too many geniuses of the loftiest order to render a place among them at all desirable, whether for its hardness of attainment or its seclusion. The highest peak of our Parnassus is, according to these gentlemen, by far the most thickly settled portion of the country, a circumstance which must make it an uncomfortable residence for individuals of a poetical temperament, if love of solitude be, as immemorial tradition asserts, a necessary part of their idiosyncrasy. [There is scarce a gentleman or lady of respectable moral character to whom these liberal dispensers of the laurel have not given a ticket to that once sacred privacy, where they may elbow Shakespeare and Milton at leisure. A transient visitor, such as a critic must necessarily be, sees these legitimate proprietors in common, parading their sacred enclosure as thick and buzzing as flies, each with 'Entered according to act of Congress' labeled securely to his back. Formerly one Phoebus, a foreigner, we believe, had the monopoly of transporting all passengers thither, a service for which he provided no other conveyance than a vicious horse, named Pegasus, who could, of course, carry but one at a time, and even that but seldom, his back being a ticklish seat, and one fall proving generally enough to damp the ardor of the most zealous aspirant. The charges, however, were moderate, as the poet's pocket formerly occupied that position in regard to the rest of his outfit which is now more usually conceded to his head. But we must return from our little historical digression.]

Mr Poe has two of the prime qualities of genius, a faculty of vigorous yet minute analysis, and a wonderful fecundity of imagination. The first of these faculties is as needful to the artist in words, as a knowledge of anatomy is to the artist in colors or in stone. This enables him to conceive truly, to maintain a proper relation of parts, and to draw a correct outline, while the second groups, fills up, and colors. Both of these Mr Poe has displayed with singular distinctness in his prose works, the last predominating in his earlier tales, and the first in his later ones. In judging of the merit of an author, and assigning him his niche among our household gods, we have a right to regard him from our own point of view, and to measure him by our own standard. But, in estimating his works, we must be governed by his own design, and, placing them by the side of his own ideal, find how much is wanting. We differ with Mr Poe in his opinions of the objects of art. He esteems that object to be the creation of Beauty,[†] and perhaps it is only in the definition of that word that we disagree with him. But in what we shall say of his writings we shall take his own standard as our guide. The temple of the god of song is equally accessible from every side, and there is room enough in it for all who bring offerings, or seek an oracle.

In his tales, Mr Poe has chosen to exhibit his power chiefly in that dim region which stretches from the very utmost limits of the probable into the weird confines of superstition and unreality. He combines in a very remarkable manner two faculties which are seldom found united: a power of influencing the mind of the reader by the impalpable shadows of mystery, and a minuteness of detail which does not leave a pin or a button unnoticed. Both are, in truth, the natural results of the predominating quality of his mind, to which we have before alluded, analysis. It is this which distinguishes the artist. His mind at once reaches forward to the effect to be produced. Having resolved to bring about certain emotions in the reader, he makes all subordinate parts tend strictly to the common center. Even his mystery is mathematical to his own mind. To him x is a known quantity all along. In any picture that he paints, he understands the chemical properties of all his colors. However vague some of his figures may seem, however formless the shadows, to him the outline is as clear and distinct as that of a geometrical diagram. For this reason Mr Poe has no sympathy with *Mysticism*. The Mystic dwells in the mystery, is enveloped with it; it colors all his thoughts; it affects his optic nerve especially, and the commonest things get a rainbow edging from it. Mr Poe, on the other hand, is a spectator *ab extra*. He analyzes, he dissects, he watches.

> – with an eye serene,
> The very pulse of the machine,

for such it practically is to him, with wheels and cogs and piston rods all working to produce a certain end. [It is this that makes him so good a critic. Nothing balks him, or throws him off the scent, except now and then a prejudice.]

This analysing tendency of his mind balances the poetical, and, by giving him the patience to be minute, enables him to throw a wonderful reality into his most unreal fancies. A monomania he paints with great power. He loves to dissect one of these cancers of the mind, and to trace all the subtle ramifications of its roots. In raising images of horror, also, he has a strange success; conveying to us sometimes by a dusky hint some terrible doubt which is the secret of all horror. He leaves to imagination the task of finishing the picture, a task to which only she is competent.

> For much imaginary work was there;
> Conceit deceitful, so compact, so kind,
> That for Achilles' image stood his spear
> Grasped in an armed hand; himself behind
> Was left unseen, save to the eye of mind.

[We have hitherto spoken chiefly of Mr Poe's collected tales, as by them he is more widely known than by those published since in various magazines, and which we hope soon to see collected. In these he has more strikingly displayed his analytic propensity.]‡

Besides the merit of conception, Mr Poe's writings have also that of form. His style is highly finished, graceful, and truly classical. It would be hard to find a living author who had displayed such varied powers. As an example of his style we would refer to one of his tales, 'The House of Usher,' in the first volume of his *Tales of the Grotesque and Arabesque*. It has a singular charm for us, and we think that no one could read it without being strongly moved by its serene and somber beauty. Had its author written nothing else it would alone have been enough to stamp him as a man of genius, and the master of a classic style. In this tale occurs one of the most beautiful of his poems. It loses greatly by being taken out of its rich and appropriate setting, but we cannot deny ourselves the pleasure of copying it here. We know no modern poet who might not have been justly proud of it.

[Quotes 'The Haunted Palace'.]

Was ever the wreck and desolation of a noble mind so musically sung?

A writer in the London *Foreign Quarterly Review*, who did some faint justice to Mr Poe's poetical abilities, speaks of his resemblance to Tennyson. The resemblance, if there be any, is only in so sensitive an ear to melody as leads him sometimes into quaintness, and the germ of which may be traced in his earliest poems, published several years before the first of Tennyson's appeared.

We copy one more of Mr Poe's poems, whose effect cannot fail of being universally appreciated.

[Quotes 'Lenore'.]

How exquisite, too, is the rhythm!

Beside his *Tales of the Grotesque and Arabesque,* and some works unacknowledged, Mr Poe is the author of *Arthur Gordon Pym*, a romance, in two volumes, which has run through many editions in London; of a system of Conchology, of a digest and translation of Lemonier's *Natural History*, and has contributed to several reviews in France, in England, and in this country. He edited the *Southern Literary Messenger* during its novitiate, and by his own contributions gained it most of its success and reputation. He was also, for some time, the editor of this magazine, and our readers will bear testimony to his ability in that capacity.

Mr Poe is still in the prime of life, being about thirty-two years of age, and has probably as yet given but an earnest of his powers. As a critic, he has shown so superior an ability that we cannot but hope that he will collect his essays of this kind and give them a more durable form. They would be a very valuable contribution to our literature, and would fully justify all we have said in his praise. We could refer to many others of his poems than those we have quoted, to prove that he is the possessor of a pure and original vein. His tales and essays have equally shown him a master in prose. It is not for us to assign him his definite rank among contemporary authors, but we may be allowed to say that we know of *none* who has displayed more varied and striking abilities.

[In the 1850 version the matter after the sentence reading 'In this tale occurs one of the most beautiful of his poems' was omitted, and the following ending substituted:]

The great masters of imagination have seldom resorted to the vague and the unreal as sources of effect. They have not used dread and horror alone, but only in combination with other qualities, as means of subjugating the fancies of their readers. The loftiest muse has ever a household and fireside charm about her. Mr Poe's secret lies mainly in the skill with which he has employed the strange fascination of mystery and terror. In this his success is so great and striking as to deserve the name of art, not artifice. We cannot call his materials the noblest or purest, but we must concede to him the highest merit of construction.

As a critic, Mr Poe was aesthetically deficient. Unerring in his analysis of dictions, meters, and plots, he seemed wanting in the faculty of perceiving the profounder ethics of art. His criticisms are, however, distinguished for scientific precision and coherence of logic. They have the exactness, and, at the same time, the coldness of mathematical demonstrations. Yet they stand in strikingly refreshing contrast with the vague generalisms and sharp personalities of the day. If deficient in warmth, they are also without the heat of partisanship. They are especially valuable as illustrating the great truth, too generally overlooked, that analytic power is a subordinate quality of the critic.

On the whole, it may be considered certain that Mr Poe has attained an individual eminence in our literature, which he will keep. He has given proof of power and originality. He has done that which could only be done once with success or safety, and the imitation or repetition of which would produce weariness.

NOTES

★ We cannot but think that this was the case in his review of W.E. Channing's poems, in which we are sure that there is much which must otherwise have challenged Mr Poe's hearty liking.—J.R.L.

† Mr. P.'s proposition is here perhaps somewhat too generally stated. – Editor, *Graham's Magazine*.

‡ [Since the publication of the *Tales of the Grotesque and Arabesque*, Mr. P. has written, for this and other journals, the following tales, independently of essays, criticisms, etc.: The Mystery of Marie Roget, Never Bet Your Head, A Tale of the Ragged Mountains, The Masque of the Red Death, The Colloquy of Monos and Una, The Landscape Garden, The Pit and the Pendulum, The Tell-Tale Heart, The Black Cat, The Man of the Crowd, The System of Doctors Tarr and Fether, The Spectacles, The Elk, The Business Man, The Premature Burial, The Oblong-Box, Thou Art the Man, Eleonora, Three Sundays in a Week, The Island of the Fay, Life in Death, The Angel of the Odd, The Literary Life of Thingum-Bob, The Descent into the Maelstrom, the 1002 d Tale of Scheherazade, Mesmeric Revelation, The Murders in the Rue Morgue, The Purloined Letter, and The Gold-Bug. He is also the author of the late Balloon-Hoax. *The Grotesque and Arabesque* included twenty-five tales.]

51. Thomas Dunn English, 'Notes About Men of Note', *Aristidean*

April 1845, 1, 153

English (1819–1902) was trained as a physician, though most of his energy went into politics and magazine work. He edited the *Aristidean* throughout its brief existence. English knew Poe in Philadelphia, and for a time in New York they were close literary associates – the *Aristidean* and the *Broadway Journal* shared the same address. In 1846, however, the two men quarrelled bitterly: Poe lampooned English in the 'Literati' papers, and English's vindictive and libellous response (the case is discussed and documented in Sidney P. Moss, *Poe's Major Crisis*) contributed much to the souring of Poe's public image.

EDGAR A. POE, ONE OF THE EDITORS OF THE *Broadway Journal*. He never rests. There is a small steam engine in his brain, which not only sets the cerebral mass in motion, but keeps the owner in hot water. His face is a fine one and well-gifted with intellectual beauty. Ideality, with the power of analysis, is shown in his very broad, high and massive forehead – a forehead which would have delighted GALL beyond measure.[1] He would have made a capital lawyer – not a very good advocate, perhaps, but a famous unraveller of all subtleties. He can thread his way through a labyrinth of absurdities, and pick out the sound thread of sense from the tangled skein with which it is connected. He means to be candid, and labours under the strange hallucination that he is so; but he has strong prejudices, and without the least intention of irreverence, would wage war with the DEITY, if the divine canons militated against his notions. His sarcasm is subtle and searching. He can do nothing in the common way; and buttons his coat after a fashion peculiarly his own. If we ever caught him doing a thing like anybody else, or found him reading a book any other way than upside down, we would implore his friends to send for a straight jacket, and a Bedlam doctor. He were mad, then, to a certainty.

NOTE

1 Poe's head was in fact a delight to the phrenologists – see Madeleine B. Stern, *Heads & Headlines: The Phrenological Fowlers* (Norman, Oklahoma, 1971), 73–7.

52. William Gilmore Simms, 'Poe's Poetry', Charleston
Southern Patriot

10 November 1845

Simms (1806–70) was an eminent novelist, poet, critic, editor, and Southern apologist. He detested what he saw as the Northern dominance of American letters, and wrote this essay in response to press attacks on Poe following his poetry reading débâcle at the Boston Lyceum. The essay was immediately reprinted by Poe in the *Broadway Journal*, and used by him to initiate a new assault upon the Boston 'Frog-Pond'.

Mr Edgar A. Poe is one of the most remarkable, in many respects, among our men of letters. With singular endowments of imagination, he is at the same time largely possessed of many of the qualities that go to make an admirable critic; – he is methodical, lucid, forcible, – well-read, thoughtful, and capable, at all times, of rising from the mere consideration of the individual subject, to the principles, in literature and art, by which it should be governed. Add to these qualities, as a critic, that he is not a person to be overborne and silenced by a reputation; – that mere names do not control his judgement; – that he is bold, independent, and stubbornly analytical, in the formation of his opinions. He has his defects also; – he is sometimes the victim of capricious moods; – his temper is variable – his nervous organization being such, evidently, as to subject his judgements, sometimes, to influences that may be traced to the weather and the winds. He takes his colour from the clouds; and his sympathies are not unfrequently chilled and rendered ungenial, by the pressure of the atmosphere – the cold and vapors of a climate affecting his moral nature, through his physical, in greater degree than is usual among literary men, – who, by the way, are generally far more susceptible to these influences, than is the case with the multitude. Such are the causes which occasionally operate to impair the value and the consistency of his judgments as a Critic. As a Poet, Mr Poe's imagination becomes remarkably conspicuous, and to surrender himself freely to his own moods, would be to make all his writings in verse, efforts of pure imagination only. He seems to dislike the merely practical, and to shrink from the concrete. His fancy takes the ascendant in his Poetry, and wings his thoughts to such superior elevations, as to render it too intensely spiritual for the ordinary reader. With a genius thus endowed and constituted, it was a blunder with Mr Poe to accept the appointment, which called him to deliver himself in poetry before the Boston Lyceum. Highly imaginative men can scarcely succeed in such exhibitions. The sort of poetry called for on such occasions, is the very reverse of the spiritual, the fanciful or the metaphysical. To win the ears of a mixed audience, nothing more is required than moral or patriotic common places in rhyming heroics. The verses of Pope are just the things for such occasions. You must not pitch your flight higher than the penny-whistle elevation of

> Know then this truth, enough for man to know
> Virtue alone is happiness below.

Either this or declamatory verse, – something patriotic, or something satirical, or something comical. At all events, you must not be mystical. You must not ask the audience to study. Your song must be such as they can read running, and comprehend while munching pea-nuts. Mr Poe is not the writer for this sort of thing. He is too original, too fanciful, too speculative, too anything in verse, for the comprehension of any but 'audience fit though few'. In obeying this call to Boston, Mr Poe committed another mistake. He had been mercilessly exercising himself as a critic at the expense of some of their favorite writers. The swans of New England, under his delineation, had been described as mere geese, and these, too, of none of the whitest. He had been exposing the shortcomings and the plagiarisms of Mr Longfellow, who is supposed, along the banks of the Penobscot, to be about the comeliest bird that ever dipped its bill in Pieria. Poe had dealt with the favorites of Boston unsparingly, and they hankered after their revenges. In an evil hour, then, did he consent to commit himself, in verse to their tender mercies. It is positively amusing to see how eagerly all the little witlings of the press, in the old purlieus of the Puritan, flourish the critical tomahawk about the head of the critic. In their eagerness for retribution, one of the papers before us actually congratulates itself and readers on the (asserted) failure of the poet. The good editor himself was not present, but he hammers away not the less lustily at the victim, because his objections are to be made at second hand. Mr Poe committed another error in consenting to address an audience in verse, who, for three mortal hours, had been compelled to sit and hear Mr Caleb Cushing in Prose.[1] The attempt to speak after this, in poetry, and fanciful poetry, too, was sheer madness. The most patient audience in the world, must have been utterly exhausted by the previous inflictions. But it is denied that Mr Poe failed at all. He had been summoned to recite poetry. It is asserted that he did so. The *Boston Courier*, one of the most thoughtful journals of that city, gives us a very favourable opinion of the performance which has been so harshly treated. 'The Poem', says that journal, 'called "The Messenger Star", was an eloquent and classic production, based on the right principles, containing the essence of *true* poetry, mingled with a gorgeous imagination, exquisite painting, every charm of metre, and a graceful delivery. It strongly reminded us of Mr Horne's *Orion*, and resembled it in the majesty of its design, the nobleness of its incidents, and its freedom from the trammels of productions usual on these occasions. The delicious word-painting of some of its scenes brought vividly to our recollection, Keats', 'Eve of St Agnes', and parts of 'Paradise Lost'.

'That it was malapropos to the occasion, we take the liberty to deny. What is the use of repeating the "mumbling farce" of having invited a poet to deliver a poem? We (too often) find a person get up and repeat a hundred or two indifferent couplets of words, with jingling rhymes and stale witticisms, with scarcely a line of *poetry* in the whole, and which will admit of no superlative to describe it. If we are to have a poem, why not have the "true thing", that will be recognized as such, – for poems being written for people that can appreciate them, it would be as well to cater for their tastes as for individuals who cannot distinguish between the true and the false.'

The good sense of this extract should do much towards enforcing the opinion which it conveys; and it confirms our own, previously entertained and expressed, in regard to the affair in question. Mr Poe's error was not, perhaps, in making verses, nor making them after a fashion of his own; but in delivering them before an audience of mixed elements, and just after a discourse of three mortal hours by a prosing orator. That any of his hearers should have survived the two-fold infliction, is one of those instances of good fortune which should bring every person present to his knees in profound acknowledgement to a protecting providence.

NOTE

1 Caleb Cushing was a local statesman; according to the *Boston Transcript*, his address was 'one laudation of U. States at the expense of Great Britain'.

TALES

1845

---

53. [Evert Augustus Duyckinck], notice in the New York *Morning News*

---

28 June 1845, p. 2

Duyckinck (1816–78) was an influential editor and critic, and the leader of the 'Young America' group of literary nationalists. He arranged the publication of *Tales*, and gave much support to Poe at this time. See further Claude Richard, 'Poe and "Young America"', University of Virginia *Studies in Bibliography*, 21 (1968), 25–58; also No. 59.

Mr Poe's tales will be welcomed in this neat and convenient form. They have hitherto been scattered over the newspapers and magazines of the country, chiefly of the South, and have been scarcely, if at all, known to Northern and Eastern readers. Singly, the most remarkable have been received with great favour. 'The Gold-Bug' received a prize of five hundred dollars.[1] 'The Fall of the House of Usher' was pirated in *Bentley's (London) Magazine*, and 'The Murders in the Rue Morgue' appeared translated in one of the Parisian journals.[2] 'The Purloined Letter' appeared in this year's *Gift*, and was not copied into any American paper, we believe, till it had been produced in *Chambers' Edinburgh Journal*, and had been republished here in *Littell's Living Age of Foreign Literature*. It is to be presumed that our American readers will not be ashamed of the volume after these circumstances. It is eminently original and characteristic of the peculiar idiosyncrasy of the author. The subtle ingenuity exhibited in the construction will strike everyone; the analysis of this power is a subject worthy of the maturest critic. 'The Gold-Bug' is a tale of Captain Kidd's treasure, the interest of which depends upon the solution of an intricate cypher. Since this tale was published the author has received historical and other papers in cypher sent to him from different parts of the country to be unmasked. We believe he has generally succeeded, but never with so brilliant and splendidly lucrative result as in the tale of the Gold-Bug.

'The Murders in the Rue Morgue', the 'History of Marie Roget' and the 'Purloined Letter' turn upon matters of police, and would do credit either to the sagacity of an Indian hunter or the civilized skill of a Fouché for their ingenuity and keenness of scent. Marie Roget is the story of Mary Rogers, the Cigar Girl, the scene being transferred from the banks of the Hudson to those of the Seine.

NOTES

1 The *Dollar Newspaper* prize was $100.
2 No trace has been found of this Paris printing. The bibliographical information here probably derived from Poe.

54. [Margaret Fuller], review in the New York *Daily Tribune*

11 July 1845, p. 1

Margaret Fuller (1810–50), editor, essayist, and critic, was one of the foremost American intellectuals of the day. She edited the *Dial* (1840–2), the chief organ of Transcendentalist opinion, and had recently published an important work on feminism – *Women in the Nineteenth Century*. As literary critic of the *Daily Tribune* (1844–6), she sought to establish fair and principled standards of reviewing. Poe admired her intelligence, but had no sympathy for her radicalism – see *Works*, 15, 73–83.

Mr Poe's tales need no aid of newspaper comment to give them popularity; they have secured it. We are glad to see them given to the public in this neat form, so that thousands more may be entertained by them without injury to their eye-sight.

No form of literary activity has so terribly degenerated among us as the tale. Now that everybody that wants a new hat or bonnet takes this way to earn one from the magazines or annuals, we are inundated with the very flimsiest fabrics ever spun by mortal brain. Almost every person of feeling or fancy could supply a few agreeable and natural narratives, but when, instead of using their materials spontaneously, they set to work, with geography in hand, to find unexplored nooks of wild scenery in which to locate their Indians, or interesting farmers' daughters, or with some abridgment of history to hunt up monarchs or heroes yet unused to become the subjects of their crude coloring, the sale-work produced is a sad affair indeed and 'gluts the market' to the sorrow of both buyers and lookers-on.

In such a state of things, the writings of Mr Poe are a refreshment, for they are the fruit of a genuine observation and experience, combined with an invention, which is not 'making up', as children call *their* way of contriving stories, but a penetration into the causes of things which leads to original but credible results. His narrative proceeds with vigor, his colours are applied with discrimination, and where the effects are fantastic they are not unmeaningly so.

The 'Murders of the Rue Morgue' especially made a great impression upon those who did not know its author and were not familiar with his mode of treatment. Several of his stories made us wish he would enter the higher walk of the metaphysical novel, and, taking a mind of the self-possessed and deeply marked sort that suits him, give us a deeper and longer acquaintance with its life than is possible in the compass of these tales.

As Mr Poe is a professed critic, and of all the band the most unsparing to others, we are surprised to find some inaccuracies in the use of words, such as these: 'he had with him many books, but rarely *employed* them.' – 'His results have, in truth, the *whole air* of intuition.'[1]

The degree of skill shown in the management of revolting or terrible circumstances makes the pieces that have such subjects more interesting than the others. Even the failures are those of an intellect of strong fibre and well-chosen aim.

NOTE

1 Poe hit back at this criticism: in his 'Literati' article on Miss Fuller, he pointed out examples of her 'ignorance of grammar' and her 'strange and continual inaccuracies' (*Works*, 15, 78–9).

55. [Charles Anderson Dana], review in the *Harbinger*

12 July 1845, 1, 73–4

Dana (1819–97) was an editor and journalist. He joined the Brook Farm Fourierist community in 1843, and became a regular contributer to the *Harbinger*, which was edited and printed there.

By what strange means the present volume finds its way into a library of American Books we are not informed, and we suppose have no right to inquire. In this land of unbounded freedom every man can name his child Benjamin Franklin or Thomas Jefferson, without any possibility of redress on the part of those injured worthies.

Mr Poe might properly have divided his book into two parts, one of Tales the other, of Philosophical Sketches. In the Tales a peculiar order of genius is apparent. It might be called the intense order. To this there is one exception in which the author lays off the tragic mantle and gives his humor an airing. But that is intense also; – our readers shall have a specimen.

'At Chalk-Farm, the next morning, I shot off his nose, – and then called upon my friends.

"Bete!" said the first.
"Fool!" said the second.
"Dolt!" said the third.
"Ass!" said the fourth.
"Ninny!" said the fifth.
"Noodle!" said the sixth.
"Be off!" said the seventh.
At all this I felt mortified and so called upon my father.'

But the full glory of the book is not seen in its wit, which

178

is merely by-play and alternation. When we come to 'the general burst of terrific grandeur', which makes our countenances 'cadaverously wan' with 'an intensity of intolerable awe', as 'a flood of intense rays rolls throughout and bathes the whole in ghastly and inappropriate splendor', we begin to be 'oppressed by an excess of nervous agitation'; but when we have fairly heard the 'one long, loud, and continuous scream, utterly anomalous and inhuman, – a howl, – a wailing shriek, half of horror and half of triumph, such as might have arisen out of hell, conjointly from the throats of the damned in their agony, and of the demons that exult in the damnation', we can't help saying to ourselves, – we now say it to the public, that Mr Poe's Tales are absolutely overwhelming.

They remind us of the blue lights, the blood and thunder, and corked eyebrows of that boast of modern dramatic achievements, the melo-drama. One more specimen.

[Quotes the final paragraph of 'The Fall of the House of Usher', *Works*, 3, 297.]

If our readers can get through this passage they have a most remarkable degree of insensibility. We had thought of introducing to them Mr Poe's Black Cat, 'with red, extended mouth, and eye of fire', but in mercy we forbear. We fear that they would be 'overpowered by an intense sentiment of horror' which might interfere with their proper attention to their business. – Among what might be called the Philosophic Sketches is one named 'Mesmeric Revelation', which we have seen before in the newspapers. We give the reader a touch of this philosophy, of which the manner is quite equal to the matter.

[Quotes Vankirk's speech beginning 'The multitudinous conglomeration of rare matter into nebulae', *Works*, 5, 252.]

But we spend too much time on this book. Its tales are clumsily contrived, unnatural, and every way in bad taste. There is still a kind of power in them; it is the power of disease; there is no health about them, they are alike in the vagaries of an opium eater. 'An excited and highly distempered ideality throws a sulphurous lustre over all.' The philosophy of the book is of a similar character.

56. Unsigned notice in the *Spectator*

2 August 1845, 18, 739

This volume contains a dozen tales, mostly tinged with a spirit of diablerie or mystery, not always of a supernatural character, but such as caterers for news delight to head 'mysterious occurrence'. To unfold the wonderful, to show that what seems miraculous is amenable to almost mathematical reasoning, is a real delight of Mr Poe; and though he may probably contrive the mystery he is about to unravel, this is not always the case – as in the tale of the murder of Marie Roget; and in all cases he exhibits great analytical skill in seizing upon the points of circumstantial evidence and connecting them together. He has also the faculty essential to the story-teller by 'the winter's fire', who would send the hearers trembling to their beds – despite a profusion of minute circumstances if not of mere words, he holds the attention of the reader and sometimes thrills him. As a novelist [*sic*], Mr Poe has little art; depending for his effects chiefly upon the character of his subject, and his skill in working out the chain of proofs to solve the mystery. Both art and effects are of a *magazinish* kind; and in an American periodical some if not all of the tales appear to have been published. The volume is an importation, though issued in London.

57. From a notice in the *Atlas*

9 August 1845, 20, 507

This is a volume of a dozen tales of a sort of genteel *Terrific Register* description.[1] They consist of startling adventures by field and flood, told in an agreeable, graphic manner; but they bear evidences that the writer is an American, scribing for American readers; indeed, this work was originally printed in the New World, and is now re-issued as one of a series which the publishers, we presume, intend to continue. We can better recommend the volume in three months' time than now, for the stories are more fitted for a Christmas-party, round a good blazing fire, than for long autumnal evenings, when the lengthened shadows might seem the phantom of horrors which the perusal of Mr POE's *Tales* would assuredly conjure up. They must be read when prickly red-holly scares away blue devils. The story called 'A Descent into the Maelström', smacks peculiarly of the marvellous; but if it be an invention, it is well imagined and vividly told. It seems that at a certain period this terrific whirlpool enjoys a cessation from its otherwise eternal labours, and at the 'time of slack' boats can pass near it in safety. Two brothers one day, however, mistook the hour, and were drawn gradually on into the frightful abyss of waters. That either should have escaped is certainly very difficult to believe, but here is a portion of the recital – .

[Quotes from 'As I felt the sickening sweep of the descent' to 'into the "grounds" of the fishermen', *Works*, 2, 241–7.]

NOTE

1 The *Terrific Register* was a London weekly devoted to sensational and sadistic accounts of murders, executions, tortures, etc.

58. Rufus Wilmot Griswold, from 'The Intellectual History, Condition and Prospects of the Country', Washington *National Intelligencer*

30 August 1845, p. 2

Griswold (1815–57), is chiefly remembered as Poe's editor and untrustworthy biographer – his 'Ludwig' obituary (No. 92), and his malicious 'Memoir' of 1850, did much to discredit Poe's reputation for years to come. But in his own day Griswold was a respected editor and critic, and his popular anthologies (especially *The Poets and Poetry of America*, 1842) made him an important arbiter of taste. In 1842 he replaced Poe as literary editor of *Graham's Magazine*; thereafter Poe generally regarded him with sour hostility, though there were periods of reconciliation. Throughout most of 1845 they were superficially friendly: Griswold solicited contributions from Poe for his forthcoming anthology of American prose, and evidently tried to place his poems with a publisher; Poe, for his part, 'puffed' Griswold and borrowed money from him. Though not strictly a review, Griswold's friendly comments were provoked by Poe's recent collection; the entire essay was reprinted as the introduction to Griswold's *Prose Writers of America* (1847).

The tales of EDGAR A. POE are unlike any I have mentioned, and in some respects are different from any others with which I am acquainted. He belongs to the first class of tale writers who have appeared since the marvel-loving Arabian first attempted fabulous history. He has a great deal of imagination and fancy, and his mind is in the highest degree *analytical*. He is deficient in humor, but humor is a quality of a different sort of mind, and its absence were to him slight disadvantage, but for his occasional forgetfulness that he does not possess it.

The reader of Mr POE's tales is compelled, almost at the outset, to surrender his mind to the author's control. As he goes forward, impalpable shadows are constantly darting on the shadows of his thought. Unlike that of the greater number of *suggestive* authors, his narrative is most minute; he has nothing superfluous – nothing which does not tend to the common centre – nothing which is not absolutely necessary to the production of the desired result. His stories seem to be written *currente calamo*, but, if examined, will be found to be the results of consummate art. No mosaics were ever piled with greater deliberation. In no painting was ever conception developed with more boldness and apparent freedom. Mr Poe. resembles BROCKDEN BROWN in his intimacy with mental pathology but surpasses that author in delineation. No one ever delighted more or was more successful in oppressing the brain with anxiety or startling it with images of horror. GEORGE WALKER, ANN RADCLIFFE, MARIA ROCHE,[1] could charm with dire chimeras, could lead their characters into difficulties and perils – but they extricated them so clumsily as to destroy every impression of *reality*. Mr POE's scenes all seem to be actual. Taking into view the chief fact, and the characteristics of the *dramatis personae*, we cannot understand how any of the subordinate incidents of his tales could have failed to happen.

NOTE

1 George Walker and Maria Roche were contemporaries of Ann Radcliffe (1764–1823), and wrote in a similar Gothic vein.

59. From notices in the London *Critic*

(a) 6 September 1845, 2, 378–80; (b) 20 September 1845, 2, 420–2

(a) We have in this volume a number of tales, many of which show the ingenuity, rather than the capacity, of the author's mind. Mr Poe is familiar to us as a poet of considerable power.[1] We remember the fine conception and the musical execution of some of his stanzas, and, with these fresh in our mind, we confess ourselves disappointed by the present volume of *Tales*. The first story, 'The Gold-Bug', is only interesting from its strangeness. It tells of the discovery of some hidden treasure, by the solving of certain enigmatical figures. Viewed with the moral, the tale *may* be useful, as showing what a patient, earnest mind may accomplish. This is barely probable, and the tale will add no more to the stock of choice literature than the thousand and one stories that yearly fill the penny novelists.

Of a piece with 'The Gold-Bug' are the 'Mystery of Marie Roget' and the 'Murders of the Rue Morgue'. The author seems here to have amused himself by following the plan of those philosophers who trace a series of references between every minute act, and so upward to the making and dethroning of kings. Mr Poe has been as assiduous in this scheme as an Indian who follows the trail of a foe. He has learned from the dwellers in the American woods a marked acuteness, which he has dealt out again to the readers in the *Tales* before us.[2] Another tale of this class is the 'Purloined Letter'. If we were called upon to recommend this story to any particular party, it would be to some Bow-street officers. Such functionaries would be sure to appreciate it, as it exhibits a quick intellect, which, from a few surmises, arrives at a chain of conclusive evidence.

Perhaps of even less utility is Mr Poe's tale of the 'Black

Cat'. The Black Cat would have been a proper inmate for the 'Castle of Otranto', and a most valuable counterpart to the mysterious plume and helmet. The beauty of WALPOLE'S inexplicable riddle would have been much enhanced by the introduction of such a sooty monster. But it may be argued that the Black Cat is a figurative personification of the dark-brooding thoughts of a murderer, murder being the climax of the story. It *may* be so urged, we repeat, but, at present, our little perception cannot perceive it; and we have not faith to believe that the generality of readers will discover what we cannot.

We object, for the most part, to the tales we have instanced because they uncurtain horrors and cruelties. It is enough, and perhaps too much, for public benefit, that minute details of murders and other horrors find their way into newspapers. They form no part of the glories of literature. The literature of the past, in a great measure, is not pure enough for the gaze of the future because of its antagonistic character. Mr Poe's *Tales* are out of place. They are things of the past, but the past has retired from them. They do not anticipate the wants of the future, and the future will take no cognizance of them. But why has Mr Poe given us so much of the scraps and the worn-out thoughts of yesterday?

Mr Poe could not possibly send forth a book without some marks of his genius, and mixed up with the dross we find much sterling ore. He is a deep thinker, and as proof of it, we give an entire story. The interest of the subject, and its masterly treatment, is an apology for its length.

[Quotes 'Mesmeric Revelation'.]

(b) Turning from these mesmeric revelations, we present our readers with a portion of a tale of a very different character. It is a descent into the Maelstrom. The description is thrilling, and the reader feels a frightful and giddy interest as if he were actually whirling in the 'hell of waters'.

[Quotes from 'A Descent into the Maelstrom', from 'our boat was the lightest feather of a thing' to 'I will bring my story quickly to conclusion', *Works*, 2, 236–46.]

Although this volume has many redeeming points of goodness, we cannot conscientiously recommend it to the libraries. We have given reasons, and we think strong ones, for this opinion, and if we have erred, it is from our squeamishness in selecting the best works for the librarian and public.

NOTES

1 'The Raven' had been printed in the *Critic* (14 June, 1845).
2 Poe retorted in the *Broadway Journal* (1 November, 1845, p. 262): 'The only objection to this theory is that we never go into the woods (for fear of the owls) and are quite sure that we never saw a live Indian in our lives.'

60. [Evert Augustus Duyckinck], review in the *American Review*

September 1845, 2, 306–9

We fear that Mr Poe's reputation as a critic, will not add to the success of his present publication. The cutting scorn with which he has commented on many authors, and the acrimony and contempt which have often accompanied his acuteness, must have provoked enmities of that kind, which are kept warm by being assiduously 'nursed'. It might be too much to expect praise from those, on whose brows he has been instrumental in fixing the brand of literary damnation; but we still think that even an enemy could be found to acknowledge, that the present volume is one of the most original and peculiar ever published in the United States, and eminently worthy of an extensive circulation, and a cordial recognition. It displays the most indisputable marks of intellectual power and keenness, and an individuality of mind and disposition, of peculiar intensity and unmistakeable traits. Few books have been published of late, which contain within themselves the elements of greater popularity. This popularity it will be sure to obtain, if it be not for the operation of a stupid prejudice which refuses to read, or a personal enmity, which refuses to admire.

These tales, though different in style and matter from the generality of such compositions, lack none of the interest of romantic narrations. Indeed, their peculiarity consists in developing new sources of interest. Addressed to the intellect, or the more recondite sympathies and emotions of our nature, they fix attention by the force and refinement of reasoning employed in elucidating some mystery which sets the curiosity of the reader on an edge, or in representing, with the utmost exactness, and in sharpest outlines, the inward life of beings, under the control of perverse and morbid passions. As specimens of subtle dialectics, and the anatomy of the heart, they are not less valuable and interesting, than as tales. Their effect is to surprise the mind into activity, and to make it attend, with a curious delight, to the unraveling of abstruse points of evidence, through the exercise of the most piercing and patient analysis. This power is employed, not on any subject apart from the story, but to relieve the curiosity of the reader from the tangled mesh of mystery, in which it is caught and confined. It like wise makes him aware of the practical value of such mental acuteness in the ascertainment of truth, where the materials for its discovery seem provokingly slight, or hopelessly confused.

The first story in this collection – a collection, we believe, that does not include more than one-sixth of what Mr Poe has written – is 'The Gold-Bug'. Few could guess at the character of this tale from the title. It is exceedingly ingenious and interesting, and full of acute and vigorous thinking. The account of the intellectual process by which a cryptograph is decyphered strikes us as a most remarkable instance of subtle observation and analysis. This is one of the author's most characteristic tales, and well illustrates his manner and his mode of arresting and fixing the attention of the reader.

The 'Murders in the Rue Morgue', 'The Mystery of Marie

Roget', and the 'Purloined Letter', are all illlustrations of forcible analysis, applied to the disentangling of complicated and confused questions, relating to supposed events in actual life. The difference between acumen and cunning, calculation and analysis, are admirably illustrated in these tales. No one can read them without obtaining some metaphysical knowledge, as well as having his curiosity stimulated and his sympathies awakened. A lawyer might study them to advantage, and obtain important hints relative to the sifting of evidence. We extract the commencement of 'The Murders in the Rue Morgue', in order that the reader may learn, from Mr Poe himself, his notion of the analytic power:

[Quotes the first three paragraphs of 'The Murders in the Rue Morgue', *Works*, 4, 146–50.]

The last sentence in this extract, referring to the imaginative element in analysis, is forcibly illustrated in the 'Purloined Letter'. In the last tale, the whole cunning and ingenuity of the Parisian police are baffled by the seeming simplicity of their antagonist. He is a poet, and, in imagination, identifies his own intellect with that of his opponents, and consequently understands what will be the course they will pursue in ferreting out the place where the letter is concealed. They act upon the principle, that every man, who has anything to hide, will follow what would be their own practice, and therefore they search for their object in the most out-of-the-way holes and corners. The man of imagination, knowing this, puts the letter in a place, the very publicity of which blinds and leads astray his cunning opponents. This identification of the reasoner's mind with that of his adversary, so as to discover what course of action he would in all probability pursue in given circumstances, is, of course, an exercise of imagination, just as much as the delineation of an imaginary character. No force or acuteness of mere understanding, could do the office of the imagination in such a case. The thousand instances which arise daily in actual life, where such a power of analysis as Mr Poe describes, might be of great practical utility, are too obvious to need comment.

'The Fall of the House of Usher', though characterized by intellectual qualities in no way dissimilar from those apparent in the tales to which we have just referred, is still one which has a more potent pictorial effect on the imagination, and touches with more subtlety the mysterious feelings of supernatural terror. In this story is a fine instance of probing a horror skillfully. It is wrought out with great elaboration, and displays much force of imagination in the representation of morbid character. Each picture, as it rose in the author's mind, we feel to have been seen with the utmost distinctness, and its relation to the others carefully planned. The kind of shuddering sympathy with which we are compelled to follow the story, and the continuity of the impression which it makes on the mind, are the best evidences of the author's design. 'A Descent into the Maelstrom' is also conceived with great power, and developed, in its details, with almost painful exactness. The singular clearness with which the scene is held up to the imagination, and the skill with which the thoughts and emotions of the author and sufferer are transferred to the reader's mind, evince uncommon intensity of feeling and purpose. In both of these compositions, it would be difficult to convey a fair idea of their merit by extracts, as the different parts bear the most intimate relation to each other, and depend for their true effect upon being read consecutively, – still we cannot refrain from giving the conclusion of the 'Fall of the House of Usher':

[Quotes the final three paragraphs, *Works*, 3, 295–7.]

'The Black Cat' is a story, exceedingly well told, illustrative of a theory, which the author has advanced in other writings, respecting perverseness, or the impulse to perform actions simply for the reason that they ought not to be performed. For this devilish spirit, Mr Poe claims the honor of being 'one of the primitive impulses of the human heart – one of the indivisible primary faculties, or sentiments, which give direction to the character of man.' The theory is ingeniously represented in the case of an imaginary character, and supported by a skillful use, or abuse, of certain facts of consciousness, revealed in morbid states of the mind. The story is not without power and interest, and is doubtless a fair exhibition of the inward life of the criminal whose motives and actions are narrated; but it is not much to our taste. The perverseness, to which the author refers, seems to us to be rightly classed, not among the original impulses of human nature, but among the phenomena of insanity. In its lighter manifestations in human character, we think that it would be possible to show that it is one of those secondary feelings, produced by the moral discord of the mind, and to be classed among the other frailties or sins of human nature. It is a moral disease, not a primitive impulse. The best illustration of it, perhaps, is Shelley's 'Cenci'.

In this review we have merely indicated some characteristics of these tales which strike us as eminently original, and as entitling them to more attention than is usually given to fictitious compositions bearing the same general name, but not belonging to the same class. We have not space to enter into any discussion respecting the justness of the author's views on some debatable questions in ethics or metaphysics, or to point out occasional offences against good taste in his mode of opposing antagonistic opinions. In a volume like the present, bearing on every page evidence of marked individuality of thought and disposition, and interesting the reader as much by the peculiarity as the force of the mind which produced it, it would not argue critical skill, so much as critical impertinence, to subject it to tests which it was never intended to bear, and try it by laws which it openly contemns. In each of the tales the author has succeeded in the object he presented to himself. From his own point of view, it would puzzle criticism to detect blunders in thought, or mismanagement in the conduct of the story. The objections to the volume will vary according to the differences of taste among its readers. But whatever may be the opposition it may meet, from persons whose nature is essentially different from that of the author, it would be vain to deny that it evinces a quickness of apprehension, an intensity of feeling, a vigor of imagination, a power of analysis, which are rarely seen in any compositions going under the name of 'tales'; and that, contemptuously tossing aside the common materials on which writers of fiction generally depend for success, the writer has shown that a story may be all the more interesting by demanding for its full development the exercise of the strongest and most refined powers of the intellect.

61. Unsigned review in *Graham's Magazine*

September 1845, 28, 143

These tales are among the most original and characteristic compositions in American letters. In their collected form, they cannot fail to make a forcible impression on the reading public. We are glad to see them in a 'Library of American Books'. 'The Gold-Bug' attracted great attention at the time it appeared, and it is quite remarkable as an instance of intellectual acuteness and subtlety of reasoning. 'The Fall of the House of Usher' is a story of horror and gloom, in which the feeling of supernatural fear is represented with great power. The pertinacity with which Mr Poe probes a terror to its depths, and spreads it out to the reader, so as it can be seen as well as felt, is a peculiarity of his tales. He is an anatomist of the horrible and ghastly, and trusts for effect, not so much in exciting a vague feeling of fear and terror, as in leading the mind through the whole framework of crime and perversity, and enabling the intellect to comprehend their laws and relations. Metaphysical acuteness characterises the whole book. 'The Murders in the Rue Morgue' and 'The Mystery of Marie Roget', are fine instances of the interest which may be given to subtle speculations and reasonings, when they are exercised to penetrate mysteries which the mind aches to know. 'A Descent into the Maelstrom', 'Mesmeric Revelation', 'The Purloined Letter', 'The Man of the Crowd', 'The Black Cat', are all characterised by force and refinement of intellect, and are all effective as tales. The volume is a great stimulation to reflection. It demands intellectual activity in the reader. There are some hardy paradoxes in it, uttered with unhesitating confidence, and supported with great ingenuity. These 'stir and sting' the mind to such a degree, that examination and reasoning become necessary to the reader's peace.

62. Thomas Dunn English/Poe, review in the *Aristidean*

October 1845, 1, 316–19

Poe seems to have been responsible for much of this review, though of course he never acknowledged it, and it was initialled by English in the *Aristidean* index. It is written for the most part in Poe's style, and he makes use of his own critical theory (for example, his emphasis on unity of plot and novelty of effect) to point out his originality and ingenuity. The review also reveals an intimate knowledge of, and peculiar interest in, the origins, composition, publication, and reception of individual tales; and it is unlikely that English would have followed the minutiae of Poe's career with such attention. The September issue of the *Aristidean* carried a brief notice of *Tales* (probably also by Poe), complaining of the inadequacy of the selection.

The great fault of American and English authors is imitation of the peculiarities of thought and diction of those who have gone before them. They tread on a beaten track because it is well trodden. They follow as disciples, instead of being teachers. Hence it is that they denounce all novelty as a

culpable variation from standard rules, and think all originality to be incomprehensible. To produce something which has
not been produced before, in their estimation, is equal to six,
at least, of the deadly sins – perhaps, the unpardonable sin
itself – and for this crime they think the author should atone
here in the purgatory of false criticism, and hereafter by the
hell of oblivion, the odor of originality in a new book is 'a
savor of death unto death' to their productions, unless it can
be destroyed. So they cry aloud – 'Strange! incomprehensible! what is it about?' even though its idea may be plainly
developed as the sun at noon-day. Especially, we are sorry to
say, does this prevail in this country. Hence it is that we are
chained down to a wheel, which ever monotonously
revolves round a fixed centre, progressing without progress.

Yet that we are beginning to emancipate ourselves from
this thraldom, is seen in the book before us, and in the
general appreciation of its merits, on both sides of the
Atlantic. It has sold well: and the press has praised it,
discriminately and yet with no stint. The British *Critic*, and
other English literary journals laud it most handsomely.
Though, as a general rule, we do not care a fig for British
criticism – conducted as it mostly is, we *do* prize a favourable
review, when it is evidently wrung from the reviewer by a
high admiration and a strong sense of justice – as in the case
before us. And all this, as we have said, proves that we are
escaping the shackles of imitation. There is just as much
chance of originality at this day, as at any other – all the
nonsense of the sophists to the contrary, notwithstanding.
'There is nothing new under the sun', said SOLOMON. In the
days of his many-wived majesty the proverb might apply – it
is a dead saying now. There is no end to the original
combinations of words – nor need there be to the original
combination of ideas.

The first tale in Mr POE's book is called 'The
Gold-Bug'. If we mistake not, it was written in competition
for a large premium, some years since – a premium
which it obtained. It made a great noise when first
issued, and was circulated to a greater extent than any
American tale, before or since. The intent of the author was
evidently to write a popular tale: money, and the finding of

money being chosen as the most popular thesis. In this he
endeavored to carry out his idea of the perfection of the plot,
which he defines as – that, in which nothing can be
disarranged, or from which we are never able to determine
whether any point depends upon or sustains any other. We
pronounce that he has perfectly succeeded in his perfect aim.
There is a marked peculiarity, by-the-by, in it, which is this.
The bug, which gives title to the story, is used only in the
way of mystification, having throughout a seeming and no
real connection with the subject. Its purpose is to seduce the
reader into the idea of supernatural machinery, and keeping
him so mystified until the last moment. The ingenuity of the
story cannot be surpassed. Perhaps it is the most *ingenious*
story Mr POE has written; but in the higher attributes – a
great invention – an invention proper – it is not at all comparable to the 'Tell-tale Heart' – and more especially to 'Ligeia',
the most extraordinary, of its kind, of his productions. The
characters are well drawn. The reflective qualities and steady
purpose, founded on a laboriously obtained conviction of
LEGRAND, is most faithfully depicted. The negro is a perfect
picture. He is drawn accurately – no feature overshadowed,
or distorted. Most of such delineations are caricatures.*

The materials of which the 'Gold-Bug' is constructed are,
apparently, of the simplest kind. It is the mode of grouping
them around the main idea, and their absolute necessity of
each to the whole – note Mr. POE's definition of plot
before given – in which the perfection of their use consists.
The solution of the mystery is the most curious part of the
whole, and for this, which is a splendid specimen of analysis,
we refer the reader to the book.

'The Black Cat' is the next tale. In our last number we
found fault with this, as a reproduction of the 'Tell-tale
Heart'. On further examination, we think ourselves in error,
somewhat. It is rather an amplification of one of its phases.
The *dénouement* is a perfect printed *tableau*.

'Mesmeric Revelation', which comes next, has excited
much discussion. A large number of the mesmerists, queerly
enough, take it all for gospel. Some of the Swedenborgians,
at PHILADELPHIA, wrote word to POE, that at first they
doubted, but in the end became convinced, of its truth. This

was excruciatingly and unsurpassably funny – in spite of the air of *vraisemblance* that pervades the article itself. It is evidently meant to be nothing more than the vehicle of the author's views concerning the DEITY, immateriality, spirit, &c., which he apparently believes to be true, in which belief he is joined by Professor BUSH.[1] The matter is most rigorously condensed and simplified. It might easily have been spread over the pages of a large octavo.

'Lionizing' which PAULDING, and some others regard with great favor, has been overlooked, in general. It is an extravaganza, composed by rules – and the laws of extravaganza are as much and clearly defined as those of any other species of composition.

'The Fall of the House of Usher', was stolen by BENTLEY, who copied it in his *Miscellany*, without crediting the source from whence he derived it. The thesis of this tale, is the revulsion of feeling consequent upon discovering that for a long period of time we have been mistaking sounds of agony, for those of mirth or indifference. It is an elaborate tale – surpassed only by 'Ligeia', in our judgement. IRVING's view of it – and he speaks of it, in italics, as *powerful*, is correct. The *dénouement*, where the doors open, and the figure is found standing without the door, as USHER had foretold, is grand and impressive. It appears to be better liked than the rest of Mr POE's productions, among literary people – though with the mass, the 'Gold-Bug', and 'Murders in the Rue Morgue', are more popular, because of their unbroken interest, novelty of the combination of ordinary incident, and faithful minuteness of detail. 'The Haunted Palace', from which we stated in our late review of his poems, LONGFELLOW had stolen, all, that was worth stealing, of his 'BELEAGUERED CITY', and which is here introduced with effect, was originally sent to O'SULLIVAN, of the *Democratic Review*, and by him rejected, because 'he found it impossible to comprehend it.'[2] In connection with the subject of rejections, there is a good thing concerning TUCKERMAN, which would show – if it needed to show the very palpable – his utter lack of discrimination, and his supreme self-esteem. When he edited the *Boston Miscellany*, POE, under the impression that the work was still conducted by HALE, sent him

'The Tell-tale Heart', a most extraordinary, and very original composition. Whereon Master TUCKERMAN, in noting its rejection, chose to say, through his publishers, that 'if Mr POE would condescend to be more quiet, he would be a valuable contributor to the press'. POE rejoined, that TUCKERMAN was the King of the Quietists, and in three months would give a quietus to the *Miscellany*. The author was mistaken in time – it took only two months to finish the work. LOWELL afterwards published the 'Tell-tale Heart', in the *Pioneer*.[3]

'A Descent into the Maelstrom', is chiefly noted for the boldness of its subject – a subject never dreamed of before – and for the clearness of its descriptions.

'Monos and Una', is one of a series of *post-mortem* reveries. The style, we think, is good. Its philosophy is damnable; but this does not appear to have been a point with the author, whose purpose, doubtless, was novelty of effect – a novelty brought about by the tone of the colloquy. The reader feels as though he were listening to the talk of spirits. In the usual imaginary conversations – LANDOR's,[4] for instance – he is permitted to see a tone of banter. He feels that the author is not in earnest. He understands that spirits have been invented for the purpose of introducing their supposed opinions.

'The Man of the Crowd', is the last sketch in the work. It is peculiar and fantastic, but contains little worthy of special note, after what has been said of others.

The three tales before the last, are 'Murders in the Rue Morgue' – 'Mystery of Marie Roget' – and 'The Purloined Letter'. They are all of the same class – a class peculiar to Mr POE. They are inductive – tales of ratiocination – of profound and searching analysis. 'The Mystery of Marie Roget' – although in this the author appears to have been hampered by facts – reveals the whole secret of their mode of construction. It is true that there the facts were before him – so that it is not fully a parallel – but the *rationale* of the process is revealed by it. The author, as in the case of 'Murders in the Rue Morgue', the first written, begins by imagining a deed committed by such a creature, or in such a manner, as would most effectually mislead inquiry. Then he applies analysis to the investigation.

'The Mystery of Marie Roget' has a locale, independent of any other interest. Every one, at all familiar with the internal history of NEW YORK, for the last few years, will remember the murder of MARY ROGERS, the segar-girl. The deed baffled all attempts of the police to discover the time and mode of its commission, and the identity of the offenders. To this day, with the exception of the light afforded by the tale of Mr POE, in which the faculty of analysis is applied to the facts, the whole matter is shrouded in complete mystery. We think, he has proven, very conclusively, that which he attempts. At all events, he has dissipated in our mind, all belief that the murder was perpetrated by more than one.

The incidents in the 'Murders in the Rue Morgue' are purely imaginary. Like all the rest, it is written backwards.

We have thus noticed the entire collection – and have only to say, by way of close, that the collection embraces by no means the best of Mr. POE's productions that we have seen; or rather it is not totally so good, as might have been made, though containing some of the best.

The style of Mr POE is clear and forcible. There is often a minuteness of detail; but on examination it will always be found that this minuteness was necessary to the development of the plot, the effect or the incidents. His style may be called, strictly, an earnest one. And this earnestness is one of its greatest charms. A writer must have the fullest belief in his statements, or must simulate that belief perfectly, to produce an absorbing interest in the mind of his reader. That power of simulation can only be possessed by a man of high genius. It is the result of a peculiar combination of the mental faculties. It produces earnestness, minute, not profuse detail, and fidelity of description. It is possessed by Mr POE in its full perfection.

The evident and most prominent aim of Mr POE is originality, either of idea, or the combination of ideas. He appears to think it a crime to write unless he has something novel to write about, or some novel way of writing about an old thing. He rejects every word not having a tendency to develop the effect. Most writers get their subjects first, and write to develop it. The first inquiry of Mr POE is for a novel effect – then for a subject; that is, a new arrangement of circumstance, or a new application of tone, by which the effect shall be developed. And he evidently holds whatever tends to the furtherance of the effect, to be legitimate material. Thus it is that he has produced works of the most notable character, and elevated the mere 'tale', in this country, over the larger 'novel' – conventionally so termed.

NOTES

* We see, by-the-by, that Willis, in one of his letters, talks about the tales having to encounter an obstacle in England, because of the word 'bug'. This is a mere affectation – but were it not, the junction with 'gold' saves it. Look at the other compounds in common English use – '*bug*bear', for instance. 'Gold-bug' is peculiarly an English – not an American word. (Poe's note)

1 George Bush was Professor of Hebrew at New York University; Poe sent him a printing of 'Mesmeric Revelation' in the *Dollar Newspaper*, asking him to comment on it – see *Letters*, 1, 273.

2 John L. O'Sullivan was a founder and editor of the *Democratic-Review*.

3 Poe seems to be copying here from a letter he sent to J. R. Lowell in 1842 – see *Letters*, 1, 220.

4 Walter Savage Landor's *Imaginary Conversations of Literary Men and Statesmen* appeared between 1824 and 1829.

63. From a review in the *Literary Annual Register*

1845, p. 163

This annual review of books was published in London; it was primarily intended for librarians.

These *Tales* also are the work of an American, they are strongly tinctured with the peculiar mannerism of the author, showing an extraordinary bias towards the analytical, so much so, that had he been an Englishman, we would unhesitatingly have set him down for an Old Bailey lawyer. He is never so happy as when unravelling cyphers that, to any one else, would seem unintelligible, or in combining the various details attendant upon some mysterious murder, till, by dint of wading through the probable and improbable, he at length discovers the real culprit. On such occasions he exhibits a degree of ingenuity that would do credit to a Ballantyne or a Clearkson.[1]

But though all these stories have the distinguishing mark of the same mint, they cannot be called either monotonous or tiresome, embracing, as they do, a variety of subjects as opposed to each other as well as can be imagined, but most of them exceedingly amusing. Thus the 'Gold-Bug' is a wild tale of hidden treasure; the 'Black Cat' is a striking but improbable story of a murderer haunted by a cat with the mark of a gallows on her breast, and finally, by her agency brought to justice; the 'Mesmeric Revelation', the 'Colloquy of Monos and Una', and the 'Conversation of Eiros and Charmion', are somewhat vague philosophical speculations; the 'Descent into the Maelstrom' is a marvellous account of a fisherman plunged into the whirlpool, and finally escaping, after having for hours been whirled round and round upon the gyrating walls of the vortex; the 'Murders in the Rue Morgue', and the 'Mystery of Marie Roget', two stories admirably calculated for the purpose of melodramatic scribblers. The first of the two last mentioned, whether fact or not, has some very peculiar features about it, and might well occupy a page in the volumes of the *Causes Célèbres*.[2] The mere outlines of the story are these.

[The plot of 'The Murders in the Rue Morgue' is briefly retold, but the murderer is not identified.]

Such are the facts, the various points of evidence, and we leave it to our readers to exercise their ingenuity in unravelling the mystery, or, what will give them less trouble, and more amusement, refer at once to the original for the solution.

NOTES

1 William Ballantyne and William Clarkson were criminal lawyers in London.
2 *Causes criminelles célèbres de XIXe siècle,* 4 vols (Paris, 1827).

64. [William Gilmore Simms], from an editorial review in the *Southern and Western Magazine*

December 1845, 22, 426–7

Simms edited the short-lived *Southern and Western* in Charleston, S.C.

...we have read with delight the fine artistic stories of Mr Edgar A. Poe, – a writer of rare imaginative excellence, great intensity of mood, and a singularly mathematic directness of purpose, and searching analysis, by which the moral and spiritual are evolved with a progress as symmetrical, and as duly dependent in their data and critieria, as any subject matter however inevitable, belonging to the fixed sciences. Certainly, nothing more original, of their kind, has ever been given to the American reader. Mr Poe is a mystic, and rises constantly into an atmosphere which as continually loses him the sympathy of the unimaginative reader. But, for those who can go with him without scruple to the elevation to which his visions are summoned, and from which they may all be beheld, he is an acknowledged master – a Prospero, whose wand is one of wonderful properties. That he has faults, are beyond question, and some very serious ones, but these are such only as will be insisted upon by those who regard mere popularity as the leading object of art and fiction. At a period of greater space and leisure, we propose to subject the writings of Mr Poe, with which we have been more or less familiar for several years, to a close and searching criticism. He is one of those writers of peculiar idiosyncrasies, strongly marked and singularly original, whom it must be of general service to analyse with justice and circumspection. We must content ourselves here, with simply regretting that, in the first tale of this collection, he has been so grievously regardless of the geographical peculiarities of his *locale*. It is fatal to the success of the tale, in the mind of him who reads only for the story's sake, to offend his experience in anything that concerns the scene of action. Every Charlestonian, for example, who does not see that the writer is aiming at nothing more than an ingenious solution of what might be held as a strange cryptographical difficulty, will be revolted when required to believe in the rocks and highlands in and about Sullivan's Island. This is a small matter, it is true – Mr Poe had only to change the scene of his action to more suitable regions, and all would have been right: – but this allowance is never made by a certain class of readers. To show them that you err in one respect, however unimportant to action and the interest, and you afford them a privilege of which they never hesitate to avail themselves. Sure of your weak point, they infer the rest, and away with your fiction, as they would with an ingenious puzzle, the key to which is already within their keeping.

65. [Martin Farquhar Tupper], review in the London *Literary Gazette*

31 January 1846, pp. 101–3

Tupper (1810–89), was a poet and journalist; his versified *Proverbial Philosophy* (1838) had great success. This review was probably arranged by Duyckinck; on 30 January Poe inquired of him: 'Have you seen Tupper 's notice of my *Tales* yet? if so – how long is it? long or short – sweet or sour? – if you have it, please lend it to me' (*Letters*, 2, 313). Poe was pleased by Tupper's efforts on his behalf – in August he told Philip P. Cooke that 'Martin F. Tupper, author of "Proverbial Philosophy" has been paying me some high compliments – and indeed I have been treated more than well' (*Letters*, 2, 329).

In the *Literary Gazette*, No. 1490, p. 528, we briefly noticed the following work, – so briefly that a valued correspondent had not observed it, and thought we had altogether neglected a volume of very considerable talent and imagination. To repair this wrong, he favoured us with his opinion of it; and agreeing with him in his estimate, we have pleasure in adopting it as our own, and thus doing more justice to a Transatlantic writer of original powers. – Ed. L.G.

'Fresh fields and pastures new' are obviously the likeliest places wherein to look for inventive genius and original power: accordingly, we are not surprised to hear that the author of this remarkable volume is an American. His work has come to our shores recommended by success upon its own; and that such success is no more than it deserves we will undertake to demonstrate to our readers, before we put the finishing point to our note of admiration.

First, however, and by way of getting a troublesome duty out of the way at once, we must qualify our coming praises, by a light and wholesome touch of censure. This, in a general way, and without descending into a specification of instances, must be held to apply to such a tale as the 'Black Cat', which is impossible and revolting; to such an argument as 'Mesmeric Revelation', which far too daringly attempts a solution of that deepest of riddles, the nature of the Deity; to such a dialogue as 'Lionizing', simply foolish; and to such a juvenile production as the 'Fall of the House of Usher'. These, though not without their own flashes of genius, might have been omitted to great advantage; and the remainder of the volume, acute, interesting, and graphic, would then have stood consistent with itself.

Induction, and a microscopic power of analysis, seem to be the pervading characteristics of the mind of Edgar Poe. Put him on any trail, and he traces it as keenly as a Blackfoot or Ojibbeway; give him any clue, and he unravels the whole web of mystery; never was blood hound more sagacious in scenting out a murderer; nor Oedipus himself more shrewd in solving an enigma. He would make a famous Transatlantic Vidocq, and is capable of more address and exploit than a Fouché,[1] he has all his wits about him ready for use, and could calmly investigate the bursting of a bombshell; he is a hound never at fault, a moral tight-rope dancer never thrown from his equilibrium; a close keen reasoner, whom no sophistry distracts – nothing foreign or extraneous diverts him from his inquiry.

But it is time to present the reader with specimens of our author's peculiarities. 'The Gold-Bug', a strange tale of treasure seeking, forcibly demonstrates how able an ally Dr Young and M. Champollion would have found in Edgar Poe, whilst engaged in deciphering Egyptian hieroglyphics. The case of the Rosetta stone is exactly parallel to the following piece of ingenious calculation:

[Quotes from 'The Gold-Bug', from 'But how did you proceed?' to 'I have solved others of an abstruseness ten thousand times greater', *Works*, 5, 130–1.]

Thereafter, at too much length for our columns, but not

for the interest of mankind at large, he reads his own riddle. Take, again, the marvellous train of analytical reasoning whereby he arrives at truth in the 'Rue Morgue Murders'; a tale wherein the horror of the incidents is overborne by the acuteness of the arguments; and is introduced by a specimen of mind-reading which Dr Elliotson's Adolphe or Okey[2] might vainly attempt to equal. 'The Mystery of Marie Roget' is similar in keenness; and to us at least the only mystery in the matter now is, – why was not the 'dark sailor' apprehended? Additional interest is given to these twin tales of terror from their historic truth; and from the strange fact that the guesser's sagacity has anticipated in the last case the murderer's confession.

Let us now turn to other pages equally brightened by genius, while they are untarnished with the dread details of crime. 'A Descent into the Maelstrom' has but one fault; it is too deliberate; there is too little in it of the rushing havoc, the awful eddying of that northern sea's black throat. Still there is magnificent writing in the tale; and a touch is given below of our author's peculiar presence of mind, which would stand him in good stead on a barrel of ignited gunpowder:

[Quotes the narrator's sensations in the vortex and his escape, *Works*, 2, 241–7.]

The 'Conversation of Eiros and Charmion' is full of terror and instruction; true to philosophy and to holy writ, it details the probable mode of the final conflagration:

[Quotes the description of the end of the World, *Works*, 4, 5–8.]

If the *Vestiges of Creation* have obtained so much celebrity from attempting to show and explain to mankind the *Beginning* of things, we may surely anticipate fame for the author who has thus, in a like philosophising excursus, depicted to us their *Ending*.

Let us, in conclusion, draw the reader's attention to the only piece of Poetry – (the pun is quite irresistible) – wherewith Mr Poe has favoured us in this book. It occurs in the otherwise condemned tale of 'Usher'; and not only half redeems that ill-considered production, but makes us wish for many more such staves. Its title is the 'Haunted Palace', and it purports to be a madman's rhapsody on his own mind:

[Quotes 'The Haunted Palace'.]

After perusing these extracts, and our own honest verdict of the book, we are sure that our readers will not long be strangers to the *Tales* of Edgar Poe.

NOTES

1 The exploits of the French detectives made popular fictional topics.
2 Dr. John Elliotson was an eminent and ardent exponent of mesmerism in England; Adolphe and the Okey sisters were mediums.

66. E.D. Forgues, from 'Studies in English and American Fiction: the *Tales* of Edgar A. Poe', *La Revue des deux mondes*

15 October 1846, pp. 341–66

Paul-Emile Daurand Forgues (1813–83) was a critic, editor of *La Revue des deux mondes*, and a prolific translator of contemporary English and American authors. His translation of 'A Descent into the Maelstrom' was published by *La Revue britannique* in September 1846; he followed this on 12 October with a version of 'The Murders in the Rue Morgue' in *Le Commerce* which provoked charges of plagiarism and culminated in a libel suit. Curiously, Poe was also engaged in a libel suit in New York at the same time.

Do you know the *Philosophical Essay on Probabilities*?[1] It is one of those books in which the audacity of the human mind is revealed at its most daring and far reaching. Since Prometheus's quest to rescue the eternal flame from the altar of the gods, the most perilous undertakings have been by men who have been willing to calculate the changing, uncertain, mysterious order of fortune; to penetrate the obscure realms of the future; to reduce to numbers the myriads of combinations of pure chance which embrace a single word – the *possible*; to introduce algebra equipped with its rigorous formulae, its inflexible deductions. The book of Laplace also exercises a real fascination over certain minds whom the power of reasoning subjugates, intoxicates, and upon whom a new truth acts like a pipe of opium, a spoonful of hashish. They make it their Gospel, they devote themselves to its propagation: I know some who travel the world peddling this marvellous treatise, like Protestants the Bible or our pious Catholics those dialogues with the *Loved-One*, composed for men who do not want to perish. This is understandable. The *Philosophical Essay* is not merely an ambitious effort by an intellect animated by a desire to know; it has moral conclusions, taking men back to the practice of good through the calculations of favourable probabilities, constantly linked to the observation of those eternal principles which establish and maintain societies.

Without quite being of that high an order, without leading to quite so noble an end, without proceeding from quite so vigorous a mind, the tales of which we shall speak bear an obvious relationship to the serious work of the learned Marquis. If the incoherent fictions of the vulgar novel manage to attract and hold you – then here you will find nothing of interest. Poetry, invention, stylistic effects, dramatic development – all are subordinate to a bizarre preoccupation – we would almost call it a monomania of the author – who seems to acknowledge but a single source of inspiration: that of reasoning; only one muse – logic, only one means of affecting his reader – doubt. For there are as many enigmas in differing forms, dressed in a diversity of costumes, as there are tales. Whether the fantastic livery of Hoffmann or the grave and magisterial costumes of Godwin refurbished by Washington Irving or Dickens, it is always the same combination which brings into conflict Oedipus and the Sphinx, the hero and the enigma; a dark event, an apparently impenetrable mystery, and the mind which is irritated by and roused to passion against the veil spread out before it, until, after unbelievable efforts minutely retold, it emerges victorious from the struggle.

In the end, you will tell me, this is the essence of more than one novel and of almost all dramas. Suppress curiosity, all doubt or fear, dispel this uncertainty as to the final conclusion of the tale which holds the reader in suspense, holding his breath, an embarrassed spectator; where do you find those conditions without which this kind of composition could not subsist? First, all novels, all dramas imply an antagonism whose doubtful vicissitudes are, according to the talent of the writer, more or less linked together by a logical bond. This syllogism is at the root of the most moving situations, and the address which moves a whole audience to applause is basically but an eloquently disguised exit. But in plays and novels logic is the hidden axis of action. It unfolds under an infinite number of details, all destined to dazzle, to lead the mind astray, and from its point of departure rushes to a conclusion too fast, by too direct a route. And to convince yourself that the accessories outweigh reality, you have only to remove the logical *substratum* from its cover made up of a thousand brilliant colours, a thousand ingenious embroideries, to see on what poor argument and miserable framework this magnificent fabric has been composed.

In contrast, in these original tales that have reached us from New York by the last packet-boat and which we would like to make known, logic reigns as queen and mistress; she dominates everyhing. Her function is no longer to support as a hidden framework, a monument to external wealth; she is herself that monument borrowing nothing or almost nothing from the other resources of art. She no longer plays the rôle of a submissive slave, lending her robust shoulders to a tottering drunken master and leading him, not without difficulty, to some dimly perceived door; she walks alone, strong in her own strength; she is the end and the means; she is cause and effect. Just as yesterday, in the hands of a scholar, she tackled the most intractable problems of speculative philosophy, so today she takes on the form of a novel so as to be accessible to the greatest possible number while giving up as little as possible of her dignity as a science.

What then did Laplace look for in his analysis of chance, and Buffon in his political arithmetic? Each one, following thousands of famous predecessors, wanted to dominate a rebellious *unkown*; to tame by means of induction the resistance it offered to thought, and to make moral consequences emulate the certainty of mathematical consequences. Thus Laplace weighs on the same scale the periodic return of a star, the chances of a lottery ticket, and the value of the historical evidence of a judicial judgement. The same reasoning serves to assure him that the effect of the moon on the sea amounts to more than double that of the sun, and that the niece of Pascal, the young Perrier, was not cured of her fistula through the direct and miraculous intervention of Divine Providence.[2] Thus, for the past, for the present, for the future, he poses systematic rules, he establishes general laws of probability.

Mr Poe also occupies himself in his own way in judging and classifying probabilities – no longer using uniform precepts but that particular instinct, that shrewdness, which is more or less certain in one man or the other, and which varies in power depending on aptitude or profession. The fundamental idea of his tales appears to have been borrowed from those first adventures of Zadig, where the young Babylonian philosopher displays such wonderful insight. The eccentric person whom Mr Poe uses as a special agent, and whose intelligence he submits to such arduous trials, would have guessed, through mere inspection of footprints, that the queen of Babylon's spaniel had only produced puppies shortly before escaping from the palace, and that the king's horse lost by a rascally stable boy had in his harness small lumps of twenty-four-carat gold.[3]

This protagonist is none other than Mr Poe hardly taking the trouble to hide himself, and in the tales in which he does not appear, he boldly substitutes himself.

Who else but this searcher after problems for resolution would have imposed upon himself the task of guessing what could be the posthumous sensations of man, or rather of the corpse, first laid out on the deathbed, then in the coffin under the humid earth, listening to his own dissolution, watching himself rot? To whom would it have occurred to tell, in a manner acceptable to reason, of the final catastrophe which will reduce this terrestrial globe to nothing? To touch upon these great secrets of mortality as well as the end of the world seems the business of the most profound thinkers, the deepest meditations, the most complete systems. For Mr Poe there is only the adaptation of a hypothesis, providing an initial fact, and making it engender among the probable consequences, those which the human spirit can grasp most easily and willingly.

Monos is dead; Una his adored mistress has followed soon after to the sombre kingdom of the departed. They meet – Una wants to know from her beloved what he had felt from the moment when near him, in distress, she contemplated him immobile, cold, disfigured, marked by the supreme seal. With life, has all thought disappeared? The divorce of body and soul, is it so quick, so complete that with the death rattle the soul escapes entirely, leaving behind only an inert mass? Common sense responds affirmatively; our writer, fearless of shocking opinion, rejects as false this hypothesis which no one could prove for certain, and constructs, helped by logic, his tale of beyond the grave.

To be fair, this is not the first time that imagination has gone beyond the limits of life, impassable by reason and in the face of which all philosophy averts its humbled gaze; but I do not believe that one has ever been offered the *memories of a dead man* with this kind of exact definition and reasoned conviction. There is no question here of fantastic adventures, of arbitrary complication, of dialogue more or less filled with humour, but rather a genuine monograph – patient, methodical, which seems to aspire to a place among documents of human knowledge. Mr Poe has deduced from the phenomena of dreams the sensibilities of the corpse; he has taken seriously that fraternity of dreams and death, of which so many poets have sung; from this he has created a philosophical dogma, and from this dogma he has drawn those truths which derive from it. One would suppose that this does not represent hack work!

[Quotes Monos's sensations after his death, from 'I breathed no longer' to 'Thus your wild sobs ...', *Works*, 4, 206–7.]

We shall prolong no further this curious quotation which, however, is indispensable to justify our earlier comment about the distinctive character which this anatomy of a dead man dissecting himself had for Mr. Poe.

The final ruin of the globe, the destruction of our planet is just as methodically treated in the dialogue of Eiros and Charmion as is the decomposition of the human being in that of Monos and Una. The principle is presented in the same way. Given the elementary fact that the air we breathe is composed of twenty-one parts of oxygen and seventy-nine parts of nitrogen, with a small part of carbonic acid; given the fact that the earth is enveloped in atmosphere approximately fifteen leagues thick, what would happen if the elipses described around the sun by a comet were to lead the latter into contact with the earth? This is precisely the supposition of Trissotin in *Les Femmes Savantes*.[4] Mr Poe does not adopt this point of view. He presents the comet not as a massive and weighty body, but as a whirlwind of subtle matter whose nucleus is of much less density than our lightest gases. The encounter does not, therefore, carry the same danger as that of two locomotives speeding on the same track; we pass without difficulty through the enemy star. But what will happen to us during this singular penetration? Oxygen, the mainspring of combustion, will develop to unnatural proportions, whereas nitrogen, in contrast, will be completely extracted from the earthly atmosphere. What consequence will this double phenomenon have? An irresistible combustion will devour everything. From this fundamental idea, once it is admitted, the tale develops its pitiless consequences and inevitable deductions with pinpoint logic. Dispute, if you wish, the main point, the premises, the point of departure; the rest is strictly unassailable.

[The story of 'The Conversation of Eiros and Charmion' is here retold in detail.]

You see then that this extraordinary tale, this unparalleled caprice of an imagination which stops at nothing, has all the appearance, if not the whole reality, of strict logic. Few people would deny that a comet and the earthly globe could meet in space. Put in this way, one must admit, at least the possibility of a conflagration of gas, a blaze of the atmosphere, a horrible end to the human race suddenly reduced to inhaling only flame.

Having once tackled this sort of problem, one is inclined to review all those for which science seems condemned forever to refuse us a solution, leaving them for God. Mr Poe is therefore driven to seek a plausible explanation both of the human soul and of the Divinity. This is the subject of a third tale entitled 'Mesmeric Revelation'. The author supposes himself at the deathbed of an unbeliever who, having arrived at the last stage of a mortal illness, resorts to treatment by magnetism. Mr Van-Kirk has doubted the immortality of the soul all his life. For only a few days, troubled by vague recollections left by his ecstasies of sleepwalking, he asks himself if, in this singular condition, a few pointed questions could not throw an entirely new light upon metaphysical truths, perhaps guessed, but badly explained, badly commented on by a philosophy impeded by the shortcomings of its ordinary resources. In fact, at the moment when magnetic action allows man to improve the imperfections of his finite organs and transports him, endowed by a miraculous perception, into the domain of creations which escape the senses, is it not very natural that the sleep walker should possess, more than any other, the power to explain to us the hidden realities of the invisible world? Having won this first point, trust the story teller to give you, by question and answer, a highly convincing theory about all that having to do with the division of soul and body, in essence that which constitutes this force, this superior order known by the name of God, the unknown relationship of the human soul, an individualized particle of the divinity, with that divinity from which it is separated forever. It goes without saying that we would in no way wish to be answerable for the system set out by the American story teller against famous representatives of modern philosophy. Much as one would like to revive, in order to defend them, the theories of the cardinal of Cusa (Nicholas Chripffs), on comprehending the incomprehensible, with which these of Mr Edgar Poe are not without some distant connection; or Giordano Bruno, who seems to play a good part in Poe's ingenious hypotheses. That which Bruno called Nature, is at once principle and element – just as a pilot can be at once pilot and passenger of the vessel he is steering. Mr Poe calls him God. He contests the separation that men have established between spirit and matter. All is matter; even God is composed only of the most rarefied matter, of that very same which acts in us under the name of soul – a separate substance, sublimated beyond anything that the human spirit can perceive, and which is not formed like the other conglomerations of particles. It fills everything, moves everything, is itself all that is understood in it, that is, the entire universe. At rest, this Substance-God is the universal soul; active, it is the creative force. This portion of ourselves which we call soul is a fragment of the universal soul which, without ceasing to belong, finds itself incarnated for a time – individualized. Only the incarnation, by giving limited organs to this fraction of divine substance, restricts the full power which would otherwise be its necessary attribute. Consequently separated from his body, Man would be God or would enter God. But this separation is not possible. Man is a creature, the creatures are God's thoughts. All thought is irrevocable by its nature.

[Quotes 'Mesmeric Revelation', from 'I do not comprehend' to 'ultimate life', *Works*, 5, 250.]

Mr Van-Kirk then explains, with a singular lucidity, what is happening during the magnetic ecstasy, in which the organs of the rudimentary being themselves paralysed, the clairvoyant medium of the ulterior body, a body too insubstantial to have organs, functions freely etc. We shall not go any further in this purely hypothetical exposé of which several passages have recalled to us the inspiration or rather the aspiration of some of our own novelists who found it charming, some fourteen or fifteen years ago, to put the visions of Jacob Boehme, of Saint Martin, of Swedenborg, even of Mme. Guyon, into 'madrigals'. Only one must note that the logic of Mr Poe has a much more precise character, much more tenacious than that of *Louis Lambert* or of *Séraphita*, the angelic hermaphrodite.[5] This logic does not waste large and cloudy words, impenetrable formulae, affected concision. Its principles, once established, deviate rarely, and are always clear and comprehensible; the reader is caught despite himself.

The time has come to return to earth and to follow this inexorable logic, over ground less favourable to the traps of style, and artistic illusion.

In 'The Gold-Bug', we shall see all the reasoning faculties of man in the grip of a cipher, apparently impenetrable, the solution of which involves a great treasure once hidden by a pirate. Here reasoning plays the rôle of a talisman which can enrich one in a few hours. Further on, in 'A Descent into the Maelstrom', Mr Poe tells us how a sound observation, a well followed argument, draws a miserable fisherman caught up in the consuming whirlpool, safe and sound, from the bottom of a Norwegian abyss. We do not assert that general plausibility has been entirely respected here, nor that a theory of gravity could ever have been improvised by a common peasant in a situation which seems to exclude the exercise of any mental faculties – that of a man carried away by the impulse of a wind dragon – but if all that is rigorously, strictly, possible, is conceivable, exceptionally by the human spirit, one can admit that extreme danger develops in a man to whom certainty of death has given complete composure, a special lucidity of the intellect, a miraculous power of observation. And this suffices for the story to fascinate like 'The Anaconda' of Lewis or the novel of *Frankenstein*, both of which are surely highly unlikely.[6]

Here is something easier to believe:

[C. Auguste Dupin's logical intelligence is summarized from 'The Murders in the Rue Morgue'.]

Apply this surprising insight, resulting from an almost superhumanly close application and a marvellous instinct, to a police operation, and you have an admirable bloodhound, an investigator whom nothing escapes, an examining magistrate such as will hardly ever be encountered. Mr Poe takes this situation and with an all American tenacity develops it to its extreme consequences.

Three or four of these tales rest upon this very simple but very effective contrivance. We only regret that the foreign narrator has thought to heighten interest by choosing a Paris of which he has not the least idea, and our present society, which is very poorly known in the United States, as the location of his ingenious hypotheses. His intention, without any doubt, was to increase the likelihood of these little dramas in the eyes of his compatriots. Such detail, unacceptable in a story set in Baltimore or in Philadelphia, becomes admissible when placed two thousand leagues from there – it does not disturb the credulity of the American reader. The marvellous and even the extraordinary need perspective. Introduce the Caliph Haroun-al-Raschid into the streets next to the Tuileries, remove from their familiar surroundings to the banks of the Yonne or the Cher the astonishing adventures which comprise the charm of *Alif-Laila*[7] – the story of Abul-Hasan and of Chems-el-Nihar, for example – and you will be surprised. Mr Poe is hence not badly advised to remove his scene in order to conceal the artifice of his 'painting', and to give it all the prestige of truth, but he should have foreseen that the French reader, having stopped in front of the same canvases, would be amazed to find the capital of France completely overturned, quarters all of a sudden moved; a blind alley Lamartine in the region of the Palais-Royal, a rue Morgue in the quartier Saint-Roch, and the gate of Roule near the Seine, 'on the banks opposite the Street Pavée-Saint-André'. He should not then have applied to our social hierarchy the ideas of a country much more egalitarian than our own, to assume that the prefect of police, having reached the end of his resources, not knowing which saint to turn to find a mysterious paper, would casually arrive one evening to smoke a cigar or two with the young observer of whom we were speaking, to ask his advice, to express his doubts, and to lay a bet on the success of the steps proposed by this officious councillor. In fact, we do not cite all the blunders, however great, which our red pencil has marked in the margins of these bizarre little tales. These blunders are explained by their foreign orgins, and also by the method adopted by the author to bring us real events chosen from among the crimes which have occupied the magistrates of New York or Boston. Thus the story of Marie Roget is an American *cause célèbre*; only the names are rendered French, the incidents could not have been. The Hudson becomes the Seine; Weehawken, the barrier of Roule; Nassau Street, the Pavée-Saint-André; and so forth. Equally Marie Roget, the so-called Parisian waif, is none other than Mary Cecelia Rogers, the cigar girl whose mysterious assassination terrified, some years ago, the population of New York. Let us tell the event as told in the *New York Mercury* or in *Brother Jonathan*. There always will be time to come back to the fiction when we have a proper idea of the reality.

[Forgues summarizes the newspaper accounts of the murder.]

Mr Poe in turn gets hold of the story and introduces into the clash of opinion this peculiar character, this living syllogism of which we have been speaking. The chevalier Dupin – this is the name that he has wrought, a name truly characteristic, and of a remarkable unlikeliness and strangeness – the cheva-lier Dupin, attentive to all contradictory versions, discusses them rigorously, submits them to the scrutiny of mathema-tical analysis. One sees that he has read, in Laplace's *Essay on Probabilities*, the chapter devoted to the probabilities of the judgements of tribunals. Laplace says in fact that one should abstain from judging if, in order to reach a definitive judgement in a criminal matter, mathematical evidence is rigorously demanded. While looking for this evidence, Mr Poe's agent seems to despair. But his calculations on probability are striking and curious. This is all that one can ask of them.

Novalis said in *Morale Ansichten*: 'There are ideal series of events which run parallel with the real ones. They rarely coincide. Men and circumstances generally modify the ideal train of events, so that it seems imperfect, and its consequences are equally imperfect. Thus with the Reformation; instead of Protestantism came Lutheranism.' By choosing this passage as the epigraph for his story, the American author explains its metaphysical design to us. When he presents the diverse hypotheses of the French (that is to say American) papers on the subject of the murders committed in New York, when he brings out the coarse mistakes of vulgar logic, improvised for the consumption of the unintelligent masses, his aim is to prove by virtue of certain principles that an ideal series, one which is purely logical, made up of facts clearly dependent one upon the other, must lead by an accumulation of mutually corroborated suppositions to the truth. He therefore destroys by an inexorable dialectic the false systems erected around him and, on perfectly cleared ground, constructs a new edifice all of a piece.

In the eyes of this terrible logic-chopper, the practice of tribunals in limiting the admission of proof to a small number of conclusive facts is highly erroneous. Modern science, which very often takes the unexpected into account and proves the known by the unknown, understands the importance of secondary incidents better, the collateral demonstrations which have to be noticed before all else. It is these apparently inessential facts and isolated accidents which have become the basis of the most complete and best established systems.

This principle once established, the consequences follow naturally. By abandoning the principal fact, in order to fall back on apparently insignificant details, the chevalier comes to appreciate several circumstances which later on will serve to enlighten him.

[Forgues relates 'The Mystery of Marie Rogêt' emphasizing throughout the logic of Poe and Dupin.]

Now that you have some idea of this American author,

and his particular preferences, I have to present him to you in a new light. We have studied him as a logician, in pursuit of abstract truths, in love with the most eccentric hypotheses, the most arduous calculations; it is right to judge him as a poet, as inventor of purposeless fantasies and purely literary caprices. For this we shall restrict ourselves to two stories which we have deliberately kept back – 'The Black Cat' and 'The Man of the Crowd'.

'The Black Cat' recalls Theodore Hoffmann's inspiration at its most sombre. Never has the Serapion club heard anything more fantastic than the history of this man, of this unfortunate maniac, in whose brain burned by strong liquors, lodged a monstrous hatred for his poor cat.

[The story of 'The Black Cat' is retold.]

'The Man of the Crowd' is not a story; it is a study, a very simple idea energetically rendered. The author supposes that as his eye passed haphazardly over the many pedestrians who passed and repassed before the windows of a café where he was seated, he distinguished a face whose appearance filled him with inexpressible curiosity; it is that of an old man, thin and pale, whose features express with unusual energy the disquiet of conscience, the anxieties of remorse.

[The plot of 'The Man of the Crowd' is retold.]

We have already compared Mr Poe's talent to that of Washington Irving, the latter being lighter, more varied, less ambitious, and to that of William Godwin, whose 'sombre and unhealthy popularity' has been so severely censured by Hazlitt. However, one has to recognize in the author of *St. Leon* and of *Caleb Williams* more real philosophic science, a tendency much less marked by purely literary paradox. So if one wanted to designate an American predecessor of Mr Edgar Poe, one could, without too much forcing of analogies, compare him to Charles Brockden Brown, who also sought sincerely, even in his most frivolous fictions, the solution of some intellectual problem; taking care, like Mr Poe, to paint those maladies of the spirit which offer so large a field of observation and so many curious phenomena to the studious constructors of metaphysical systems.

Brockden Brown, it is true, wrote novels, and we know only very short stories by Mr Poe – some of which are no more than six or seven pages; but time would be wasted, it seems to us, classifying in order of extent compositions of this type. It is so easy to prolong indefinitely a series of facts, and so difficult to condense into a few words, in the form of a tale, a whole abstract theory, all the elements of an original conception. Today, when the least scribbler begins with a melodrama in ten or twenty volumes, Richardson himself, if he returned to earth, would in the interest of his glory, be obliged to summarize his characters, to trim his interminable dialogues, and to divide into finely drawn medallions the numerous figures of his huge canvases. Victory yesterday went to the big battalions; tomorrow it will belong to the crack troops. From the great novels which amused Mme de Sévigné followed the tales of Voltaire and Diderot. A caprice of fashion has honoured the *Clélie* and the *Astrée* of the 17th century;[8] but for all that, one has forgotten neither *Candide* nor the *Amis de Bourbonne*, and time, which has removed nothing from those enduring classic tales, will certainly bring back the taste for simple, laconic, deliberately concentrated forms. The diamond is never very large, perfume never fills huge casks, and tales like those by Mr Poe offer more substance to the spirit, open more new horizons, than twenty volumes such as those formerly fabricated by the hundred by Courtilz de Sandras, de Baculard D'Arnaud, and de Lussan,[9] precursors and prototypes of many contemporary serial story writers. Between these latter and the American author, we take care not to draw a parallel. It would be opportune and useful to compare them when time will have consolidated the growing reputation of the foreign story teller and – who knows? – shaken a little that of our prolific novelists.

NOTES

1 The Marquis de Laplace's *Philosophical Essay on Probabilities* (1814) was a popular version of his comprehensive work *Analytic Theory of Probability* (1812).

2 This 'miracle' was rationalized by Laplace in chapter XI of the *Philosophical Essay on Probabilities*.

3 The 'eccentric person' is of course C. Auguste Dupin; the stories of the queen's spaniel and king's horse are told in chapter 3 of Voltaire's *Zadig*.

4 One must note that this conclusion meets with objections and one of the gravest is an example or, as one now says, a precedent. There exist, as a matter of fact, four, so-called *telescopic*, planets – Pallas, Juno, Ceres and Vesta, which appear to be merely four fragments of a larger planet shattered by a cause to this day unknown. Cotin's hypothesis, supported by the arguments of Laplace, is thus not entirely improbable. [Forgues's note.]

Trissotin in Molière's play satirized the notions of the Abbé Charles Cotin promulgated in a work entitled *Gallant Dissertation upon the Comet which Appeared in December 1664 and January 1665.*

5 *Louis Lambert, Séraphita, La Fille aux yeux d'or*, together with *Le Proscrits*, make up the *Livre Mystique* of Balzac. They were published together in 1835.

6 'The Anaconda' by 'Monk' Lewis appeared in *Romantic Tales* (1808); it was translated into French in 1822.

7 This is the actual title of the collection known as *The Thousand and One Nights*. [Forgues's note.]

8 *Clélie* (1654), a novel by Madeleine de Scudéry; *L'Astrée* (1647), a novel by Honoré d' Urte.

9 Popular novelists of the eighteenth century.

67. [William Henry Smith], from a review of 'The American Library' in *Blackwood's Edinburgh Magazine*

November 1847, 62, 582–7

Smith (1808–72), a poet and critic, was a frequent contributor to *Blackwood's*.

No one can read these tales, then close the volume, as he may with a thousand other tales, and straightway forget what manner of book he has been reading. Commonplace is the last epithet that can be applied to them. They are strange – powerful – more strange than pleasing, and powerful productions without rising to the rank of genius. The author is a strong-headed man, which epithet by no means excludes the possibility of being, at times, wrong-headed also. With little taste, and such analytic power, one would rather employ such an artist on the anatomical model of the Moorish Venus, than intrust to his hands any other sort of Venus. In fine, one is not sorry to have read these tales; one has no desire to read them twice.

They are not framed according to the usual manner of stories. On each occasion, it is something quite other than the mere story that the author has in view, and which has impelled him to write. In one, he is desirous of illustrating Laplace's doctrine of probabilities as applied to human events. In another, he displays his acumen in unravelling or in constructing a tangled chain of circumstantial evidence. In a third ('The Black Cat') he appears at first to aim at rivalling the fantastic horrors of Hoffmann, but you soon observe that the wild and horrible invention in which he deals, is strictly in the service of an abstract idea which it is there to illustrate. His analytic observation has led him, he thinks, to detect in men's minds an absolute spirit of 'perversity', prompting them to do the very opposite of what reason and mankind pronounce to be right, simply because they *do* pronounce it to be right. The punishment of this sort of diabolic spirit of perversity, he brings about by a train of circumstance as hideous, incongruous, and absurd, as the sentiment itself.

There is, in the usual sense of the word, no passion in these tales, neither is there any attempt made at dramatic dialogue. The bent of Mr Poe's mind seems rather to have been towards reasoning than sentiment. The style, too, has nothing peculiarly commendable; and when the embellishments of metaphor and illustration are attempted, they are awkward, strained, infelicitous. But the tales rivet the attention. There is a marvellous skill in putting together the close array of facts and of details which make up the narrative, or the picture; for the effect of his description, as of his story, depends never upon any bold display of the imagination, but on the agglomeration of incidents, enumerated in the most veracious manner. In one of his papers he describes the Maelstrom, or what he chooses to imagine the Maelstrom may be, and by dint of this careful and De Foe-like painting, the horrid whirlpool is so placed before the mind, that we feel as if we had seen and been down into it.

'The Gold-Bug' is the first and most striking of the series, owing to the extreme and startling ingenuity with which the narrative is constructed. It would be impossible, however, to convey an idea of this species of merit, without telling the whole story; nor would it be possible to tell the story in shorter compass, with any effect, than it occupies here. 'The Murders in the Rue Morgue' and 'The Mystery of Marie Roget', both turn on the interest excited by the investigation of circumstantial evidence. But, unlike most stories of this description, our sympathies are not called upon, either in the fate of the person assassinated, or in behalf of some individual falsely accused of the crime; the interest is sustained solely by the nature of the evidence, and the inferences to be adduced from it. The latter of these stories is, in fact, a transfer to the city of Paris of a tragedy which had been really enacted in New York. The incidents have been carefully preserved, the scene alone changed, and the object of the author in thus re-narrating the facts seems to have been to investigate the evidence again, and state his own conclusions as to the probable culprit. From these, also, it would be quite as impossible to make an extract as it would be to quote a passage from an interesting case as reported in one of our law-books. The last story in the volume has, however, the advantage of being brief, and an outline of it may convey some idea of the peculiar manner of Mr Poe. It is entitled 'The Man of the Crowd'.

[The plot is summarized.]

In this description it would be difficult to recognise the topography of London, or the manners of its inhabitants. That *Square* brilliantly illuminated and thronged with promenaders, the oldest inhabitant would scarcely find. He closes his gin-palace at the hour when, we believe, it would be about to re-open; and ejects his multitude from the bazaar and the theatre about the same time. When he lays his scene in Paris there is the same disregard to accuracy. There is no want of names of streets and passages, but no Parisian would find them, or find them in the juxtaposition he has placed them. This is a matter hardly worth remarking; to his American readers an ideal topography is as good as any others; we ourselves should be very little disturbed by a novel which, laying its scene in New York, should misname half the streets of that city. We are led to notice it chiefly from a feeling of surprise, that one so partial to detail should not have more frequently profited by the help which a common guide-book, with its map, might have given him.

Still less should we raise an objection on the manifest improbability of this vigilant observer, a convalescent too, being able to keep upon his legs, running or walking, the whole of the night and of the next day, (to say nothing of the pedestrian powers of the old man). In a picture of this kind, a moral idea is sought to be portrayed by imaginary incidents purposely exaggerated. The mind passing immediately from these incidents to the idea they convey, regards them as little more than a mode of expression of the moral truth. He who should insist, in a case of this kind, on the improbability of the facts, would find himself in the same position as that hapless critic who, standing before the bronze statue of Canning, then lately erected at Westminster, remarked that 'Mr Canning was surely not so tall as he is there represented', the proportions, in fact, approaching to the colossal. 'No, nor so green', said the wit to whom the observation had been unhappily confided. When the artist made a bronze statue, eight feet high, of Mr Canning, it was evidently not his stature nor his complexion that he had designed to represent.

Amongst the tales of Mr Poe are several papers which, we suppose, in the exigency of language, we must denominate philosophical. They have at least the merit of boldness, whether in the substratum of thought they contain, or in the machinery employed for its exposition. We shall not be expected to encounter Mr Poe's metaphysics; our notice must be here confined solely to the narrative or inventive portion of these papers. In one of these, entitled 'Mesmeric Revelation', the reader may be a little startled to hear that he has adopted the mesmerised patient as a vehicle of his ideas on the nature of the soul and of its immortal life; the entranced subject having, in this case, an introspective power still more reasonable than that which has hitherto revealed itself only in a profound knowledge of his anatomical structure. As we are not yet convinced that a human being becomes supernaturally enlightened – in mesmerism more than in fanaticism – by simply losing his senses; or that a man in a trance , however he got there, is necessarily omniscient; we do not find that Mr Poe's conjectures on these mysterious topics gather any weight whatever from the authority of the spokesman to whom he has intrusted them. We are not quite persuaded that a cataleptic patient sees very clearly what is going on at the other side of our own world; when this has been made evident to us, we shall be prepared to give him credit for penetrating into the secrets of the next.

In another of these nondescript papers, 'The Conversation of Eiros and Charmion', Mr Poe has very boldly undertaken to figure forth the destruction of the world, and explain how that great and final catastrophe will be accomplished. It is a remarkable instance of that species of imaginary matter of fact description, to which we have ventured to think that the Americans show something like a natural tendency. The description here is very unlike that with which Burnet closes his 'Theory of the Earth'; it is confined to the natural history of the event; but there is nothing whatever in Mr Poe's manner to diminish from the sacredness or the sublimity of the topic. With some account of this singular and characteristic paper we shall dismiss the volume of Mr Poe.

[The story is summarized and several lengthy passages cited.]

THE RAVEN AND OTHER POEMS

1845

68. [George Pope Morris], review in the New York *Evening Mirror*

21 November 1845

Morris (1802–64) was a poet, editor, and journalist; he is best remembered for his sentimental poem, 'Woodman, Spare That Tree!'. The *Evening Mirror*, a daily for 'the upper ten thousand', was started by Morris and his co-worker, N.P. Willis, in October 1844. Willis had recently left for Europe, but Morris was also friendly to Poe: on 18 November he reprinted Poe's 'Preface' to *The Raven and other Poems*, adding, 'We like the spirit that dictated it.'

In spite of Mr Poe's majestic disclaimer of any great interest in this book, we must venture to think it contains a good deal of that which we call poetry – an element too rare in these days of frigid verse-making to be treated with disregard. Whatever makes the heart beat quicken and the eyes fill, bringing before the mind in flitting pictures, the scenes and feelings of the past – calling up from the depth of memory the freshness so long departed from the present – must possess an essence very different from that which pervades much of that would-be poetry of the day. This last is like our pyramids of ice-cream – sweet enough, and delicately rose tinted; but forced into shape and there frozen, and desperately flat if you try to restore it to its original condition to ascertain its ingredients. Mr Poe's creations are more like firelight reviews,

> Where glowing embers through the room
> Teach light to counterfeit the gloom –

the very light to see sheeted ghosts by, and to fancy that the loved and lost

> Come and take the vacant chair.

Tall shadows and a sighing silence seem to close around us as we read. We feel dream-land to be more and more touching than the actual life we had left, and not the unpleasing sadness of the spirit, a better test of the poet's power than all the formal criterions that were ever penned. 'The Raven', for instance, which we have been surprised to hear called, in spite of its exquisite versification, somewhat aimless and unsatisfactory, leaves us with no such impression; but on the contrary, the shadowy and indistinct implied resemblance of the material and immaterial throughout, gives an indescribable charm to the poem, producing just the effect upon the imagination that the author designed artistically to produce. The reader who cannot feel some of the poet's 'fantastic terrors', hear the 'whisper'd word, LENORE', perceive the air grow denser 'perfum'd from an unseen censer', and at last catch some dim vanishing glimpse of 'The rare and radiant maiden' mourned so agonisingly, can have pondered but little over those 'quaint and curious volumes of forgotten lore' which so well introduce this 'stately raven of the saintly days of yore'. We recommend to him a year's regimen of monkish legends, and chronicles with which Wharton and Scott fed the poetic fire, and from which no bard of modern times has disdained to draw elements of power and passion.

The ballad of 'Lenore' is in the same tone – a wild wail, melancholy, as the sound of the clarion to the captive knight who knew that its departing tones bore with them his last earthly hope. 'Mariana' is not more intensely mournful. The *'Peccavimus'*, the passing bell, the hair natural and life-like above closed eyes hollow with the death-change – leave pictures and echoes within the heart, which allows no doubt as to the power of the poet.

The remainder of the poems in this neat volume we shall leave to the regular critic with his foot-rule and his metronome; 'simple, passionate and sensuous', Coleridge's list of poetic requisites, all must allow to apply to Mr Poe's verses; and although it is true that in one's own country one must not expect much honor, yet he is right, and those who read to enjoy rather than to criticise, will not disappoint him. Thus much is bare justice to the author, whose pardon we entreat if we have offended him by 'paltry commendation'.

69. [Margaret Fuller], review in the New York *Daily Tribune*

26 November 1845

Mr Poe throws down the gauntlet in his preface, by what he says of 'the paltry compensations or more paltry commendations of mankind'. Some champion might be expected to start up from the 'somewhat sizeable' class embraced, or more properly speaking, boxed on the ear, by this defiance, who might try whether the sting of Criticism was as indifferent to this knight of the pen as he professes its honey to be.

Were there such a champion, gifted with acumen to dissect, and a swift glancing wit to enliven the operation, he could find no more legitimate subject, no fairer game than Mr Poe, who has wielded the weapons of criticism, without relenting, whether with the dagger he rent and tore the garment in which some favored Joseph had pranked himself, secure of honor in the sight of all men, or whether with uplifted tomahawk he rushed upon the new-born children of some hapless genius, who had fancied and persuaded his friends to fancy that they were beautiful and worthy a long and honored life. A large band of these offended dignitaries and aggrieved parents must be on the watch for a volume of 'Poems by Edgar A. Poe', ready to cut, rend and slash in turn, and hoping to see his own Raven left alone to prey upon the slaughter of which it is the herald.

Such joust and tournament we look to see and, indeed, have some stake in the matter so far as we have friends whose wrongs cry aloud for the avenger. Nevertheless we could not take part in the *melée*, except to join the crowd of lookers-on in the cry – Heaven speed the right!

Early we read that fable of Apollo who rewarded the critic, who had painfully winnowed the wheat, with the chaff for his pains. We joined the gentle Affirmative School, and have confidence that if we indulge ourselves chiefly with the appreciation of good qualities, Time will take care of the faults. – For Time holds a strainer like that used in the diamond mines, – have but patience and the water and gravel will all pass through and only the precious stones be left. Yet we are not blind to the uses of severe criticism, and of just censure, especially in a time and place so degraded by venal and indiscriminate praise as the present. That unholy alliance, that shameless sham, whose motto is

'Caw me
And I'll caw thee'

That system of mental adulation and organized puff which was carried to such perfection in the time and may be seen to the life in the correspondence of Miss Hannah More,[1] is fully represented in our day and generation. We see that it meets a counter agency, from the league of Truthtellers, few, but each of them mighty as Fingal or any other hero of the sort. Let such tell the whole truth, as well as nothing but the truth, but led their sternness be in the spirit of Love. Let them seek to understand the purpose and scope of an author, his capacity as well as his fulfilments, and how his faults are made to grow by the same sunshine that acts upon his virtues, for this is the case with talents no less than with character. The rich field requires frequent and careful weeding; frequent, lest the weeds exhaust the soil; careful, lest the flowers and grain be pulled up along with the weeds.

Well! but to return to Mr Poe; we are not unwilling that cavil should do her worst on his book, because both by act and word he has challenged it, but as this is no office for us, we shall merely indicate, in our usual slight way, what, naturally and unsought, has struck ourselves in the reading of these verses.

It has often been our case to share the mistake of Gil Blas, with regard to the Archbishop. We have taken people at their word, and rejoicing that women could bear neglect without feeling mean pique, and that authors, rising above self-love, could show candor about their works and magnanimously meet both justice and injustice, we have been rudely awakened from our dream, and found that Chanticleer, who crowed so bravely, showed himself at last but a dunghill fowl. Yet Heaven grant we never become too worldly-wise thus to trust a generous word, and we surely are not so yet, for we believe Mr Poe to be sincere when he says:

In defence of my own taste, it is incumbent upon me to say that I think nothing in this volume of much value to the public or very creditable to myself. Events not to be controlled have prevented me from making, at any time, any serious effort in what, under happier circumstances, would have been the field of my choice.

We believe Mr Poe to be sincere in this declaration; if he is, we respect him; if otherwise, we do not. Such things should never be said unless in hearty earnest. If in earnest, they are honorable pledges; if not, a pitiful fence and foil of vanity. Earnest or not, the words are thus far true; the productions in this volume indicate a power to do something far better. With the exception of 'The Raven', which seems intended chiefly to show the writer's artistic skill, and is in its way a rare and finished specimen, they are all fragments – *fyttes* upon the lyre, almost all of which leave us something to desire or demand. This is not the case, however, with these lines:

[Quotes 'To One in Paradise'.]

This kind of beauty is especially conspicuous, then rising into dignity, in the poem called 'The Haunted Palace'.

The imagination of this writer rarely expresses itself in

pronounced forms, but rather in a sweep of images, thronging and distant like a procession of moonlight clouds on the horizon, but like them characteristic and harmonious one with another, according to their office.

The descriptive power is greatest when it takes a shape not unlike an incantation, as in the first part of 'The Sleeper' where

> I stand beneath the mystic moon.
> An opiate vapour, dewy, dim,
> Exhales from out her golden rim,
> And, softly dripping, drop by drop,
> Upon the quiet mountain top,
> Steals drowsily and musically
> Into the universal valley.

Why '*universal*'? 'resolve me that, Master Moth'.

And farther on, 'the lily *lolls* upon the wave.'

This word '*lolls*', often made use of in these poems, presents a vulgar image to our thought; we know not how it is to that of others.

The lines which follow about the open window are highly poetical. So is the 'Bridal Ballad' in its power of suggesting a whole tribe and train of thoughts and pictures by few and simple touches.

The Poems written in youth, written indeed, we understand, in childhood, before the author was ten years old, are a great psychological curiosity. Is it the delirium of a prematurely excited brain that causes such a rapture of words? What is to be gathered from seeing the future so fully anticipated in the germ? The passions are not unfrequently felt in their full shock, if not in their intensity, at eight or nine years old, but here they are reflected upon,

> Sweet was their death – with them to die was rife
> With the last ecstacy of satiate life.

The scenes from 'Politian' are done with clear, sharp strokes; the power is rather metaphysical than dramatic. We must repeat what we heretofore said, that we could wish to see Mr Poe engage in a metaphysical romance. He needs a sustained flight and a fair range to show what his powers really are. Let us have from him the analysis of the Passions, with their appropriate Fates; let us have his speculations clarified; let him intersperse dialogue or poem as the occasion prompts, and give us something really good and strong, firmly wrought, and fairly blazoned. Such would be better employment than detecting literary larcenies, not worth pointing out if they exist. Such employment is quite unworthy of one who dares vie with the Angel.

[Quotes 'Israfel'.]

NOTE

1 Published in 1834.

70. Thomas Dunn English, review in the *Aristidean*

November 1845, 1, 399–403

Quite a controversy is being carried on, at the present time, between the critics, concerning the merits of Mr POE, as a poet. It appears that Mr POE was invited to deliver a poem before the Boston Lyceum, on the same evening during which Mr CALEB CUSHING was to deliver an address. The poet, dilatory as he usually is, neglected until too late to write anything original for the occasion; and, in order to test the judgement of the Bostonians, who, to trust their words, are judges of everything, he recited a poem of his, which had been written and published at the age of ten. As a psychological curiosity, the poem was very wonderful, but as a poem, it is such as a juvenile production might have been expected to be. It took very well with the audience, who, deny it if they dare, applauded most furiously. That same night, over a bottle of Madeira, the poet let out the secret; and BOSTON – that is, the transcendental donkeys who call themselves BOSTON – has been in a ferment ever since. 'Straight jackets wouldn't howld 'em, for the rage they were in, when they found themselves diddled.' They began to abuse POE, who spoke back; and, dirt began to fly lustily from both parties. That Mr POE was wrong in performing such a trick, we assert without hesitation; but the less the *clique* in BOSTON say about critical judgement the better. According to their own story, they invited a poet, whom they now assert has no claims to the title to deliver a poem before the best of their *literati*. Why, they should now take such uncommon pains to prove themselves donkeys, we cannot, for the life of us, conceive.

The book opens with 'The Raven', a peculiar and extraordinary production. It is an evident attempt to evolve interest from a common-place incident, and by means of the mechanism of verse, to throw beauty around a simple narration, while the very borders of the ludicrous are visited. So far, it is successful in the highest degree. The reader is interested and borne away in spite of himself by what, on a cool examination, appears to be nothing. The peculiar arrangement of the lines and metre, is not original with Mr. POE, the same thing being found – with the exception of the repetition, in meaning, of half the last line of each stanza – in Miss BARRETT's book. On this repetition, however, much of the poem's effect depends.

'The Raven' commences with a simple narration, rather inclined to the ludicrous. The poet is seated, upon a dreary midnight, poring over an old volume, when he hears a faint tapping at his chamber door. This he supposes to be some visitor, and he distinctly remembers it because

> – it was in the bleak December,
> And each separate dying ember wrought its
> ghost upon the floor –

and he was immersed in sorrow, through the loss of his LENORE. The rustling of the silken curtains, the hour, the memory of the dead, and the otherwise stillness, filled his heart with vague terror. So he stood, and repeated, in order to quiet his own alarm, that it was some late visitor entreating entrance. After a minute, his heart grew stronger, and opening the door, he entreated pardon of the unseen visitor, for detention – alleging that he was napping, and the tapping was so light that he was scarcely sure that he heard it. But there was no reply, and no one was to be seen; he peered into the darkness.

But the silence was unbroken, and the darkness gave no token, and the whispered word 'LENORE!' was murmured back by the echo. Turning into the chamber, he heard another tapping, somewhat louder, and going to his lattice, flung open the shutter. In stalked an old raven, who perched on a bust of PALLAS, over the chamber door. Amused by its strange and grave appearance, the poet jocularly inquired its name, and the raven answered – 'Nevermore'. The poet marvelled at this apparently meaningless answer; but the bird answered nothing else, and sat in quiet. To a mournful anticipation of the poet, that the bird would leave him, as other friends had, the bird replied with the same word, and the poet began to believe that the bird's apparently only stock of language had been caught from some unhappy master, whom disaster had followed, until that word had become the only burthen of his song. Again smiling at the quaint manner of the bird, he sat himself down in an easy chair, and began guessing the meaning – if meaning there was – in what he heard. From this point out, let the poet tell his own story:

[Quotes the last six stanzas.]

That much of the effect depends upon the mode of construction, and the peculiar arrangement of words and incidents, there can be no doubt; but, the power to conceive and execute the effect, betokens the highest genius. We hold a poem to be of high merit, which can effect our mind as 'The Raven' did, and does; and that the common-place has been raised from its degradation by a master-hand, is sufficient to place Mr POE in a high rank. It requires more power to raise a demon to heaven, than to drag an angel down to hell.

Of the other poems, in the first part, there are some

inserted for no other purpose, that we can conceive, than to fill up the book. The commencement of 'The Sleeper', is one of the finest pictures of sleepy calm, in the language. For instance –

> I stand beneath the mystic moon.
> An opiate vapor, dewy, dim,
> Exhales from out her golden rim,
> And, softly dripping, drop by drop,
> Upon the quiet mountain top,
> Steals drowsily and musically,
> Into the universal valley.
> The rosemary nods upon the grave;
> The lily lolls upon the wave:
> Wrapping the fog about its breast,
> The ruin moulders into rest;
> Looking like Lethe, see! the lake
> A conscious slumber seems to take,
> And would not, for the world, awake.

'The Coliseum', written at an early age, has force – and contains well-managed apostrophe and antithesis. The close is unsatisfactory and incomplete. 'Lenore' is musical and melancholy – it tells a tale without seeming to attempt narration. 'Israfel', is a very pretty specimen of fiddle-de-dee. 'Dream-land', 'The City in the Sea', 'The Haunted Palace', and 'The Conqueror Worm', are well managed allegories – the first and last, especially fine, The scenes from 'Politian', are not of any great account. They are very well in their way – and their way, is not remarkable. The 'Sonnet – To Zante' is beautiful. So much for the first part of the work.

The second portion of the volume is the reprint of a volume published by Mr POE, at an incredibly early age; and as far as we understand it, is re-published, to discredit one of the foreign reviewers, who charged Mr POE with being an imitator of TENNYSON. The charge was ridiculous – the poets being unlike; and Mr POE had better let that sleep. As a curiosity – as we said before – the poem is well enough – nothing more. It is in most respects puerile, and so deeply transcendental that no one can tell what it is all about. Yet it is wonderful that a mere child could have written such lines as the following – and we are satisfied, as true as it is wonderful.

[Quotes 'Al Aaraaf', Part 2, lines 16–27.]

But these and several other forcible lines, by no means compensate for doses of such stuff as the following, which is given *ad nauseam*, through the poem:

> Oh! nothing earthly save the ray
> (Thrown back from flowers) of beauty's eye,
> As in those gardens where the day
> Springs from the gems of Circassy –

and so on, and so on.

Yet, throwing these things aside, and taking the first part of the volume, as a fair selection from the poet's writings, we cannot help pronouncing Mr POE, the first poet of his school – a school peculiar, in some measure to himself – in this country. As such we admire him, and look with wonder on his productions; yet they have little power over our spirit. The sensations we feel in reading his poems are more those of admiration than sympathy. We feel *at*, rather than *with* him; if that expression will convey our sentiments, with sufficient clearness. They are not fitted for every mood. It is only in the dim twilight, or by the dim light of a flickering candle, about to die in its socket, that they should be read. Then – we can even *feel* them – can wonder with him at the unearthly beauty of the sleeper – contemplate in awe the wonders of the ruined Coliseum – wander

> By a route obscure and lonely,
> Haunted by ill angels only,
> Where an Eidolon, named Night,
> On a black throne reigns upright;

Contemplate the

> (Time-eaten towers that tremble not)

in the city in the sea; behold with awe the 'haunted palace' of the human mind; or thrill to see a play of hopes and fears , in a theatre, where

> Mimes in the form of God on high,
> Mutter and mumble low,
> And hither and thither fly –

Mere puppets they, who come and go
At bidding of vast formless things
   That shift the scenery to and fro,
Flapping from out their Condor wings
   Invisible Wo!

But we cannot take him up, at all seasons, with satisfaction. He is the poet of the idler, the scholar and dreamer. He has nothing to do with every day life. He is of the ether, etherial. He is not like BRYANT, calm and coldly correct; not WHITTIER, fiery and turgid; nor like WILLIS, passionate and *à la mode*; nor like HALLECK, nervous and imitative. He is neither the poet of out-door nature; nor the poet of every day humanity. He is the poet of the ideal; and sings to his own soul, having no care to sing to the souls around him.

71. Unsigned review in the *Boston Post*

1 December 1845, 27, 1

The good people who heard Edgar Allan Poe deliver what he called a 'poem', though not a *di-dac-tic* one, before the Boston Lyceum, will doubtless be gratified to see the volume under notice. The identical and wonderful composition to which we have alluded, is included in the 'other poems' of the collection. We have read it carefully through, but we do not understand it any better than when we heard it delivered from the honored lips of the author, we have nothing to say about it in particular.

'The Raven' which heads the list of poems, is worthy of notice as an ingenious specimen in versification and the use of language. Like Mr Poe, it is peculiar and eccentric, but one can scarcely praise those qualities when allied to no other and more meritorious ones. 'The Bridal Ballad' is, perhaps, the best piece in the book. It means something, and its expression is full of spirit and delicacy. A short address to 'F.S.O.,' is prettily turned. The remaining portions of the volume, in our opinion, range from mediocrity to absolute nonsense. Numberless times have we praised, and sincerely, the prose tales of Mr Poe and we believe we have ever given to his 'Raven' all the praise which its author would ever claim for it. On the appearance of this volume of poems, therefore, we looked for something as peculiar, eccentric and self-conceited, it may be, as the prose writings of the same man, and for something as wild, as ingenious and as fanciful. We did not expect to see such a parcel of current trash as is contained in the volume in question. In the preface he himself says that 'it is not of much value to the public or very creditable' to himself, and sure enough, this affectation of the writer is, in this instance, but the sorry truth. He also says, that with him 'poetry is not a purpose but a passion'. One fears that if his passion be *true poetry*, it has not been over indulged. We trust it may not 'burst in ignorance.'

72. John Sullivan Dwight, review in the *Harbinger*

6 December 1845, I, 410–11

Dwight (1813–93) was an early member of the Transcendental Club, and contributed important music criticism to the *Dial* and the *Harbinger*. Poe actively resented Dwight's attack on him: he reprinted the review in the *Broadway Journal* (13 December), together with a point by point reply to what he mockingly called the 'Snook Farm Phalanx' – see *Works*, 13, 27–32.

Mr Poe has earned some fame by various tales and poems, which of late has become notoriety through a certain blackguard warfare which he has been waging against the poets and newspaper critics of New England, and which it would be most charitable to impute to insanity. Judging from the tone of his late articles in the *Broadway Journal*, he seems to think that the whole literary South and West are doing anxious battle in his person against the old time-honoured tyrant of the North. But what have North or South to do with affairs only apropos to Poe! He shows himself a poet in this, at least, in this magnifying mirror of his own importance. To him facts lose their barren literality; to him a primrose is more than a primrose; and Edgar Poe, acting the constabulary part of a spy in detecting plagiarisms in favourite authors, insulting a Boston audience, inditing coarse editorials against respectable editresses,[1] and getting singed himself the meanwhile, is nothing less than the hero of a grand mystic conflict of the elements.

The present volume is not entirely pure of this controversy, else we should ignore the late scandalous courses of the man, and speak only of the 'Poems'. The motive of the publication is too apparent; it contains the famous Boston poem, together with other juvenilities, which, he says, private reasons' – some of which have reference to the sin of plagiarism, and others to the date of Tennyson's first poems – have induced him to republish. Does he mean to intimate that he is suspected of copying Tennyson! In vain have we searched the poems for a shadow of resemblance. Does he think to convict Tennyson of copying *him*? Another of those self-exaggerations which prove, we suppose, his poetic imagination.

In a sober attempt to get at the meaning and worth of these poems as poetry, we have been not a little puzzled. We must confess they have a great deal of power, a great deal of beauty, (of thought frequently, and always of rhythm and diction,) originality, and dramatic effect. But they have more of *effect*, than of *expression*, to adopt a distinction from musical criticism; and if they attract you to a certain length, it is only to repulse you the more coldly at last. There is a wild unearthliness, and unheavenliness, in the tone of all his pictures, a strange unreality in all his thoughts; they seem to stand shivering, begging admission to our hearts in vain, because they look not as if they came from the heart. That ill-boding Raven, which you meet at the threshold of his edifice, is a fit warning of the hospitality you will find inside. And yet 'The Raven' has great beauty, and has won the author some renown; we were fascinated till we read it through; we hated to look at it, or think of it again: why was that? There is something in it of the true grief of a lover, an imagination of a broken-heartedness enough to prove a lover in earnest, a power of strange, sad melody, which there is no resisting. So there is in all his poems. Mr Poe has made a critical study of the matter of versification, and succeeded in the art rather at the expense of nature. Indeed the impression of a very *studied* effect is always uppermost after reading him. And you have to study him to understand him. This you would count no loss, if, when you had followed the man through his studies, you could find anything in them beyond the man and his most motiveless moods, which lead you no where; if you could find anything better at bottom than the pride of originality. What is the fancy which is merely fancy, the beauty which springs from no feeling, which neither illustrates nor promotes the great truths and purposes of life, which glimmers strangely only because it is aside from the path of human destiny? Edgar Poe does not write for Humanity; he has more of the art than the soul of poetry. He affects to despise the world while he writes for it. He certainly has struck out a remarkable course: the style and imagery of his earliest poems mark a very singular culture, a judgement most severe for a young writer, and a familiarity with the less hacknied portions of classic lore and nomenclature. He seems to have had an idea of working out his forms from pure white marble. But the poet's humility is wanting; a morbid egotism repels you. He can affect you with wonder, but rarely with the thrill of any passion, except perhaps of pride, which might be dignity, and which therefore always is interesting. We fear this writer even courts the state described by Tennyson:

> A glorious devil, large in heart and brain,
> That did love beauty only, (beauty seen

In all varieties of mould and mind.)
And knowledge for its beauty; or if good,
Good only for its beauty, seeing not
That Beauty, Good, and Knowledge, are three sisters
That doat upon each other, friends to man,
Living together under the same roof,
And never can be sundered without tears;
And he that shuts Love out, in turn shall be
Shut out by Love, and on her threshold lie
Howling in utter darkness.[2]

NOTES

1 The lady in question was Cornelia Wells Walter, editress of the Boston *Transcript*.
2 From 'To –' first published in 1832.

73. [Freeman Hunt], notice in the *Merchant's Magazine and Commercial Advertiser*

January 1846, 14, 107

Hunt (1804–58) was the founder and editor of the *Merchant's Magazine*. For a discussion of his friendship with Poe, see Burton R. Pollin, 'Freeman Hunt, and Four Unrecorded Reviews of Poe's Works', *Texas Studies in Literature and Language*, 16 (Summer 1974), 305–13

This is the second volume of Mr Poe's productions that have
appeared in Wiley and Putnam's American Library. The
characteristics of his poetry are a quick, subtle conception,
and a severe taste of what is harmonious in expression.
Exhibiting all the nervous, impatient marks of true genius,
an unbridled playfulness of fancy, it is, while seemingly
riding havoc in thought, meter and harmony, restrained
throughout by a skilful rein; that guides sentiment and style
by well defined rules, never allowing it to border upon the
ridiculous, or ill-judged sublimity. This union of the faculties
of a critic and genius, making cultivation a second nature,
and unconsciously governing the style, is a rare gift and
power in a writer. The passion and sentiment are also
original, while the style has a fragmentary character, like the
architecture of the ruins of Chiapas, where frescoes, and rude
but beautiful workmanship, are scattered about in the wildest
profusion. 'The Raven' is rather a production of artistic
cleverness than genius, while the poems that follow breathe
such pure passion, and are embodied in such beautiful
imagery, and the etherial speculations given with so much
descriptive, thought-awakening power, that we regret Mr
Poe should do aught else than write poetry.

74. [Lewis Gaylord Clark], review in the *Knickerbocker Magazine*

January 1846, 27, 69–72

The author of this slender volume is of course one of the
'sundry citizens of this good land, meaning well, and hoping
well, who, prompted by a certain something in their nature,
have trained themselves to do service in various essays,
poems, histories, and books of art, fancy and truth;' for we

find this very remarkable passage as a motto on the cover of his poems. But the 'certain something' which has prompted him to publish, according to his preface, is not the 'paltry compensations nor the more paltry commendations of mankind.' These have been powerful 'somethings' with most poets, but we think that the author of 'The Raven' has wisely chosen to regard them as nothings; for the amount of either likely to be bestowed upon him as a poet by the 'mankind' he esteems so lightly we fear will be small. Mr POE says in his preface: 'Events not to be controlled have prevented me from making, at any time, any serious efforts in what, under happier circumstances, would have been the field of my choice. With me poetry has not been a purpose, but a passion.' This is very pitiable, but entirely incomprehensible. According to the biographies of Mr POE, he must be very near the age at which BYRON died, and beyond that at which all the great poets produced their greatest works; and according to his own story, he began writing poetry at an age much earlier than any poet of whom we know anything. His whole life has been spent in literary pursuits, and here we have the results of his poetical career. At what period he commenced writing verses we do not know; but he tells us in a note that it was in his 'earliest boyhood', which begins we believe with the jacket-and-trousers, generally at three or four years. If Mr POE wrote the 'Ode to Science' at that early period, he was certainly a remarkable boy, but hardly a poet. We have heard that, in the paper of which he is the editor, he has stated that he wrote 'Al Aaraaf', the poem with which he professes to have humbugged the poor Bostonians, in his tenth year. The *Boston Post* thought it must have been produced at a much earlier age. We have no opinion on the subject ourselves, not having read it, but are disposed to believe the author, and should believe him if he said the same of the poems which we have read. We see no reason why they might not have been written at the age of ten: children are more apt, in remembering words, than men; and as there have been infant violinists, pianists, mimics and dancers, we see no reason why there should not be an infant rhythmist. A talent for versification may exist without a genius for poetry; and according to our own estimate of Mr POE's abilities, his poetical constitution is nothing more than an aptitude for rhythm. We should judge as much, from reading his criticisms of poetry, which seem to have been written after a very thorough cramming of BLAIR's lectures and the essays of Lord KAMES. In several instances he has asserted that there cannot be such a thing as a didactic poem. This demolishes at one swoop about nine-tenths of what the world has heretofore considered the highest poetry. If we can glean any distinct meaning from Mr POE's criticisms and verses, respecting his ideas of what constitutes a poem, it is this: a poem is a metrical composition without ideas. 'The Haunted Palace' and other of his best performances were certainly composed upon such a principle; and the same might be said of many of his prose essays, words being the sole substance in them. One of the reasons which he gives for publishing the 'poems written in youth' is a 'reference to the date of TENNYSON's first poems'. Whether he means by this to clear his own or TENNYSON's skirts from the taint of plagiarism, we do not understand. But we do not believe that anybody has ever dreamed of charging Mr POE with imitating TENNYSON in any of these 'poems written in youth'. It will not be a very easy matter, however, for him to convince the readers of TENNYSON that he did not draw largely upon that poet when he wrote 'Lenore'. It is a much more palpable imitation than LONGFELLOW's in his 'Midnight Mass for the Dying Year', which Mr POE has made so much noise about. Mr POE's tendency to extreme vagueness, which is the antipodes of poetical expression, shows itself plainly in the titles of his poems: one is addressed 'To the River——', as though there were something mighty private or naughty in his address to a running stream, which might compromise its character, if known. There are poems addressed 'To——', which, according to our author's theory, is a highly poetical designation, '——' being hazy to the last extreme: there is a poem addressed 'To F——' and another 'To F——s S. O——d'. This last is suggestive of a lady's name, FRANCES S. OSGOOD, and being a poetess herself, we extract the poem, both as a specimen of Mr POE's matured powers, and of the kind of epistle which a poet sends to a poetess:

Thou wouldst be loved? – then let thy heart
From its present pathway part not!
Being every thing which now thou art,
Be nothing which thou art not.
So with the world thy gentle ways,
Thy grace, thy more than beauty,
Shall be an endless theme of praise,
And love – a simple duty.

This is not one of the poems 'written in youth', but this which follows is:

'To——'

The bowers whereat, in dreams, I see
The wantonest singing birds,
Are lips, and all thy melody
Of lip-begotten words:

Thine eyes, in Heaven of heart enshrined,
Then desolately fall,
O God! on my funereal mind
Like starlight on a pall.

Thy heart! *thy* heart! I wake and sigh
And sleep to dream till day,
Of the truth that gold can never buy,
Of the baubles that it may.

'The child is father of the man', but the father in this case is superior to the offspring. There are probably very few boys who have enjoyed the privilege of a common-school education who have not written scores of verses like these; but it is a very rare occurrence for verses 'To——' to be published by their authors when they become men. This, however, is a mere matter of taste.

We have no disposition to criticise Mr. POE's poems: such as they are, we give them welcome. His reputation as a poet rests mainly upon 'The Raven', which, as we have already said, we consider an unique and musical piece of versification, but as a poem it will not bear scrutiny. If we were disposed to retort upon Mr POE for the exceedingly gross and false statements which, upon an imaginary slight, he made in his paper respecting this Magazine, we could ask for no greater favour than to be allowed to criticise his volume of poems. Surely no author is so much indebted to the forbearance of critics as Mr POE, and no person connected with the press in this country is entitled to less mercy or consideration. His criticisms, so called, are generally a tissue of coarse personal abuse or personal adulation. He has praised to the highest degree some of the paltriest writers in the country, and abused in the grossest terms many of the best. But criticism is his weakness: 'to that music he rises and flutters'. In ladies' magazines he is an ARISTARCHUS, but among men of letters his sword is a broken lath.

We are not much disappointed in the quality of Mr POE's poems, but the meagreness of his volume as to quantity is really surprising. He is one of the few authors by profession known to American readers; and considering that poetry is 'a passion' with him, and 'not a purpose', the little of any kind that he has produced is a thing to be wondered at. We do not know what the unhappy circumstances may be which have prevented him from making any 'serious effort' in his favorite pursuit; but his hinderances can hardly be greater than those under which the greater part of that which the world calls poetry has been produced. Has he been blind, like MILTON; has he been mad, like TASSO; been starved, like CHATTERTON; persecuted, like DANTE; exposed, like BYRON; harassed, like BURNS; depressed, like COWPER? Has he labored like ELLIOT; fought, like KORNER; been neglected, like BUTLER; bent, like DRYDEN, or tempted, as many noble poets have been, by luxury and sloth? A real poet will never tell of the hinderances to effort. It is overcoming hinderances which gives the surest testimony of ability. Nothing will excuse a poet for non-production but non-ability. Let the author produce his talent and say, ''Tis the best I could do'; excuses for not doing better will avail him nothing. Indeed, we are believers in CARLETON's Irish paradox, and think it as applicable to poets, 'who dare have it in them,' as to any body else; namely, that 'more men have risen in the world from the enmity of their enemies than from the kindness of their friends.' Poets, like other men, may become 'blue-moulded for want of a *batin*''. Whatever circumstances the true poet may be placed in, whether worried by affluence or depressed by misery, he will be a poet in spite of them; and his overcoming difficulties will be the best evidence of his 'passions'. Mr POE's passion for poetry must be a very tender one, or he would not come before the world at his age with such a volume, and with such an excuse for its meagreness. The history of genius hardly affords an instance of one born upon 'the field of his choice'. Shepherds have become astronomers, shoemakers mathematicians, barbers commanders, physicians architects, ploughmen poets, tailors statesmen, weavers artists. Judging from Mr POE's memoirs, which must be correct, since he circulates them himself, his opportunities for cultivating his passion have been superior to those enjoyed by any writer of reputation among us. But 'every heart knoweth its own bitterness', and we doubt not that Mr. POE's complaint is well founded. It is a painful reflection, however, that we have a great poet among us in such unhappy circumstances that he cannot develop his genius, nor make a serious effort in that kind of composition for which he has a consciousness of being qualified by nature. The circumstances must indeed be exceedingly unhappy and distressing, which would cause a poet to accept an invitation from a learned society to deliver an original poem at its annual meeting, and after receiving pay therefore, to read a rhapsody composed and published in his tenth year, and afterward bring forward, as proof of the stupidity of his audience, that they listened to him with civil attention. 'But something too much of this.'

75. [Lucius Alonzo Hine], 'Edgar A. Poe', Cincinnati *Quarterly Journal and Review*

January 1846, 1, 92–6

Hine (1819–1906), was trained as a lawyer, but became interested in radical religious and social ideas, which he promoted in a series of short-lived magazines – the *Quarterly Journal and Review* lasted only one year.

Edgar A. Poe occupies a conspicuous position in the literary world. He has attained considerable reputation as a prose and poetical writer. He is – what can be said of few – *sui generis*, stamped with his own originality. It seems to have been his aim to do and be something different from anyone else. In this, we think, he has rather strained himself, and overdone the thing. He has presumed largely on his own reputation to give credit to anything he might write, on the one hand, and largely on the gullibility of the people, on the other, to swallow his imaginings for realities. How far he has succeeded, his reputation answers. He has done many things well. His peculiar characteristic is wildness – etheriality, – though his celestial journies are not in circles, as are the flights of most other heavenly bodies; but in tangents – so that it is difficult, at all times, to find him. His mind is peculiarly nervous by nature. We never saw him, but can conceive him to be, in height about five feet nine, – in weight, about one hundred and thirty, – in age about forty – pale, cadaverous and Cassius looking, – with a large black eye, overhung with prominent perceptive faculties, and black, heavy eyebrows, – in demeanor, rather cold and unsocial, arising from his inattention to externals, and constant musings and dreamings with himself. His sleep is, doubtless, anything but quiet, owing to the chimeras, hobgoblins and spectres that dance in his visions. Mr. Poe has high claims to a substantial reputation as a critic. He has served in this capacity faithfully, as many an aspirant for fame can testify. He has clapped up more poetry than all the other critics of the land put together, and many a worshipper of the muse has shivered and shuddered before his words, as though they were a shower of brickbats.

On the whole, we regard him as no ordinary genius. He is a man of genius rather than talents, – though were his genius less, and his talents greater, he would do more for the good of the world, and his own reputation.

Now for the poems before us. Some of them are excellent. The author says in his preface, that his poems are collected chiefly to 'redeem them from the improvements to which they have been subjected in going the rounds of the press.' He confessess that they are of little value to the public, or credit to himself. He also says that poetry has been, with him, a passion, 'and the passions must be held in reverence; they must not – they cannot at will, be excited,' &c. This is modest enough, but not a very fair apology for discreditable and valueless poetry, for if he possesses the 'passion', and writes only when it impels, his effusions ought to be nothing else than good and soul-stirring.

The leading poem is 'The Raven', from which title few would conjecture its nature. It is a perfect original, and will live longer than its author.

The scene of 'The Raven' is his study, on a dreary midnight in bleak December. The author, weak and weary, pondered over the volumes of forgotten lore, until, beginning to nod, he heard a tapping at his door. Then follow ghosts, dancing on the floor – rustling of the purple curtains, as though they concealed some direful shape. He was thrilled, and trembled with fantastic terrors. He sorrowed for his radiant maiden, the lost Lenore. At length he summoned courage enough to peer into the darkness, though with much shivering, quivering, and dreaming dreams no mortal ever dared to dream before. But all was silent and dark, save the whispered word 'Lenore'. He turned back into his chamber, but still the tapping was louder than before. He then threw up the window-shutter, when, with many a flirt and flutter, stepped in a 'stately raven of the saintly days of yore,' which perched upon the bust of Pallas, above his chamber door.

> 'Though thy crest be shorn and shaven, thou,' I said, 'art sure
> no craven,
> Ghastly grim and ancient raven wandering from the Nightly
> shore –
> Tell me what thy lordly name is on the Night's Plutonian
> shore!'
> Quoth the raven, 'Nevermore'.

This reply, of course, occasions surprise, as no mortal had ever been known to be blessed with a talking-bird, sitting above his chamber door, named 'Nevermore'. The thought arises that he will leave him on the morrow, as 'other friends have flown before' – but the bird said 'Nevermore'.

[Quotes 'The Raven', stanza 11.]

Then began an earnest thinking what this ghastly ominous bird 'meant in croaking "Nevermore"'. After guessing, and fancying, and thinking awhile, –

[Quotes 'The Raven', stanzas 14–18.]

One objection we have to its general tenor, is that it associates the author with people of ancient times, when the fate of man was seen by the perverted imagination in the flight and song of ominous birds, or in the appearance of the intestines of the beasts sacrificed to the gods; and with those old women of the days of witchcraft, who were haunted, night and day, by horrid shapes and ghastly spectres. Only think, Edgar A. Poe – a thinker of the nineteenth century – the scourge of all who aspire to poesy – Edgar A. Poe frightened at the approach of a witch on a broomstick! See him tremble with affright, and quiver like an aspen leaf! See each 'particular hair stand on end, like quills upon the fretful porcupine.' If he had personified in this piece one of those curious beings who are startled at every rustling – afraid in the dark – unable to pass a graveyard, between sunset and dark, without fainting, and whose disordered brain reels with spectral delusions, he would have written more sensibly. However, we may be in error, – for perhaps he has represented himself with more truth than fiction, and the whole matter is natural.

With a word or two we dismiss 'The Raven'. In the fifth stanza

> Deep into that darkness peering, long I stood there wonder-
> .ing, fearing,
> Doubting, dreaming dreams no mortal ever dared to dream
> before;

We ask the reader to fancy Poe all shrivelled up, glaring wildly, and reaching forward to peer into the darkness to see what 'scared him'; ready, with hand on bolt, to dodge back and bolt the door, should he make a discovery in the *'darkness'*. 'Dream no mortal ever dared to dream before,' – we thought dreams were involuntary, and those we would least dare to dream, we are most apt to dream. Again, in the seventh verse, he flung up the shutter, and in there stepped a stately raven. Now, considering the chills that had crawled over him, while hearing the tapping at the door, the rustling of the curtains, and peering into the darkness, we should naturally expect a perfect congelation on the advent of the raven; but, on the contrary

> Then this ebony bird beguiling my sad fancy into smiling,
> By the grave and stern decorum of the countenance it wore,

Ah, Poe! this won't do; – let us have the whole thing, and not a jumbled up inconsistency. In another stanza his sad soul is beguiled into smiling by the same object 'whose fiery eyes *burned into his (sic) bosom's core*', and further on he represents himself as being haunted with horror, all of which will hardly sing on the same key with smiling. In the last stanzas quoted above, it has been asked where the lamp could have stood to stream its light over the raven sitting above his chamber door, and throw its 'shadow on the floor'?

'The Valley of Unrest', the second piece in this volume, is destitute of every mark of poetry, except its rhyme, which is very imperfect and the capitals that commence each line. The 'Bridal Ballad', is passable. 'The Sleeper' is imperfect in harmony, and we protest against the lines quoted below:

> My love, she sleeps! Oh, may her sleep,
> As it is lasting, so be deep!
> Soft may the worms about her creep.

Wretched must be the taste that relishes the last line in connection with the other two. Oh, Edgar!

'The Coliseum' is excellent. It carries us back to the ruins of Eld, and makes us feel the

> Vastness and Age! and memories of Eld!
> Silence! and Desolation! and dim Night!

that surround them.

The poem 'Israfel', is unworthy the talents of E.A. Poe. 'Dream-Land', 'To One in Paradise', and 'The Conqueror Worm', are of a high order for short poems. There are many other pieces in this volume, but none particularly striking except 'Scenes from Politian', an unpublished drama. The part given forces a desire to see the whole; which we hope Mr Poe will not be backward in handing over to the printer. In passing we must quote the following address of Lalange to a mirror:

[Quotes 'Politian', scene 4, lines 59–73.]

We had prepared an extended notice of this drama, but it proved too long for insertion in this number. It is, indeed, a readable production – but it is questionable whether it is adapted to the stage. As to this, however, we cannot judge until the whole be published. We close by asking Mr Poe's pardon for the liberty we have taken with his poems, and assuring him that a more careful examination would have enabled us to speak of them more justly.

76. [Thomas Kibble Hervey], review in the London *Athenaeum*

28 February 1846, pp. 215–16

Hervey (1799–1859) edited the *Athenaeum* (1846–53); his review was reprinted in *Littell's Living Age*, 9 (April 1846).

Much that calls itself poetry – and some that *is* so – comes to us from America; yet we have waited in vain for American poetry. Even what has reached us of the true ore has not the mark of the American mint – no peculiar stamp of the great continent – nothing to characterize it as American currency. The transatlantic poets give us back our own coin, thinned and deteriorated by the transit. As if America had not the ore of song in all her rivers, and a mint of her own on every mountain, she does little more for the service of the Muse than melt down our English gold and recast it in British forms.

It is Mr Poe's fancy to be original, – and it might, therefore, have been hoped that he would choose to be so after a native fashion. The instinct of borrowing must be unconquerable amongst a people who borrow even their *originality*. In the poetical department of mind it seems that England must grow even the singularities and absurdities of her distant brethren. In nearly all the other walks of intellect, America has shown itself quite equal to her own production alike of great things and of follies. Electing to be mystical, we should have been grateful to Mr Poe for a mysticism caught up on his own mountains, – fed on the far prairie, – watered by the mighty rivers of the land, – toned by the voice of the giant cataracts, – coloured by the hues of the transatlantic heaven, – and ministered to by those new and peculiar moral influences which should have an exponent in every utterance

251

of the American mind. But Mr Poe has taken his mystical degree in one of the worst of our London schools; where the art, as taught, consists in saying plain things enough after a fashion which makes them hard to be understood, and commonplace in a sort of mysterious form which causes them to sound oracular. This is to be regretted, because Mr Poe has a sense of picture and of music; and now and then, from out of the cloud, of a familiar pattern, in which it is his pleasure to involve himself, come an echo and a sign which there is no difficulty in recognizing as a breathing of the Muse. It is a pity still further, because Mr Poe is not a very successful cultivator of the formulae of his school; and there are too many times when he has probably desired to go no further in its ways than into the obscure – where the utmost extent of his ambition has been to be unintelligible – that he approaches dangerously near to the verge of the childish, and wanders on the very confines of the absurd. It might not, perhaps, be quite fair to allude to the scenes from 'Politian', an unpublished drama; because the excess of the puerile, there, amounts to dramatic imbecility, – and there are faults of different kinds, the absence of which in the other poems of the writer suggests that these are an early production, which the commonest exercise of discretion would have excluded from the volume. But Mr Poe is the author of a volume of *Tales;* to which allusion may be made here, as collateral illustrations at once of the merits and defects of his poetry. With very considerable powers of description, there is yet a fondness for the mystical in subject and manner – a constant straining after effect in intention, to which he has not the art of communicating an air of spontaneity by the covering of a warm and glowing style, – which make his prose the twin-brother of his poetry, though the older and more instructed brother of the two. Yet, as we have said, the poet, too, has occasional whispers from dreamland; and there are times when, from the maze of his eccentricities, a quaint spirit looks out, to whom these seem even to add something of character – when the very curiosities and crookednesses in the form of the instrument appear to lend something towards the fashioning of the wild and peculiar tone that issues through it. We are tempted to quote 'The Raven', as a strange specimen of the author's mannerisms, – yet involving a poetical feeling, of which the mannerisms themselves seem almost to make a part.

[Quotes 'The Raven'.]

That the author has both music and imagination may be gathered from his own poem of –

[Quotes 'Dream-land'.]

Into the region of Tycho Brahe's lost star – which appeared in the heavens for a few days only, and, after attaining a brilliancy surpassing that of Jupiter, disappeared as suddenly as it came, and has never since been seen – we confess our inability to follow our author. Something of the mystery that involves the planet has communicated itself to the poem – which, perhaps, the author may think a merit; but it has the disadvantage of not enabling the reader to judge of the amount of that merit. The sense of the vague and mysterious, no doubt, may be conveyed by mysterious music; but the character and meaning of the mystery wants some more intelligible exponent. The best advice which we can give to Mr Poe is to be simple and natural: – and, above all, to strike his harp amid the grand novelties which his own country presents. Their mere expression will be found to be rich in the effects which he seeks by means less legitimate; and to give an air of originality to his Muse which she will never wear in the most curiously-fashioned garment that can be furnished by the schools.

77. [William Gilmore Simms], review in the *Southern Patriot*

2 March 1846

It is a great error of the multitude to confound poetry with those things and arts upon which a judgement is easily made up. If the standards of poetry be fixed, as must be the case with all human arts before we can possibly or wisely sit in judgement upon them, it is equally certain that its varieties are endless, and each calls for standards of its own. The vulgar disregard of this necessity, is at the bottom of all the thousand blunders which presumption commits, whenever it places its beefy bulk in the *fauteuils* of literary criticism. There it sits, dispensing judgment with the most vulgar air of authority, without the slightest consciousness of the true nature of the case before it. Without dreaming of the true principles involved, and making the arbitrary dicta of its narrow experience or comprehension, the code by which to judge of principles and performance wholly foreign to all which it has ever known or understood. Thus, to the person who pins his faith to the style of composition peculiar to Pope and Dryden, this volume of Mr Poe will seem the most arrant nonsense. Such a person will be utterly at a loss to conceive the possibility of a human and sane reason having been present with the writer of the verses before us at any one moment during the performance of his whole task. The wild, fanciful and abstract character of these poems, will prove incomprehensible to him who requires that poetry shall embody an axiom in morals, or a maxim in philosophy or society, and the seemingly purposeless character – wholly purposeless in an economical and practical sense – of these phantasies, will seem to him worthy only of the inmates of a cell in Bedlam. Without going so far as to approve wholly of the scheme and tenor of Mr Poe's performances in verse, we must beg to caution those who, habituated to certain dissimilar kinds of composition, would utterly reject, or refuse any faith in their merits, that in making up their judgments, regard must be had to the not always understood varieties of poetry – to its wonderful flexibility – the numerous classes of style conception and utterance which it enjoys, – and the still more infinite forms in which it may hereafter, and in the hands of future artists be found to embody itself. We are apt, however wise, experienced and indulgent, to insist, after a certain age upon a certain routine in the course of our studies and reading; and to object to the novel and the unusual for no better reason than its singularity. Now, it is in poetry and the indefinite arts alone, that originality can be found or fancied, and a refusal to make the exception in respect to these has been the cause of all those unfortunate cases of judgement, which have had their decisions reversed by posterity. Mr Poe is a fantastic and a mystic – a man of dreamy mood and wandering fancies. His scheme of poem requires that his reader shall surrender himself to influences of pure imagination. He demands as a preliminary that you should recognize totally unreal premises – that you should yield yourself wholly to the witch element, as implicitly as Mephistopheles requires it of Faust, ascending the wizard eminences of the Brocken. Unless you can make him this concession you had better have nothing to do with his volume. At all events, for your mutual sakes, do not venture to pass any opinion upon it. He has not written for you, and you are not the critic for him.

We have already more than once had occasion to declare our high opinion of Mr Poe, as a largely endowed imaginative writer. It is not within the limits of a journal like this that we can be expected to go into any detailed consideration of his qualities. To say that he does justice to his endowments, however, must not be understood of us now when we declare our high respect for, and our great interest in their exercise. The training of Mr Poe has been unfavorable to his peculiar genius. He has been too much his own master; and his moods are too capricious, and his purpose is too desultory, to afford sufficient opportunity to his various resources for the exercise of art in fiction. And still, even with these qualifications to success, it is wonderful with what symmetry – a severe symmetry, we may call it – he can carry out a plan at once ingenious and exactly. How intensely he can pursue, to its close, a scheme of the imagination – imagination purely – rigidly defining his principles as he goes, step by step, and maintaining to the sequel, the most systematic combinations of proprieties and dependencies. Some of his stories are the most remarkable specimens of the power of *intensifying* a conception of pure romance, to the exclusion of all the ordinary agents of fiction, which have been written. – His poems are less elaborate, but belong to the same order of writings. 'The Raven', which in part gives its title to this volume, and the merits of which, more than any thing besides, has drawn the attention of the public recently to the claims of this writer, is a happy specimen of the manner in which his genius enables him to use a very simple and common place, incident for the purposes of pure imagination. A bird which has been taught by its owner to repeat a single word, wanders away from its keeper, and is heard tapping at the window of a melancholy student, who is sadly musing over the recent loss of a beloved one. He hears the tapping, opens the window, and the dark and glossy visitor glides in, musing aloud on the singularity of the visit, he is surprised to hear from the throat of the raven, a word which strangely accords with the subject of his musings. His superstitions are awakened and he apostrophizes the bird, – speaks of the dear one he has lost – declares his sombre meditations, and glimpses at the future. To all of these topics, the single utterance of the gloomy strayer is an appropriate and impressive answer. The beauty of the poem is in its picturesque, in the novelty of the conception, and the ingenuity with which the poet has so framed the language of the student, as to adapt it to the single word which is the only one in the vocabulary of the raven.

We can give but a single extract from this volume, which will exhibit equally the merits and faults of our author as a poet. It is not the best, by far, in the collection, but its character will perhaps, as well as any other, illustrate what we have been saying about the peculiarities of his genius as any other, and is short enough for our limits. The music of the verse, the vagueness of the delineation, its mystical character, and dreamy and spiritual fancies, are all highly characteristic:

[Quotes 'The Valley of Unrest'.]

78. Unsigned review in the London *Literary Gazette*

14 March 1846, pp. 237–8

This review was probably by William Jerdan (1782–1869), proprietor and editor of the *Literary Gazette*.

The genius of Edgar Poe, such as it is, had its full exposition and place assigned to it in the *Literary Gazette* of 31st January. Upon that critique we were favoured with the following letter:

To the Editor of the Literary Gazette.

Sir, – Having just read a review of Edgar Poe's Romances in the *Literary Gazette* of January, p. 101, allow me to advert to a curious misconception, in scientific point of view, which the author has fallen into. In describing his whirling *in the Maelstrom*, he says: 'On looking out when half-way down, the boat appeared hanging, as if by magic, *upon the interior surface* of a funnel of vast circumference and prodigious depth,' &c.... 'My gaze fell instinctively *down-wards*.... The smack hung on the *inclined surface of the pool, which sloped at an angle* of more than forty-five degrees; so that we *seemed* to be lying on our beam-ends,' &c.

Now, with all deference, I would submit: 1st. That our only notions of *up* and *down* are derived from the direction of gravity. When, therefore, the direction of gravity is changed by centrifugal force, *that* direction will still *appear* to be *down*. 2nd. That our only sense of motion is *relative*; when, therefore, all that is visible is rotating along with ourselves, we shall have no sense of motion; and in few cases do we ever *ourselves* appear to be the moving objects (witness the case of railway travelling). The only apparent motion will be the slight *difference of motion* between the various objects and ourselves.

Whence it appears, that the gentleman in the predicament described would, on looking about him, see a vast funnel of water apparently *laid on its side*, with its lower side horizontal, at which lower part his boat would *always appear to be lying*; the heavens appearing *at one end horizontally, and apparently rotating*; while the chaotic abyss and foam would be at the opposite end; the waters appearing (full of local currents, no doubt) stretching in a miraculous archway or tunnel, *almost motionless*, about and over the boat, and apparently supported by nothing; and objects nearer the entrance would appear to rotate vertically in a *slowly* retrograde direction; while objects would appear to have an opposite rotation, more and more rapid, towards the misty tumultuous end; the real velocity of the whole being unperceived, except by the contrary apparent rotation of the heavens. This would indeed be a wondrous spectacle, though scarcely sufficing to induce a personal experiment by your humble servant.

WILLIAM PETRIE.[1]

If such objections can justly be raised against his prose, we fear we must allow that some of his poetry is not less wild; or, in other words, that there is not so much method in his *furor* as could be desired by readers not inflamed and carried away by his vague thoughts and diction. It is true the author himself says of them:

'In defence of my own taste, nevertheless, it is incumbent upon me to say, that I think nothing in this volume of much value to the public, or very creditable to myself. Events not to be controlled have prevented me from making, at any time, any serious efforts in what, under happier circumstances, would have been the field of my choice. With me poetry has been not a purpose, but a passion; and the passions should be held in reverence: they must not, they cannot at will be excited with an eye to the paltry compensations, or the more paltry commendations, of mankind.'

This is the Ercles vein, and we have no disposition to

quarrel with it. If Mr Poe published to please only himself, he has a perfect right to be his own critic, and to despise all others. We shall merely offer an example and an opinion or two. From 'The Sleeper' we take the annexed, as a specimen of bad taste and exaggeration:

[Quotes 'The Sleeper', lines 45–60.]

Here is another sample of the morbid:

[Quotes 'The Conqueror Worm'.]

Scenes from 'Politian', an unpublished drama, lead to some compositions of youthful days; but we do not meet with aught to tempt us to farther extract.

The volume is dedicated to Elizabeth Barrett Barrett, whose style, as well as Tennyson's, seems to have considerable influence on Mr Poe. The two volumes of that lady² lie before us, evidences of her powers, who said of poetry that it had been as serious a thing as life itself to her: the consequences of which feeling is the high elevated tone of her compositions, whose devoted earnestness is only slightly affected by somewhat of the masculine and pedantic; her lofty aspirations tend to this result, the use of strange language and the strange application of words, as if they had any meaning she wished, and not their common acceptation. Daring, and almost able enough to bend the bow of Milton; as when she tells us, when Adam and Eve flee into the wilderness, 'there is a sound through the silence, as of the falling tears of an angel!' and this, with the deep religious reverence, renders it easy to conceive how her writings should affect the imaginative mind of the American author. In some points it might have been better had he studied her more closely.

NOTES

1 William Petrie was a chemist, civil engineer, and surveyor.
2 Published by Moxon in 1844.

79. Unsigned review in the London *Critic*

4 April 1846, 3, 257–8

In an early number of the *Critic* we presented to our readers a very remarkable poem, entitled 'The Raven', which had been sent to us from America. It was its first appearance in England, and it attracted a great deal of notice, and went the round of the provincial papers.[1] Mr POE, the author, has now published it in a volume, as the foremost of a collection of poems written by him for divers periodicals, and which his friends have deemed worthy of being rescued from the rapid oblivion of the journals.

Mr POE is intensely American; but, unfortunately, we cannot employ this term in the same sense in which we use the words 'German', 'English', 'French', and so forth, as applied to literature. These latter mean a certain individuality of thought as well as of language; but when we speak of a literature or a style as American, we mean a strain of thought, utterly without nationality, and a style peculiarly its own. It is the fault of all the authors America has produced, with the exception of BRYANT, that, for aught in their subjects or the manner of treating them, they might have been born and brought up in any part of the world. Their country does not colour their thoughts or mould their imagery; they are essentially imitative; they echo the ideas wafted to them from England, and with the feebleness of echoes. The characteristic of American literature is, the absence of a character.

But we beg pardon – we must modify this assertion. The style is peculiar; it is marked by diffuseness, as if words were thoughts, and consequent feebleness. To weave smooth sentences and rounded periods appears to be the aim, as if they were ignorant of the force frequently obtained by the introduction of discords. It must, however, be conceded to

them, that they have a musical ear, and that we seldom find
in American poetry the sins against metre and rhyme so
constantly offending in the works even of those of our own
poets who may claim a respectable position. Mr POE has not
escaped the error of his countrymen. The poems before us
are all marked by the peculiarities we have noticed. He is, as
we gather from the indications afforded by the subjects
selected and the manner of treating them, a young man, we
suspect a very young man. If so, there is good stuff in him.
He has the foundation of the poet, and industry and
experience may raise a structure that will be an honour to his
own country, and the admiration of ours. But to accomplish
this, he must work hard, and aim at excellence; he must look
at what he has done as only dim intimations of what he is to
do – at the lowest steps of the ladder, he must climb before he
will be admitted into the temple of fame. He must write
much, and blot much, and burn much – without remorse or
hesitation; and from this time forth resolve to give to the
world only the *best* productions of his brain; and for these to
rely upon the approval of a judicious friend, rather than upon
his own judgment; the parent of a poem, like the father of a
child, being apt to love best his most rickety bantling.

That Mr POE has something in him, but that he wants
pruning and training, will be apparent from the singular
poem of 'The Raven', for which the reader is referred to the
first volume of the *Critic*, as from the following, which are
among the most favourable specimens of his genius contained in the collection before us.

First, for a poem that reminds us forcibly of TENNYSON.

[Quotes 'The Valley of Unrest'.]

Undoubtedly there is poetry in this. And the next is after
the manner of COLERIDGE. Although we must acknowledge
its beauty, it will be observed that it illustrates the remarks
previously made as to the imitative character of American
literature.

[Quotes 'The Sleeper'.]

There is power of painting in

[Quotes 'Dream-Land'.]

More than half the volume is occupied with 'Poems written in youth'. They serve, at least, to mark the great progress the author has made; otherwise they are not worth the paper on which they are printed.

We shall be glad to meet Mr POE again, both in prose and poetry. His volume of tales we reviewed some time since.

NOTE

1 The *Critic* copied 'The Raven' from the *American Review* in its issue of 14 June 1845, 2, 148. The only provincial printing so far located is that in the *Birmingham Journal*, 28 June 1845, p.3.

80. [Nathaniel Parker Willis], review in the *National Press: A Home Journal*

10 October 1846, 2, 3

Willis and George P. Morris founded the *National Press: A Home Journal* in February 1846; in November it began to appear under its more familiar subtitle. On his return from Europe in March 1846, Willis found Poe in a pitiful condition: he was ill, poverty-stricken, hounded and ridiculed by his enemies over the 'Literati' papers, and deep in scandal and litigation. Willis's article was less a review than a gesture of friendship and support for Poe (*The Raven and Other Poems* had been in print for almost a year); and it was followed by a well-meaning but insensitive plea in the *Home Journal* (26 December 1846) for Poe to be treated as an object of public charity, and placed in a special 'Hospital for Disabled Labourers with the Brain' – see Sidney P. Moss, *Poe's Major Crisis*, pp. 139–42.

We take this work, not so much with a view to a particular examination of its merits, as for the purpose of saying to Mr Poe, how much greater pleasure it gives us to meet him in his own proper field of poetical creation, than in the uncomfortable regions of criticism and controversy.

Mr Poe is, unquestionably, a man of genius. Narratives which rivet the interest, and sway the passions, as powerfully as his do, indicate a vigour of imagination that might send its productions forward far along the line of future life. Many of these tales we have no doubt, will long survive, as among the ablest and most remarkable of American productions. In the perfect contrivance of the plans, which, though complex, are never embarrassing or perplexing, and in the orderly evolvement of all the incidents, they bear a resemblance to the dramatic plots of Ben Jonson, which of themselves, without reference to the treasures which they wrap up in them, have been considered as giving him a very eminent rank. Of the talents such as Mr Poe is blessed with, the true employment is in original composition; in a genial exercise of the creative faculties of imagination and feeling, in extending through a space which is else void and silent, the limits of the region of living and lovely forms, and augmenting the trophies of the genius of his nation and his race. To one who possesses the powers of close, logical reasoning and of pointed and piercing sarcasm, the *torpe voluptas* of literature and social controversy is often a fatal fascination. But a man who is conscious within himself of faculties which indicate to him that he was born, not to wrangle with men of his own times, but to speak truth and peace to distant ages and a remote posterity, ought to make a covenant with himself, that he will be drawn aside by no temptation, however vehement from that calm dedication of his thoughts to literary art, which is the service he owes to that spirit which has given him power to become one of its ministers.

As an analytical critic, Mr Poe possesses abilities, in our opinion, quite unrivalled in this country, and perhaps on either side of the water. We have scarcely ever taken up one of his more critical papers, on some author or work worthy of his strength, without a sense of surprise at the novel and profound views from which his inquiries began, nor followed their development without the closest interest, nor laid the essay down without admiration and respect for the masculine and acute understanding with which we had coped during the perusal. But in the case of inventive genius so brilliant and vigorous as is shown in these poems, and in the tales to which we have alluded, we feel that even criticism of the highest kind is an employment below the true measure of its dignity, and, we may say, its duty; for to be tender of the light in another man's tomb, is no fit occupation for one who is able to kindle a lamp of his own, whose ray may abide against all the forces of night, and storms, and time. The poet's is a consecrating gift. A man who can produce such a work as 'The Raven', ought to feel that it was his office to afford subjects, and not models, to criticism.

81. William Gilmore Simms, 'From Our Correspondent', *Southern Patriot*

20 July 1846

Simms's letter from New York covers the literary happenings of the summer; only the portion dealing with Poe is reproduced here.

... Among the petty excitements common to authorship is that which Mr Edgar A. Poe is producing by his pencil sketches of the New York Literati in *Godey's Lady's Magazine*. He has succeeded most happily (if such was the object), in fluttering the pigeons of this dove cote. His sketches, of which we have seen but a few, are given to a delineation as well of the persons as of the performances of his subjects. Some of them are amusing enough. I am not prepared to say how true are his sketches, but they have caused no little rattling among the dry bones of our Grub street. Of Poe, as a writer, we know something. He is undoubtedly a man of very peculiar and very considerable genius – but is irregular and exceedingly mercurial in his temperament. He is fond of mystifying in his stories, and they tell me, practises upon this plan even in his sketches; more solicitous, as they assert, of a striking picture than a likeness. Poe, himself, is a very good looking fellow. I have seen him on two or three occasions, and have enjoyed a good opportunity of examining him carefully. He is probably thirty three or four years old, some five feet eight inches in height, of rather slender person, with a good eye, and a broad intelligent forehead. He is a man, clearly, of sudden and uneven impulses, of great nervous susceptibility, and one whose chief misfortune is not to have been caught young and trained carefully. The efforts of his mind seem wholly spasmodic. He lacks habitual industry, I take it, which, in the case of the literary man who must look to his daily wits for his daily bread, is something of a deficiency. He, also, is in obscurity somewhere in the country, and sick, according to a report which reached me yesterday, of brain fever.[1]

NOTE

1 The rumour that Poe was deranged was circulating in New York at the time.

82. [Evert Augustus Duyckinck], 'An Author in Europe and America', *Home Journal*

9 January 1847

This piece was written at Poe's request: on 30 December he had sent letters and notes on his publications to Duyckinck, asking him to 'make a paragraph or two for some one of the city papers', adding, 'Willis or Morris will put in anything you may be kind enough to write; but as the *Home Journal* has already said a good deal about me, some other paper would be preferable' (*Letters*, 2, 336). Evidently Duyckinck was unable to satisfy Poe's preference.

While Mr Poe, an author of understood merits, quite unique and apart from the rest of the literary race in his literary productions, which are all his own, *paid for by himself in actual experience of heart and brain*, is pestered and annoyed at home by penny-a-liners whom his iron pen has cut into too deeply, and denied all ability and morality whatever – it is curious to contrast this with his position abroad, where distance suffers only the prominent features of his genius to be visible, and see what is made of his good qualities in Europe.

Why the American press should be so intolerant of the original authors of the country, and battle with them at every step, while the most liberal good words are freely accorded to mediocrity, and imitative talents, is one of those little problems of human nature, well enough for Rochefoucauld to pry into, but which we have too much of the wisdom of the serpent and the good feeling of the dove to meddle with. The fact is, that our most neglected and best abused authors, are generally our best authors.

The reception of Mr Poe's tales in England is well known. The mystification of M. Valdemar was taken up by a mesmeric journal as a literal verity, and enquiries were sent on here, to be supplied (in case the historian of the event were not accessible) by personal solicitation of the poor victim's neighbours at Harlem, where the scene was laid.[1] A London publisher has got it out, in pamphlet, under the title of 'Mesmerism in Articulo Mortis',[2] and a Scotchman in Stonehaven has recently paid a postage by steamer, in a letter to the author, to test the matter-of-factness of the affair. We can conceive of nothing more impressive in the way of curiosity.[3] Miss Barrett, by the way, paid the author a handsome compliment on this story. After admiring the popular credulity, she says 'The certain thing in the tale in question, is the power of the writer, and the faculty he has of making horrible improbabilities seem near and familiar.'[4]

The tale of the 'Murders in the Morgue' [*sic*], is giving rise to various editorial perplexities, in Paris. It has been translated by the feuilletons, local personal allusions discovered and the American authorship denied. One of the journals says 'if there turn out to be such an American author, it will prove that America has at least one novelist besides Mr Cooper' – and this, in France, is praise. The *Revue des deux Mondes*, in the meantime, has an elaborate review of the *Tales*. The *North American Review* of the same date calls them trash.[5]

Besides a peculiar vein of invention, Mr Poe has a style, a clearness, cleanness and neatness of expression, which, together, will always make their way. They are unmistakeable classic elements. By them Mr Poe will live. A writer so ready in *new resources* as Mr Poe, should command his own terms and full employment from the trade. It is a duty they owe the world, to astonish it now and then by some clever performance, and a duty they owe to their own families to put money in their pockets. An occasional book from Mr Poe would unite these desirable conditions.

NOTES

1 See No. 49.
2 *Mesmerism 'in Articulo Mortis'. An Astounding and Horrifying Narrative Shewing the Extraordinary Power of Mesmerism in Arresting the Process of Death, By Edgar A. Poe, Esq. of New York*, was published by Short & Co. (London, 1846), price three pence.
3 The man in question was Archibald Ramsay, a druggist, who dabbled in the 'new sciences' – see *Works*, 17, 268–9.
4 This is from a private letter, not a review – see *Works*, 17, 229–30.
5 *North American Review*, 63 (October 1846), 359.

83. Philip Pendleton Cooke, 'Edgar A. Poe', *Southern Literary Messenger*

January 1848, 14, 34–8

Poe suggested that Cooke should revise Lowell's memoir of him for his projected book on 'The Living Literati of the U.S.': he wrote on 16 April 1846, 'I fancy that you appreciate me – estimate my merits & demerits at a just value' (*Letters*, 2, 314). Cooke did not reply until 4 August, but then he did agree to 'continue the memoir' (*Works*, 17, 262–4), and Poe supplied him with some further information – see *Letters*, 2, 327–30. Poe's book never appeared.

[The following paper is a sequel to Mr Lowell's memoir, (so called,) of Mr Poe, published two or three years since in *Graham's Magazine*. Mr P. edited the *Messenger* for several years, and the pages of that Magazine would seem therefore a proper place for the few hurried observations which I have here made upon his writings and genius. P.P.C.]

Since the memoir of Mr Poe, written by James Russell Lowell, appeared, Mr P. has written some of his best things; amongst them 'The Raven', and 'Dreamland' – poems – and M. Valdemar's case – a prose narrative.

'The Raven' is a singularly beautiful poem. Many readers who prefer sunshine to the weird lights with which Mr Poe fills his sky, may be dull to its beauty, but it is none the less a great triumph of imagination and art. Notwithstanding the extended publication of this remarkable poem, I will quote it almost entire – as the best means of justifying the praise I have bestowed upon it.

The opening stanza rapidly and clearly arranges time, place, etc., for the mysteries that follow.

[Quotes the first stanza of 'The Raven'.]

Observe how artistically the poet has arranged the circumstances of this opening – how congruous all are. This congruity extends to the phraseology; every word is admirably selected and placed with reference to the whole. Even the word 'napping' is well chosen, as bestowing a touch of the fantastic, which is subsequently introduced as an important component of the poem. Stanza 2d increases the distinctness and effect of the picture as already presented to us. The 'Midnight Dreary' is a midnight 'in the bleak December', and the 'dying embers' are assuming strange and fantastic shapes upon the student's hearth. We now pass these externals and some words of exquisite melody let us into the secret of the rooted sorrow which has led to the lonely night-watching and fruitless study.

> Vainly I had sought to borrow
> From my books surcease of sorrow – sorrow
> for the lost Lenore –
> For the rare and radiant maiden, *whom the angels name Lenore,*
> *Nameless here forever more.*

A death was never more poetically told than in the italicised words. The 'tapping' is renewed –

[Quotes stanza 3 of 'The Raven'.]

After some stanzas, quaint and highly artistical, the raven is found at the window; I quote now continuously to the end.

[Quotes the rest of 'The Raven'.]

The rhythm of this poem is exquisite, its phraseology is in the highest degree musical and apt, the tone of the whole is wonderfully sustained and appropriate to the subject, which, full as it is of a wild and tender melancholy, is admirably well chosen. This is my honest judgement; I am fortified in it by high authority. Mr Willis says:–

[Quotes Willis's introduction to 'The Raven' in the *Evening Mirror*.]

Miss Barrett says: – 'This vivid writing! – this power *which is felt!* "The Raven" has produced a sensation – a "fit horror" here in England. Some of my friends are taken by the fear of it, and some by the music. I hear of persons *haunted* by the Nevermore, and one acquaintance of mine, who has the misfortune of possessing a bust of Pallas, never can bear to look at it in the twilight. Our great poet, Mr Browning, author of *Paracelsus*, etc., is enthusiastic in his admiration of the rhythm.... Then there is a tale of his which I do not find in this volume, but which is going the rounds of the newspapers, about mesmerism, throwing us all into most "admired disorder", or dreadful doubts as to whether it can be true, as the children say of ghost stories. The certain thing in the tale in question is the power of the writer, and the faculty he has of making horrible improbabilities seem near and familiar.'[1]

The prose narrative, 'M. Valdemar's Case' – the story of which Miss Barrett speaks – is the most truth-like representation of the impossible ever written. M. Valdemar is mesmerized *in articulo mortis*. Months pass away, during which he appears to be in mesmeric sleep; the mesmeric influence is withdrawn, and instantly the body becomes putrid and loathsome – *he has been many months dead*. Will the reader believe that men were found to credit this wild story? And yet some very respectable people believed in its truth firmly. The editor of the Baltimore *Visiter* republished it as a statement of facts, and was at the pains to vouch for Mr Poe's veracity. If the letter of a Mr Collier [*sic*], published just after the original appearance of the story, was not a quiz, he also fell into the same trap. I understand that some foreign mesmeric journals, German and French, reprinted it as being what it purported to be – a true account of mesmeric phenomena.[2] That many others were deceived in like manner by this strange tale, in which, as Miss Barrett says, 'the wonder and question are, can it be true?' is very probable.

With Mr Poe's more recent productions I am not at all acquainted – excepting a review of Miss Barrett's works, and an essay on the philosophy of composition. The first of these contains a great deal of noble writing and excellent criticism; the last is an admirable specimen of analysis. I believe Mr P. has been for some time ill – has recently sustained a heavy domestic bereavement – and is only now returning to his literary labours. The public will doubtless welcome the return of so favorite an author to pursuits in which heretofore he has done so much and so well.

Unnecessary as the labor may be, I will not conclude this postscript to Mr Lowell's memoir, without making some remarks upon Mr Poe's genius and writings generally.

Mr P.'s most distinguishing power is that which made the extravagant fiction of 'M. Valdemar's Case' sound like truth. He has De Foe's peculiar talent for filling up his pictures with minute life-like touches – for giving an air of remarkable naturalness and truth to whatever he paints. Some of his stories, wrtitten many years ago, are wonderful in this fidelity and distinctness of portraiture; 'Hans Phaall', 'A Descent into the Maelström', and 'MS. Found in a Bottle', show it in an eminent degree. In the first of these a journey to the moon is described with the fullness and particularity of an ordinary traveller's journal; entries, astronomical and thermical, and, on reaching the moon, botanical, and zoölogical, are made with an inimitable matter-of-fact air. In 'A Descent into the Maelström' you are made fairly to feel yourself on the descending round of the vortex, convoying fleets of drift timber, and fragments of wrecks; the terrible whirl makes you giddy as you read. In the 'MS. Found in a Bottle' we have a story as wild as the mind of man ever conceived, and yet made to sound like the most matter-of-fact veracious narrative of a seaman.

But in Mr Poe, the peculiar talent to which we are indebted for Robinson Crusoe, and the memories of Captain Monroe, has an addition. Truthlike as nature itself, his strange fiction shows constantly the presence of a singularly adventurous, very wild, and thoroughly poetic imagination. Some sentences from them, which always impressed me deeply, will give full evidence of the success with which this rare imaginative power is made to adorn and ennoble his truthlike pictures. Take this passage from 'Ligeia', a wonderful story, written to show the triumph of the human will even over *death*. Ligeia, in whom the struggle between the will to live, and the power of death, has seemed to terminate in the defeat of the passionate will, is consigned to the tomb. Her husband marries a second wife, 'the fair-haired and blue-eyed Lady

Rowena'. By the sick bed of this second wife, who is dying from some mysterious cause, he sits.

[Quotes from 'Ligeia', from 'I sat by the side of her ebony bed,' to 'three or four large drops of a brilliant and ruby-colored fluid', *Works*, 2, 262–3.]

Again take this passage from 'The Fall of the House of Usher':

From that chamber, and from that mansion, I fled aghast. The storm was still abroad in all its wrath as I found myself crossing the old causeway. Suddenly there shot along the path a wild light, and I turned to see whence a gleam so unusual could have issued – for the vast house and its shadows were alone behind me. *The radiance was that of the full, setting, and blood-red moon, which now shone vividly through that once barely-discernible fissure of which I have before spoken, as extending from the roof of the building, in a zig-zag direction to the base.*

These quoted passages – the 'white and ghastly spectrum of the teeth' in 'Berenice' – the visible vulture eye, and audible heart-beat in the 'Tell-Tale Heart' – the resemblance in 'Morella' of the living child to the dead mother, becoming gradually fearful, until the haunting eyes gleam out a terrible *identity*, and prove as in 'Ligeia' the final conquest of the will over death – these and a thousand such clinging ideas, which Mr P's writings abound in, prove indisputably that the fires of a great poet are seething under those analytic and narrative powers *in which no living writer equals him.*

This added gift of a daring and wild imagination is the source of much of the difference between our author and De Foe. De Foe loves and deals always with the homely. Mr Poe is nervously afraid of the homely – has a creed that Beauty is the goddess of the Poet: – not Beauty with a swelling bust, and lascivious carriage, exciting passions of the blood, but Beauty sublimated and cherished by the soul – the beauty of the Uranian, not Dionean Venus. De Foe gives us the cheerful and delightful story of his colonist of the desert isles, (which has as sure a locality in a million minds as any genuine island has upon the maps,) a clear, plain, true-sounding narrative of matters that might occur any day. His love for the real makes him do so. The 'real' of such a picture has not strangeness enough in its proportions for Mr Poe's imagination; and, with the same talent for truth-like narrative, to what different results of creation does not his imagination, scornful of the soberly real, lead him! Led by it he loves to adventure into what in one of his poems he calls –

> a wild weird clime
> Out of space, out of time; –

deals in mysteries of 'life in death,' dissects monomania, exhibits convulsions of soul – in a word, wholly leaves beneath and behind him the wide and happy realm of the common cheerful life of man.

That he would be a greater favorite with the majority of readers if he brought his singular capacity for vivid and truth-like narrative to bear on subjects nearer ordinary life, and of a more cheerful and happy character, does not, I think, admit of a doubt. But whether with the few he is not all the more appreciable from the difficult nature of the fields which he has principally chosen, is questionable. For what he has done, many of the best minds of America, England and France, have awarded him praise; labors of a tamer nature might not have won it from such sources. For my individual part, having the seventy or more tales, analytic, mystic, grotesque, arabesque, always wonderful, often great, which his industry and fertility have already given us, I would like to read one cheerful book made by his *invention*, with little or no aid from its twin brother *imagination* – a book in his admirable style of full, minute, never tedious narrative – a book full of homely doings, of successful toils, of ingenious shifts and contrivances, of ruddy firesides – a book healthy and happy throughout, and with no poetry in it at all anywhere, except a good old English 'poetic justice' in the end. Such a book, such as Mr Poe could make it, would be a book for the million, and if it did nothing to exalt him with the few, would yet certainly *endear* him to them.

Mr Lowell has gone deeply and discriminatingly into Mr Poe's merits as a poet. Any elaborate remarks of mine on the same subject, would be out of place here. I will not, however, lose this opportunity of expressing an admiration which I have long entertained of the singular mastery of certain externals of his art which he everywhere exhibits in his verse. His rhythm, and his vocabulary, or phraseology, are perhaps perfect. The reader has perceived the beauty of the rhythm in 'The Raven'. Some other verses from poems to which Mr Lowell has referred are quite as remarkable for this beauty. Read these verses from 'Lenore': –

Come let the burial rite be read – the funeral song be sung! –
An anthem for the queenliest dead that ever died so young –
A dirge for her the doubly dead that ever died so young.

        *   *   *

The sweet Lenore hath gone before, with hope that flew
    beside,
Leaving thee wild, for the dear child, that should have been
    thy bride –
For her the fair, and debonair, that now so lowly lies,
The life upon her yellow hair, but not within her eyes –
The life still there upon her hair, – the death upon her eyes.

        *   *   *

Avaunt! to-night my heart is light. No dirge will I upraise,
But waft the angel on her flight with a Paean of old days!

        *   *   *

And take these, in the most graceful of all measures – they are from 'To one in Paradise'.

And all my days are trances
   And all my nightly dreams
Are where thy dark eye glances,
   And where thy footstep gleams –
In what etherial dances,
   By what etherial streams.

Along with wonderful beauty of rhythm, these verses show the exquisite taste in phraseology, the nice sense of melody and aptness in words, of which I spoke. We have direct evidence of this nice sense of verbal melody in some quotations which are introduced into the dramatic fragment 'Politian'. Lalage reads from a volume of our elder English Dramatists:

[Quotes from 'Politian', scene four, lines 5–19; *Poems*, pp. 260–1.]

I must conclude these insufficient remarks upon a writer worthy of high and honourable place amongst the leading creative minds of the age.

As regards the Wiley & Putnam publication of Mr Poe's tales – a volume by which his rare literary claims have been most recently presented to the public – I think the book in some respects does him injustice. It contains twelve tales out of more than seventy; and it is made up almost wholly of what may be called his analytic tales. This is not *representing* the author's mind in its various phases. A reader gathering his knowledge of Mr Poe from this Wiley & Putnam issue would perceive nothing of the diversity and variety in their *full* force; but much more might have been done to represent his mind by a judicious and not wholly one-toned selection.

NOTES

1 This extract from a private letter from Miss Barrett to Poe dated April 1846 (*Works*, 17, 229–30) is made to read as if it were a review.
2 Dr Robert H. Collyer wrote to Poe on the 'Valdemar' case, and Poe published his letter in the *Broadway Journal* – see, *Works*, 17, 225–6. No French or German printings have been located.

EUREKA

1848

84. John Henry Hopkins, report on 'The Universe' in the New York *Evening Express*

4 February 1848

In a letter to George W. Eveleth (29 February 1848), Poe declared: 'The only report... which approaches the truth, is the one I enclose – from the *Express* – written by E.A. Hopkins [*sic*] – a gentleman of much scientific acquirement – son of Bishop Hopkins of Vermont – but he conveys only my general idea, and his digest is full of inaccuracies' (*Letters*, 2, 361). Poe, however, confused E.A. Hopkins with his brother, Reverend John Henry Hopkins Jr (1820–91), who was at that time preparing for the ministry. Hopkins was a confidant of Poe's friend Mrs Shew, and after hearing Poe's lecture, he took a special interest in *Eureka* – see his letter of 1875 to Mrs Shew (then Mrs Houghton) printed in John Carl Miller, *Building Poe Biography* (Baton Rouge and London, 1977), pp. 100–1; also No. 87.

Mr Poe's lecture on the Universe, at the Society Library Room, on Thursday evening, we regard as beyond all question the most elaborate and profound effort we ever listened to in the shape of a lecture; one evincing a more extensive investigation, a more original train of thought, a greater complexity of detail, all subjected to the one great unity of fundamental thought, than we ever had thought it possible to compress into one evening's discourse. The work has all the completeness and oneness of plot required in a poem, with all the detail and accuracy required in a scientific lecture. The fundamental conception is one which was generated in the highest regions of the pure imagination, and radiating thence seemed to illumine with its light all the facts that experiment and observation could throw in its way. Starting from the Deity, as a comet from the Sun, it went careering onward in its march through infinite space, approaching more and more closely the comprehension of man, until bending its course gradually homeward at length, it drew nearer and nearer, grew brighter and brighter, until it buried itself in a blaze of glory from whence it had its birth. It would be impossible to give any respectable report of this extraordinary work of Art without devoting several columns to it, and even then justice could not be done. For the immense ground covered by the Lecturer rendered compression and close condensation one of the leading characteristics of his performance, so in reality it should be published as delivered in order to present it fairly to the mind of the reader. We can therefore give only a meagre outline, but one sufficient to show to an intellect capable of comprehending such subjects what must have been made of so sublime a theme by the searching analysis, the metaphysical acumen, the synthetic power and the passion for analogical and serial development of idea according to preconceived law, all which qualities are exemplified by Mr Poe to a degree unsurpassed in this country, at least, so far as we are acquainted.

[Then follows a digest of Poe's lecture.]

The conclusion of this brilliant effort was greeted with warm applause by the audience, who had listened with chained attention throughout. We regret that the audience was not more numerous, for seldom is there an opportunity to hear a production like this; a production which proves not only that its author is a man of uncommon powers, but that those powers are growing stronger and deeper as they are further developed, and that the goodly tree bids fair to bring forth still nobler fruit than has ever yet been shaken from its flowery and fragrant boughs.

85. Unsigned notice in the New York *Evening Express*

12 July 1848

A most extraordinary essay upon the material and spiritual Universe, – but one to which we are at this moment unable to do anything like adequate justice, – the work itself having barely made its appearance from the press of Mr Putnam. Those of our readers who remember a report of Mr Poe's Lecture at the Society Library, a few months ago, which appeared in this journal at the time, may gather some idea of the work before us from the fact that the lecture has been expanded, with really consummate art – but this was to be expected from the admitted genius of its author – into an elegant volume of nearly 150 pages, in which the ideas which were then set forth with such novelty and effect, have been carefully arranged in a more elaborate form for the public eye. We shall be greatly surprised if this work does not create a most profound sensation among the literary and scientific classes all over the union – displaying as it does a reasoning power and grasp of thought which cannot possibly fail to excite the 'Special Wonder' of even the most careless reader. In respect of novelty, Mr Poe's new theory of the Universe will certainly attract universal attention, in as much as it is demonstrated, so to speak, with a degree of logical acumen which has certainly not been equalled since the days of Sir Isaac Newton, and can hardly be said to have been excelled even by that great philosopher. But we must bring a brief notice of this extraordinary book to a hurried close here – earnestly recommending it to everyone of our readers as one that can in no event fail to shed an unfailing lustre upon the American name, as a work of almost unequalled power in respect to philosophical research and speculative force. Mr Poe has appropriately dedicated it 'With very profound respect,' to Alexander von Humboldt, whose well known

Cosmos he very justly ranks higher than any other work upon the same subject.

86. [Epes Sargent], notice in the Boston *Transcript*

20 July 1848

According to a clipping in the Ingram Collection, University of Virginia, the reviewer was Sargent (1813–80), the Boston author and journalist who succeeded Cornelia Walter as editor of the *Transcript*.

The author says in his preface, 'What I here propound is true: – therefore it cannot die: or if by any means it be now trodden down so that it die, it will "rise again to the life everlasting."' To all of which the knowing reader, if he be one of the vulgar, will be apt to reply by placing his forefinger on the side of his nose, and ejaculating humph! Mr Poe proposes here to give us an essay on the material and spiritual universe, and he dedicates his work 'with very profound respect' to Alexander von Humboldt. So ingeniously does he smatter of astronomical systems, concentric circles, centrifugal forces, planetary distances, the Nebular theory and the star Alpha Lyrae, that we should not be surprised if the great cosmogonist himself were to be dismayed by the lavish ostentation of scientific lore, and of conceits, which if not philosophical, will be likely to pass for such with the mass of readers even as paste settings pass for diamonds of the purest water. There is talent unquestionably in these fanciful speculations, and we are occasionally reminded of that remarkable work the *Vestiges of Creation* by the character and tendency of the author's scientific romancing.[1] But the vital element of sincerity is wanting. The mocking smile of the hoaxer is seen behind his grave mask. He is more anxious to mystify and confound than to persuade, or even to instruct; and there are passages,

> Which read and read, you raise your eyes in doubt,
> And wonder what the deuce 'tis all about.

If Mr Poe is not a philosopher he is the most adroit of mimics. He will discourse to you in technical phrase of the mechanism of the universe, its existing phenomena and ultimate annihilation as glibly as a Lyceum lecturer will dilate upon the constitution of the steam engine. But it is as a 'poem' that Mr Poe wishes *Eureka* to be judged 'after he is dead'. We trust that he will live much longer than his book – live to exercise his really fine talents upon something more profitable to himself and his readers.

NOTE

1 In a letter of February 1848, Poe denied having read *Vestiges of the Natural History of Creation* – see *Letters*, 2, 362–4.

87. [John Henry Hopkins], review in the *Literary World*

29 July 1848, 3, 502

Hopkins visited Poe at Fordham in April 1848, when they argued about pantheism; on 15 May he informed Poe that he had seen the MS. of *Eureka* in Putnam's office, and warned that he would have to attack it (MS. in Boston Public Library). Moreover, he advised Mrs

Shew to break off her relationship with Poe – see *Letters*, 2, 364–5. Poe believed that Hopkins, the 'Student of Theology', was the author of this review, and he wrote an indignant reply to the editor of the *Literary World*, Charles Fenno Hoffmann – see *Letters*, 2, 379–82.

This is a strange work – a very strange work, and will excite quite a sensation in certain circles, both at home and abroad. It presents a two-fold appearance – as a poem, and as a work of science. It is only as the former, the author tells us, he would wish his work to be judged after he is dead; – leaving us at liberty, as it may be inferred, to judge of it as the latter so long as he shall still be on earth to see that it has fair play. In both respects much might be said both for and against various portions of *Eureka*, but except an occasional allusion, we shall let the Poetry take care of itself, and confine our remarks to the work in so far as it purports to be truth – Scientific, Metaphysical, or Theological.

The book opens, after the introduction, with an extract from a letter purporting to have been found in a bottle floating on the *Mare tenebrarum*, an ocean 'but little frequented in modern days unless by the Transcendentalists and some other divers for crotchets.' Now it is singular that with the sensible and supreme contempt expressed by Mr Poe for the Transcendentalists, he should have gone to the Shadowy Sea, frequented but by them, for a defence of the principle on which his whole discovery rests. This letter is a keen burlesque on the Aristotelian and Baconian methods of ascertaining truth, both of which the writer ridicules and despises, and pours forth his rhapsodical ecstasies in glorification of the third mode – the noble art of *guessing*. Now we have nothing to say against guessing in scientific matters. It certainly has antiquity and universality in its favor, especially as regards the formation of Cosmogonies, and our witty correspondent from the 'Sea of Shadows', so far from making any new discovery, has only been advocating what has ever been more or less the practice all the world over, being always in highest vogue where ignorance and barbarism most prevailed. All the nonsense put forth by Hindoos,

Scandinavians, Greeks, Romans, North American Indians, and Negroes, to say nothing of the philosophers and poets, has been the result of this ancient and noble art of guessing, and surely they all had as much right to guess as Mr Poe. It must be granted, however, that *guessing* is as good a plan as any other, – provided it *hits*; but in order to tell whether it hits or not, we are compelled to resort to that slow and troublesome process called 'demonstration', a plan much decried by those who excel rather in wit than wisdom. We hope that on some of his subsequent excursions to the Ocean of Shadows, Mr Poe may find another bottle which may enable him to *guess* his *demonstrations* also. That would be something *new*.

As we have already said, we think a guess as good as anything else, provided it *hits*. The question is: does Mr Poe's guess hit? We think that partly it does, and partly it does not. And here we can do nothing but indicate the *results* of our reflection on the theories propounded by Mr. Poe. To argue the point would require a volume far larger than *Eureka*. The great point of the Discovery claimed by Mr Poe, is his mode of accounting for the principle of the Newtonian Law of Gravity. This may be stated in general terms as follows: The Attraction of Gravitation, which acts with a force inversely proportional to the squares of the distances, is but the reaction of the original act of creation, which was effected by irradiating the atoms of which the universe is composed from one centre of unity, with a force directly proportional to the squares of the distances (reaction being action conversed), and that this was the mode of distributing the original matter is shown on geometrical principles. The development of electricity, and the formation of stars and suns, luminous and non-luminous, moons and planets with their rings, &c., is deduced, very much according to the nebular theory of La Place, from the principle propounded above.* In this, and perhaps in some other parts, such as the scheme for the final destruction of the Universe, the guess seems to *hit*, or at least comes apparently near the mark. Kepler's laws, it is well known, were guessed, and have been received as true, not because the principle of those laws was demonstrated by him or by anybody else, but merely because observed and known facts all agreed with them. And Mr Poe's *guess* is in some parts substantiated by the *same kind and the same degree of proof as the other,* – that is, *perfect harmony with ascertained facts.* So far as this can be *shown*, his theory must and will stand. Where it fails, his guess will return to the Sea of Shadows from whence it came.

In many respects it would be very easy to show a close correspondence between this theory and the Mosaic account. It would require no more ingenuity than has been already displayed by the geologists in accommodating Scripture to their Science. But there are several points which Mr Poe discusses in which he reminds us of a certain class of philosophers who, like himself, draw largely on the Ocean of Shadows. 'There are people, I am aware, who, busying themselves in attempts at the unattainable, acquire very easily, by dint of the jargon they emit, among those thinkers – that – they – think with whom darkness and depth are synonymous, a kind of cuttle-fish reputation for profundity; but the finest quality of thought is its self-cognisance;' – and to judge by the accuracy of the description, Mr Poe possesses this 'finest quality of thought' in a high degree of perfection. If further proof of this be needed, look at the system of Pantheism which is more or less interwoven into the texture of the whole book, but displays itself most broadly at the end. Yet the whole is most absurdly inconsistent. On pp. 28, 29, Mr Poe speaks of 'God' and 'the Godhead' as a Christian or a deist might speak – being One. On p. 103 he has the 'hardihood' to assert that we have a right to infer that there are an infinity of universes (?) such as ours, of which 'Each exists, apart and independently, in *the bosom of its proper and particular god.'* This makes Mr Poe a polytheist – a believer in an *infinite* number of *proper and particular* gods, existing *apart and independently.* On page 141 it appears that this infinity of gods is forgotten, and Mr Poe cannot conceive 'that anything exists *greater than his own soul;*' he feels 'intense and overwhelming dissatisfaction and rebellion at the thought; he asserts that this feeling is superior to any demonstration;' and that each soul is therefore 'its *own god, its own creator'*. All this is extraordinary nonsense, if not blasphemy; and it may very possibly be *both.* Nay we have

Mr Poe's own authority for saying so – authority which seems to be 'divine' with him. After all these contradictory propoundings concerning 'God' we would remind him of what he lays down on page 28. 'Of this Godhead, in itself, he alone is not imbecile – he alone is not impious, who propounds – *nothing*.' A man who thus conclusively convicts himself of imbecility and impiety needs no further refutation.

To conclude our brief and imperfect notice of this strange and in many respects original production, we should say that much of its physical portion may be true, – and we commend this particularly to the attention of scientific men. Its Metaphysical part, including ideas about the Spiritual portion of the universe, its being 'Repulsion' while matter is 'Attraction', whereas nevertheless Electricity is the Spiritual principle, and 'Attraction and repulsion' (taken together), and 'Matter' are convertible terms: – all this, we say, with much more of the same sort, is simply unintelligible, and smacks of the cuttle-fish. The Theological portion is intolerable. Mr Poe has guessed. In some respect we may grant that we also 'guess so'. In others we most decidedly 'guess *not*'. We agree with him, that when his 'theory has been corrected, reduced, sifted, cleared little by little, of its chaff of inconsistency – until at length there stands apparent an unencumbered *Consistency*,' it will be acknowledged 'to be an absolute and unquestionable *Truth*;' but in this case, we opine, the sifters will discover an original, ingenious, profound, and abundant quantity of chaff.

NOTE

* Further than this, Mr. Poe's claim that he can account for the existence of all organised beings – men included – merely from those principles on which the origin and present appearance of suns and worlds, are explained, must be set down as mere bald assertion, without a particle of evidence. In other words, we would term it *arrant fudge*, were it not for a shrewd suspicion which haunts us, that the whole essay is nothing more nor less than an elaborate quiz upon some of the wild speculations of the day – a scientific hoax of the higher order which few men are capable of executing more cleverly than the ingenious author of 'The Murders of the Rue Morgue', 'The Descent into the Maelstrom', &c, &c.

88. Unsigned notice in the New York *Daily Tribune*

3 August 1848

This is one of the most remarkable books we have read in a long time. As a poem, it has the quality of a bold and exhaustless force of imagination; as an essay on the Material and Spiritual Universe, which it would more properly be termed, it is marked with the keenest analysis and the most singular ingenuity. The greater part of the work, with the central Idea, around which the author's veiling web of argument is so skillfully twined, was contained in a lecture on 'The Universe', which he delivered last Winter, in the City. – It is here wrought out into a more perfect shape, with some additional illustrations. The most powerful *mental passion*, (we know not how else to express it,) to which the highest condition of Man's nature is subject, has been seized upon by the author and ministered to with the most startling propositions which a reasoning imagination ever conceived. The seriousness, and we doubt not sincerity, with which he asserts their truth, adds to the effect he desires to produce, and although the soul, from its very *knowledge* of abstract truth, (which he regards as superior to any logical demonstration,) rejects a great deal of his theory, there is no part of it which does not chain the attentive and excite the inquiring. The tenacity with which he pursues the subject along the farthest brink of finite knowledge, and the daring with which he throws aside all previous systems of philosophers and theologians, constitute the chief merit of the book. The preface is terse and striking, and the dedication, to Alexander von Humboldt, exceedingly appropriate. We do not admire, however, the attempt at humor, in his description of the contents of a bottle floating in the *Mare tenebrarum*; it degrades the high aim with which the work sets out. His theory of the Universe is too intricate to be told in a few lines, and we will not do injustice to it by a partial description; but we will give the following wild conjecture with which the book concludes, recommending all who take an interest in the subject, to procure and read the whole of it:

[Quotes *Eureka,* from 'On the Universal agglomeration and dissolution' to '*seems, because it is*', *Works,* 16, 311–12.]

89. 'Mr. Poe's *Eureka*', *Home Journal*

12 August 1848

In his 'Memoir', Griswold ascribed this notice to Willis.

The application of rhetoric and imagination to science is a novel feature in modern culture. The domains of natural philosophy and poetry were once considered, if not antagonistic, at least totally dissimilar. Men of genius, however, in this age, have demonstrated that the perceptive organs are not the only means of reading the secrets of nature, nor mechanical details the exclusive process for communicating them to the world. The *Astronomical Discourses* of Dr Chalmers indicated to the popular mind the relation of siderial wonders to Christian truth; and to borrow an illustration nearer home, what fiction or poem can be more attractive, in its way, than one of Dr Draper's *Introductory Lectures on Chemistry*?[1] This tendency to elucidate scientific truth by addressing the sense of beauty, and calling in imagination and pure reflection, instead of mere observation and memory, is full of promise, both in regard to its own advancement and the highest enlightenment of mankind.

In the spirit of bold speculation and ideal thought, Mr Poe has undertaken, in the little treatise before us, to expound a theory of the universe. He begins by repudiating the idea that the arcana of nature are to be completely explored by induction. He recognizes the intuitive and unconscious process as the source of discovery, and eloquently protests against that slavery to the Baconian system which has so long prevailed. Kepler, he says, *guessed*, that is, *imagined*, the vital laws he promulgated. Accordingly, Mr Poe deems, and with justice, that besides patient induction, a certain power of seizing upon great truths is required in the philosopher. In a word, he believes in a kind of *scientific inspiration*; and history – as well as individual consciousness – confirms this faith. So much for his general views. As to the particular theory developed in *Eureka*, the whole book (and it is not voluminous, though written with extreme conciseness,) should be read, in order to be appreciated. Mr Poe recognizes but two absolute principles in the universe – attraction and repulsion. He assumes a unit or particle as the germ of all subsequent creation, and imagines an innate power – which he identifies with divine volition – to have projected from this atom an infinity of other atoms into space, and that gravitation is only an attempt on the part of those to return to their central unity.

There is doubtless as much fantasy as fact developed in the course of this prose-poem, as the author properly calls *Eureka*. It is not a demonstrative so much as a suggestive work. It contains many striking figures and brilliant rhetorical passages. Some parts are very ingenious – others very fanciful. There is no great novelty in the scientific ideas advanced. We have been constantly reminded, while reading the work, not by any precise similitude, but a certain correspondence of tone, of the *Vestiges of Creation*; and in Swedenborg's writings, the idea of the Infinite is revealed upon with a more rich and clear significance. Without adopting the author's theory, or sympathizing in the sublimated materialism of his cogitations, we can sincerely advise such of our readers who have a poetic, metaphysical or philosophic tendency, to ponder *Eureka*.

NOTE

1 Thomas Chalmers. *A Series of Discourses on the Christian revelation, viewed in connection with the Modern Astronomy (1817)* went through

many reprints; John William Draper's *Introductory Lecture to a Course of Chemistry* was published in New York in 1845.

90. Unsigned review in the *New Church Repository, and Monthly Review*

August 1848, 1, 508–9

The *New Church Repository* was 'conducted' in New York by the Rev. George Bush (1796–1859), Swedenborgian scholar and controversialist, who probably wrote this review himself.

The poet here enters upon profound speculations, shooting ahead of the Newtons, Laplaces, Herschels, and Nicholses,[1] in the solution of the great problems of the Universe. He calls his work a poem, perhaps because, with Madame De Stael, he regards the Universe itself as more like a poem than a machine, and therefore to be treated *poematically*. Others might say it was because he had invested the subject with all a poet's imagination. But this would be, we think, to withhold its due meed of praise from the vein of rich philosophic thought which runs through it. It is a book devoted indeed to a theory, but a theory by no means to be despised nor lacking in some of the higher elements of scientific probability. We might perhaps feel the want of a certain property termed *demonstration* as a buttress to his reasonings, but that the author has effectually estopped any such inconvenient demand in his case by the peremptory position that 'in this world, at least, there is *no such thing* as demonstration' – that such affairs as axioms or self-evident truths are 'all in my eye', mere figments and phantasies. Waving, however, the application of this sweeping *negatur* to his own speculations, we refuse not to concede that the work before us does offer some hints towards solving no less a problem than that of the *cause of gravitation*, before which the grandest geniuses have shrank abashed. Of this we can scarcely make the barest *statement* in a manner which shall do full justice to the propounder's thought, but we may afford an inkling of it by saying that he assumes a created unitary and irrelative particle as the first principle or germ of the Universe, and supposes an internal force, identical with the Divine volition, to have radiated or projected all but an infinity of minimal atoms from this parent particle into the regions of space, and that the attraction of gravitation is nothing else than a *conatus* on the part of these atoms to return to the central unity. It would doubtless be easy to suggest a multitude of difficulties that weigh upon this theory in the form in which it is proposed by the poet-philosopher, but we may take the main position apart from all the accessories by which it is surrounded and give it the credit of at least a very plausible and sagacious guess. The hypothesis of the generation of the universe from a *simple monad* – not however the monad of Leibnitz – plainly approximates, in several of its features, to the view given by Swedenborg in his philosophical works, of the evolution of all things from 'the first natural point', and Mr Poe will recognize a striking analogy between his own theory and that presented in the following paragraph from the *Outlines on the Infinite:*

[Quotes a paragraph from Swedenborg.]

Indeed, we have no doubt that Mr Poe would be vastly surprised upon reading Swedenborg's *Outlines on the Infinite* to see to what extent many of the prominent ideas of his own work had been anticipated in that masterly dissertation on the origin of the Universe and 'the final case of creation'. We trust too that if he should ever turn his attention to this work, he may feel the force of Swedenborg's reasoning in regard to the being and agency of a God distinct from nature, in which, if we understand Mr P. he is disposed to sink the Universal Cause. Its pantheistic tendency is the worst feature of his book, and it is felt the more from the contrast between the passages where this is broadly avowed, and those in which he speaks of the Divine volition as if he regarded the subject from a Christian stand-point. With all abatements, however, the book will repay perusal.

NOTE

1 J.P. Nichol was a Scottish writer on astronomy. His *Views of the Architecture of the Heavens* (1837) influenced *Eureka*, and in January 1948 he had lectured in New York on 'Views of Astronomy'.

91. [John Milton Emerson], from a review in the Amherst College *Indicator*

February 1849, 1, 193–9

Emerson (1826–69) a member of the Class of 1849, was a contributing editor of the *Indicator*. He later practised law in New York City.

EUREKA This is the very modest title of a book written by Mr Edgar A. Poe of 'Raven' notoriety. Like the sage of Samos he comes forth shouting 'Eureka'. Not seldom is it nowadays that we hear this cry. Even now it is ringing in our ears from the distant Californian El Dorado.

But what is it that Mr Poe has found? Is it the fountain of youth, the elixir of life, the philosopher's stone?

None of these. Mr Poe's discovery is one before which, all other discoveries of all time must 'hide their diminished heads'. Mr Poe has found the key, hear him announce it, of the 'Physical, Metaphysical, and Mathematical, of the Material and Spiritual Universe, of its Essence, Origin, Creation, Present Condition and its Destiny.' Shades of Pythagoras, Kepler, and Newton! We conjure you, leave not the Elysian bowers, revisit not the 'glimpses of the moon', if ye would not see your glories eclipsed in the splendor of this new luminary.

To be candid and serious now, we have always considered Mr Poe to be the most conceited, impudent fellow in existence. His works are all 'thunder in the index', and strut in the preface. We have had from him one or two short poetical pieces of superior excellence, as 'Dream Land' and 'The Raven', but by far the greater portion of his writings, consists of the most harsh and bitter criticism, of monstrous tales and hoaxing stories. His genius delights in whatever is *outré* and extravagant. He has not that simplicity and naturalness about him, which ever belongs to the highest order of intellect. Mr Poe has once or twice before, deliberately hoaxed people, (witness the story about the case of Monsieur De Somebody, that came out in the *Whig Review*, a year or two since,)[1] and it was not without some suspicions therefore, that we took up *Eureka*. We have read it quite through, and it is our conviction that this time, Mr Poe has egregiously hoaxed – not his readers – but himself. His iniquities have returned upon his own head.

However, the book shall speak for itself. We have done our best to extract the kernel of the nut, and will endeavor to serve it up to our readers, in such a way as to save them the inconvenience of smashing their fingers in getting at it.

[The main arguments of *Eureka* are summarized sceptically.]

To this final conclusion, we are led by this wonderful treatise. And now what shall be the verdict? We have a way of reading the preface of a book, just as the author writes it, – the last thing. We had about decided to call it a physico Metaphysico Mathematical Rhapsody, when in reading the preface, we came upon these words. 'It is only as a poem, that I wish this work to be judged after I am dead.' If the work is to be judged at all after the death of Mr Poe, we fear that his sands are nearly run. Still, we are good natured enough to hope that he is destined to outlive this, and some of his other works, as well as a good share of his impudence and conceit. But, supposing him dead for a moment, upon what grounds can we call it a poem? He gives us a definition of poetry, himself. 'Poetry is truth, and truth is poetry.' This is about as true as it would be to say that all the light God ever made, is moonshine. According to this definition, we might indeed reckon this work a poem, provided that we admitted the truth of another proposition which he advances, viz: 'What I here propound is true.' But there's the rub. Martinus Scriblerus in his treatise Πεξι Βαθουζ, tells the world that 'Poetry is a morbid secretion from the brain.' Since Mr Poe wishes to have his book considered as a poem, we are bound in courtesy, to force it into that category if possible. Martinus' definition seems to afford us the only means of doing so, and we avail ourselves of it with thankfulness. That Mr Poe has talents, we do not deny. The ingenious author of the 'Fable for Critics', puts him down as 'three-fifths genius'. Judging of him by the book before us, we should be inclined to reckon him as three-fifths genius and six-fifths 'sheer fudge'. We cherish no ill will towards Mr Poe, and to prove it, we promise, the very next time he publishes a book, to take no notice of it whatever. He evidently considers himself one of the favored class who according to Coleridge, are blessed with an extra faculty, – the Metaphysical faculty. Whatever may be our opinion as to his Metaphysics, we shall not hesitate long about his Mathematics or his Logic. But the great fault with this as well as with most of his works, is that inordinate vanity and egotism which leads him to be constantly thrusting *himself* upon the reader, and so contrary to the intention, has the effect of reminding us constantly that 'I one Snug, a joiner am,' and no lion at all.

NOTE

1 'The Facts in the Case of M. Valdemar'.

OBITUARY NOTICES

92. [Rufus Wilmot Griswold], 'Death of Edgar Allan Poe', New York *Daily Tribune*

9 October 1849

This notice was signed 'Ludwig', though it was soon common knowledge that Griswold had written it. Griswold's dislike of Poe is obvious, his reasons less so; but he must have been riled by Poe's lack of respect for his compilations, and he may also have been jealous of his romantic relationship with Mrs Osgood, whose favors he, too, later enjoyed. Griswold was not, however, responsible for the biographical errors: he merely took his facts from the fanciful and inaccurate notes Poe had sent to him in 1841 – see *Works*, 1, 343–6.

Edgar Allan Poe is dead. He died in Baltimore the day before yesterday. This announcement will startle many, *but few will be grieved by it*. The poet was well known personally or by reputation, in all this country; he had readers in England, and in several states of Continental Europe; *but he had few or no friends* and the regrets for his death will be suggested principally by the consideration that in him literary art lost one of its most brilliant, but erratic stars.

The family of Mr Poe, we learn from Griswold's *Poets and Poetry of America*, from which a considerable portion of the facts in this notice are derived, was one of the oldest and most respectable in Baltimore. David Poe, his paternal grandfather, was a Quartermaster-General in the Maryland line during the Revolution, and the intimate friend of Lafayette, who during his last visit to the United States, called personally upon the General's widow, and tendered her acknowledgments for the services rendered to him by her husband. His great-grandfather, John Poe, married in England, Jane, a daughter of Admiral James McBride, noted in British naval history, and claiming kindred with some of the most illustrious English families. His father and mother, – both of whom were in some way connected with the theatre, and lived as precariously as their more gifted, and more eminent son, – died within a few weeks of each other, of consumption, leaving him an orphan at two years of age. Mr John Allan, a wealthy gentleman of Richmond, took a fancy to him, and persuaded his grandfather to suffer him to adopt him. He was brought up in Mr Allan's family; and as that gentleman had no other children, he was regarded as his son and heir. In 1816 he accompanied Mr and Mrs Allan to Great Britain, visited every portion of it, and afterward passed four or five years in a school kept at Newington, near London, by Rev. Dr Bransby. He returned to America in 1822, and in 1825 went to the Jefferson University, at Charlottesville, in Virginia, where he led a very dissipated life, the manners of the college at that time being extremely dissolute. He took the first honors, however, and went home greatly in debt. Mr Allan refused to pay some of his debts of *honor*, and he hastily quitted the country on a quixotic expedition to join the Greeks, then struggling for liberty. He did not reach his original destination, however, but made his way to St Petersburg, in Russia, when he became involved in difficulties, from which he was extricated by the late Henry Middleton, the American Minister at that Capital. He returned home in 1829, and immediately afterwards entered the Military Academy at West Point. In about eighteen months from that time, Mr. Allan, who had lost his first wife while Mr Poe was in Russia, married again. He was sixty-five years of age, and the lady was young; Poe quarreled with her, and the veteran husband, taking the part of his wife, addressed him an angry letter, which was answered in the same spirit. He died soon after, leaving an infant son heir to his property, and bequeathing Poe nothing.

The army, in the opinion of the young poet, was not a place for a poor man; so he left West Point abruptly, and determined to maintain himself by authorship. He printed, in 1827, a small volume of poems, most of which were written in early youth. Some of these poems are quoted in a reviewal by Margaret Fuller, in *The Tribune* in 1846, and are justly regarded as among the most wonderful exhibitions of the precocious developments of genius. They illustrated the character of his abilities, and justified his anticipations of success. For a considerable time, however, though he wrote readily and brilliantly, his contributions to the journals attracted little attention, and his hopes of gaining a livelihood by the profession of literature was nearly ended at length in sickness, poverty and despair.

But in 1831, the proprietor of a weekly gazette, in Baltimore, offered two premiums, one for the best story in prose, and the other for the best poem.

In due time Poe sent in two articles, and he waited anxiously for the decision. One of the Committee was the accomplished author of *Horseshoe Robinson*, John P. Kennedy, and his associates were scarcely less eminent than he for wit and critical sagacity. Such matters were usually disposed of in a very off-hand way; committees to award literary prizes drink to the payer's health, in good wines, over the unexamined MSS., which they submit to the discretion of the publisher, with permission to use their names in such a way as to promote the publisher's advantage. So it would have been in this case, but that one of the Committee, taking up a small book in such exquisite calligraphy as to seem like one of the finest issues of the press of Putnam, was tempted to read several pages, and being interested, he summonsed the attention of the company to the half-dozen compositions in the volume. It was unanimously decided that the prizes should be paid to the first of geniuses who had written legibly. Not another MS. was unfolded. Immediately the confidential envelope was opened, and the successful competitor was found to bear the scarcely known name of Poe.

The next day the publisher called to see Mr Kennedy, and

gave him an account of the author that excited his curiosity and sympathy, and caused him to request that he should be brought to his office. Accordingly he was introduced; the prize money had not yet been paid, and he was in the costume in which he had answered the advertisement of his good fortune. Thin, and pale even to ghastliness, his whole appearance indicated sickness and the utmost destitution. A tattered frock-coat concealed the absence of a shirt, and the ruins of boots disclosed more than the want of stockings. But the eyes of the young man were luminous with intelligence and feeling, and his voice and conversation, and manners, all won upon the lawyer's regard. Poe told his history, and his ambitions, and it was determined that he should not want means for a suitable appearance in society, nor opportunity for a just display of his abilities in literature. Mr Kennedy accompanied him to a clothing store, and purchased for him a respectable suit, with changes of linen, and sent him to a bath, from which he returned with the suddenly regained bearing of a gentleman.

The late Mr Thomas W. White had then recently established *The Southern Literary Messenger*, at Richmond, and upon the warm recommendation of Mr Kennedy, Poe was engaged at a small salary – we believe of $500 a year – to be its editor. He entered upon his duties with letters full of expression of the warmest gratitude to his friends in Baltimore, who in five or six weeks were astonished to learn that with characteristic recklessness of consequence, he was hurriedly married to a girl as *poor as himself.* Poe continued in this situation for about a year and a half, in which he wrote many brilliant articles, and raised the *Messenger* to the first rank of literary periodicals.

He next moved to Philadelphia, to assist William E. Burton in the editorship of the *Gentleman's Magazine,* a miscellany that in 1840 was merged in *Graham's Magazine,* of which Poe became one of the principal writers, particularly in criticism, in which his papers attracted much attention by their careful and skilful analysis, and general caustic severity. At this period, however, he appeared to have been more ambitious of securing distinction in romantic fiction, and a collection of his compositions in this department, published in 1841, under the title of *Tales of the Grotesque and Arabesque*, established his reputation for ingenuity, imagination and extraordinary power in tragical narration.

Near the end of 1844 Poe removed to New York, where he conducted for several months a literary miscellany called the *Broadway Journal*. In 1845 he published a volume of *Tales* in Wiley and Putnam's 'Library of American Books'; and in the same series a collection of his poems. Besides these poems he was the author of *Arthur Gordon Pym*, a romance; *Eureka*, an essay on the spiritual and material universe; a work which he wishes to have 'judged as a poem'; and several extended series of papers in the periodicals, the most noteworthy of which are 'Marginalia', embracing opinions of books and authors; 'Secret Writing', 'Autography'; and 'Sketches of the Literati of New York'.

His wife died in 1847, at Fordham, near this city, and some of our readers will remember the paragraphs in the papers of the time, upon his destitute condition. We remember that Col. Webb collected in a few moments fifty or sixty dollars for him at the Metropolitan Club; Mr Lewis, of Brooklyn, sent a similar sum from one of the courts, in which he was engaged when he saw the statement of the poet's poverty;[1] and others illustrated in the same manner the effect of such an appeal to the popular heart.

Since that time Mr Poe has lived quietly, and with an income from his literary labors sufficient for his support. A few weeks ago he proceeded to Richmond, in Virginia, where he lectured upon the poetical character, etc., and it was understood by some of his correspondents here that he was this week to be married, most advantageously, to a lady of that city, a widow, to whom he had been previously engaged while a student in the University.

The character of Mr Poe we cannot attempt to describe in this very hastily written article. We can but allude to some of the more striking phases.

His conversation was at times almost supramortal in its eloquence. His voice was modulated with astonishing skill, and his large and variably expressive eyes looked reposed or shot fiery tumult into theirs who listened, while his own face glowed or was changeless in pallor, as his imagination quickened his blood, or drew it back frozen to his heart. His imagery was from the worlds which no mortal can see but with the vision of genius. Suddenly starting from a proposition exactly and sharply defined in terms of utmost simplicity and clearness, he rejected the forms of customary logic, and in a crystalline process of accretion, built up his ocular demonstrations in forms of gloomiest and ghostliest grandeur, or in those of the most airy and delicious beauty, so minutely, and so distinctly, yet so rapidly, that the attention which was yielded to him was chained till it stood among his wonderful creations – till he himself dissolved the spell, and brought his hearers back to common and base existence, by vulgar fancies or by exhibitions of the ignoble passions.

He was at times a dreamer – dwelling in ideal realms – in heaven or hell, peopled with creations and the accidents of his brain. He walked the streets, in madness or melancholy, with lips moving in indistinct curses, or with eyes upturned in passionate prayers (never for himself, for he felt, or professed to feel, that he was already damned), but for their happiness who at that moment were objects of his idolatry; or with his glance introverted to a heart gnawed with anguish, and with a face shrouded in gloom, he would brave the wildest storms; and all night, with drenched garments and arms wildly beating the wind and rain, he would speak as if to spirits that at such times only could be evoked by him from that Aidenn close by whose portals his disturbed soul sought to forget the ills to which his constitution subjected him – close by that Aidenn where were those he loved – the Aidenn which he might never see but in fitful glimpses, as its gates opened to receive the less fiery and more happy natures whose listing to sin did not involve the doom of death. He seemed, except when some fitful pursuit subjected his will and engrossed his faculties, always to bear the memory of some controlling sorrow. The remarkable poem of 'The Raven' was probably much more nearly than has been supposed, even by those who were very intimate with him, a reflection and echo of his own history. He was the bird's

> – unhappy master,
> Whom unmerciful disaster

Followed fast and followed faster
Till his song the burden bore –
Melancholy burden bore
Of 'Nevermore', of 'Nevermore'.

Every genuine author in a greater or less degree leaves in his works, whatever their design, traces of his personal character; elements of his immortal being, in which the individual survives the person. While we read the pages of 'The Fall of the House of Usher', or of 'Mesmeric Revelation', we see in the solemn and stately gloom which invests one, and in the subtle metaphysical analysis of both, indications of the idiosyncrasies, – of what was most peculiar – in the author's intellectual nature. But we see here only the better phases of this nature, only the symbols of his juster action, for his harsh experience had deprived him of all faith in man or woman.

He had made up his mind upon the numberless complexities of the social world, and the whole system was with him an imposture. This conviction gave a direction to his shrewd and naturally unamiable character. Still though he regarded society as composed of villains, the sharpness of his intellect was not of that kind which enabled him to cope with villainy, while it continually caused him overshots, to fail of the success of honesty. He was in many respects like Francis Vivian in Bulwer's novel of *The Caxtons*. 'Passion, in him, comprehended many of the worst emotions which militate against human happiness. You could not contradict him, but you raised quick choler; you could not speak of wealth, but his cheek paled with gnawing envy. The astonishing natural advantage of this poor boy – his beauty, his readiness, the daring spirit that breathed around him like a fiery atmosphere – had raised his constitutional self-confidence into an arrogance that turned his very claims to admiration into prejudice against him. Irascible, envious – bad enough, but not the worst, for these salient angles were all varnished over with a cold repellant cynicism while his passions vented themselves in sneers. There seemed to him no moral susceptibility; and what was more remarkable in a proud nature, little or nothing of the true point of honor. He had, to a morbid excess, that desire to rise which is vulgarly called ambition, but no wish for the esteem or love of his species; only the hard wish to succeed – not shine, not serve – succeed, that he might have the right to despise a world which galled his self-conceit.'[2]

We have suggested the influence of his aims and vicissitudes upon his literature. It was more conspicuous in his later than his earlier writing. Nearly all that he wrote in the last two or three years – including much of his best poetry – was in some sense biographical; in draperies of his imagination, those who had taken the trouble to trace his steps,· could perceive, slightly covered, the figure of himself.

There are perhaps some of our readers who will understand the allusions of the following beautiful poem. Mr Poe presented it in MS. to the writer of these paragraphs, just before he left New York recently, remarking it was the last thing he had written.

[Quotes 'Annabel Lee'.]

We must omit any particular criticism of Mr Poe's works. As a writer of tales it will be admitted generally, that he was scarcely surpassed in ingenuity of construction or effective painting; as a critic, he was more remarkable as a dissector of sentences than as a commentator upon ideas. *He was little better than a carping grammarian.* As a poet, he will retain a most honorable rank. Of his 'Raven' Mr Willis observes, that in his opinion, 'it is the most effective single example of fugitive poetry ever published in this country, and is unsurpassed in English poetry for subtle conceptions, masterly ingenuity of versification, and consistent sustaining of imaginative lift'. In poetry, as in prose, he was most successful in the metaphysical treatment of the passions. His poems are constructed with wonderful ingenuity, and finished with consummate art. They illustrate a morbid sensitiveness of feeling, a shadowy and gloomy imagination, and a taste almost faultless in the apprehension of that sort of beauty most agreeable to his temper.

We have not learned of the circumstance of his death. It was sudden, and from the fact that it occurred in Baltimore,

it is presumed that he was on his return to New York.
'After life's fitful fever he sleeps well.'

NOTES

1 Sylvanus Lewis was the lawyer husband of Sarah Anna 'Stella'
Lewis, whose poetry Poe was paid to promote – see *Letters*, 2, 451.
2 In his 'Memoir' Griswold removed the quotation marks from this
passage, thus relating it more directly to Poe's character.

93. 'Edgar A. Poe', unsigned obituary in the New York *Journal of Commerce*

9 October 1849

Our readers will observe, under our telegraphic head, the
announcement of the death of this well known author. For
some years past he has been more or less ill, and the
announcement of his death is not unexpected, though none
the less melancholy on that account.

Few men were his equals. He stands in a position among
our poets and prose writers which has made him the envy of
many and the admiration of all. His life has been an eventful
and stormy one, and if anyone shall be found to write its
history, we venture to say that its simple truths will be of
more thrilling interest than most romances.

During the early part of his life he wandered around the
world, wasting the energies of a noble mind. Subsequently
he returned to his native country, but his heart seemed to
have become embittered by the experiences of life, and his
hand to be against every man. Hence he was better known as

a *severe* critic than otherwise; yet Mr Poe had a warm and noble heart, as those who best knew him can testify. He had been sadly disappointed in his early years. Brilliant prospects had been dashed away from before him, and he wandered over the world in search of a substitute for them. During the latter part of his life it has seemed as if his really high heart had been weighed down under a heavy load, and his own words best express the emotions of his soul:

> Alas, alas for me,
>   Ambition – all is o'er!
>   No more, no more, no more,
> (Such language hath the solemn sea
>   to the sands upon the shore,)
> Shall bloom the thunder blasted tree,
>   The stricken eagle soar!

It will not be denied, even by his enemies, that Mr Poe was a man of great ability, – and all other recollections of him will be lost now, and buried with him in the grave. We hope he has found rest, for he needed it.

94.   'Death of Edgar A. Poe', *Baltimore Patriot*

9 October 1849

This notice was reprinted in the *Richmond Whig* (11 October) with the following introduction: 'For the gratification of the numerous friends of this lamented gentleman, we publish, in another column, a notice from the Baltimore *Patriot*. The writer has fallen into two slight errors. Mr Poe (we learn from those who have the best right to know) was forty-four not thirty

eight [*sic*], and he was never at William & Mary, but at
the University of Virginia.'

We sincerely regret to hear of the melancholy death of EDGAR
A. POE, who expired in this city on Sunday morning about
five o'clock, at the early age of 38 years, after an illness of
about a week. His disease was congestion of the brain.

Mr Poe was equally remarkable for his genius and his
acquirements. He enjoyed uncommon advantages of early
education, having spent his boyhood at a school in the
neighborhood of London, and afterwards received instruction at William and Mary College, and at West Point. These
advantages were improved with considerable assiduity, and
by the time he reached his majority he had acquired
accomplishments rarely attained by men far more advanced
in years. He was acquainted, in a greater or less degree, with
the ancient languages, and with French, Spanish, Italian and
German, and had an accurate knowledge of most branches of
science and art. His acquirements in Astronomy, Natural
Philosophy, Natural History, Botany, Chemistry &c. are
said to have been both extensive and accurate, and there were
few branches of human knowledge to which he had not
directed his attention, and with which he had not, at least,
such familiarity as to enable him in his writings, to draw
upon them for the purposes of illustration, with aptness and
effect. Mr Poe's writings, both in prose and poetry, have for
several years past, had an established reputation. They were
peculiar, and far from being without striking faults; but there
is scarcely one of them that can be read by a person of
judgement, without leading him to the conclusion that the
author was a man of genius truly original, of a taste refined
by diligent study and comparison; and of information,
varied, comprehensive and minute. It is greatly to be
regretted that his extraordinary capacity was not more
appropriately employed than in the field of literary labour, to
which circumstances obliged him to confine himself. For,
under better auspices, he might have produced works that
would have been of enduring value to posterity. His writings
disclose the most remarkable power of analysis, and had his

efforts been steadily and judiciously directed, he would have left behind him a reputation inferior to that of no other American writer whatever. As it is, what he has written will not fail to be rescued from the common fate of the ephemeral productions of the day. The learning, genius, taste, originality and nice discrimination exhibited in his prose, and the artistical construction, mellifluous flow, and often exquisite imagery of his verse, will never cease to be acknowledged and admired. His criticisms of his contemporaries were universally admitted to discover the most acute perception of the faults as well as merits of those whom he reviewed; and although often impeached in wanting in impartiality, are now generally conceded to have been equally just and discriminating.

Mr Poe is said to have been a man of polished manners, fine colloquial powers, warm and amiable impulses, and of a high and sometimes haughty spirit. It is deeply to be deplored that his great powers, which might have enabled him to soar so high and to have acquired for himself so much of fame and prosperity, were obscured and crippled by the frailties and weaknesses which have too often attended eminent genius in all ages.

It may be regarded as a singular coincidence, that several days ago we received a note from a 'Lady Friend', asking us to publish two poems by Mr Poe, 'The Raven' and 'Ulalume', and that we had prepared to publish the former, on this very day, and even were on the point of sending it to the compositor, when we heard of his death. We still publish it in connection with the above notice of his decease. 'The Raven' on the first publication about five years ago, excited a deep interest, and was copied far and near, at home and abroad. It is a rare effort of the peculiar genius of the writer, and is one of the most remarkable and metrical poems ever written.

['The Raven' is printed.]

95. 'Death of a Poet', New York *Organ*

9 October 1849, 9, 133

The *Organ* was a temperance magazine; it was subtitled 'A Family Companion Devoted to Pure Literature, Temperance, Morality, Education and General Intelligence'. For the temperance movement's response to Poe, see Burton R. Pollin, 'The Temperance Movement and its Friends Look at Poe', *Costerus*, 2 (1972), 119–44.

Edgar A. Poe, whose writings, both prose and poetical, have attracted marked attention in this country, is numbered with the dead. He possessed genius of a peculiar and striking order, and had he not, like too many other gifted men, yielded to the snare of intemperance, he might have trodden a luminous pathway to immortality. Quite recently he appears to have renounced the enemy of his peace and usefulness, and was received as a member of a Division of the Sons of Temperance in Virginia. His friends and admirers were indulging the most favorable anticipation from this change in his course, when he again yielded, broke his pledge, and died of *mania a potu* in the Baltimore hospital. An awful warning comes up from the grave of this unhappy, self-ruined man. Would that it might make its due impression. – Think of Poe's miserable end, and then resolve to touch not, taste not the cup that poisoned him. When tempted to break your pledge, point to that grave and answer, No, never!

96. Nathaniel Parker Willis, 'Death of Edgar A. Poe', *Home Journal*

20 October 1849

This notice was reprinted in Griswold's edition of Poe's *Works* (1850); also in Willis's *Hurry-Graphs* (1851).

The ancient fable of two antagonistic spirits imprisoned in one body equally powerful and having the complete mastery by turns – of one man, that is to say, inhabited by both a devil and an angel – seems to have been realized, if all we hear is true, in the character of the extraordinary man whose name we have written above. Our own impression of the nature of Edgar A. Poe differs in some important degree, however, from that which has been generally conveyed in the notices of his death. Let us, before telling what we personally know of him, copy a graphic and highly finished portraiture, from the pen of Dr Rufus W. Griswold, which appeared in a recent number of the *Tribune*:

[Quotes paragraphs 1 and 13–17 of the 'Ludwig' article.]

Apropos of the disparaging portion of the above well-written sketch, let us truthfully say: –

Some four or five years since, when editing a daily paper in this city, Mr Poe was employed by us, for several months, as critic and sub-editor. This was our first personal acquaintance with him. He resided with his wife and mother at Fordham, a few miles out of town, but was at his desk in the office from nine in the morning till the evening paper went to press. With the highest admiration for his genius, and a willingness to let it atone for more than ordinary irregularity, we were led by common report to expect a very capricious attention to his duties, and occasionally a scene of violence and difficulty. Time went on, however, and he was

307

invariably punctual and industrious. With his pale, beautiful, and intellectual face as a reminder of what genius was in him, it was impossible, of course, not to treat him always with deferential courtesy, and to our occasional request that he would not probe too deep in a criticism, or that he would erase a passage colored too highly with his resentments against society and mankind, he readily and courteously assented, – far more yielding than most men, we thought, on points so excusably sensitive. With the prospect of taking the lead in another periodical, he at last voluntarily gave up his employment with us, and through all this considerable period we had seen but one presentment of the man, – a quiet, patient, industrious, and most gentlemanly person, commanding the utmost respect and good feeling by his unvarying deportment and ability.

Residing as he did in the country, we never met Mr Poe in hours of leisure; but he frequently called on us afterwards at our place of business, and we met him often in the street, – invariably the same sad-mannered, winning, and refined gentleman such as we had always known him. It was by rumor only, up to the day of his death, that we knew of any other development of manner or character. We heard, from one who knew him well (what should be stated in all mention of his lamentable irregularities), that, with a *single glass* of wine, his whole nature was reversed, the demon became uppermost, and, though none of the usual signs of intoxication were visible, his *will* was palpably insane. Possessing his reasoning faculties in excited activity at such times, and seeking his acquaintances with his wonted look and memory, he easily seemed personating only another phase of his natural character, and was accused, accordingly, of insulting arrogance and bad-heartedness. In this reversed character, we repeat, it was never our chance to see him. We know it from hearsay, and we mention it in connection with this sad infirmity of physical constitution, which puts it upon very nearly the ground of a temporary and almost irresponsible insanity.

The arrogance, vanity, and depravity of heart of which Mr Poe was generally accused seem to us referable altogether to this reversed phase of his character. Under that degree of intoxication which only acted upon him by demonizing his sense of truth and right, he doubtless said and did much that was wholly irreconcilable with his better nature; but when himself, and as we knew him only, his modesty and unaffected humility, as to his own deservings, were a constant charm to his character. His letters (of which the constant application for autographs has taken from us, we are sorry to confess, the greater portion) exhibited this quality very strongly. In one of the carelessly written notes of which we chance still to retain possession, for instance, he speaks of 'The Raven', – that extraordinary poem which electrified the world of imaginative readers, and which has become the type of a school of poetry of its own, – and, in evident earnest, attributes its success to the few words of commendation with which we had prefaced it in this paper. It will throw light on his sane character to give a literal copy of the note: –

Fordham, April 20, 1849.
MY DEAR WILLIS, – The poem which I enclose, and which I am so vain as to hope you will like, in some respects, has been just published in a paper for which sheer necessity compels me to write, now and then. It pays well, as times go – but unquestionably it ought to pay ten prices; for whatever I send it I feel I am consigning to the tomb of the Capulets. The verses accompanying this, may I beg you to take out of the tomb, and bring them to light in the *Home Journal*? If you can oblige me so far as to copy them, I do not think it will be necessary to say 'From the ——', – that would be too bad; – and, perhaps, 'From a late – paper' would do.

I have not forgotten how a 'good word in season' from you made 'The Raven', and made 'Ulalume', (which, by-the-way, people have done me the honor of attributing to you) – therefore I *would* ask you, (if I dared), to say something of these lines – if they please you.

Truly yours ever,
EDGAR A. POE.

In double proof of his earnest disposition to do the best for himself, and of the trustful and grateful nature which has been denied him, we give another of the only three of his notes which we chance to retain: –

Fordham, January 22, 1848.

MY DEAR WILLIS, – I am about to make an effort at re-establishing myself in the literary world, and *feel* that I may depend·upon your aid.

My general aim is to start a Magazine, to be called 'The Stylus'; but it would be useless to me, even when established, if not entirely out of the control of a publisher. I mean, therefore, to get up a Journal which shall be *my own*, at all points. With this end in view, I must get a list of, at least, five hundred subscribers to begin with: – nearly two hundred I have already. I propose, however, to go South and West, among my personal and literary friends – old college and West Point acquaintances – and see what I can do. In order to get the means of taking the first step, I propose to lecture at the Society Library, on Thursday, the 3d of February – and, that there be no cause of *squabbling*, my subject shall *not be literary* at all. I have chosen a broad text – 'The Universe'.

Having thus given you *the facts* of the case, I leave all the rest to the suggestions of your own tact and generosity.

Gratefully – *most* gratefully –

Your friend always,
EDGAR A. POE.

Brief and chance-taken as these letters are, we think they sufficiently prove the existence of the very qualities denied to Mr Poe, – humility, willingness to persevere, belief in another's kindness, and capability of cordial and grateful friendship! Such he assuredly was *when sane*. Such only he has invariably seemed to us, in all we have happened personally to know of him, through a friendship of five or six years. And so much easier is it to believe what we have seen and known than what we *hear of* only, that we remember him but with admiration and respect, – these descriptions of him, when morally insane, seeming to us like portraits, painted in sickness, of a man we have only known in health.

But there is another, more touching and far more forcible, evidence that there *was goodness* in Edgar A. Poe. To reveal it, we are obliged to venture upon the lifting of the veil which sacredly covers grief and refinement in poverty; but we think it may be excused if so we can brighten the memory of the poet, even were there not a more needed and immediate service which it may render to the nearest link broken by his death.

Our first knowledge of Mr Poe's removal to this city was by a call which we received from a lady who introduced herself to us as the mother of his wife. She was in search of employment for him, and she excused her errand by mentioning that he was ill, that her daughter was a confirmed invalid, and that their circumstances were such as compelled her taking it upon herself. The countenance of this lady, made beautiful and saintly with an evidently complete giving up of her life to privation and sorrowful tenderness, her gentle and mournful voice urging its plea, her long-forgotten but habitually and unconsciously refined manners, and her appealing and yet appreciative mention of the claims and abilities of her son, disclosed at once the presence of one of those angels upon earth that women in adversity can be. It was a hard fate that she was watching over. Mr Poe wrote with fastidious difficulty, and in a style too much above the popular level to be well paid. He was always in pecuniary difficulty, and, with his sick wife, frequently in want of the merest necessities of life. Winter after winter, for years, the most touching sight to us, in this whole city, has been that tireless minister to genius, thinly and insufficiently clad, going from office to office with a poem, or an article on some literary subject, to sell – sometimes simply pleading in a broken voice that he was ill, and begging for him – mentioning nothing but that 'he was ill', whatever might be the reason for his writing nothing; and never, amid all her tears and recitals of distress, suffering one syllable to escape her lips that could convey a doubt of him, or a complaint, or a lessening of pride in his genius and good intentions. Her daughter died, a year and a half since, but she did not desert him. She continued his ministering angel, – living with him, caring for him, guarding him against exposure, and, when he was carried away by temptation, amid grief and the loneliness of feelings unreplied to, and awoke from his self-abandonment prostrated in destitution and suffering, *begging* for him still. If woman's devotion, born with a first love, and fed with human passion, hallow its object, as it is allowed to do, what does not a devotion like this – pure, disinterested, and holy as the watch of an invisible spirit – say for him who inspired it?

We have a letter before us, written by this lady, Mrs. Clemm, on the morning in which she heard of the death of this object of her untiring care. It is merely a request that we would call upon her; but we will copy a few of its words, sacred as its privacy is, to warrant the truth of the picture we have drawn above, and add force to the appeal we wish to make for her: –

I have this morning heard of the death of my darling Eddie.... Can you give me any circumstances or particulars?... Oh! do not desert your poor friend in this bitter affliction....Ask Mr——to come, as I must deliver a message to him from my poor Eddie....I need not ask you to notice his death and to speak well of him. I know you will. But say what an affectionate son he was to me, his poor desolate mother....

To hedge round a grave with respect, what choice is there between the relinquished wealth and honours of the world and the story of such a woman's unrewarded devotion! Risking what we do, in delicacy, by making it public, we feel – other reasons aside – that it betters the world to make known that there are such ministrations to its erring and gifted. What we have said will speak to some hearts. There will be those who will be glad to know how the lamp, whose light of poetry has beamed on their far-away recognition, was watched over with care and pain, that they may send to her, who is more darkened than they by its extinction, some token of their sympathy. She is destitute and alone. If any, far or near, will send to us what may aid and cheer her through the remainder of her life, we will joyfully place it in her hands.

97. Henry Beck Hirst, 'Edgar Allan Poe', McMakin's *Model American Courier*

20 October 1849, 19, 2

Hirst (1817–74) was a Philadelphia lawyer, journalist, and poet, with a reputation for eccentricity. Hirst and Poe were friendly in Philadelphia, and they collaborated on Poe's *Saturday Museum* biography of 1843. Hirst always remained proud of his friendship with Poe, even though he suffered from the delusion that Poe plagiarized from him – see *Works*, 13, 209–13; *Poems*, ed. T.O. Mabbott, p. 355.

Edgar A. Poe is no more. We knew him well, perhaps better than any other man living, and loved him, despite his infirmities. He was a man of great and original genius, but the sublime *afflatus* which lifted him above his fellows, made him a shining mark for the covert as well as the open attacks of literary rivals, and alas! that it should be so, eventually proved his ruin. So much we gather from the unwritten history of his later years. His was a life of strange vicissitudes. His father and mother, while he was yet an infant, died within a few weeks of each other, of consumption. He was then adopted by Mr Richard [*sic*] Allan, a wealthy gentleman, almost a millionaire, of Richmond, Virginia, who at once announced his intention of educating him as his heir. Mr Allan took him with him to England, and he received the first rudiments of his fine classical education at Stoke Newington, near London. The Rev. Dr Bransby was his tutor. Dr Bransby's school is very forcibly described in 'William Wilson', one of Mr Poe's most powerful stories. He subsequently returned to America, and passed some time

313

at the Jefferson University, in Virginia. He graduated,
although a careless student, with the first honors. His life, at
that institution, was full of romance. At even-fall he
wandered away among the mountains, seeking inspiration.

In silence, desolation and dim night.

During the day, frequently for weeks together, he passed
his hours in studies which were only pursued in chambers
litten with sepulchral lamps, of various colored chemical
fires, which he afterward described in the spirit-haunted
apartment of the Lady Rowena of Tremaine, in his terribly
imaginative tale of 'Ligeia'. He was a poet at the age of
twelve, and some of his finest still-existing poems were
written at that time.

Shortly after he left college, owing to some pecuniary
difficulties with Mr Allan, he ran off on an expedition to join
the Greeks, who were then struggling for their liberty, and
actually made his way as far as St Petersburg, in which place
he again became involved in difficulties. He was sent back by
the American Consul. On his return home, he found Mr
Allan married to a young wife. The old gentleman was then
65 years of age. Much against his inclination he went to West
Point, to which place he was recommended by General
Scott. Mr Allan became the father of a son. Young Poe at
once saw that all his hopes of fortune had fallen to the
ground, and wrote for leave to resign. It was refused. He
applied to General Scott, who seconded Mr Allan. Poe then
refused to perform any duty, and covered the walls of the
institution with pasquinades on the Professors. One, Mr
Joseph Locke, was particularly obnoxious to the students,
and he became the principal victim. Mr Locke was rather a
Martinet; he never failed to appear on the parade ground, and
he invariably reported a delinquent. A report, at West Point,
is a matter of no small moment, for whenever the bad marks
amount to a certain number, we forget what it is, charges are
preferred against the cadet, the consequences of which are
expulsion. We quote one of these satires from memory:

'John Locke is a notable name,
Joe Locke is a greater in short,

The former was well known to fame,
The latter *well known* – TO REPORT.

Another:

As for Locke – he is all in my eye,
May the devil right soon for his soul call;
He never was known to *lie* –
In bed, at a reveille roll call.

Ridicule is a weapon few can withstand, and the affair ended in the way that Mr Poe wished. Charges were preferred against him, the specifications amounting to only 152 in number. He at once pleaded guilty, and left the institution. Mr Allan instantly abandoned his protégé, and Poe was left penniless. Mr A. soon after died, and without a reconciliation.

Mr Poe bankrupt in everything except genius, entered the arena of authorship. Some time after, in 1831, the proprietor of a literary weekly paper, in Baltimore, offered two premiums, the one for the best prose story, the other for the best poem. Poe entered into competition, and took both prizes. His 'MS. Found in a Bottle' – such is our recollection – was the tale; the 'Coliseum', the poem. John P. Kennedy, Esq., author of *Horse Shoe Robinson*, was one of the Committee, who unanimously united in publishing a card in the *Gazette*, expressive of the high sense they entertained of his literary abilities. But Mr Kennedy did not stop here; he applied to the late Thomas W. White, who was then engaged in publishing the *Southern Literary Messenger*, and Mr W. immediately wrote to Poe, offering him the editorship of that periodical. Poe accepted, and the *Messenger*, under his care, took the first rank in American literature. He subsequently left Richmond, and came to Philadelphia to take charge of the *Gentleman's Magazine*, afterwards *Graham's*. On its being merged with *Graham*, he assumed the editorship of the latter Monthly, which attained its present unequalled reputation under his care. When his engagement with *Graham's Magazine* terminated he removed to New York, where he edited, during its brief but brilliant existence, the *Broadway Journal*. Since that time, some two or three years, he has remained unconnected with the press.

Soon after the decease of his young and beautiful wife, the 'Lenore' of the muse, Mr Poe removed to a little cottage on the banks of the romantic Bronx, in the vicinity of New York, where he supported himself and his aged mother-in-law, by the occasional use of his brilliant pen. The death of his wife, who was his cousin, and whom he had loved from youth, clouded his fine intellect, and he almost sank under the blow. Adversity hung like a lean and hungry bloodhound on his trail, and he yielded. On a visit to the South, while on his return home, in Baltimore, he succumbed to the destroying angel, and descended into charnel, there to become a prey to the 'Conqueror Worm'.

Poe had his faults – who has not his errors? We are none of us infallible; but had his opportunities equalled his genius and ambition, he would have died a universally esteemed great man. As it is, the world of authors and author-lovers, with some few pitiful exceptions, will mourn a departed brother. His name, under any circumstances, cannot be forgotten. His tales are without existing equals in English literature, and his 'Raven', the personification of his own despair at the loss of his wife, has made him immortal.

Poor Poe! Hour by hour have we listened to his delightful abstractions, poured forth in a voice so remarkable in the peculiarity of its intonation as to incline to the extraordinary in tone. He was unfortunate in every sense of the word. When miserable authors of still more miserable love stories and puling poems, were winning gold from the Magazines of the day, he was rarely able to 'sell an article', and was always suffering in the iron grasp of penury, and that, too, when the brilliant corruscations of his genius were eagerly sought for by the public *in vain*. Poe wielded too formidable a pen; he was no time server, and as a critic he could not, and would not, *lie*. What he thought he wrote, and, as a consequence, he made enemies, – like carping muck-worms in the barnyards, of literature, whose very odor offended the nostrils of his genius. But their number was legion – and he was only one. Gulliver was in the hands of the Lilliputians; they triumphed – he fell. Few could imagine the occupational sufferings under the awful wrong of undeserved poverty, for Poe was an industrious man, who would and did toil, delving, when his labors demanded, imperishable gold from the California of his heart – gold which was exchanged for copper in the Jewry of American literature. And with all his talent how little was he understood. We saw him twice and thrice a day, for two years. We sat night by night, a welcome guest at his often meagre, but when fortune smiled on him, his well-filled board. In all that time, in all our acquaintance, we never heard him express one single word of personal ill-feeling against any man, not even in his blackest hours of poverty.

His criticisms of individuals, and they were nervous enough, referred only to their literary merits, and he was always just and *always right*. Unamiable he was not; he was otherwise to a fault; and always ready to forget and forgive. But his philippics against pretenders in literature, which he loved as an art, and for its own sweet sake, have been misunderstood; they were the expression of the artist, not the man; the object of them would have found a brother in the individual, who, as a critic, would have weeded him from the garden of song, with joy that he had done so much toward perfecting its parterres. Poor Poe!

98. George Lippard, notice in the *Quaker City*

20 October 1849

Lippard (1822–54) was a prolific Philadelphia journalist and novelist with strong populist sympathies. He presumably named his weekly paper after his sensational novel of life in Philadelphia – *The Quaker City; or, The Monks of Monk Hall* (1844). Lippard saw himself as an outsider and felt affinity with Poe, whom he assisted on his last 'spree' in Philadelphia – see *Letters*, 2, 455–6. For further comment on the Poe – Lippard relationship, see Emilio De Grazia, 'Poe's Devoted Democrat, George Lippard', *Poe Studies*, 6 (June 1973), 6–8; Burton R. Pollin, 'More on Lippard and Poe', *Poe Studies*, 7 (June 1974), 22–3.

Edgar Allan Poe died, in the city of Baltimore, on Sunday, nearly two weeks ago. He is dead, and we are conscious that words are fruitless to express our feelings in relation to his death. Only a few weeks ago we took him by the hand, in our office, and heard him express himself in these words – 'I am sick – sick at heart. I have come to see you before I leave for Virginia. I am home-sick for Virginia. I don't know why it is, but when my foot is once in Virginia, I feel myself a new man. It is a pleasure to me to go into her woods – to lay myself upon her sod – even to breathe her air.' These words, the manner in which they were spoken, made a deep impression. They were the words of a man of genius, hunted by the world, trampled upon by the men whom he had loaded with favours, and disappointed on every turn of life. Poe spent the day with us. He talked of the time we had first met, in his quiet home in Seventh Street, Philadelphia, when it was made happy by the presence of his wife – a pure and beautiful woman. He talked also of his last book *Eureka*, well named a 'Prose Poem', and spoke much of projects for the future. When we parted from him in the cars, he held our hand for a long time, and seemed loth to leave us – there was in his voice, look and manner something of a Presentiment that his strange and stormy life was near its close. His look and his words were vividly impressed upon our memory, until we heard of his death and the news of that event brought every look and word home to us as keenly as though only a moment had passed since we parted from him. We frankly confess that, on this occasion, we cannot imitate a number of editors who have taken upon themselves to speak of Poe, and his faults, in a tone of condescending pity! That Poe had faults we do not deny. He was a harsh, a bitter, and sometimes an unjust critic. But he was a man of genius – a man of high honor – a man of good heart. He was not an intemperate man. When he drank, the first drop maddened him; hence his occasional departures from the line of strict propriety. But he was not an habitual drinker. As an author, his name will live, while three-fourths of the bastard critics and mongrel authors of the present day go down to nothingness and night. And the men who now spit upon his grave, by way of retaliation for some injury which they imagined they have received from Poe living, would do well to remember, that it is only an idiot or a coward who strikes the cold forehead of a corpse. On some occasion – when the lapse of time shall allow us to express ourselves freely – we shall speak more fully of the gifted dead. For the present we can only say, that his death adds another name to that scroll on which neglect and misfortune has already written the names of John Lofland and Sumner Lincoln Fairfield.[1]

NOTE

1 The names of John Lofland, 'The Milford Bard' (1798–1849), and Sumner Lincoln Fairfield (1803–44) were commonly thought of in relation to Poe by contemporaries: the lives of both poets were marked by illness, instability, and neglect.

99. [Charles J. Peterson], 'Mr Poe's Last Poem', Philadelphia *Saturday Gazette*

20 October 1849

Peterson, then editor of the *Saturday Gazette*, had known Poe when they worked together on *Graham's Magazine*.

Edgar A. Poe Esq., who died in Baltimore, on the 7th inst., was one of the most remarkable of the literary men of the United States. He was a native of Baltimore [sic], had enjoyed unusual advantages of education, and left many poems and fugitive prose pieces of marked genius. With considerable capacity for continued mental labor, he yet produced no great works on which to build his name; and the consequence is that in fifty years his reputation, like that of Dennie,[1] will be merely traditionary. The characteristic of his mind was its wonderful analytical power. This was the great secret of his literary success. He would take a great poem mentally to pieces, just as a mechanician would take to pieces a watch, and thus learn, like the artisan, how to construct a similar one. We were associated together, in 1842, in editing *Graham's Magazine*; and we speak from observation, therefore, when we describe the manner in which he produced his prose and poetical articles. His wonderful poem of 'The Raven' was evidently thus written. His analytical faculty rendered him also a superior critic, and when not prejudiced, no man was his equal as a reviewer. But, though not mercenary Mr Poe had strong likings and antipathies, which always colored his criticisms, and which, unfortunately for his consistency, frequently led him to censure and praise the same person at different times. In his private life, his sensibility, joined with many misfortunes, rendered him eminently unhappy; we think we never knew a man to whom life was so little of a pleasure. Over whatever follies he had, or may have been charged with, however, we draw a veil. The dead are sacred.

We quote below a poem by Mr Poe, probably one of the last he ever wrote. It appears in *Sartain's Magazine* for November, and when analysed, renders fully evident his manner of composition. The subject is a trite one, nor are the thoughts themselves fresh, yet with what novelty and art they are handled! No man indeed could make so much out of a subject as Mr Poe. The wild and irregular style of the verse in the following poem; the skill with which the author avails himself of the subtle force that lies sometimes in the reiteration of a word; and many other peculiarities, none the result of chance, but all of the most careful thought, prove

Mr Poe to have been the greatest master of the *mere art* of composition, which this country, or perhaps this century, has produced.

[Quotes 'The Bells'.]

NOTE

1 Joseph Dennie (1768–1812) was a conservative essayist and critic then considered old-fashioned.

100. Edward H.N. Patterson, 'Death of Poe', and 'Literary Fame', Oquawka *Spectator*

(a) 24 October 1849; (b) 7 November 1849

Patterson (1828–?) was editor of the *Spectator*, a weekly 'Family Newspaper' recently started by his father in Oquawka, Illinois. During 1849 Poe and he made grandiose plans to establish the 'Stylus' magazine; meanwhile Patterson published Poe's work in the *Spectator*. See further M.D. McElroy, 'Poe's Last Partner: E.H.N. Patterson of Oquawka, Illinois', *Papers on Language and Literature*, 7 (1971), 252–71.

(a) Edgar A. Poe is dead! He died at Baltimore on the 7th inst., after a few days illness. We at first hoped that this was a mistake, but the announcement of the fact in the papers of that city deprives us of the solace of such a hope.

Although not young, being but 38 years old, Mr Poe had attained an enviable position among our Literati, and was justly distinguished for his great learning, his excellence as a

Poet, and his acuteness and analytical power as a Critic. Some of his productions have never been surpassed for originality of thought, and singularity yet beauty of style. Although his 'Raven' has been pronounced the best, as well as the most remarkable poem ever written in America, yet it is most probable that we have never had anything from his pen, which has displayed the great intellectual powers that he possessed, to their full extent; at least this was his own conviction. He has had to struggle, nearly all his life with poverty, and has not had those advantages which more leisure, and a comfortable living, would have afforded him for displaying his powers. In the Department of Criticism he has obtained his greatest celebrity, yet even in this he has been cramped – never having had a periodical under his exclusive control.

The doings of the Supreme One are incomprehensible, and it is not for frail man to impugn His motives, else we might wonder why the lamented poet was removed so soon – and when he was upon the eve of realizing the cherished hope of his life!

Had he lived, arrangements had been completed by which he was, next year, to have been placed at the head of a large Magazine, which would have been entirely under his control. This statement may surprise even many of his friends, but it is nevertheless true. We are personally knowing to the whole arrangement. But death has removed him from us, and we can only lament the sad event which has deprived us of a noble and eminent man. His life was a sad succession of trials and disappointments, but death has released his soul from its thraldom to live forever with its Creator above.

(b) 'With considerable capacity for continued mental labor, he yet produced no great works on which to build his name; and the consequence is that in fifty years his reputation, like that of Dennie, will be merely traditional.'

We copy the above from an article relative to Edgar A. Poe which we find in the *Saturday Gazette*, for the purpose of expressing our disagreement from the conclusion at which the editor of that paper has arrived. That Mr Poe's fame will ever become 'merely traditional' we cannot believe; so long as our language endures will that remarkable poem – the 'Raven' – continue to be read with interest.

An author's reputation must not be estimated by his capacity for producing voluminous works; the cumbrous folios which have been, from time to time, foisted upon the public, only to be laid aside as useless embodyments of the dullness of the drones who produced them, serve to point out the folly of making mere *bulk* our criterion in estimating an author's fame. It is the display of that highest order of intellect – Genius – that will insure to its possessor, in its display, an undying fame: Gray, for instance, will never be forgotten while man is capable of appreciating true poetry; and it is not saying too much to assert that his *fame* rests solely upon his 'Elegy in a Country Churchyard'. There is in this brief poem all the elements of true poetic talent, and it will never cease to be read – nor will it ever be read without eliciting the conviction that its author was a poet of the highest order of talent. The same may be said of Poe's 'Raven'; it bears all the essential marks of *greatness*, which, combined with its *originality* of versification, renders it one of the most remarkable poems ever written. That such a poem as this, distinguished for its originality, its beauty of style, its melody of versification, and the extraordinary display of genius made manifest in its composition, can ever be suffered to go out of print, is a supposition founded in an erroneous estimate of the human mind. The 'Raven' cannot become obsolete – it is destined to remain coexistent with our language, and the fame attached to its author will ever be green in the hearts of its reader. – Poe's *Eureka: or System of the Universe* is another work, not so well known as the 'Raven', but equally deserving of the epithet 'great', – not great in bulk, but in the extraordinary display of the imagination, and for the deep and almost incontrovertible train of reasoning, founded upon the proposition that Beauty and Consistency constitute Truth, which renders *probable* that which before seemed *impossible*.

But this subject affords ample room for an essay, which our want of space will not permit us to occupy; it is enough for our present purpose if we are judged to be correct in our proposition that a truly great work is one in which a mighty intellect is displayed – that literary fame rests not upon the size of an author's books but upon their *character*. Gray's 'Elegy' is great work – such, the 'Raven' – such, Halleck's 'Marco Bozzaris', which will be read and admired when his other poems are forgotten.

The grave may hide the wasted form of the penury-smitten and unhappy Poe – Heaven may become the resting place of the soul of the gifted poet, but the great intellect which he possessed, the name which he bore, and the great poem which he has left us, no Lethean wave can ever obliterate from the tablets of human memory.

101. John Reuben Thompson, 'The Late Edgar A. Poe', *Southern Literary Messenger*

November 1849, 15, 694–7

Thompson (1823–73) was a poet and journalist who owned and edited the *Messenger* (1847–60). He met Poe in Richmond in 1849 and presumed much on a rather slight acquaintance. He later expanded this notice into a popular lecture on 'The Genius and Character of Edgar Allan Poe' – ed. and arranged by James H. Whitty and James H. Rindfleisch (Richmond, 1929) – but he was often an unreliable witness.

So much has been said by the newspaper press of the country concerning this gifted child of genius, since his recent death, that our readers are already in possession of the leading incidents of his short, brilliant, erratic and unhappy career. It is quite unnecessary that we should recount them in this place. We feel it due to the dead, however, as editor of a magazine which owes its earliest celebrity to his efforts, that some recognition of his talent, on the part of the *Messenger*, should mingle with the general apotheosis which now enrols him on the list of 'heroes in history and gods in song.'

Mr Poe became connected with the *Messenger* during the first year of its existence. He was commended to the favorable consideration of the proprietor, the late T. W. White, by the Honorable John P. Kennedy who, as Chairman of a Committee, had just awarded to Poe the prize for the successful tale in a literary competition at Baltimore. Under his editorial management the work soon become well-known everywhere. Perhaps no similar enterprise ever prospered so largely in its inception, and we doubt if any, in the same length of time – even *Blackwood* in the days of Dr Maginn,[1] whom Poe in some respects closely resembled – ever published so many shining articles from the same pen. Those who will turn to the first two volumes of the *Messenger* will be struck with the number and variety of his contributions. On one page may be found some lyric cadence, plaintive and inexpressibly sweet, the earliest vibrations of those chords which have since thrilled with so many wild and wondrous harmonies. On another some strange story of the German school, akin to the most fanciful legends of the Rhine, fascinates and astonishes the reader with the verisimilitude of its improbabilities. But it was in the editorial department of the magazine that his power was most conspicuously displayed. There he appeared as the critic, not always impartial, it may be, in the distribution of his praises, or correct in the positions he assumed, but ever merciless to the unlucky author who offended by a dull book. A blunder in this respect he considered worse than a crime, and visited it with corresponding rigor. Among the nascent novelists and newly-fledged poetasters of fifteen years ago he came down 'like a Visigoth marching on Rome'. No elegant imbecile or conceited pedant, no matter whether he made his avatar under the auspices of a Society, or with the *prestige* of a degree, but felt the the lash of his severity. *Baccalaurei baculo potius quam laureo digni* was the principle of his action in such cases, and to the last he continued to castigate impudent aspirants for the bays. Now that he is gone, the vast multitude of blockheads may breathe again, and we can imagine that we hear the shade of the departed crying out to them, in the epitaph designed for Robespierre,

> Passant! ne plains point mon sort,
> Si je vivais, tu serait mort!*

It will readily occur to the reader that such a course, while it gained subscribers to the review, was not well calculated to gain friends for the reviewer. And so Mr Poe found it, for during the two years of his connection with the *Messenger*, he contrived to attach to himself animosities of the most enduring kind. It was the fashion with a large class to decry his literary pretensions, as poet and romancer and scholar, to represent him as one who possessed little else than

> th' extravagancy
> And crazy ribaldry of fancy –

and to challenge his finest efforts with a chilling *cui bono*; while the critics of other lands and other tongues, the *Athenaeum* and the *Revue des deux Mondes*, were warmly recognizing his high claims. They did not appreciate him. To the envious obscure, he might not indeed seem entitled to the first literary honors, for he was versed in a more profound learning and skilled in a more lofty minstrelsy, scholar by virtue of a larger erudition and poet by the transmission of a diviner spark.

Unquestionably he was a man of great genius. Among the litterateurs of his day he stands out distinctively as an original writer and thinker. In nothing did he conform to established custom. Conventionality he condemned. Thus his writings admit of no classification. And yet in his most eccentric vagaries he was always correct. The fastidious reader may look in vain, even among his earlier poems – where 'wild words wander here and there' – for an offence against rhetorical propriety. He did not easily pardon solecisms in others; he committed none himself. It is remarkable too that a mind so prone to unrestrained imaginings should be capable of analytic investigation or studious research. Yet few excelled Mr Poe in power of analysis or patient application. Such are the contradictions of the human intellect. He was an impersonated antithesis.

The regret has often been expressed that Mr Poe did not bring his singular capacity to bear on subjects nearer ordinary life and of a more cheerful nature than the gloomy incidents of his tales and sketches. P.P. Cooke, (the accomplished author of the *Froissart Ballads*, who, we predict, will one day take, by common consent, his rightful high position in American letters,) in a discriminating essay on the genius of Poe, published in this magazine for January, 1848, remarks upon this point,

For my individual part, having the seventy or more tales, analytic, mystic, grotesque, arabesque, always wonderful, often great, which his industry and fertility have already given us, I would like to read one cheerful book made by his *invention*, with little or no aid from its twin brother *imagination* – a book in his admirable style of full, minute, never tedious narrative – a book full of homely doings, of successful toils, of ingenious shifts and contrivances, of ruddy firesides – a book happy and healthy throughout, and with no poetry in it at all anywhere, except a good old English 'poetic justice' in the end.

That such a work would have greatly enhanced Mr Poe's reputation with the million, we think, will scarcely be disputed. But it could not be. Mr Poe was not the man to have produced a *home-book*. He had little of the domestic feeling and his thoughts were ever wandering. He was either in criticism or in the clouds, by turns a disciplinarian and a dreamer. And in his dreams, what visions came to him, may be gathered to some extent from the revealings he has given – visions wherein his fancy would stray off upon some new Walpurgis, or descend into the dark realms of the Inferno, and where occasionally through the impenetrable gloom, the supernal beauty of Lenore would burst upon his sight, as did the glorified Beatrice on the rapt gaze of the Italian master.

The poems of Mr Poe are remarkable above all other characteristics, for the exceeding melody of the versification. 'Ulalume' might have been cited as a happy instance of this quality, but we prefer to quote 'The Bells' from the last number of the *Union Magazine*. It was the design of the author, as he himself told us, to express in language the exact sound of bells to the ear. He has succeeded, we think, far better than Southey, who attempted a similar feat, to tell us 'how the waters came down at Lodore.'

[Quotes 'The Bells'.]

The untimely death of Mr Poe occasioned a very general feeling of regret, although little genuine sorrow was called forth by it, out of the narrow circle of his relatives. We have received in our private correspondence, from various quarters of the Union, warm tributes to his talent, some of which we take the liberty of quoting, though not designed for publication. A friend in the country writes –

Many who deem themselves perfect critics talk of the want of *moral* in the writings and poetry of Poe. They would have everyone write like Aesop, with the moral distinctly drawn at the end to prevent mistake. Such men would object to the meteor, or the lightning's flash, because it lasts only for the moment – and yet they speak the power of God, and fill our minds with the sublime more readily than does the enduring sunlight. It is thus with the writings of Poe. Every moment there comes across the darkness of his style a flash of the spirit which is not of earth. You cannot analyse the feeling – you cannot tell in what the beauty of a particular passage consists; and yet you feel that deep pathos which only genius can incite – you feel the trembling of that melancholy chord which fills the soul with pleasant mournfulness – you feel that deep yearning for something brighter and better than this world can give – that unutterable gushing of the heart which springs up at the touch of the enchanter, as poured the stream from

Horeb's rock, beneath the prophet's hand.

I wish I could convey to you the impression which the 'Raven' has made upon me. I read it hastily in times gone by without appreciation; but now it is a study to me – as I go along like Sinbad in the Valley of Diamonds, I find a new jewel at every step. The beautiful rhythm, the mournful cadence, still ring in the ear for hours after a perusal – whilst the heart is bowed down by the outpourings of a soul made desolate not alone by disappointed love, but by the crushing of every hope, and every aspiration.

In a recent letter the following noble acknowledgement is made by the first of American poets – Henry W. Longfellow – towards whom, it must be said, Mr Poe did not always act with justice. Mr. Longfellow will pardon us, we trust, for publishing what was intended as a private communication. The passage evidences a magnanimity which belongs only to great minds.

'What a melancholy death', says Mr Longfellow, 'is that of Mr Poe – a man so richly endowed with genius! I never knew him personally, but have always entertained a high appreciation of his powers as a prose-writer and a poet. His prose is remarkably vigorous, direct and yet affluent; and his verse has a particular charm of melody, an atmosphere of true poetry about it, which is very winning. The harshness of his criticisms, I have never attributed to anything but the irritation of a sensitive nature, chafed by some indefinite sense of wrong.'

It was not until within two years past that we ever met Mr Poe, but during that time, and especially for two or three months previous to his death, we saw him very often. When in Richmond, he made the office of the *Messenger* a place of frequent resort. His conversation was always attractive, and at times very brilliant. Among modern authors his favorite was Tennyson, and he delighted to recite from 'The Princess' the song 'Tears, idle tears'; a fragment of which –

> *when into dying eyes*
> *The casement slowly grows a glimmering square*

he pronounced unsurpassed by any image expressed in writing. The day before he left Richmond, he placed in our hands for publication in the *Messenger*, the MS. of his last poem, which has since found its way (through a correspondent of a northern paper with whom Mr Poe had left a copy) into the newspaper press, and has been extensively circulated. As it was designed for this magazine, however, we publish it, even though all our readers may have seen it before:

[Quotes 'Annabel Lee'.]

In what we have said of Mr Poe, we have been considering

329

only the brighter side of the picture. That he had many and sad infirmities cannot be questioned. Over these we would throw in charity the mantle of forgetfulness. The grave has come between our perception and his errors, and we pass over them in silence. They found indeed a mournful expiation in his alienated friendships and his early death.

NOTE

* We translate it freely,

Traveller! forbear to mourn my lot,
Thou would'st have died, if I had not.

1 William Maginn (1793–1842) was an important contributor to *Blackwood's Magazine*.

102. [Charles Frederick Briggs], preview in *Holden's Dollar Magazine*

December 1849, 4, 765–6

Briggs (1804–77) was a journalist and novelist well known under his pen name 'Harry Franco'. He founded the *Broadway Journal*, but Poe pushed him out, and abused him in a 'Literati' sketch – see *Works*, 15, 20–3. Briggs was a friend of Lowell, and an associate of Poe's enemies in the *Knickerbocker* clique. He was at this time editor of *Holden's Dollar Magazine* in New York.

The prominent topic of conversation in literary circles, during the past month, has been the death of that melancholy man Edgar A. Poe. Mr Poe left his home, in Westchester County, in this State, early in the Summer on a visit to the South, and we were told at the time that his mother-in-law, Mrs Clemm, who was his sole companion, had no expectations of ever again seeing him return. He arranged all his papers so that they could be used without difficulty in case of his death, and told her that if he never came back she would find that he had left everything in order. But there was no cause to apprehend that the termination of his career was so close at hand. He went to Richmond where he delivered a series of lectures and was well received by his old friends; he renewed his attachment to a wealthy widow in that city, whom he had known before his or her marriage, and was on his way home to make arrangements for his marriage to her, when he had a relapse of his besetting infirmities in Baltimore, and died miserably.

A biography of Mr Poe is soon to be published with his collected writings, under the supervision of Rev. Rufus W. Griswold; but it will be a long while, if ever, before the naked character of the sad poet will be exposed to public gaze. There is a generous disposition on the part of those who knew him intimately, to bury his failings, or rather personal characteristics, in the shade of forgetfulness; while nothing is dwelt upon but his literary productions. He was a psychological phenomenon, and more good than harm would result from a clear, unprejudiced analysis of his character. But when will any one be found bold enough to incur the risk of an imputation of evil motives, by making such a revelation as the task demands? Like all other writers, Mr Poe developed himself in his literary productions, but to understand his writings it was necessary to be possessed of the key of his personal acquaintance. Knowing him thoroughly, you could thoroughly comprehend what he wrote, but not otherwise. He was an intellectual machine without a balance wheel; and all his poetry, which seems perfect in itself, and full of feeling, was mere machine work. It was not that spontaneous outgushing of sentiment, which the verse of great poets seems to be, but a carefully constructed mosaic, painfully elaborated, and designedly put together, with every little word in its right place, and every shade of thought toned down to its exact position. There is nothing of the 'fine frenzy' about it, which marks the poetry of those who warble their native wood notes wild. – His last poem, the 'Bells', is a curious example of his way of jingling words to make them sound like music:

Bells, bells,
Bells, bells, bells, bells.

This was the burden of the song. Yet, ever and anon, in this strange jingling and clanging of words, there struck upon the ear sounds of a real sadness, which touched the heart and produced the feeling produced by the strain of the true poet. But, was not Poe a true poet? That remains for the world to decide. If he was a poet, he cannot be deprived of criticism of his rightful fame. His merits as a critic were very slender, he was a minute detector of slips of the pen, and, probably, was unequalled as a proof reader. But such was his sensitiveness to small imperfections, that it incapacitated him from taking a comprehension or liberal survey of a literary subject. He was of the Doctor Blair school of critics, and while measuring the lines of a poem was indifferent to their meaning. One of the strange points of his strange nature was to entertain a spirit of revenge towards all who did him a service. His pecuniary difficulties often compelled him to solicit aid, and he rarely, or never, failed to malign those who befriended him. It was probably this strange propensity which caused him to quarrel with his early benefactor, and forfeit the aid which he might have received from that quarter. He was altogether a strange and fearful being, and a true history of his life would be more startling than any of the grotesque romances which he was so fond of inventing.

103. George Ripley, review in the New York *Daily Tribune*

19 January 1850

Ripley (1802–80) was a writer on religious and philosophical matters and a central figure in the Transcendentalist movement. He was a book reviewer for the *Tribune*.

If we were disposed to point a moral with the exhibition of the errors of wasted genius, we could not be furnished with more fruitful materials than are presented in these volumes. Judging from their contents, which is the only means we possess of forming an estimate of Mr Poe, he was a man of extraordinary boldness and originality of intellect, with a power of sharp and subtle analysis that has seldom been surpassed, and an imagination singularly prolific both in creations of beauty and of terror. The ingenuity, with which he combines the delicate filaments of thought into what seems a compact and substantial texture, is a perpetual surprise. His ability in the sphere of artistic invention was sufficient to have insured him a permanent fame as a writer of romance or dramatic poetry, had the truthfulness of his intellect been in proportion to its energy. The skill with which he throws an air of probability over the most absurd, and often the most horrible and revolting situations – the apparent good faith with which he weaves up a tissue of complicated details into a plot which beguiles the reader, until he arrives at the audacious denouement, is equaled only by the exquisite propriety and force of the language, which he always selects with the unerring instinct of genius. With these rare gifts of invention and expression, Mr Poe might have attained an eminent rank in literature, and even have been classed among the intellectual benefactors of society.

Unhappily he had no earnestness of character, no sincerity of conviction, no faith in human excellence, no devotion to a high purpose, – not even the desire to produce a consummate work of art, – and hence, his writings fail of appealing to universal principles of taste, and are destitute of the truth and naturalness, which are the only passports to an enduring reputation in literature. He regarded the world as an enormous humbug, and, in revenge, would repay it in kind. His mind was haunted with terrific conceptions, which he delighted to embellish and work up, by the aid of his preternatural analysis, into the strangely plausible fictions, which at length disgust the reader with their horrible monstrosities. The effect of his writings is like breathing the air of a charnel house. The walls seem to sweat with blood, we stumble on skulls and dead men's bones, and grinning spectres mock us in the dim, sepulchral light. There is no smell of the fresh earth, we see no Spring blossoms or

Autumn fruits, we hear no cattle lowing on the hills, the song of forest birds is hushed, all the blessed sights and sounds of Nature are no more, and some foul, accursed demon is throttling us with his infernal grasp. Even the title of many of Mr Poe's tales is a nightmare.

If these grim, ghastly creations contributed to any true aesthetic effect – if they were redeemed by any touches of humanity – if their lurid blackness were intended to highten the splendor of any celestial dawn, one might forgive such a horrible play of the imagination to the purposes of the artist. But there is no such apology. Mr Poe luxuriates in the wantonness of his ingenuity, and evokes the most terrific spectres merely for terror's sake. This would be fatal in any kindred spheres of Art. Conceive of one of those demoniacal scenes being embodied in painting or sculpture! It is equally fatal in literature. And hence these writings (we refer particularly to the prose articles) bear the seal of early death upon their face.

Many of the poetical pieces contained in these volumes are of a different character. Some of them are remarkable for their limpid smoothness and sweetness. But they are destitute of the freedom, the gushing spontaneity, the inspired, ecstatic burst of soul, which are essential to an immortal song. They show a profound study of the theory and resources of versification, but seem to be composed as an intellectual experiment, not the expression of the rapt spirit, to which poetry is as natural as the 'wood notes wild' to the bird. Their prevailing characteristic is an extreme artificiality, a certain cunning skill in construction, and displays of artistic force which have no merit but their ingenuity, like the singular conceit of enveloping the name of a favorite in the mazes of a sonnet. No one can find it till he knows the trick, and when known, it loses its interest.

Mr Poe's own account of the composition of his most popular piece, 'The Raven', lets us into the secret of his methods, unless, indeed, this very confession is a quiz, which, with his monomaniacal love of mystification, is very likely to be the case. At all events, however, it is too curious a specimen of analysis, too characteristic of Poe's refining, hair splitting intellect, not to reward a moment's attention.

[Then follows a summary of Poe's account of how he wrote 'The Raven' from 'The Philosophy of Composition'.]

Whether this psychological revelation is to be taken in just or earnest – historically or as a shrewd afterthought, – it is singularly illustrative of the tendency of mind, to which we have before alluded, and which formed such a disproportionate element in Mr Poe's intellectual composition.

The announcement on the title page of these volumes that they are to contain notices of the life and genius of their author by J.R. Lowell, N.P. Willis and R.W. Griswold is not fulfilled in a manner to satisfy the reasonable expectations of the reader. Mr Lowell contributes only a short essay written for one of the magazines a few years since at the request of Mr Poe. It abounds in admirable criticisms, and fully meets the object for which it was originally designed. But it is not the tribute of one poet to another which we had the right to look for from the announcement. Mr Willis gives nothing but an article published in the *Home Journal* soon after Mr Poe's death, into which are interwoven some paragraphs of Mr Griswold's notice of that event in *The Tribune*. We wonder that these gentlemen should have allowed the use of their names to authorise a promise of which there is such a meager fulfilment.

In spite of the criticisms, which we could not avoid making, if we noticed the subject at all, we need not say that these volumes will be found rich in intellectual excitements, and abounding in remarkable specimens of vigorous, beautiful, and highly suggestive composition. They are all that remains to us of a man whose uncommon genius it would be folly to deny, and which alone justifies our protracted consideration of his brilliant errors as a literary artist. We cannot doubt that the edition will command a rapid and extensive sale, no less by reason of the undeniable interest of the work than of the beneficent object to which its avails are consecrated.

104. [Evert Augustus Duyckinck], reviews in the *Literary World*

(a) 26 January 1850; (b) 21 September 1850

(a)   From the announcement we expected a somewhat fuller account of the life of Mr Poe than is furnished in the few pages prefixed to this collection of his writings. If we had considered carefully the character of the man's talent this expectation would have been found to be ill-founded. Poe was strictly impersonal; as greatly so as any man whose acquaintance we have enjoyed. In a knowledge of him extending through several years, and frequent opportunities, we can scarcely remember to have had from him any single disclosure or trait of personal character; anything which marked him as a mover or observer among men. Although he had traveled in distant countries, sojourned in cities of our own country, and had, at different times, under favourable opportunities, been brought into contact with life and character of many places, he had no anecdote to tell, no description of objects, dress, or appearance. Nothing, in a word, to say of these things. Briefly, he was what Napoleon named an ideologist – a man of ideas. He lived entirely apart from the solidities and realities of life: was an abstraction; thought, wrote, and dealt solely in abstractions. It is this which gives their peculiar feature to his writings. They have no color, but are in pure outline, delicately and accurately drawn, but altogether without the glow and pulse of humanity. His genius was mathematical, rather than pictorial or poetical. He demonstrates instead of painting. Selecting some quaint and abstruse theme, he proceeded to unfold it with the closeness, care, and demonstrative method of Euclid; and you have, to change the illustration, fireworks for fire; the appearance of water for water; and a great shadow in the place of an actual, moist, and thunder-bearing sky. His indifference to living, flesh and blood subjects, explains his

337

fondness for the mechanism and music of verse, without reference to the thought or feeling. He is therefore a greater favorite with scholars than with the people; and would be (as a matter of course) eagerly followed by a train of poetastering imitators, who, to do them justice in a familiar image, 'hear the bell ring and don't know where the clapper hangs.' Poe is an object of considerable, or more than considerable size; but the imitation of Poe is a shadow indescribably small and attenuated. We can get along, for a while, on a diet of common air – but the exhausted receiver of the air-pump is another thing! The method and management of many of Mr Poe's tales and poems are admirable, exhibiting a wonderful ingenuity, and completely proving him master of the weapon he had chosen for his use. He lacks reality, imagination, everyday power, but he is remarkably subtle, acute, and earnest in his own way. His instrument is neither an organ nor a harp; he is neither a King David nor a Beethoven, but rather a Campanologian, a Swiss bell-ringer, who from little contrivances of his own, with an ingeniously devised hammer, strikes a sharp melody, which has all that is delightful and affecting, that is attainable without a soul. We feel greatly obliged to Messrs. Willis, Lowell, and Griswold, for helping to wheel into public view this excellent machine; to which Mr Redfield has furnished an appropriate cloth and cover, with the performer's head, as large and as true as life, stamped on its front, in an excellent daguerreotype portrait.

(b)   The Rev. Dr Griswold[1] appears to have been employed to let off the late Mr Poe's posthumous blunderbuss, on the principle involved in Dr Johnson's saying with regard to Mallet's publication of the infidel writings left by Bolingbroke:[2] a job to which the Reverend Executor seems to have been by no means disinclined, inasmuch as the parties whom it seemed to the late Mr Poe desirable to 'shoot down', are the very persons whom, from his known relations to them, the Reverend Executor himself would like 'to have a crack at'.

As we find the Rev. Dr Griswold and the late Mr Poe standing at the front door of the volume, in the title-page, in close conjunction, and as they both lift up their voices together, promising 'honest' opinions, with only 'occasional' words of personality, we are bound, on a full inspection of the work, to charge both the dead Poe and the living Griswold with introducing themselves to our attention under false pretences. The opinions, we find, are about as dishonest as they well can be, and the 'words of personality' are by no means 'occasional', but constant, there being, we should say, on a fair estimate, at least twelve hundred personalities in the six hundred pages. Now we would inquire, if any interest can attach to a work from an author whose editor and executor asserts, in introducing this very book to the public, that 'a volume might be filled with passages to show that his criticisms were guided by no sense of duty, and that *his opinions were so variable and so liable to be influenced by unworthy considerations, as to be really of no value whatever.*' – If, after this unhesitating avowal of the utterly worthless and unprincipled character of the work he is editing, we can bring ourselves to regard it with any other feeling than that of simple indifference, we would ask the Reverend Editor one or two questions to which the public, we are quite confident, would like to have answers. Was this book left by its author, Poe, to be published in its present form? or is it a compilation made by Griswold, from unedited material left by Poe? If made by Griswold, on what principle has he selected hostile criticisms, where there were later favourable criticisms written by Poe on the same parties? Are these honest opinions printed *literatim et verbatim*, as written by Poe, or have they undergone editorial revisal? As to Poe's criticisms themselves, which the Rev. Dr Griswold has been at such pains to edit, at the same time that he charges the author with an utter want of conscience and principle – and which proceeding we would like to have the Rev. Editor reconcile to decency and common sense: as to Poe's critical libels or 'honest opinions', which Griswold has made his own, they have not the slightest earthly value. Poe was, in the very centre of his soul, a literary attorney, and pleaded according to his fee. To omit, when properly invited to do so, to retain Poe, by an advance of his *peculium*, was to incur his everlasting hostility; and it is a striking illustration of this, that the author, who is made the most consistent occasion, throughout these six hundred pages, of malevolent abuse and misrepresentation, is one who, both from principle and necessity, never allowed himself to be taxed by the late Poe to the extent of a dollar. And yet the author of 'The Literati' was not without a gleam of consciousness of the peculiar course he was pursuing. For instance, we have here, by favor of Dr Griswold, resurrectionized from *Graham's Magazine* of 1840, or thereabouts,[3] a particularly personal and impertinent review of the 'Wakondah' of Cornelius Mathews; which Poe himself, subsequently, when sober, characterized, in a letter to Mr Mathews now before us, – 'Could I imagine that, at any moment, you regarded a certain *impudent and flippant* critique as more than a matter to be laughed at, I would proffer you an apology on the spot. Since I scribbled the article in question, you yourself have given me fifty good reasons for being ashamed of it.' We would like to learn from Dr Griswold why this repudiated article now appears in print, after a lapse of eight or ten years, to the exclusion of criticisms of the same author of a friendly tenor? And why, on the other hand, the work is carefully purged of any unhandsome references to Dr Griswold, of whom it is well known the late Mr Poe was not sparing, during many of the years over which this collection extends? On the contrary, we find the Doctor, throughout this fat 12mo., steadily treated with the most profound gravity and decorum, while such small creatures as Henry Fielding, Margaret Fuller, Tobias Smollett, and John Neal, are thrown to the dogs: and one Robert Burns, a Scotch poet of some little repute, is coolly spoken of as 'the puppet of circumstance.'...

[Examples of Poe's 'personality' criticism are cited and quoted.]

...Of the parties ill used by these random curryings of the late Mr Poe, we think the Rev. Dr Griswold has the best cause to complain: we can imagine no meaner use for a Reverend Doctor of Divinity, of great critical activity and a desire to have his universal hand in everything of that kind going forward, than to be overawed by the ghost of a dead Aristarch into the editing of a work like this. Nothing but a dread of the potent deceased, and a fear of his return to avenge the neglect, could have prompted the reverend editor to bestir himself in giving publicity to so many uncivil, so many absurd, so many purposeless and worthless critical statements. The testamentary behest of the critic seems to act upon the Doctor pretty much as the ring-master's whip on the clown's hide – which causes that lively gentleman to jump about and busy himself immediately with the utterance of all sorts of common-place Millerisms and mouldy balderdash. We trust the next time we meet Dr Griswold it will be in better company. He may learn, if he does not know, that to play the usher to a man of talent without principle is the surest course to work the greatest injury to himself; that in this case he has lent himself to an enterprise where no honor can be acquired, and where, for the momentary gratification of his own personal feelings, he has wrought a lasting hurt to whatever of character his principal had left behind him. He has presented himself with a lucky-bag in hand, with a half bushel of decayed potatoes to one single-bladed penknife.

As for the publisher, *he* has done his duty by presenting these interesting and amiable twins in a clean frill and jacket: the book being well printed and substantially bound; and, whether good, bad, or indifferent, one likely, from the number of persons introduced in its pages, to excite general curiosity and secure a wide sale. It is a peculiarity of Mr Redfield that he is not afraid to publish books: and that he is willing to let the character of the publication rest where it should, with the author and editor.

NOTES

1 Griswold was a licensed Baptist preacher, but took little active part in church life. During 1844–5, however, he was editor of the virulently anti-Catholic *Quarterly Review of the American Protestant Association*, and for this he was awarded an honorary DD by a Baptist institution in Illinois. Duyckinck probably used the titles ironically.
2 David Mallet was Bolingbroke's literary executor.
3 The review appeared in February 1842. Duyckinck's single-minded conviction that Mathews was a literary genius was a curious and well-known foible; Poe's recantation was less sincere than opportunistic.

105. George Washington Peck, from a review in the *American Whig Review*

March 1850, 27, 301–15

Peck (1817–59) was a journalist with a special interest in music criticism.

... In the first place, then, Poe, in all his writings included here, appears as a pure minded gentleman – of a strange fancy, it is true, but never low or mean. He always addresses his readers in a scholarly attitude. He interests them through the better nature; he holds the mind's eye with singular pictures, or draws the understanding into curious speculations, but in the wildest of his extravagancies he does not forget his native dignity. Considering how difficult, not to say how impossible, it would have been for him to have done this amidst all the excitements of his feverish life, had it not been real and natural to him, we cannot but believe him to have been actually and in his very heart, what he appears in his pages.

Secondly, he seems to us to have been originally one of the most sensitive of men, and subject to peculiar nervous depressions; at the same time so constituted that his normal and healthful condition was one which required a great elevation of the spirits. If we imagine an extremely sensitive boy, full of fun and harmless mischief, suddenly chilled into a metaphysician, but with his early state still clinging to him, we think we have Poe precisely. No human being can be more ill-fitted for the struggle of life than such a one. The realities of existence overwhelm him; what excites others to press onward crushes him; their joy is his grief; their hope his despair; all his emotions become so intense and intolerable that he cannot endure them, and wildly endeavors to stifle feeling. Charles Lamb was constituted very much after this manner: he cried at weddings and laughed at funerals; but he had habits of study, the influence of strong intellects, duty to his sister, and, perhaps, the fear of insanity, to restrain him.

Besides, Lamb's mind, though clear, was anything but mathematical in its tendencies; while with Poe's, this was a marked trait. Originally gifted with peculiar perceptions of the beauty of form, and of a disposition apt to perceive symmetrical relations both in things and ideas, Poe, when the blight came, found refuge in following out chains of thought in harmony with the gloom that enshrouded him. Instead of avoiding the shadow he would boldly walk into it and analyse it. Hence comes his peculiar power. No writer ever understood better how to work upon the nervous system. He must have been able, one would think, to master the horror of the most awful night-mare that ever visited a dyspeptic couch, to have faced his own conceptions, and yet we can see often in his tales, glimpses of the native boyish glee that must have once been his life, and which still lurks behind his haunted imagination. And not only in his fancy, but apparently in his whole nature did the actual press upon him so heavily that his original youth was borne down, and he appeared to the world as through an inverting lens. The necessities from without, arising in part from his inward constitution,

> Shook so his single state of man, that function
> Was smothered in surmise; and nothing was,
> But what was not.

He himself, in reasoning upon it, seems to have reproached himself for it as a crime, when it was no more a crime than the despondency of Cowper. Several passages in his tales, though they touch the individual experience of every reader, seem to come from him like confessions. For example:

[Quotes Poe's analysis of 'perverseness' from 'The Black Cat' and 'The Imp of the Perverse', *Works*, 5, 146; 6, 148–50.]

There can be no doubt that this infirmity was experienced by Poe, almost as intensely as he has here represented it.

With the superficial there is only one name for any mental affliction which prevents a man from laboring when he has apparently every motive to labor, and every necessary ability. They call it 'idleness', and they fancy that he who is thus afflicted is enjoying the luxury of repose, at the very moment when he is powerless under the torture of anxiety....

But Poe, with all this depression or over-excitement, call it what we please, bearing upon him, inverting his original nature and rendering him incapable of self-control, was anything but an idle man. These tales and poems are not the offspring of an indolent brain. They are wrung from a soul that suffered and strove; from a fancy that was driven out from the sunny palaces of youth and hope, to wander in

> A wild weird clime that lieth, sublime,
> Out of space – out of Time

Even the bulk of what he has written is considerable, as here collected, and these are only the cream of a great mass of writing.

Estimated by its quality, however, and compared with the productions of any of our writers of the same age, we think that Poe did his work as well as the best of them. The material he wrote in was finer. The class of readers whom he will find most favor with, are those of delicate fancies and who are subject to gloomy forebodings – a more numerous class than is often supposed, and of far more consequence – for though the politicians, the hard, noisy, impudent, and ambitious, do the work of governing the earth, it is the meek and patient who inherit it.

With Poe, as with all men of genius, there was an ever-abiding consciousness of the presence of Death. He delighted to look the destroyer in the face and to trick him out in theatrical horrors. With some there is a constant gnawing fear of the monster, and they avert their eyes from him, or now and then steal shuddering glances askance; with others there seems to be an utter inability to realize that they are immortal – that after a few years at most, of inevitably decreasing capacity for enjoyment, their souls will be in heaven or hell, and their bodies in the grave – the sun shining above and the throng of the living pressing on as before. For either of these kinds of readers, Poe's stories must be healthy diet; for the first, because he goes beyond their utmost agonies of apprehension, and stales and tames them; for the second, because he frightens their consciences – makes them wake and shudder and form good resolutions, in the still watches of the night.

In several passages in his tales Poe has unintentionally personated himself: 'My fancy grew charnal. I talked of worms, of tombs and epitaphs.' And again, in the same sketch, he takes us into the very gates of death:

[Quotes from 'The Premature Burial', *Works*, 5, 263, last paragraph.] .

Even where he does not deal directly with Death, he delights to take up and drape elaborately some one of those gloomy clouds that roll upward from the dark abyss. This is so well known to be his *forte* that we need give only one or two examples, and those such as will also illustrate presently a remark on his manner and style. The opening of 'The Fall of the House of Usher', is wilder and profounder than the introduction to *Der Freyschutz*:[1]

[Quotes the first paragraph of 'The Fall of the House of Usher', *Works*, 3, 273–4.]

What a Salvator Rosa-like landscape is that which occurs in the course of 'The Gold-Bug':

[Quotes from 'The Gold-Bug', *Works*, 5, 108–9, paragraphs 2–3.]

And in 'MS. Found in a Bottle', we have a sea view from an ocean that had not been visited before, since the voyage of the Ancient Mariner:

[Quotes from 'MS. Found in a Bottle', *Works*, 2, 5.]

It is good to remain as child-like in our perceptions and affections as we can. Children are the most catholic of readers: only interest them and nothing comes amiss. One who can, like them, pass from the lively dialogue of Dumas, to these pictures of concentrated mysterious apprehension, and find amusement in both, will be likely never to die of *ennui*.

Many of these tales, if not all, were hastily written, and, they are therefore often fragmentary and imperfect. Sometimes the plot is too obvious and the secret is out too soon; in others, the particular horror is too horrible to be contemplated, however artistically it might be veiled. But in all, wherever Poe gives his dreaming fancy any play, it never fails to paint vividly. Take its pictures altogether, and they belong to a new school of grotesque *diablerie*. They are original in their gloom, their occasional humor, their peculiar picturesqueness, their style, and their construction and machinery. Of their gloom we have just spoken.

The balloon of Hans Pfaall, seen by the citizens of Rotterdam, and made of dirty newspapers, is a touch of Poe's original playfulness. So is the negro in 'The Gold-Bug'; the 'Balloon Hoax', is the work of a born quiz; 'Some Words With a Mummy', 'Hop Frog', 'Bon Bon', 'The Devil in the Belfrey', 'Lionizing', and many more, show how full he naturally was of boyish feeling. They are mere trifles to please children; but then he was a child who wrote them – he never got over being a child.

The fate of Mr Dammit, in the sketch 'Never Bet the Devil Your Head', is an awful warning – one which even now it is impossible to contemplate without emotion. He bet the Devil his head that he could leap over a certain style; it happened that above the style was a thin flat bar of iron, which he did not perceive, and which shaved his head clean off. Our author gives the conclusion:

[Quotes final paragraph of 'Never Bet the Devil Your Head', *Works*, 4, 225–6.]

What a bold comparison we have in 'The Duc de L'Omelette', where the hero is taken by Baal-Zebub into the enchanted chamber.

It was not its length nor its breadth, but its height; oh, that was appalling! There was no ceiling, certainly none; but a dense whirling mass of fiery colored clouds. His Grace's brain reeled as he glanced upwards. From above hung a chain of an unknown blood-red metal, its upper end lost, like the city of Boston, *parmi les nues*.

In the 'Rationale of Verse', a not very clear essay, but one abounding in acute suggestion, we have plenty of examples of a like pleasant sarcasm. Indeed, throughout these writings there is enough to show that their author, as is generally true of such spirits, was no less sensitive to the laughable than to the horrible. Indeed, had life gone happily with him, it is possible he might have been only known as one of the gay spirits of fashionable society.

With respect to Poe's style, the extracts above given from 'The Gold-Bug', 'The MS. Found in a Bottle', &c., exhibit his affluence of musical variety in expression, and command of words.

One more extract we must give, not only for its eloquence, but in illustration of our theory, that Poe was one originally so sensitive, the first breath of the world withered him; so that he was benumbed, and fancied he had outlived his heart:

[Quotes from 'Eleonora', *Works*, 4, 237–8.]

Poor Poe! It was a sad day for him when he was forced from dreams like these into the real world, where there are so many 'far wiser' than he. No wonder he sometimes lost heart and temper, and soon died!

We have observed that Poe is original, not only in his gloom, his humor, and so forth, but also in the construction of his tales. Indeed, it is for this he has been found most fault with. It is said he wrote his things 'on a plan'. It is not denied that he contrives to get up an interest; but it is objected that he does it systematically, foreseeing the end from the beginning, laying out his work, and deliberately going through it.

But is not this really an argument in his favor? The painter composes 'on a plan'; he touches not his canvas till his whole design is sketched, or laid out perfectly, in his mind; he *must* do so. Still more is this true (though we are aware it is not generally thought so) with the musical composer; everything is calculated beforehand, the composition may be said to exist in his mind, exactly in reverse order; in the freest style, the climax is the first thing conceived, and to which the rest is adjusted. And in writing plays, must not the plot be first established, and then elaborated? Does any one suppose that Shakespeare did not foreknow the action of *Hamlet*, when he sat himself to write it? or that he *improvised Macbeth*? or that he could elaborate that singular texture of plots, the *Midsummer Night's Dream*, by the Dumas process of accretion? Surely those who think so cannot understand any, the simplest work of art, in its entirety. For a work of art is not a heap of things built up, and to which more may be joined; it is, like the French Republic, 'one and indivisible'. If you take away aught from it, it is incomplete; if you add, you put on what does not belong to it. Even so simple a work of art as a house, must be built 'on a plan', or it will be only a conglomeration of rooms; and whenever it is completed, whatever is added is very properly styled an 'addition'. The pen in our hand, we could not have made it without definite design. Why should we not have tales constructed on such plots as it will best excite a continued interest to unravel?...

Again; it has been objected to Poe's stories and poems, that they are abstract, unlike anything in real life, out of all experience, and touching no human sympathy. As to the abstractness and remoteness from experience, if these be faults, God help the wicked! for the author of *Paradise Lost* is surely damned; but as to their coldness and incapacity to touch human sympathy, that we utterly deny. We are unable to perceive, from these harmless little sketches and verses, a reason for all that has been said of Poe's coldheartedness, 'cynicism', want of moral sense, and so on. It must be admitted, however, that if the friendship manifested in these biographical prefixes was the warmest he could inspire, he was certainly one of the most unfortunate men that ever lived. But to judge him purely as he appears in his own writing, we do not see but that he had as much 'heart' as other men – as much, at least, as other literary men who have resided as long as he did in this 'commercial metropolis'. To be sure, his disposing of the remains of his friend Mr Toby Dammit in the manner he did, after the transcendentalists refused to bear the expenses of that gentleman's funeral, was out of the common way; but whoever heard Dr Southwood

Smith accused of inhumanity for dissecting his friend Jeremy
Bentham?

All these objections and accusations appear to us to have
arisen from two sources; first, his success in gaining, at once,
what so many would give their eyes for, viz.: a reputation;
and, secondly, his frankness, or want of self-respect. This
leads us to speak of his poetry, and what he has related
respecting his mode of writing it.

Coleridge, speaking of some of his own poems, observes:
'In this idea originated the plan of the *Lyrical Ballads*; in which
it was agreed that my endeavors should be directed to
persons and characters supernatural, or, at least, romantic;
yet so as to transfer from our inward nature a human interest
and a semblance of truth sufficient to procure for these
shadows of imagination that willing suspension of disbelief
for the moment, which constitutes poetic faith.' – 'With this
in view I wrote "The Ancient Mariner", and was preparing
among other poems, "The Dark Ladie", and the "Christabel",
in which I should have more nearly realized my ideal, than I
had done in my first attempt.'[2]

From this extract we learn that even the most fanciful of
modern poems, the 'Ancient Mariner', was written in
conformity with a specific purpose, if not 'on a plan'.
Doubtless, also, had it served its author's purpose to
enlighten us concerning the manner of his composition, he
could have done so; for, the existence of a design argues
forethought in execution. How certain words, rhymes, and
similes, came into his mind, he could not have told; but why
he chose that particular metre, or, at least, *that* he chose a
metre, he could have told, and also many other incidents of
the poem's composition.

Poe has done this with regard to 'The Raven'; a much
shorter piece, and on admitting a more regular ingenuity of
construction – but still a poem full of singular beauty. His
opening remarks in this analysis show the perfect frankness,
or indifference with which he sets to work to dispel his own
conjurations:

[Quotes from 'The Philosophy of Composition', from 'I
have often thought' to '*literary histrio*', *Works*, 14, 194–5.]

In what follows, wherein he goes minutely into his process of composition, though, in general, true, he was probably misled by the character of his mind, his love of speculation, his impatience of littleness, the 'perverseness' we have claimed for him, and a secret delight in mystifying the foolish – to make it appear that he wrote the whole poem, as he would have demonstrated a problem, and without experiencing any state or phase of elevated feeling. The poem itself is so sufficient an evidence to the contrary, and Poe, in his explanation, in its mode of construction, 'The Philosophy of Composition', has carried his analysis to such an absurd minuteness, that it is a little surprising that there should be any verdant enough not to perceive that he was 'chaffing'. He was enough a boy in his feelings to take delight in quizzing. What are most of his stories, but harmless hoaxes? Horrible faces grin at us in them out of the darkness; but at the end comes the author, shows them to be nothing but pumpkin lanterns, and cries 'sold!' in our faces.

Probably there is not, in all poetry or prose, an instance where language is made to present a more vivid *picture* to the fancy than in this poem. The mysterious introduction, the 'tapping', the appearance of the Raven, and all his doings and sayings, are so perfectly *in character*, (we were once, many years ago, the 'unhappy master' of one of these birds, who, it was evident, were in league with the devil,) that we seem actually to see him:

[Quotes 'The Raven', stanzas 7–8.]

Perhaps Poe would tell us that, in writing these stanzas, having determined, upon good reasons, to introduce the Raven in some fantastic manner, he then considered what motions a bird of that species would be likely to make, and finally concluded to choose the most natural, as being the most fantastic; and thus, at length, after looking his dictionary, pitched upon the word 'flirt', which Johnson defines to mean 'a quick, elastic motion', as most suited to his purpose; then, finally, connected with it 'flutter', not so much to add to the meaning, as for the convenience of the rhyme with 'shutter'. And for such harmless 'philosophy of

composition' as this, he must be set down for a man of no
heart!

To our apprehension, it is quite impossible that most of the
words and phrases in these two stanzas could have been
chosen in any other than an elevated state of feeling – a
condition when

> The poet's eye in a fine frenzy rolling,
> Doth glance from heaven to earth, from earth to heaven,
> And, as imagination bodies forth
> The forms of things unknown, the poet's pen
> Turns them to shapes, and gives to airy nothing
> A local habitation and a name.

The 'stately Raven', coming in with 'many a flirt and flutter';
the 'saintly days of yore' – what days? where? when?; the
'obeisance', 'mien of lord or lady', how picturesque! And in
the second stanza every line is the offspring of the highest
power of poetic vision; 'grave and stern decorum' and

> Ghastly grim and ancient Raven wandering from
>   the Nightly shore,
> Tell me what thy lordly name is on the Night's
>   Plutonian shore!

– where is this 'Nightly shore', which we recognize as
familiar, like the scenery of a dream that we never saw
before? We seem to have heard of it and to know of it, and
yet it is a perfectly new region. There is an indescribable
power in the sound of these words, as also in the march of the
lines which precede it. As the product of a pure vividness of
fancy, and a sustained intense feeling, they are as remarkable
as any similar passages in our poetic literature.

[Then follows a general discussion on language and music.]

Coleridge's 'Kubla Khan' is the first instance, that we are
aware of, in which an attempt is made by an *assumed,* yet not
unnatural, indistinctness of meaning, to portray a phase of
feeling too subtle and evanescent to be touched with
definites. About this time, the same thing was done by
Beethoven in music; among his trifles, 'bagatelles', as they
are rightly named, for the piano, are some which begin

sanely and run off into actual wildness; in his last symphony, and in some of his posthumous works, he is thought to have ventured too far unintentionally. In painting, too, the notion of aiming at only a single effect has arisen, and is a favorite one with a numerous class of artists. And in literature, we have at last, Poe, who writes poems that move us deeply, but in which the meaning is only hinted at, and even that sometimes so obscurely that it is impossible to find out an unbroken connection; but there is always an evident design and an extremely artistic construction. And to counterbalance, him, we have, as before observed, writers, and their name is legion, whose minds appear to have lost the power of sequent thought, whose writing is bald, unjointed, without form, and void.

Between all such as these (a portion of whom even declined, as we have seen, to reimburse him for the funeral expenses of his friend Mr D.) and Poe, there was, necessarily, a wide gulf. Poe's mind, though it would have to do only with fragilest ideas, and though ever grasping, and never comprehensive, yet worked beautifully within its range, while it remained unbroken, When he chose, there is no writer who ever had a more perfect command of his native style, or could pursue a flight of subtle thoughts more closely and rapidly. The minuteness of his description never wearies. His taste, also, was like the tunica conjunctiva of the eye, sensitive to the least motes; we never know, in 'The Gold-Bug', whether the *scarabeus* is a supernatural insect or only a mechanical contrivance; we never know who sent the Raven from 'the Night's Plutonian shore!' it would have been less mysterious in either case if we had been told. In some of his later things we see where his physical strength was failing him, and his mental power getting enfeebled through 'too much conceiving'; we see it, as we can see it, in a greater or less degree, in the working of all minds which are or have been overwrought. But even in these things – even in *Eureka* – to read is like wandering through the ruins of a fair city that has been pillaged by barbarians; there are sacred things wantonly mutilated, beautiful images broken and scattered, yet still enough left to show the original structure.

What rank Poe is to take in the catalogue of our poets, Time will assign him, in the face of all that might be urged by the most sagacious reviewer. But as Time never tells his secrets till they are found out, we may be excused for offering an opinion.

That Poe will long be considered, as he is now, a poet of singular genius, there can be no question. What he attempted, had never been attempted before; and he succeeded in it. He wrote poems addressed to the feelings, wherein the meaning is designedly vague and subordinate. As long as our language retains its present shape and inflection, we think the musical effects of these poems will be felt and acknowledged. But when the next change comes over it – and that might be very soon, by the sudden uprising of a great poet, with a new song in his mouth, – they will be forgotten. For they have no power to stay change. Their indistinctness does not arise, like the indistinctness of Milton and Shakespeare, from the reader's ignorance, and hence there is nothing in them to keep them forever in the world's eye; no learning, nor any powerful burden of true philosophy to overawe the majority who have no perception of poetic beauty. Hence, also, though Poe succeeded, marvellously succeeded, yet we cannot find it in our heart to wish what he accomplished ever to be undertaken again. We would prefer to keep the old lines distinct; to have neither poetry nor music, the brother or the sister, infringe upon each other's domain. The mind is never permanently satisfied with single effects; when the first glow has passed, we look deeper, and if there is no fuel the fire goes down, Hence, also, again, though we now feel the excellence of Poe so strongly, it is with a sort of misgiving that we may outgrow or become indifferent to him hereafter.

We will quote one or two of his pieces, which may be new to our readers, to illustrate an observation upon some of his peculiarities of construction. The following has much of the form and effect of a wild rondo in music:

[Quotes 'Dream-Land'.]

The repetition with which the third stanza, or strophe, commences, 'By the lakes that thus outspread,' &c., is one of

Poe's obvious peculiarities. It occurs in every stanza of 'The Raven',

> From my books surcease of sorrow – sorrow for the
>   lost Lenore –
> *For a rare and radiant maiden whom the angels name*
>   *Lenore.*

The same repetition makes 'Ulalume' nearly twice as long as it would be without it:

> The skies were ashen and sober;
>   The leaves they were crisped and sere,
>   *The leaves they were withering and sere.*

We observe it also in 'The Bells,' 'Annabel Lee', 'Eulalie' and other pieces – indeed, indications of a tendency to a similar form may be traced in his prose.

This form was natural to Mr Poe because it is the natural expression of intense feeling. A fine example of it is suggested by Wordsworth from the song of Deborah, *'At her feet he bowed, he fell, he lay down; at her feet he bowed, he fell; where he bowed, there he fell down dead'*.

There is some reason for supposing that this form is peculiarly suited to the melody of our language. For it is so uniform a peculiarity of all ancient English tunes to commence the second strain with a repetition of the last phrase of the first, that they may be readily distinguished by it as Scottish or Irish tunes by their characteristics. The tune of Chevy Chase (always sung, or rather murdered, by the grave-digger in *Hamlet*) has this form; another, the words of which begin, 'When I was bound apprentice in famous Lincolnshire,' &c., is perhaps a more familiar instance. * The third stanza of 'Dream-Land' is but an imitation in language of a new strain in melody.

Where this repetition is at shorter intervals, and with variations, as in 'Ulalume' *passim*, it bears a curious analogy to the structure of the phrases in very many of Beethoven's melodies. One little point is taken up, repeated, augmented, varied, and so beaten upon the brain with the force of the most intense passion. We think of no instance likely to be known to the general reader; the opening to the andante of the first symphony may be remembered by some.

But, indeed, this repetition, growing out of 'imitation', runs through all music, and is at once the symmetry of its movement and the life of its expression. Poe has a singular paragraph upon music which is worth quoting in this connection:

[Quotes from 'The Rationale of Verse', *Works*, 14, 219, paragraph 2.]

It would appear from this, that Poe had very acute perceptions of the relations in sound arising from consecution, but not of those growing out of consentaneousness; he could analyse the drawing but not the color.

This is the secret of his peculiarities of style and construction. But beyond and above all this there was a soul of poetry in him. As we glance over these volumes to satisfy ourself that we have said all we intended (for even this article, gentle reader, is constructed 'on a plan') there are two short things which it would be unjust not to quote. The first is less peculiar in structure than most of his pieces, but it is full of exquisite fancy:

[Quotes 'The Haunted Palace'.]

As we write these lines a review of Poe lies before us, which we were pained to see, and in which the writer says he has been led to believe Poe 'mainly destitute of moral and religious principle,' and 'certain it is that the most careful student of his works will search them vainly for elevated and generous sentiment.' We cannot see any reason in these volumes for so harsh an opinion; and we feel very sure the world will not, either. As to sentiment, it was not Poe's province to deal in sentiment; but surely he could give expression to elevated emotion. As to his morality, we see not but that he writes like a gentleman; (always excepting what he relates of his conduct to the remains of his friend Mr D.) he did not undertake to write sermons. His poetry and prose are full of pure beauties; he could paint 'rare and radiant maidens', and express those affections for such which only gentle hearts can feel. Nay, one need not be of the Roman faith to feel a loftier aspiration in the following:

[Quotes 'Hymn'.]

NOTES

* In this the second strain only reverses the phrases of the first; thus: 1, 2, –2, 1.
1 Weber's opera (1821).
2 *Biographia Literaria,* Ch. 14.

106. [John Moncure Daniel], review in the *Southern Literary Messenger*

March 1850, 16, 172–87

Daniel's tirade caused some controversy: John R. Thompson, editor of the *Messenger,* issued an embarrassed editorial apology to Griswold and Willis; meanwhile, Willis produced a Richmond correspondent who replied to Daniel's 'frightful caricature' – see Quinn, p. 667. Baudelaire drew heavily on Daniel's review for his knowledge of Poe – see W.T. Bandy, 'New Light on Baudelaire and Poe', *Yale French Studies,* No. 10 (1953), 65–9.

Here we have at last the result of the long experiment; the residuum in the retort; the crystals in the crucible; the ashes in the furnace; the attainment of fiery trial and of analysis the most acute. How much bitter misery went to write these pages; – what passion, what power of mind and heart were needed to strike these impressions – the only footprints on

the sands of time of a vitality in which the lives of ten
ordinary men were more than condensed – will never be
known save to those who knew in person the man they
embody.

These half told tales and broken poems are the only records
of a wild, hard life; and all that is left of a real genius, – genius
in the true sense of the word, unmistakable and original. No
other American has half the chance of a remembrance in the
history of literature. Edgar Poe's reputation will rest on a
very small minority of the compositions in these two
volumes. Among all his poems, there are only two or three
which are not execrably bad. The majority of his prose
writings are the children of want and dyspepsia, of printer's
devils and of blue devils. Had he the power of applying his
creative faculties – as have had the Miltons, the Shakespeares
and all the other demiurgi – he would have been a very great
man. But there is not one trace of that power in these
volumes; and his career and productions rather resemble
those of the Marlowes, the Jonsons, the Dekkers, and the
Websters, the old dramatists and translunary rowdies of the
Elizabethan age, than the consistent lives and undying
utterances of those who claim the like noble will and the
shaping imagination. Had Mr Poe possessed mere *talent*,
even with his unfortunate moral constitution, he might have
been a popular and money-making author. He would have
written a great many more good things than he has left here;
but his title to immortality would not and could not have
been surer than it is. For the few things that the author has
written which are at all tolerable, are coins stamped with the
indubitable die. They are of themselves, – *sui generis*, – unlike
any diagrams in Time's Kaleidoscope, – and gleam with the
diamond hues of eternity.

But before passing to a consideration of the amber,
convention and circumstance require an examination of the
dirty little fleas and flies who have managed to enbalm
themselves therein. The works of Edgar Allan Poe are
introduced to the world by no less than three accredited
worldlings – or as the public would have us say no less than
three celestial steeds of the recognized Pegasean pedigree are
harnessed to drag the *caput mortuum* of the unfortunate Poe

into the light of public favour. Mr Rufus Griswold had seen the poor 'fellow'. Mr N.P. Willis had also seen and pitied the man; had gone so far as to give him the post of *sub-critic* to himself – N.P. Willis, Esq. – in one of his newspapers; Mr James Russell Lowell had found his sable sympathies sufficiently extensive as to take in the distressed master of the Raven, in spite of his colour and birth-place; – he could spare enough affection from Brother Frederick Douglass and Brother William Brown to make a Brother Poe out of him too.[1] The three felt quite pitifully sentimental at his dog's death; and with the utmost condescension they hearkened to the clink of the publisher's silver, and agreed to erect a monument to the deceased genius, in the shape of Memoir and Essay preliminary to his works. Their kindness and generosity has been published to the world in every newspaper. The bookseller's advertisement, that all persons possessing letters and correspondence of Poe should send them straightway to him, has gone with the news. The publication of the works of Poe were kept back from the public for a long time, that they might be brought out in a blaze of glory by this mighty triumvirate of patrons. Troy was not built; composition like theirs is not finished in a day. Here it is at last – and duty compels us to say, that this is the rawest, the baldest, the most offensive, and the most impudent humbug that has ever been palmed upon an unsuspecting moon-calf of a world. These three men have managed to spin into their nineteen pages and a half of barren type more to call forth the indignation of all right feeling and seeing people than we have ever seen before in so little space; and they have practised in the publication as complete a swindle on the purchaser as ever sent a knave to the State prison. Mr Rufus Griswold we know to be the dispenser of literary fame – the great Apollo of our literary heavens. Through the successive editions of those big little books, the *Prose and Prose Writers of America*, and the *Poets and Poetry* of the same, he lifts either the head of the miserable American to the stars, or sinks him into the ignominious chills and shadows of Hades. Why his name goes forth to the world on the title page of these volumes we are totally unable to say; – for not one word of his do they contain. We are forced to believe that he is struck into the frontispiece for the purpose of giving respectability to the author whose writings follow. As Smollett, Voltaire, Johnson and other names celebrated on the doorposts of booksellers, were wont, for so much a volume, to grant the privilege of their names to miserable translations, and to compiled memoirs still more miserable – so doth the eminent Griswold give his *imprimatur* to the amaranthine verse and to the fadeless prose of Edgar Poe! The life, &c., with the details of Poe's adventures in Russia, his letters, and his personal history, which were repeatedly promised through the press, and for which those already owning nearly all of Poe's writings have been induced to purchase this new edition – is nowhere. In the place thereof, we have a counterfeit shinplaster, ragged, dirty, ancient and worn, which Mr James Russell Lowell had palmed upon the publisher of a Magazine very many years ago. Mr James Russell Lowell belongs to a minute species of literary insect, which is plentifully produced by the soil and climate of Boston. He has published certain 'Poems'; they are copies of Keats, and Tennyson, and Wordsworth; and baser or worse done imitations the imitative tribe have never bleated forth. He has also written some very absurd prose – a volume entitled *Conversations on the Old Dramatists*, &c. Into this he has managed, together with a great deal of false sentiment and false criticism, to stow a large amount of transcendentalism, socialism, and abolition. For Mr Lowell is one of that literary set, which has grown up in the Northern States of this Union, who find no delight in the science and philosophy of this earth save when it is wrong and wicked – save when it sets common sense and common humanity at defiance. If there is anything that ought not to be believed, these people go and believe it for that very reason. But the book and its teachings are alike forgotten and unknown. With the name of Mr James Russell Lowell the public is better acquainted from its frequent appearance in the proceedings of abolitionist meetings in Boston, cheek by jowl with the signatures of free negroes and runaway slaves. His seven pages in this present compilation contain none of his great political principles, but they contain not one single fact of Poe's history accurately stated. They furnish a very happy exemplification of the style in which his *Conversations* are written – which is that of a broken merchant's ledger, all figures signifying nothing save the number and variety of his pickings and stealings.

Six pages by the man milliner of our literature, Mr N.P. Willis, constitutes in reality the only original writing in the be-heralded 'Notices of Edgar A. Poe by Rufus Griswold, James Russell Lowell, and N.P. Willis', – and of these six, three are taken up with extracts from the New York *Tribune*. The rest are occupied rather with N.P. Willis than with Edgar Allan Poe. It is here explained how all Poe's celebrity came from the good-natured patronage of N.P. Willis – and how N.P. Willis rescued the 'Raven' from oblivion and spread its wings to all the world by consenting to its insertion in his *Home Journal*, – the weekly newspaper of mantua-maker's girls, and of tailor's boys. Such is the tone and air of the entire editorial work of this publication. These three horny-eyed dunces came before the world as the patrons and literary vouchers of the greatest genius of the day. But with all their parade, as we before mentioned, these editors make no pretence of informing the reader in relation to the facts of Mr Poe's life. So far as we are able it shall be our endeavour to supply the deficiency. The sketch which follows is a compilation of the facts contained in the New York *Tribune's* obituary of Poe; in Griswold's *Prose Writers*; one or two others which we pick from Mr Willis's three pages; and several furnished by our own recollections of and conversations with the subject of discourse.

[Here Daniel gives an account of Poe's 'disastrous battle of life', stressing his activities in Richmond.]

It is now purposed to throw together certain detached fragments of information relative to Mr Poe's personal habits and history, some remarks on his genius and writings, and also to delineate, in some degree, the traits of his *morale*. Before sitting down to the task, the writer has reflected, with some perplexity, upon the proper tone and colour to give it. Mr Poe's life contained many blemishes: – the foregoing narrative has fully informed the reader of that. These blemishes, we are compelled to say, were the results of character rather than of circumstance; and in aught that pretends to be a picture of the man, some dark shades are indispensable. Yet it appears hard and unfeeling in the extreme to speak aught that is ill of the newly dead. *De mortuis nil nisi bonum* is the sentiment universal, in every rightly constituted mind and heart; and the writer is not an advocate for the stoical emendation of *nil nisi verum*. The considerations which have determined him to write this article without reserve, are a recollection of the long notoriety of the worst to all who possess the slightest knowledge of Mr Poe either by personal intercourse or by report, — and the absolute necessity of mentioning them to give a distinct conception of this most brilliant and original individual. It is hoped, therefore, that no one will attribute the evil points of character brought forward in any part of this article to a carelessness of the memory of the dead, or to sinister sentiment towards his living connections.

In person Mr Edgar Poe was rather below middle height, slenderly but compactly built. His hands and feet were moderately large, and strongly shaped, as were all his joints. Before his constitution was broken by dissipation and consequent ill health, he had been capable of great feats of strength and endurance. He once swam from the Rocketts wharf of this city seven miles in the James River, and walked back through a burning summer day, for a wager, and without any consequent ill effects. Countenance, person, gait, everything about him, when he was sober, distinguished Mr Poe as a man of mark. His features were not large, were rather regular, and decidedly handsome. His complexion was clear and dark — when the writer knew him. The general expression of his face beyond the ordinary abstraction was not pleasant. It was neither insolent, rude, nor angry. But it was decidedly disagreeable, nevertheless. The color of his fine eyes generally seemed to be dark grey; but on closer examination, they seemed to be that neutral violet tint, which is so difficult to define. His forehead was, without exception, the finest in its proportions and expression that we have ever seen. It did not strike one as being uncommonly large or high, but seemed to bulge forth with the protuberance of the reflective and constructive organs. The perceptive regions were not deficient, but seemed pressed out of the way by the growth and superiority of causality, comparison and construction. Close to them rose the arches of ideality, the dome where beauty sat weaving her garlands. Yet the head, as a whole, was decidedly a bad one.[2] When looked at in front, the bold and expressive frontal development took up the attention, and the beholder did not observe the want of cranium above. A profile view showed its deficiencies in a very strong light. There was an immense mass of brain in front and in rear, with little or none above or between these two masses. Or to speak more succinctly, the basilar region possessed immense power, both intellectual and animal; the coronal region was very deficient. It contained little moral sense and less reverence. This was one key to many of his literary characteristics. With more reverence, conjoined with other traits of craniology, Mr Poe would have been a mocker and a sneerer. Such was the head of Voltaire, whose organ of reverence equalled that of Wesley or Howard,—but which only served as a guide to his mirthfulness and combativeness, in consequence of the still greater predominance of his animal organs. But Mr Poe wanted the perception of reverential things to give them sufficient importance to be mocked. The same fact accounts for an absence of that morbid remorse and sense of duty unfulfilled which marks so distinctly all the writings of Byron, and of most modern authors of distinction. In Poe's writings there is despair, hopelessness; and the echoes of a melancholy extremely touching to those who read with a remembrance of his broken life; but nowhere in them does 'conscience roused, sit boldly on her throne'. The ideas of right and wrong are as feeble in his chains of thought as in the literature of Ancient Greece.

But we anticipate our subject. Mr Poe's hair was dark, and when we knew him, seemed to be slightly sprinkled with grey. He wore a heavy and ill-trimmed moustache. He dressed uniformly in good taste, simple and careless, the attire of a gentleman. His manners were excellent, unembarrassed, polite, and marked with an easy repose. His conversation was the very best we have ever listened to. We have never heard any other so suggestive of thought, or any from which one gained so much. On literary subjects, books,

authors, and literary life, it was as superior to all else that we
have heard or read, even the best, as the diamond is to other
jewels. It cut into the very gist of the matter. It was the
essence of correct and profound criticism divested of all
formal pedantries and introductory ideas – the kernel clear of
the shell. He was not a 'brilliant talker', in the common
after-dinner sense of the term, – was not a maker up of fine
points or a sayer of funny things. What he said was prompted
entirely by the moment, and seemed uttered for the pleasure
of uttering it. But when he became well roused, when his
thought was well worked up, and the juice all over it; he
would *say more*, send out more pithy ideas, driving straight
and keen as arrows to their mark, than any man we ever
heard speak. He was very fond of talking, and not at all
exclusive in his audiences. Whether his hearers understood
his acute abstractions or appreciated the glorious conceptions
that perpetually flashed and sparkled across his mental sky,
was no care of his. He would sit himself down in a tavern
porch beside any dirty dunce, and unfold to him the great
designs of the most wonderful book, *Eureka*, with the same
abstracted earnestness as if it was an amanuensis to whom he
was dictating for the press, or a Kepler, or a Bacon – who
alone, beside himself, could have written it. This carelessness of
companionship constituted a trait of his character. If any man
ever was perfectly emancipated from all trammels of society,
cared not ten straws what was thought of him by the passer,
cared not whether he was admitted freely into upper-
tendom, or denied access to respectable grog-shops, it was this
singular and extraordinary man. And this want of all
conception and perception of the claims of civilized society,
and the inevitable penalties which attend violations of its
laws – for there *are* penalties which attend violations of the
laws of human society, (which are none other than the laws
of nature) as *necessarily* as those attending violations of the
laws of the physical elements – was one of the causes which
rendered Mr Poe's life so unfortunate. Few men of literary
powers so marked, of genius so indubitable as his, could fail
of living at least tolerably well in the nineteenth century, – if
they conducted themselves at all in accordance with the
behests of society. As we shall presently show, true genius

does not now receive its meed of *fame* from its generation nor ever will; but it can now make books that will sell, and will keep its owner above want if he chooses to use it with ordinary discretion. *Talent* is still better than genius in such matters; but genius of such force, we repeat, always obtains a competency, if nothing intervenes. That which intervened between Mr Poe's genius and competency, was Mr Poe himself. His changeable humors, his irregularities, his caprices, his total disregard of everything and body, save the fancy in his head, prevented him from doing well in the world. The evils and sufferings that poverty brought upon him, soured his nature, and deprived him of faith in human beings. This was evident to the eye – he believed in nobody, and cared for nobody. Such a mental condition of course drove away all those who would otherwise have stood by him in his hours of trial. He became, and was, an Ishmaelite. His place of abode was as uncertain and unfixed as the Bedouins. He was equally well known in New York, Philadelphia, Boston, Baltimore and Richmond.

His habits of intoxication were another reason for his want of success in life. From all that we can learn he fell into them early in life, and they caused his death. Thousands have seen him drunk in the streets of this city. In all his visits save the last, he was in a state approaching mania. Whenever he tasted alcohol he seldom stopped drinking it so long as he was able. He did drink most barbarously. Most men, even the most inveterate, make their bad habits a source of pleasure – luxury – voluptuousness, a means of excitement or a gratification of the palate. Such was not the case with Edgar Poe. His taste for drink was a simple disease – no source of pleasure or excitement. When once the poison had passed his lips, he would go at once to a bar and drink off glass after glass as fast as its tutelar genius could mix them, until his faculties were utterly swallowed up. His long fits of intoxication, and the consequent ill health and listlessness, of course diminished the quantity of Mr Poe's intellectual products, and interfered with their perfection. But wonderful as it may seem, we do not believe that the force of his intellect was at all impaired thereby. He was a greater man at the time of his death than he had ever been before. His greatest work is his last. It is somewhat singular that this and several other of his best works either immediately preceded or succeeded long and fearful fits of his unhappy disease. He came to this city immediately after the appearance of *Eureka*, and plunged into the very depth of his woe. And we learn through an eye witness, that on the morning 'The Raven' saw the light in the pages of the *Whig Review*, when all New York was just agog about it, when the name of Poe was in every mouth, he saw him pass down Broadway in such a state that he reeled from side to side of the pavement at every yard he advanced.

We pass to the writings of Mr Poe, the portion of our subject we are much more willing to contemplate. About them there is no doubt. The true gold rings in that coin. Many things that he has written are children of hunger and haste; much more is marked with the flatness and inanity which makes up nine days in ten of a dissipated life. His multifarious outpourings, as collected in the mass before us, are unequal and uneven, gothic and grotesque; but of great weight as a whole and of inestimable value in parts.

This we are convinced is the opinion of everyone who possesses sufficient originality of mental conformation, or of research into the powers of expression and the fields of imagination, to constitute him a judge of an author entirely new, and of fruit entirely distinct from all ordinary species. The writer is well aware that the multitude of well-educated readers, and the multitude also of gentlemen who 'write with ease', will set down his sentence as extravagant and untenable in the extreme, Edgar Poe has not yet reached his proper seat in the temple of fame – nor will for many a long year. These writings are too new and too great to be taken at once into the popular mind. The temporary success of TALENT and GENIUS, is the same alike in the achievements of reason and of imagination – though the vulgar error would confine the rule to the first. For the fact is well known and sufficiently admitted, melancholy though it be, that nearly all those who have blessed mankind with great discoveries have lived and died miserably. The men who have that degree of mind which we denominate *talent*, who make a good use of the store of knowledge already in the world, and who carry the discoveries which others have made, but a short distance forward, (not so far as to be out of sight of the age in which they live,) are treated with honor by the world. Such men the world can understand and estimate. But those who are *cursed* with that high and peculiar intellect, that strange thing called *genius,* that power of seizing on great truths – or images – or expressions, which lie beyond the ken of all but themselves – in short, the men who go ahead of their age – are invariably either treated with neglect and stupid scorn, by the mob of common-place respectabilities who compose the enlightened public – or they are stoned and trampled underfoot....

[Here Daniel digresses for about a page, on how Genius is invariably neglected in its own time.]

If called upon to name the trait which distinguishes this writer from other writers of equal genius, we should say it was the metaphysical nature of all his productions and of every line of them. He is emphatically an 'ideologist' – his creations and his expressions are essentially abstractions. Edgar Poe had travelled much, – seen cities, climes, governments – known great numbers of distinguished and remarkable people; but they never appeared in his conversations or in his writings. His conversations contained no allusions to incidents, no descriptions of places, no anecdotes. In his animated moods he threw off brilliant paradoxes; and if he talked of individuals, his ideas ran upon their moral and intellectual qualities, – never upon the idiosyncrasies of their active physical phenomena, or the peculiarities of their manner. His writings contain no descriptions – or next to none – of real life or landscape. When he sketches natural scenery, the trees, the rocks, the waters, the walls are phantasms, – it is from distorted, thin, strange and morbid sick-dreams of trees, rocks, waters, and walls, that he draws. Take 'The Fall of the House of Usher' for instance – examine the natural scenery in that tale for an illustration of what we have been saying. In short, Edgar Poe is a painter of ideas, not of men and things. He had precisely the same relations to Dickens, Thackeray, and the like, that the mad artist Blake, to whom the apparition of William Wallace and the ghost of a flea (vide, Cunningham's *British Painters and Sculptors,* art.

Blake,) were wont to sit for portraits, – held to Hogarth and Reynolds.

This is the distinctive element of these volumes. It is not merely the distinctive element, but also the essential element of everything in them. The ideas are ideas *par excellence*. There is not the faintest odor of flesh and blood about them – no earthly smell. They have all the same thin, immaterial and intangible outline. They have no more atmosphere about them than the cliffs and peaks of the moon. No earthly thing can live there. The things called men and women who inhabit the tales of Poe, are no more like the beings of our world, than the strange and colorless creatures we can imagine as the denizens of the sun, passing and repassing in rays of light, homogeneous with the elements themselves, pre-existent to, and superior to organization and to the laws of existence as we know them.

This elementary quality infects every faculty of his mind – his ideality – his hate – his love – his taste. Look at its manifestations in his wit. The writings before us are not by any means destitute of those qualities in their abstract constitution. On the contrary, parts of *Eureka*, and very many of the tales exhibit them, and the disposition to indulge them in the greatest strength. But the humour never makes us laugh, and the wit never pleases while it surprises us by its scintillations. Both faculties depend for means of manifestation upon human beings as they appear to the eye, and can never be successful when separated from those phenomena. Edgar ˝Poe's wit and humour, in consequence of his superlatively metaphysical nature, becomes the pure *grotesque*. Passages which would be witty and humorous in the hands of an earthy man – of a real human being – upon his pages resemble only fantastic aperies, – the grimaces of some unknown species of goblin monkey, twistings and quaint gesticulations which we cannot understand at all. It is too far removed from fleshly sympathies to excite the nerves of laughter – or the odd surprise and smiling titilations which follow the natural exercises of wit.

From the writers of our new and unfinished country, the works of Poe, that is, the good things among them – are distinguished by another remarkable quantity: – their finish of

style. This superior finish consists not merely in that clear
perfection of arrangement which comes naturally with the
best thoughts and good hours of a first rate mind; but also in
the charms of a mastery in the art of writing greater than
those possessed by any other American author. Mr Poe was a
learned man. In spite of his irregular life, he managed to
master both literature and science to an extent reaching far
beyond any American we have known. He had, without
doubt, gotten possession of many critical tools and springs
not commonly in use. At one time in his life – we are unable
to fix the period – Mr Poe is said to have lived in London.
How he got the means and how he lived while there, no one
knows. Little relative thereto, could be got out of him, save
that he saw nothing of the great world in any sense of the
word. He had been heard to mention Hunt and Hook as two
of those whom he knew there; and it is supposed that he lived
very much with that class of men – the men like himself,
possessed of genius but down in the world, dragging out a
precarious existence in garrets, doing drudge work, writing
for the great presses and for the reviews whose world wide
celebrity has been the fruit of such men's labours. From these
he is thought by some to have learned much relative to the
literary profession, comparatively unknown in this new
country. Here too he may have gained acquaintance with
many fields of learning, which are *terra incognita* to American
students, for want of the books and machinery to explore
them.[3] But be this as it may, it is certain that in his
compositions may be observed things that are far in advance
of the profession on this side of the water.

We shall now proceed to remark upon the matter of these
volumes in particular. Mr James Russell Lowell thinks that as
a critic Edgar Poe was 'aesthetically deficient'. Very like, –
for Poe was incapable of appreciating Mr James Russell
Lowell and his set. But as a critic we prefer what remains of
Edgar Poe to anything after Hazlitt. In his paragraphs are no
inanities, no vague generalities, no timorous and half-way
work. His points are ever concrete and tangible. When he
gave chase to an absurdity, he ran it into the earth. When he
sets up a principle for a critical law, he demonstrates it with
such clearness that you can all but see it. The reader must not

estimate his critical writings by the specimens given in these volumes. For some reason or other, the editors have republished only the very dull stuff he had been putting forth for bread in the magazines of the last few years, under the headings of 'Marginalia' &c. All that is poor enough. But while he conducted the *Southern Literary Messenger*, he poured forth quantities of critical writing that was really 'great'. The volumes of this periodical, which were published under his management, are worth an examination even at this late day. It was this writing which established the *Messenger* and gave it an early celebrity. Newspapers of the times denounced it hugely; so did all the small authors about New York and Philadelphia; and all the *niminee piminee* people everywhere joined in the cry. The burden of that cry was 'wholesale denunciation', 'abuse', &c., &c. He did lay on with the most merciless severity, crucifying many. But he did not condemn one whit too much. The objectors should recollect this great truth: as there are a great many more bad than good people in this world, just so are there many more bad than good books in the world. We go not too far – no, not half enough – in saying that for every one good book one hundred volumes which are utterly worthless are published. This is a fact. From the imperfection of human things it is so. The reviewer who pretends to treat the literature of his age with justice, must needs condemn a hundred times as much as he praises. The contrary is the characteristic of American reviewing at present. The press deluges every thing with *eau sucrée*. Mr Poe dealt out nothing but justice to the dunces. He flayed them alive. He was in those days like one possessed of a divine fury; tore right and left with an envenomed tooth; like some savage boar, broken into a hot-house of pale exotics, he laid about him with white foaming tusks, uprooting all. His writing then attracted universal attention. At the same time it made him an immense number of enemies among literary men. This was a cause why his merit was never acknowledged, even by his own profession in this country. He was not recognized by the popular mind, because it did not comprehend him. He was not recognized by the writers, because they hated him of old.

As a poet, we must contemplate in this author an

unfinished column. He wanted money too often and too much to develop his wonderful imagination in verse. But there is one poem in which he succeeded in uttering himself; but on its dusky wings he will sail securely over the gulf of oblivion to the eternal shore beyond.

There is still such a difference of opinion in relation to this unique production, that it is entitled to a separate notice at our hands. With the learned in imaginative literature, 'The Raven' has taken rank over the whole world, as the very first poem manufactured upon the American continent. In their eyes, but one other work of the western world can be placed near it: – that is the 'Humble Bee' of Ralph Waldo Emerson. This last is admitted to be the superior of 'The Raven' in construction and perfect elaboration; the latter possesses a greater merit as a work of *pure art*. But while 'The Raven' maintains this exalted position upon the scale of all the class that possesses a taste sufficiently cultivated to be catholic, there is yet a large majority of those denominated 'well educated people' who make it matter of special denunciation and ridicule. Those who have formed their taste in the Pope and Dryden school, whose earliest poetical acquaintance is Milton, and whose latest Hammond and Cowper – with a small sprinkling of Moore and Byron – cannot relish a poet tinged so deeply with the dyes of the nineteenth century. 'The Raven' makes an impression on them which they are not able to explain – but that irritates them. Criticism and explanation are useless with such. In spite of our pleas, such will talk of the gaudiness of Keats, and the craziness of Shelley, until they see deep enough into their claims to forget or be ashamed to talk so. This class angrily pronounce 'The Raven' flat nonsense. Another class are disgusted therewith because they can see no purpose, no allegory, no 'meaning'; as they express it, in the poem. These people – and they constitute the majority of our practical race – are possessed of a false theory. They hold that every poem and poet should have some moral notion or other, which it is his 'mission' to expound. That theory is all false. To build theories, principles, religions, &c., is the business of the argumentative, not of the poetic faculty. The business of poetry is to minister to the sense of the beautiful in human minds. That sense is a simple element in our nature – simple, not compound; and therefore the art which ministers to it may safely be said to have an ultimate end in so ministering. This 'The Raven' does in an eminent degree. It has no allegory in it, no purpose – or a very slight one – but it is a 'thing of beauty', and will be a 'joy forever', for that and no further reason. The last stanza is an image of settled despair and despondency, which throws a gleam of meaning and allegory over the entire poem – making it all a personification of that passion – but that stanza is evidently an afterthought, and unconnected with the original poem.

'The Raven' itself, is a simple narrative of simple events. A bird which had been taught to speak by some former master, is lost in a stormy night, is attracted by the light of a student's window, flies to it and flutters against it. Then against the door. The student fancies it a visitor; opens the door; and the chance word uttered by the bird suggests to him memories and fancies connected with his own situation and his dead sweetheart or wife. Such is the poem. The last stanza is an accident and an afterthought; and the worth of 'The Raven' is not in any 'moral', nor is its charm in the construction of its story. Its great and wonderful merits consist in the strange, beautiful and fantastic imagery and colors with which the simple subject is clothed – the grave and supernatural tone with which it rolls on the ear, – the extraordinary vividness of the word painting, – and the powerful, but altogether indefinable appeal which is made throughout to the organs of ideality and marvellousness. Added to these is a versification indescribably sweet and wonderfully difficult – winding and convoluted about like the mazes of some complicated overture by Beethoven. To all who have a strong perception of tune, there is a music in it which haunts the ear long after reading. These are great merits. They render 'The Raven', in the writer's esteem, a gem of art. It is engraved with the image of true genius – and of genius in its happiest hour. It is one of those things an author never does but once.

This author has left very little poetry that is good; but that little contains traces of merits transcendent – though undeveloped. Most of his collected pieces were written in early youth. They are not above the usual verse of newspapers. He

retained them along with 'The Raven', 'Lenore', and his two
or three other jewels, only because of the attachment of early
association. Just before his death, he wrote some things
worthy of 'The Raven' and of 'Ulalume'. The chief of these is
the poem of 'The Bells', first published in *Sartain's Magazine*.
The design of the verse is to imitate the sound of bells; and it
is executed with a beauty, melody, and fidelity, which is
unsurpassed among compositions of its nature. Southey's
famous account of 'How the waters come down at Lodore',
is not for a moment comparable to it – either in the perfection
of imitation, or poetical imagery. No man ever owned the
English language more completely than Edgar Poe. In all its
winding bouts, in all its delicate shades and powerful tones,
from the most voluptuous sensualities of Moore, and from
the oddest combinations of Charles Dickens's lingo, up to the
full organ notes of Milton, he was master of it. His poems
contain evidence that any thing that could be done in English
he could do. The following lines are well known in literary
history as an example of the convertibility of the French
language:

> Quand une cordier, cordant, vent corder une corde
> Pour sa corde, trois cordons il accorde;
> Mais si des cordons de la corde descorde
> La corde descordant fait descorder la corde.

Dr Wallis, (the mathematician – the universal language
man,) translated these lines so literally as to take away the
Frenchman's triumph and boast over the superior convertibility of his tongue: –

> When a twister a-twisting will twist him a twist,
> For the twisting his twist he three times doth entwist:
> But if one of the twists of the twist doth untwist,
> The twine that untwisteth untwisteth the twist.

Among the writings of Poe may be found many examples
of the convertibility of the English language superior to
either of these. The Bell-ringing verses before alluded to are
eminently such. We do not quote them, because it is but
lately that we laid them before the reader. 'The Raven' is
familiar to everyone as the most wonderful and beautiful

example which the world affords of the complicated power of words, and of the more solemn and elevated music of verse.

A very remarkable quality in these poems is one which can scarcely be defined better, than as the *'epicurianism'* of language. It is a delicate and most extraordinary style, which is the peculiar property of our author. 'Ulalume' and 'Annabel Lee' – the last thing he ever wrote – are good illustrations of this quality. There is another poem in this collection, which is a most perfect specimen, but which has not been properly appreciated by the world – it is the fragment entitled 'Dreamland'. That poem is a fanciful picture of the phantasmagoria of dreams, of the broken and fantastic images which swim before the half-closed eye of mind, when the senses and the judgement are enveloped in sleep. We wish we had room for its insertion here.

As a tale writer, the name of Edgar Poe is best known. The collection published by Wiley & Putnam has been exceedingly popular. But the things which are most remarkable and peculiar to the author, his real wonders, are not those that have attracted attention to that volume. It is not the Maelstrom, the House of Usher, or Eros and Charmion, that are best known in it, but the Gold Bug, La Rue Morgue, and the Purloined Letter. The extraordinary specimens of analysis in these have caused the book's sale. The collection was made up by a gentleman of a decided analytic turn. He selected those among Poe's pieces which contained most exhibitions of his analytic power. This, although not the most peculiar and most original of Mr Poe's powers, was one of the most remarkable. He possessed a capacity for creating trains of thought astonishingly – painfully acute. A memorable example is to be found in the volume referred to, (121–24) where the method by which the mind can pursue the association of ideas, is exhibited with wonderful metaphysical accuracy and clearness. Mr Poe himself did not think half so much of this collection as he did of his *Tales of the Grotesque and Arabesque*; but in his estimate of these we cannot side with him. We agree to the popular verdict upon them. A criticism their author once made to us upon the German Fantastic Literature of which Hoffmann was Corypheus, may justly be applied to them – 'the gold in that hard ore is not worth the digging for it.' They are too goblin-like, too entirely unnatural, to be relished by anybody but their author. The great defect of Poe, as an author, was his want of sympathy with, and indeed of likeness to, the human kind. He could not paint men well because he did not understand them; and he did not understand them because he was not at all like them. All his peculiar compositions were marked by that galvanic and unnatural character which marks the movements of Shelley's mind.

He was certainly incapable of producing a novel presenting human life and character in any of its ordinary phases; but his chief fictitious work, the *Narrative of Arthur Gordon Pym*, has been unjustly disparaged and neglected. That narrative is the history of some sailors, who were becalmed on a wreck in the South Pacific until they were obliged to eat one another. Among those terrible scenes, and in strange descriptions of undiscovered islands and unknown savages, the temper and genius of this author revel undisturbed. The execution of the work is exceedingly plain and careless – perhaps it is purposely so, as it purports to be the log book of a common sailor. But the concluding pages we take to be one of the most remarkable and characteristic passages in all his writings.

The book has been long out of print; and the publishers of this 'new edition of Poe's Works' have omitted it from their collection. We shall therefore present the reader with an extract. The vessel has become unmanageable, and the provision and water having long ago given out, the sailors are reduced to cannibalism. While in this condition a brig approaches:

[Quotes the description of the death-ship, *Works*, 3, 110–13.]

We find ourselves in an awkward position. Our theme has seduced us from our limits. We have traversed the wilderness of this man's writings only to find that the span of magazine existence will never suffice to reach our goal and his Canaan. *Eureka*, that divine work, the Parthenon of pure reason, we may not enter in this article. We have reviewed the long lines and columns of marble and jasper, arabesque and antic, which form its propylon, and stand upon its terrace, but we can only point the reader to its portal and leave him to explore it alone. *Eureka* is an attempt to develop the process and demonstrate the law by which the universe assumed its visible phenomena and present organization; and to demonstrate further, how this same law, or principle, and process, must evidently reduce all things to the vague, imperceptible, immaterial chaos of pure matter or spirit from which it arose. The theme is manifestly one which possesses little bearing on the world we live in, and is of little practical importance in the present state of human knowledge. The author leads us to the extreme boundary of reason's horizon. His *dramatis personae* are ideas and shapes, which have never yet walked the halls of experimental science. The senses furnish no data on which to erect the edifice; and the senses furnish no test of its finished solidity. The materials are dug from the mines of the exact sciences. But if there be certainty in mathematics, or reliability on mathematical reasoning, or in the logical concatenation of self-evident ideas, this book and its conclusions are true. It is a globule of crystalline clearness, *teres ac rotundus*. Few have read it. The plan of the work is one which, in him who would read its labyrinth, requires an extensive knowledge of the entire cycle of material and metaphysical knowledge, and those who possess such knowledge are too much occupied with the tangible results of diurnal experiment, to walk with a companion so strange and wild in these regions, the most solitary and remote of the intellectual realm. It was thus with Kepler; and Copernicus, dying, left the world a book which it regarded with the same indifference and the same idle curiosity. But princes, and popes, and sages came forward to take up that book. And when the day comes, as it will come, when experimental science shall have so far enlarged its boundaries, as to catch a view of, and see the need of the grand generalities which this poor drunkard has strewn to the winds and waters, *Eureka* will tower like a monumental obelisk before the world's great eyes. It was thus with Copernicus; it was so with Kepler. In the presence of these grand recollections, we can sympathize at least with him who wrote these words: '*I care not whether my work is read now, or by posterity. I can afford to wait a century for readers, when God himself has waited six*

thousand years for an observer. I triumph. I have stolen the golden
secret of the Egyptians. I will indulge my sacred fury.'

NOTES

1 Following Griswold, Daniel believed that Poe had been born in
Baltimore; Lowell's abolitionist sentiments were anathema to
him.
2 Daniel is here thinking in phrenological terms.
3 Poe, of course, did not visit Europe as an adult.

107. George Rex Graham, 'The Late Edgar Allan Poe', *Graham's Magazine*

March 1850, 36, 224–6

Graham (1813–94) was a magazine entrepreneur in
Philadelphia. He employed Poe as literary editor of
Graham's Magazine from 1841 to 1842, and writes from
his personal knowledge of him at that time. Although
not strictly a review, Graham's open letter to Willis was
clearly inspired by Griswold's edition.

MY DEAR WILLIS, – In an article of yours which accomp-
anies the two beautiful volumes of the writings of
Edgar Allan Poe you have spoken with so much truth and
delicacy of the deceased, and with the magical touch of genius,
have called so warmly up before me the memory of our lost
friend as you and I both seem to have known him, that I feel
warranted in addressing to you the few plain words I have to say
in defence of his character as set down by Mr Griswold.

Although the article, it seems, appeared originally in the New York *Tribune*, it met my eye for the first time in the volumes before me. I now purpose to take exception to it in the most public manner. I knew Mr Poe well, far better than Mr Griswold; and by the memory of old times, when he was an editor of *Graham*, I pronounce this exceedingly ill-timed and unappreciative estimate of the character of our lost friend, *unfair and untrue*. It is Mr Poe as seen by the writer while laboring under a fit of the nightmare, but so dark a picture has no resemblance to the *living* man. Accompanying these beautiful volumes, it is an immortal infamy, the death's head over the entrance to the garden of beauty, a horror that clings to the brow of morning, whispering of murder. It haunts the memory through every page of his writings, leaving upon the heart a sensation of utter gloom, a feeling almost of terror. The only relief we feel is in knowing that it is not true, that it is a fancy sketch of a perverted, jaundiced vision. The man who could deliberately say of Edgar Allan Poe, in a notice of his life and writings prefacing the volumes which were to become a priceless souvenir to all who loved him, that his death might startle many, '*but that few would be grieved by it*', and blast the whole fame of the man by such a paragraph as follows, is a judge dishonored. He is not Mr Poe's peer, and I challenge him before the country even as a junior in the case.

[Quotes Griswold's description of Poe as Bulwer Lytton's Francis Vivian.]

Now, this is dastardly, and, what is worse, it is false. It is very adroitly done, with phrases very well turned, and with gleams of truth shining out from a setting so dusky as to look devilish. Mr Griswold does not feel the worth of the man he has undervalued; he had no sympathies in common with him, and has allowed old prejudices and old enmities to steal, insensibly perhaps, into the coloring of his picture. They were for years totally uncongenial, if not enemies, and during that period Mr Poe, in a scathing lecture upon 'The Poets of America,' gave Mr Griswold some raps over the knuckles of force sufficient to be remembered. He had, too, in the exercise of his functions as critic, put to death summarily the literary reputation of some of Mr Griswold's best friends; and their ghosts cried in vain for him to avenge them during Poe's lifetime; and it almost seems as if the present hacking at the cold remains of him who struck them down, is a sort of compensation for duty long delayed, for reprisal long desired, but deferred. But without this, the opportunities afforded Mr Griswold to estimate the character of Poe occurred, in the main, after his stability had been wrecked, his whole nature in a degree changed, and with all his prejudices aroused and active. Nor do I consider Mr Griswold *competent*, with all the opportunities he may have cultivated or acquired, to act as his judge, to dissect that subtle and singularly fine intellect, to probe the motives and weigh the actions of that proud heart. His whole nature, that distinctive presence of the departed, which now stands impalpable, yet in strong outline before me, as I knew him and *felt* him to be, eludes the rude grasp of a mind so warped and uncongenial as Mr Griswold's.

But it may be said, my dear Willis, that Mr Poe himself deputed him to act as his literary executor, and that he must have felt some confidence, in his ability at least, if not in his integrity, to perform the functions imposed, with discretion and honor. I do not purpose, now, to enter into any examination of the appointment of Mr Griswold, nor of the wisdom of his appointment, to the solemn trust of handing the fair fame of the deceased, unimpaired, to that posterity to which the dying poet bequeathed his legacy, but simply to question its faithful performance. Among the true friends of Poe in this city – and he had some such here – there are those, I am sure, that *he* did not class among *villains*; nor do *they* feel easy when they see their old friend dressed out, in his grave, in the habiliments of a scoundrel. There is something to them in this mode of procedure on the part of the literary executor that does not chime in with their notions of 'the true point of honor.' They had all of them looked upon our departed friend as singularly indifferent to wealth for its own sake, but as very positive in his opinions that the scale of social merit was not of the highest; that mind, somehow, was apt to be left out of the estimate altogether; and, partaking somewhat

378

of his free way of thinking, his friends are startled to find they have entertained very unamiable convictions. As to his 'quick choler' when he was contradicted, it depended a good deal upon the party denying, as well as upon the subject discussed. He was quick, it is true, to perceive mere quacks in literature, and somewhat apt to be hasty when pestered with them; but upon most other questions his natural amiability was not easily disturbed. Upon a subject that he understood thoroughly, he felt some right to be positive, if not arrogant, when addressing pretenders. His 'astonishing natural advantages' *had* been very assiduously cultivated; his 'daring spirit' was the anointed of genius; his self-confidence the proud convicton of both; and it was with something of a lofty scorn that he *attacked*, as well as repelled, a crammed scholar of the hour, who attempted to palm upon him his ill-digested learning. Literature with him was religion; and he, its high priest, with a whip of scorpions, scourged the money-changers from the temple. In all else, he had the docility and kind-heartedness of a child. No man was more quickly touched by a kindness, none more prompt to return for an injury. For three or four years I knew him intimately, and for eighteen months saw him almost daily, much of the time writing or conversing at the same desk, knowing all his hopes, his fears, and little annoyances of life, as well as his high-hearted struggle with adverse fate; yet he was always the same polished gentleman, the quiet, unobtrusive, thoughtful scholar, the devoted husband, frugal in his personal expenses, punctual and unwearied in his industry, *and the soul of honor* in all his transactions. This, of course, was in his better days, and by them *we* judge the man. But even after his habits had changed, there was no literary man to whom I would more readily advance money for labor to be done. He kept his accounts, small as they were, with the accuracy of a banker. I append an account sent to me in his own hand, long after he had left Philadelphia, and after all knowledge of the transactions it recited had escaped my memory. I had returned him the story of 'The Gold-Bug,' at his own request, as he found that he could dispose of it very advantageously elsewhere: –

We were square when I sold you the 'versification' article, for which you gave, first, $25, and afterwards $7 – in all	$32.00
Then you bought 'The Gold Bug' for	52.00
	————
I got both these back, so that I owed	$84.00
You lent Mrs. Clemm	12.50
	————
Making in all	$96.50
Brought over	$96.50

The review of Flaccus was $3\frac{3}{4}$ pp., which $4, is	$15.00	
Lowell's poem is	10.00	
The review of Channing, 4 pp., is $6, of which I got $6, leaving	10.00	
The review of Halleck, 4 pp., is $16, of which I got $10, leaving	6.00	
The review of Reynolds, 2 pp.	8.00	
The review of Longfellow, 5 pp., is $20, of which I got $10, leaving	10.00	
So that I have paid in all	59.00	
	————	
Which leaves still due by me		$37.50

This, I find, was his uniform habit with others as well as myself, carefully recalling to mind his indebtedness with the fresh article sent. And this is the man who had 'no moral susceptibility,' and little or nothing of the 'true point of honor.' It may be a very plain business view of the question, but it strikes his friends that it may pass as something, as times go.

I shall never forget how solicitous of the happiness of his wife and mother-in-law he was whilst one of the editors of *Graham's Magazine* his whole efforts seemed to be to procure

the comfort and welfare of his home. Except for their
happiness, and the natural ambition of having a magazine of
his own, I never heard him deplore the want of wealth. The
truth is, he cared little for money, and knew less of its value,
for he seemed to have no personal expenses. What he
received from me, in regular monthly instalments, went
directly into the hands of his mother-in-law for family
comforts, and *twice* only I remember his purchasing some
rather expensive luxuries for his house, and then he was
nervous to the degree of misery until he had, by extra
articles, covered what he considered an imprudent indebtedness. His love for his wife was a sort of rapturous worship of
the spirit of beauty which he felt was fading before his eyes. I
have seen him hovering around her when she was ill, with all
the fond fear and tender anxiety of a mother for her
first-born, her slightest cough causing in him a shudder, a
heart-chill that was visible. I rode out, one summer evening,
with them, and the remembrance of his watchful eyes eagerly
bent upon the slightest change of hue in that loved face
haunts me yet as the memory of a sad strain. It was the
hourly *anticipation* of her loss that made him a sad and
thoughtful man, and lent a mournful melody to his undying
song.

It is true, that later in life Poe had much of those morbid
feelings which a life of poverty and disappointment is so apt
to engender in the heart of man – the sense of having been
ill-used, misunderstood, and put aside by men of far less
ability, and of none, – which preys upon the heart and clouds
the brain of many a child of song. A consciousness of the
inequalities of life, and of the abundant power of mere
wealth, allied even to vulgarity, to override all distinctions,
and to thrust itself, bedaubed with dirt and glittering with
tinsel, into the high places of society, and the chief seats of
the synagogue; whilst he, a worshipper of the beautiful and
true, who listened to the voices of angels and held delighted
companionship with them as the cold throng swept disdain-
fully by him, was often in danger of being thrust out,
houseless, homeless, beggared, upon the world, with all his
fine feelings strung to a tension of agony when he thought of
his beautiful and delicate wife, dying hourly before his eyes.

What wonder that he then poured out the vials of a long-treasured bitterness upon the injustice and hollowness of all society around him. The very natural question 'Why did he not work and thrive?' is easily answered. It will not be *asked* by the many who know the precarious tenure by which literary men hold a mere living in this country. The avenues through which they can profitably reach the country are few, and crowded with aspirants for bread, as well as fame. The unfortunate tendency to cheapen every literary work to the lowest point of beggarly flimsiness in price and profit, prevents even the well-disposed from extending anything like an adequate support to even a part of the great throng which genius, talent, education, and even misfortune, force into the struggle. The character of Poe's mind was of such an order as not to be very widely in demand. The class of educated mind which he could readily and profitably address was small – the channels through which he could do so at all were few – and publishers all, or nearly all, contented with such pens as were already engaged, hesitated to incur the expense of his to an extent which would sufficiently remunerate him; hence, when he was fairly at sea, connected permanently with no publication, he suffered all the horrors of prospective destitution, with scarcely the ability of providing for immediate necessities; and at such moments, alas! the tempter often came, and as you have truly said, '*one glass*' of wine made him a madman. Let the moralist, who stands upon 'tufted carpet,' and surveys his smoking board, the fruits of his individual toil or mercantile adventure, pause before he let the anathema, trembling upon his lips, fall upon a man like Poe, who, wandering from publisher to publisher, with his fine, print-like manuscript, scrupulously clean and neatly rolled, finds no market for his brain – with despair at heart, misery ahead, for himself and his loved ones, and gaunt famine dogging at his heels, thus sinks by the wayside, before the demon that watches his steps and whispers *oblivion*. Of all the miseries which God, or his own vices, inflict upon man, none are so terrible as that of having the strong and willing arm struck down to a childlike inefficiency, while the Heart and Will have the purpose of a giant's outdoing. We must remember, too, that the very organization of such a mind as that of Poe – the very tension and tone of his exquisitely strung nerves – the passionate yearnings of his soul for the beautiful and true, utterly unfitted him for the rude jostlings and fierce competitorship of trade. The only drafts of his that could be honored were those upon his brain. The unpeopled air – the caverns of ocean – the decay and mystery that hang around old castles – the thunder of wind through the forest aisles – the spirits that rode the blast, by all but him unseen – and the deep, metaphysical creations which floated through the chambers of his soul – were his only wealth, the High Change where only his signature was valid for rubies.

Could he have stepped down and chronicled small beer, made himself the shifting toady of the hour, and, with bow and cringe, hung upon the steps of greatness, sounding the glory of third-rate ability with a penny trumpet, he would have been fêted alive, and *perhaps* been praised when dead. But, no! his views of the duty of the critic were stern, and he felt that in praising an unworthy writer he committed dishonor. His pen was regulated by the highest sense of *duty*. By a keen analysis he separated and studied each piece which the skilful mechanist had put together. No part, however insignificant or apparently unimportant, escaped the rigid and patient scrutiny of his sagacious mind. The unfitted joint proved the bungler – the slightest blemish was a palpable fraud. He was the scrutinizing lapidary, who detected and exposed the most minute flaw in diamonds. The gem of first water shone the brighter for the truthful setting of his calm praise. He had the finest touch of soul for beauty – a delicate and hearty appreciation of worth. If his praise appeared tardy, it was of priceless value when given. It was true as well as sincere. It was the stroke of honor that at once knighted the receiver. It was in the world of *mind* that he was king; and, with a fierce audacity, he felt and proclaimed himself autocrat. As a critic, he was despotic, supreme. Yet no man with more readiness would soften a harsh expression at the request of a friend, or if he himself felt that he had infused too great a degree of bitterness into his article, none would more readily soften it down after it was in type – though still maintaining the justness of his critical views. I do not believe that he wrote to give pain; but in combating what he conceived to be error, he used the strongest word that presented itself, even in conversation. He labored not so much to reform as to *exterminate* error, and thought the shortest process was to pull it up by the roots.

He was a worshipper of *intellect* – longing to grasp the power of mind that moves the stars – to bathe his soul in the dreams of seraphs. He was himself all ethereal, of a fine essence, that moved in an atmosphere of spirits – of spiritual beauty, overflowing and radiant – twin-brother with the angels, feeling their flashing wings upon his heart, and almost clasping them in his embrace. Of them, and as an expectant archangel of that high order of intellect, stepping out of himself, as it were, and interpreting the time he revelled in delicious luxury in a world beyond, with an audacity which we fear in madmen, but in genius worship as the inspiration of heaven.

But my object, in throwing together a few thoughts upon the character of Edgar Allan Poe, was not to attempt an elaborate criticism, but to say what might palliate grave faults that have been attributed to him, and to meet by facts unjust accusation; in a word, to give a mere outline of the man as he lived before me. I think I am warranted in saying to Mr Griswold that he must review his decision. It will not stand the calm scrutiny of his own judgment, or of time, while it must be regarded by all the friends of Mr Poe as an ill-judged and misplaced calumny upon that gifted son of genius.

Yours truly,
GEO. R. GRAHAM.

108. John Neal, from 'Edgar A. Poe', *Portland Daily Advertiser*

26 April 1850, 20, 2

Better late than *never*, says the proverb. May be so but, perhaps, a safer reading in most cases, would be, better *late* than ever. Early opinions are seldom good for much, and easily forgotten – Later opinions, being of course better considered, riper, and juster, are sometimes worth remembering.

So much has been said of late, over the *man*, Edgar A. Poe, which ought never to have been said at all, and which never would have been said, but for his early and terrible death; and so many questions have been asked, and so many old speculations hazarded, through the newspapers, and otherwise, by people, who are anxious to know the whole truth about him, now that their knowledge can be of no use to the poor fellow, and very little to themselves, that I, for one, though I never saw his face in my life, and only know him on paper, find it no easy matter to keep still.

To the question, 'what do you think of him?' I answer thus. I believe Edgar A. Poe to have been greatly misunderstood, and greatly misrepresented, for many years before he vanished from our midst – I do not say died, for such people never die; and by men too, who were big enough to know better, like the elephant that was cudgelled in a menagerie for kicking up a dust, and half blinding his companions in the cages about him. And now that he is beyond their reach – or perhaps it were better to say, that they are beyond his reach – I believe him to be cruelly belied.

My notion of the poor fellow has been, from the first, that he was always taken advantage of by others, and therefore, he got soured, resentful and suspicious. I do not mean by this, that everybody cheated him, for he was, to my knowledge, handsomely paid for some of his writings: but that he was not discouraged in the very outset of two or three very foolish enterprises, by his friend Graham and others, who knew that he would never be a popular Magazine-writer, although, as a man of genius, every man of genius he touched, would thrill with acknowledgement.

I believe, that after he had to do with the *Southern Literary Messenger*, and failed in two or three literary adventures, one after another, which, as a matter of business, ought never to have been thought of seriously, for a single day, nor ever entered upon, but with a large capital, and a party who would like to spend a few thousands just for the fun o' the thing, his whole outward character changed.

I hold that he was a creature of wonderful power; concentrated, keen, finished and brilliant: rather Horne Tooke-ish in his literary slope; but with ten times the imagination of Tooke, even while drawing the polished steel bow, with the poisoned arrow, mentioned by Hazlitt, and so characteristic of the 'little person', that Junius took such delight in following up and pinching, while he made faces through the window, at all the passers by.

That Edgar A. Poe understood poetry – felt poetry – and sometimes wrote poetry of amazing beauty and strength, nobody will deny; or nobody, whose opinions will ever be cared for. But his very best doings in that way, are not those which have got him a name with the people.

That he saw farther, and looked more steadily and more inquisitively into the elements of darkness – into the sha-dowy, the shifting and the mysterious – than did most of the shining brotherhood about him; and that, by a process, which amounted to a sort of self-combustion – a troubled ever changing, inward light – a fiery and passionate foreshadowing – he often saw 'the hand you cannot see', and 'princely visions rare, go stepping through the air' I believe – notwithstanding the testimony of Mr R.W. Gris-wold, to the same effect.

I believe too, that he was by nature, of a just and generous temper, thwarted, baffled, and self-harnessed by his own willfulness to the most unbecoming drudgery; and that he went about for whole years, with his hood wings rumpled, soiled and quenched, where they were wholly unheeded, like sumptuous banners trailed along the crowded thoroughfares of life, in a March drizzle.

I believe too that he was a very honest fellow, and very sincere, though incapable of doing justice to anybody he might happen to dislike no matter why; or to anybody he thought over-cuddled by the monthlies, or over-slobbered by the weeklies; while his reverend biographer would seem to be incapable of doing justice to anybody else.

That his natural temper changed before death, and that he saw the world at last, with other eyes than he was born with; and that, instead of the unearthly brightness that broke forth, in flashes, every time he lifted the wings of his boyhood, like a seraph, he delighted for the last few years of a weary life, in 'raying darkness', upon the people about him, is clear enough.

But to the books themselves. There are two volumes entitled *The Works of Edgar A. Poe*, and they certainly give one a very just idea of his character as a writer. The biographical notices are just and wise, and excellent, so far as they go, with one single exception, that of the Rev. R.W. Griswold; a book-wright and compiler by the cart-load, to whom the dying poet bequeathed his papers, and his character, to be hashed over, and served up, little by little, with a *sauce piquante*, resembling the turbid water, in which very poor eggs have been boiled to death.

But for the following passages, printed in italics, to be found in a newspaper sketch by this gentleman – the literary executor – I had well nigh said executioner – of Edgar A. Poe, before he had stiffened in his winding sheet, I should have supposed him, though honest enough perhaps, when he had no temptation to be otherwise, and rather willing to tell the truth, if he knew how, and it was likely to pay, yet wholly unfitted for the solemn duty he had undertaken so rashly; because, in my judgment, wholly incapable of understanding or appreciating Poe – dead or alive – and by no means of a temper to forget that he had ever been out-generalled or out-blazed, or not listened to by such a man as Poe, and therefore not likely to do him justice after death, when he would have no longer anything to fear from the poet's 'glittering eye', and searching words.

The passages referred to, however, being not only poetry – but exalted poetry – poetry of astonishing and original strength, passionate and characteristic – I am led to suppose one of two things, namely – that the Rev. gentleman is a poet, himself, that he *did* understand Poe, and that therefore he has no excuse for so misrepresenting him; or that, as in all that he has ever been suspected of writing hitherto, there is absolutely nothing to be compared with the passages italicised, either in thought or language, it is quite clear that he has begged, borrowed, or stolen them, from somebody else; and most likely from Poe, as they are fragments of the man himself. They are instinct with *his* vitality. They burn with *his* brightness, and with no other; vehement, cloudy, flashing and fitful. Perhaps too they were appropriated without any just idea of their value, or weight – warmth or massiveness, and the Rev. biographer did it all ignorantly, like the man who was met running away from a fire with a grindstone on his back, and being stopped and questioned, swore he didn't know he had it.

Perhaps too – for I am anxious to find a passable explanation of the gentleman's very strange behavior – perhaps, he had become disqualified for the duties he had the presumption to undertake, and wanted the manliness to refuse, by a too long, and much too intimate a companionship with Poe – for it cannot be denied that in some cases familiarity *does* breed contempt – followed by a misunderstanding, which blighted all his ancient sympathies, and withered all his better hopes. Under a show of impartiality, he is a judge, who leans against the prisoner at the bar. Edgar A. Poe is the arraigned poet, offering no plea, no excuse, no palliation for the 'deeds done in the body' – but standing mute, stiff and motionless, at the bar – his glorious eyes quenched forever, and his fine countenance overspread with the paleness of death; and the Rev. R.W. Griswold, a Radamanthus, who is not to be bilked of his fee, a thimble-full of newspaper notoriety. Laboring to be very perpendicular, ostentatiously upright, lest peradventure he might be suspected of a friendly inclination toward the memory of a man who had trusted him on his death-bed; with no measure about him – above – or below – to compare himself with, or to steady himself by, he leans backward, with a simper and a strut, such as you may see every day of your life in little, pompous, fidgetty men, trying to stand high in the world, in spite of their Creator.

While pronouncing a judgment upon the dead body of his old associate, who had left the world in a hurry, and under a mistake, which the Reverend gentleman took the earliest opportunity of correcting – by telegraph – at a penny a time, for a newspaper, and in such a way, as to leave it doubtful whether, in his opinion, Edgar A. Poe had ever had any business at all here, and whether on the whole, it were not better for himself, and for the world, that he had never been born – with that millstone round his neck, which had just fallen off – he seems to take it for granted that all this parade of sympathy will not be seen through – that, when he lifts the handkerchief to his eyes, and snuffles about poor Poe, and his melancholy want of principle – the ancient grudge still burning underneath this show, will be forgotten – and that he, at least, will have credit for whatsoever Poe had not. Peradventure he may find it so; for most assuredly, the reverse of the proposition is true. Whatsoever Edgar A. Poe had – that Mr R.W. Griswold had not.

Among the passages, or fragments above referred to, as part and parcel of the dead poet, and altogether above the dreary level of his Executor, are the following. They are printed in italics, the rest, with one or two exceptions bear no stamp of individuality, whereby their parentage may be guessed at.

'His conversation was at times almost supra-mortal, in its eloquence. His voice was *modulated with astonishing skill*, and his *large and variably expressive eyes* looked repose, or shot fiery tumult into theirs who listened, while his own face glowed, or was *changeless in pallor,* as his imagination quickened his blood, or drew it back *frozen to his heart.* His *imagery was from the worlds* which *no mortal can see,* but with the vision of genius. Suddenly starting from a proposition *exactly and sharply defined* in terms of utmost *simplicity and clearness*, he rejected the forms of customary logic, and by a crystaline process of accretion' – that's Griswold all over – 'built up his ocular demonstrations – (ditto, ditto – *ditto!*) – in forms of *gloomiest and ghastliest grandeur,* or in those of the most *airy and delicious beauty.'* ✱✱✱ *'He walks the streets in madness of melancholy, with lips moving* in indistinct curses, *or with eyes upturned in passionate prayer* ✱✱✱ He would brave the wildest storms, and all night, *with drenched garments, and arms beating the winds and rains,* would speak as if to spirits.' ✱✱✱*'The astonishing natural advantages of this poor boy – his beauty,* his readiness, the *daring spirit that breathed round him like a fiery atmosphere'* &c. &c.

The thoughts I have underscored are Poe's – and so is the very language – every word of it, in most cases. I cannot be mistaken. As well might you try to palm off a patch from Boswell's every day trowsers – I don't like to say breeches – for a bit of this ponderous armor cast away by the giant he used to straddle about with, for a show, as to persuade any mortal man acquainted with the writings of Edgar A. Poe, and Rufus W. Griswold, that the passages above cited were his, or that they were not Poe's. It is the sunshine of Poe playing through the green turf – with a basket of chips emptied over it.

Nor, if the truth could be known, should I be greatly astonished to find them scattered through some rejected article of Poe's, written for Graham, while Mr R.W. Griswold had to do with the editorship: or that they had been carefully pinched out, and put aside, from some hurried letter to the Reverend gentleman himself, while the author and he were on the best possible terms, together.

But why waste words on such a subject. Mr George R. Graham who, it is clear enough, knew the Rev. R.W. Griswold, as well as Edgar A. Poe – has done both justice; and a paper which appeared on a fly-sheet of his last monthly, where it was altogether out of place, for it should have been foremost, has got a reputation for himself as a writer, which, a long life spent in the drudgery of a *Chiffonier,* or compiler, would only serve to diminish. He has approved himself a man – by entering upon the defence of a buried friend, with a wise and careful discrimination. He has approved himself a thinker, whose good opinion will be worth having, by the unstudied sincerity and warmth of his language.

Lowell's outline sketch, though written for Graham years

ago, and well worth enlarging, is faithful clear and satisfactory; rather crowded perhaps, and a little too high finished for strength, but capital nevertheless, and worth dilating into fifty pages; and so too are the generous and well timed though very brief, testimonials furnished by Willis. Would they had both written more, for they had both talked with him face to face, and I had not. Such men honor themselves by honoring a brother like Edgar A. Poe; and to confirmation of what both say about his kindly and yielding temper – his willingness to be told his faults, his gentle aptitude – his thankfulness – notwithstanding his haughty self-respect, and trembling sensitiveness – and his impatient anxiety to show a right appreciation of plain dealing, and straight-forward honest reproof, *coming from the right quarter*, you will permit me to offer the following evidence. I do this to show the man's heart; for with his head, I have nothing to do here. That, anybody could see into, and most people through, for it was cold and clear and transparent as crystal; even while the heart, poor fellow! was forever in blast, sending off fire and smoke and frankincense and myrrh and gentle music, and thunder and lightning, no mortal knew where to look for the laboratory itself or the furnace – or what to understand by its revelations. Let the incident I mention be put on record, that our people, who are beginning to take a large, if not a deep interest in the literary reputation of the dead – I wish I could say as much for the living – may be prepared for the next, whose memory, after he has gone down to the chambers of death, may be found rotting by the wayside, under the special guardianship of some literary Executor.

In September 1829, the following notice appeared in the *Yankee*.

[The notice is cited – see No. 2 (a).]

Now this, it will be acknowledged, was not very flattering, nor very soothing. And when I add, that E.A.P. had written me a letter, offering to dedicate a volume of these poems to me – and that I had said, no for his sake, believing that he could meet with no sale if he did, and telling him so – it will be admitted perhaps that he had good reason for being out of temper with me. But how did he behave? Like a man of true genius. He saw – it could not be otherwise – he saw, that in my opinion at least, he had strangely over-rated himself; and yet he was encouraged. With that sublime self-confidence which will not be intimidated, nor thwarted, nor disheartened, nor too rudely questioned, he answered, by preparing the poems for publication; and, writing me another letter, which is referred to thus, in the *Yankee* of December 1829.

[The notice is cited – see No. 2 (b).]

And this, according to the Rev. R.W. Griswold, was the 'naturally unamiable man' – claiming relationship to another, simply because both loved a common Father, and bowing his head patiently to exasperating ridicule – 'Without faith in man or woman', yet loving even 'the natural blue sky and the sunshining earth,' and putting such entire faith in a stranger, as to be guided by him for a long while, notwithstanding the mortifications he had inflicted – 'crastible – envious – impatient of contradiction – without moral susceptibility, and with little or nothing of the true point of honour.' God forgive his calumniator!

Yet more. The poems were published, with certain alterations I had suggested in favourite passages – and here is a letter he sent with a presentation copy.

[Cites Poe's letter of 29 December 1829, omitting the first paragraph – see *Letters*, 1, 35.]

And again, a long while after – I cannot fix the year, and the letter itself is dated only June 4th; but it was written from Philadelphia, and referring to 'my friend Thomas', I take it for granted that it was after he had left the *Literary Messenger* and thought of setting up for himself in that tranquilizing community.

[Cites Poe's letter of 4 June 1840 – see *Letters*, 1, 137.]

And this, look you, is the man who had no faith in his fellow-men – no faith in women – though he died broken hearted, because a wife and a mother-in-law, who had been devoted to him, were wanting the comforts, perhaps the necessaries of life, the every-day comforts of impoverished hope. But enough, the Poet is no more; yet his character is safe notwithstanding the eulogy of his Executor.

109. Unsigned review in *Peterson's Magazine*

November 1850, 18, 214–15

The reviewer was probably Charles J. Peterson, owner and editor of the magazine, which was a rival of *Godey's*.

This is a collection of criticisms, by the late Edgar A. Poe, on a number of American authors. The articles were written during different periods of Poe's career; and while some are indisputably able and candid, others are weak and personal. We knew Poe well. He was a strange, eccentric creature, with many and great faults; yet, on the whole, a man to be pitied rather than condemned. But his reviews were not to be relied on as always just. With many of the qualities of a first-rate critic, he yet wanted a rigid sense of justice; and hence personal prejudice, or the desire of writing a slashing article, or some whim of the moment would often induce him to abuse where he should have praised. The editor of the present volume, Rufus W. Griswold, knew this well, and, therefore, ought not to have republished these criticisms. But this is not the only fault we have to find with the volume. The book is prefaced by a biography of Poe, which paints his character in the darkest colours, and gives, we sincerely believe, an altogether wrong impression of Poe. It is bad enough, under any circumstances, to misrepresent the dead; but when the traducer is the deceased's literary executor, it is a breach of trust. If the friend to whom the departed man has confined his reputation, betrays his good name to obloquy, what may be expected from the world at large? We never, during Poe's life-time, hesitated to speak of his habits of plagiarism, or his want of candor as a critic; but we would cut off our right hand before we would write such a memoir as this, which his pretended friend has written. We speak thus severely because this is the first instance, in American literary history, of such a breach of trust.

VIEWS FROM ABROAD

110. From 'Recent Poets of America', *London Quarterly Review*

June 1854, 2, 453-9

This extensive article reviewed works by Long-fellow, Lowell, and Poe; the Poe texts were: *The Poetical Works of Edgar Allan Poe* (London: Addey & Co., 1853), and *Poe's Tales of Mystery and Imagination; and Poems* (London: Clarke, Beeton & Co., 1852).

It may seem strange that utilitarian America should have been the birth-land of one who, perhaps of all poets, exhibits the most exquisite rhythmic treatment, and whose verse borrows least from without, is least dependent upon external aids and associations. Such, nevertheless, is the case: the man was EDGAR POE. This name is already known to many in this country; but it is rather regarded as the prefix to a life of moral turpitude and a premature death, than as the emblem of the rarest genius. Few there are who appreciate Poe; and, of them, some endeavour to separate the writer from the man; whilst others, unwilling to believe evil of one to whom they are compelled to do reverence, seek to palliate his conduct, believe accounts to be exaggerated, and that Poe was no worse than his neighbours, but that the brightness of his genius made any moral *peccadillo* he might commit more conspicuous. From each of these courses we are compelled to dissent. That brief and frightful history is far too well authenticated, and, we must add, in one of the peculiar temperament of Poe, far too *likely*, to be explained away or denied. And to separate from the productions of a writer that

395

knowledge of his character which is to be gained from his career, is to abandon the key to the right understanding of the former. Poe belonged to a class. There are a few, appearing now and then upon the earth, whose life is one habitual tension of soul, a ceaseless watch maintained by the spirit over the perceptive nature, a self-concentration and col-lectedness, which draws and moulds into itself every thing around. These are the true 'heritors of unfulfilled renown', – the men who never sleep, who become the slaves of morbid habits, who die young. Possessed of splendid temper, often of extraordinary *physique,* in mental sensibility and energy the most perfect of the race, endowed, as if by instinct, with universal knowledge, they yet do little, are only passively affected by the movements of society, and seem to pass through life as through a vivid dream. It is seldom that circumstances induce them to clothe their own fine and infinitely subtle intuitions in the grosser garb of language. Then they let fall a few words as a memory, which, like the dreamy mutterings of sleep, serve to show the whereabouts of the thoughts, – are half a concealment, half a revelation, of the mysteries of the inner spirit. Neither in their errors, nor in their perfections, are such men to be judged by any ordinary standard. Whatever they write, is a psychological memoir of themselves: they are absolutely the prey of their own minds; they never escape themselves; all their thoughts are interior sensations. And the very perfection of their faculties, the taste which lies at the centre of their being, insures that these sensations shall be purely aesthetic. A certain amount of moral insensibility, an isolation from the movements of the world, are the inevitable results of a mind so entirely aesthetic. 'Would', we involuntarily exclaim, 'that this nature could be imbued with a feeling of philanthropy, that this mind were gifted with an active moral sense, that these fiery passions could be fashioned into use!' It has not been so yet; and that man, in his most perfect form, has not yet fully spoken to man, is a reflection full of hope to the world. Of this order was Poe a type. His ardent passions seem to have existed for nothing else than to be subjects for the experimenting of his intellect; and this has invested their wildest freaks with an indescribable *finesse* and grace. His career is a terrible instance of what one may become whose course is guided by such a principle as this. More reckless expenditure of energy, more utter disregard of the claims of others, of the world, it is impossible to imagine. Into the details of that life we need not enter: they have already often enough pointed the moral of critic and biographer. We have only to do with them so far as regards an estimate of the writings of Poe.

America had little share in the formation of his character. His education was European. When very young, he travelled all over England, and remained for five years at school near London. Thence returning home, he entered the University at Charlottesville, where, says his biographer, 'the remarkable ease with which he mastered the most difficult studies kept him in the first rank for scholarship; and he would have graduated with the highest honours, had not his gambling, intemperance, and other vices induced his expulsion from the University'. This, and subsequent misconduct, occasioned a rupture with his friends, and he again repaired to Europe 'on a Quixotic expedition to join the insurgent Greeks'. His Grecizing enthusiasm probably evaporated with the voyage; at all events, he never reached his destination. But at this time he traversed nearly the whole of Europe, visiting Russia, France, and Italy. Of such an education his genius was the counterpart: it was European; it was Italian. He belonged in spirit to that land in which nature – the art of God – is so blended with human works and associations, as to become almost the art of man, – a symbol of human faculties, and no longer an appeal to human consciousness. So, the great characteristic of Poe's poetry is – we will not say, science, but—conscious art. Had he not been a poet, he would have been the most consummate critic that ever lived. Every piece that he ever wrote, with all its seeming spontaneity and living grace, is yet the product of the most inexorable taste, of the theoretic principles of poetry existing in his own mind; and every part, when examined, will assume an air of rigid and inviolable connexion. There is no ebulience in him; nothing foreign to his purpose occurs; a digression, however beautiful, he would have considered a blemish. Each of his little poems is a study, designed to illustrate some aesthetic principles upon which the ever-musing spirit was at the time engaged. 'The Raven', his most known poem, the only one which he laboured to render universally appreciable, with all its mastery of passion, its weird and unearthly effect, is no more than this. In the paper entitled 'The Philosophy of Composition', he has left us a minute account of the process of its formation, – consequently, a portraiture of himself. He gives a quiet, admirably perspicuous detail of each succeeding step: how he resolved to write a poem which should embody a certain effect, produce a certain impression; how he deliberately analyzed the various modes which might be employed for this purpose, selecting the best: how from these *data* he excogitated all the paraphernalia of his poem, and, with his thinking finished, his plan elaborated to the *denouement*, first set pen to paper in the composition of the last stanza but two. There is one short sentence which reveals the whole man. After mentioning that he began with the stanza, –

> 'Prophet', said I, 'thing of evil, prophet still, if bird or devil,
> By the heavens that bend above us, by the God we both adore,
> Tell this soul with sorrow laden, if within the distant Aidenn,
> It shall clasp a sainted maiden, whom the angles name Lenore,
> Clasp a rare and radiant maiden, whom the angels name Lenore?'
> Quoth the Raven, 'Nevermore'.

He adds, 'Had I been able, in the subsequent composition, to construct more vigorous stanzas, I should have purposely enfeebled them, so as not to interfere with the climacteric effect'. Could any one else have said that?

It is scarcely possible to over-estimate the artistic merits of Poe. Not only were such faculties as he had, possessed in an eminent degree, – but he possessed all the faculties of the artist. His numbers, moving to a purpose under the guidance of an unfailing taste, resemble the trained battalions of an Alva or a Cromwell; which, we are told, 'marched to victory with the rigid precision of machines, whilst burning with the wildest enthusiasm of Crusaders'. There is in them no stiffness, no appearance of elaboration; free scope is given to an invention, that is, an imagination, in the highest sense of the word, *'creative'*; and this is ever accompanied by a power

of analysis the subtlest and most minute, by which every
thing is reduced to congruity: no room is left for the
improbable; and we are enwrapped in a true dream-
atmosphere, where, dream-like, nothing jars, every faculty is
excited and gratified; and the result is a delightful, unresisting
abandonment of the whole soul to the guidance of the poet,
whose amazing skill we only pause to examine at the end,
when striving to ascertain what it is that has so spelled us.
The joint operation of these two qualities has made Poe the
most original of modern poets. He struck out for himself a
path far divergent, and it has never since been followed. He
has not even an imitator. His 'Raven' is the completest
example of conscious art that has ever been exhibited. We
have already seen how everything in it is toned down to suit a
proposed climacteric effect; and we must further refer those
who wish to understand the genius of the author, to his own
astonishing account of its elaboration. Another wonderful
little poem is that entitled, 'For Annie'. This is a flight of
thinking almost superhuman, yet how lightly and easily
sustained! A still life, haunting the body after 'the fever called
living' is past, – the apparently inanimate clay, yet instinct
with a passive consciousness, like the awakening from a
trance, and visited by slight things, half memories, half new
and pleasant fancies, which never surprise: could such a
conception have entered any other brain? Who can read these
exquisitely *naive* lines, remembering that they are supposed as
written by a dead man, without a start? –

> And I lie so composedly
>   Now in my bed,
> That any beholder
>   Might fancy me dead;
> Might start at beholding me,
>   Thinking me dead.

There are other pieces, such as 'Dreamland', 'The Haunted
Palace', 'The Sleeper', 'Ulalume', which we should be
disposed to dwell on, but can only name. These have
afforded us infinite amazement at the inspired art of the poet,
mingled with a regret and melancholy, springing from their

very tone, and which have centred naturally upon his untimely fate.

A perception so refined of the essentials of art led Poe to pay particular attention to the graces both of rhythm and metre. In these respects he is unrivalled. It is no exaggeration to say, that the finest ear ever formed for rhythm was possessed by him. The full harmonious flowing, the light and exquisite poise, of his verses, are unequalled in the language. His very roughnesses have meaning; they give relief, they delight, like the daring dissonances of a skilled musician. We may instance, in particular, 'Annabel Lee', a lovely little lyric, which goes dancing along, like a light boat on a summer sea. He is singular, again, for his mastery over metres. Every metre which he uses is modified by his peculiar touch, assumes an original appearance, and is enwoven with the very nature of his theme. In this last particular, we know of no modern poet to compare with him, except Tennyson. How admirably managed are the changes, the slightly varied repetitions *da capo*, by which this effect of originality is wrought! But some of the metres in which he writes are actually original; that of the 'Raven,' for instance, is an elaborate piece of invention. It is this, more than any thing else, that stamps Poe as a great poet. How little is ever done in the way of stanzical combination! what an event is a new metre! Poe himself seems to have been astonished at it. In the paper from which we have already quoted, he roundly affirms, that 'no man for centuries has ever done, or seemed to dream of doing, an original thing in verse'. We think there is no great cause of astonishment. It is not once in centuries that an entirely new phase of human consciousness is brought to light, and requires a sheerly novel form of expression. The majority even of those who are accounted great original poets, traverse again and again the same field, make their discoveries in an old region. However they may twist the kaleidoscope, they use the same colours still. Hence, they confine themselves to metres, already sanctioned by association to their own subjects. These they vary and modify to an accordance with their own state of feeling, just as they view the same sphere of thought from different points; but it is the exhibition of a totally new metre which alone signifies a caste of mind hitherto unexpected.

The same dispassionate passionateness, the same ceaseless watch maintained by the subtle intellect over the sentient nature, the same marvellous power of analysis, cold, bright, cruel, as the Greek painter, who, in order to gain a grander ideal of agony for his Prometheus, tortured his prisoner to death, – pervade the 'Tales'. Poe's writing are like his life, – they are the result of a series of experiments upon his own nature. A continual self-production runs through them: he is a very Byron in this. Himself may be recognised in the Legrand and Dupin of his first series of tales. The singular faculty of solution possessed by them, – a faculty apparently intuitive, yet really 'the very soul and essence of method', – is a description of one of the main attributes of the author's own mind. He lets us still further into the mystery of that self-absorption, which was at once the bane and the perfection of his character, in his tale of 'The Assignation'. The hero of this tale, – that 'ill-fated and mysterious man', who, 'squandering away a life of magnificent meditation in that city of dim visions', Venice, lived apart in a 'habit of intense and continual thought, pervading even his most trivial actions, intruding upon his moments of dalliance, and interweaving itself with his very flashes of merriment, like adders which writhe from out the eyes of the grinning masks around the temple of Persepolis'; who enveloped himself in a boudoir of more than regal magnificence, the embodiment of his own fancy, where, in defiance of timid decorism, 'the chastity of Ionia was offended by antediluvian devices, and the sphynxes of Egypt outstretched upon carpets of gold', where the senses were steeped in the tremblings of an unseen music, and the mingled perfumes of 'strange convolute censers'; whose acquirements embraced the sum of human knowledge, but who took a singular pleasure in concealing them: *who to an English birth added an Italian life*; finally, who, his spirit 'writhing in fire', departed so abruptly to the 'land of real dreams', – he, we say, is no other than the poet himself. Again: perchance, at a later, darker period, is Poe personified in the pitiable hypochondriac, 'Usher': certainly that air, rather than song, 'The Haunted Palace', is the very

strain of morbid consciousness. There is a strong significance
in the invariable form of these narratives: they are related by a
second person, – a type of that psychal duality to which we
have already often alluded as the characteristic of Poe's
temperament. The whole tone and manner of the tales give
evidence of an unhealthily stimulated mind. We stand
appalled at the preternatural acumen which could construct
such an astounding succession and complication of incident,
and draw a magnetic circle of such enthralment. It is as
though a madman should lay before us in logical outline the
whole grotesque of delirium. In that peculiarly modern
species of literature, – the literature of the horrible, which
seems to be the offspring of the human craving after
preternatural excitement, driven from the belief in ghoul and
goblin, and discovering that the true horrors of man are in
himself, – Poe stands almost alone. No one is more at home
in the glooms and shadows of the inner world; no one is
more skilful in the dissection of human agony, the sensations
of nerve haunted disease, the moods in which the mind is
conquered by the fancies it has conjured up. There is in him,
to use his own words, 'a species of energetic concision',
which unfalteringly traverses the whole range of the morbidly excited mind, from its most fairy phantasies to its most
gruesome horrors.

This tendency, which renders his 'Tales' the most perfect
of their kind, exercise a fascinating, but deleterious,
influence upon his poetry. It greatly narrows his sphere: to
reverse a sentence of his editor, 'his circle, though a magic,
was a narrow, one.' We have already remarked on the
insensibility to human interests occasioned in Poe by an
exclusively aesthetic bent. He fell into 'that true hell of
genius', where art is regarded not as a means, but as an end.
His poetry derives nothing from the world of man, reflects in
no degree the agitations of society, is fraught with none of
the enthusiastic philanthropy of the age, never even implies a
moral; therefore it will never be popular. It is not meant for
universal approbation; it is a sacrifice upon the altar of taste.
Hence there is imparted to it a certain fantastic character, as
to a musical performance confined to a few notes; and this
sometimes betrays a touch of madness, a sort of mental *hysteria*.

He has written madness, – deliberate, concinnate madness, but still madness; his guarded glance, ever retorted upon himself, is terrible, like the vivid, yet serpent, glance of the madman's eye. To read these poems is to be melancholy. They are the broken fragments of a being once of unmatched glory and beauty, the scant remains of, potentially, the greatest word-artist of modern times.

It is lamentable to think of the degraded and unhappy life of such a man; but it would be criminal to omit all references to its striking moral. The lesson so often repeated in literary history, but ignored, if not denied, in the present day, is here written as it were in blood and tears; to wit, the total insufficiency of art or mental culture, be they never so complete, to rescue man from the fatal proclivity of his nature. We commend to a certain class, 'religious philosophers' of the day, – worshippers of genius and of science, – the study of Edgar Poe. From his life and writings they may gather some curious illustrations of 'the intuitive religion of the heart.'

111. Charles Baudelaire, from 'Edgar Allan Poe: His Life and Works', introduction to *Les Histoires extraordinaires*

1856

Baudelaire (1821–67) probably first became interested in Poe through reading Mme Isabelle Meunier's translations of 'The Black Cat' and 'The Murders in the Rue Morgue' in a Paris paper in 1847. Baudelaire later said that these 'fragments' aroused in him 'singular excitement' and 'incredible sympathy'. He translated 'Mesmeric Revelation' in 1848; but he did not become fully aware of Poe's symbolic importance until he read John Daniel's review essay in the *Southern Literary Messenger* in 1850. This essay became the basis of Baudelaire's own 'Edgar Allan Poe, sa vie et ses ouvrages', published in the *Revue de Paris* in 1852. By this time, Poe was a central figure in Baudelaire's imagination – a doomed, alienated artist in a materialistic society – and he began to translate his work with a missionary zeal. The first volume of *Les Histoires extraordinaires*, prefaced by a revised version of the 1852 study, appeared in 1856; other volumes followed in 1857, 1858, 1863, and 1865.

There have been several translations of Baudelaire's essay into English; the earliest, which is printed in part here, was done by the critic, Henry Curwen, and introduced a selection of the *Works of Edgar A. Poe* (London: J.C. Hotten, 1872).

Much has been written on the Poe/Baudelaire relationship; especially important are Patrick F. Quinn, *The French Face of Edgar Poe* (Carbondale, 1957), and Claude Richard, *Edgar Allan Poe, journaliste et critique* (Paris, 1978).

Unhappy Master, whom unmerciful Disaster
Followed fast, and followed faster, till his songs one burden bore –
Till the dirges of his Hope that melancholy burden bore
Of 'Never – nevermore!'
'The Raven'

I

Not long ago, there was brought before one of our tribunals a criminal whose forehead was tattooed with the singularly strange device – *Never a chance.* Thus as a book bears its title, he carried above his eyes the etiquette-law of his life, and the cross-examination proved this curious writing to be cruelly veracious. There are, in the history of literature, many

404

analogous destinies of actual damnation, – many men who bear the word *Luckless* written in mysterious characters in the sinuous folds of their foreheads. The blind angel of Expiation hovers forever around them, punishing them with rods for the edification of others. It is in vain that their lives exhibit talents, virtues or graces. Society has for them a special anathema, accusing them even of those infirmities which its own persecutions have generated. What would Hoffmann not have done to disarm Destiny? what Balzac not attempted to compel Fortune? Does there, then, exist some diabolic Providence which prepares misery from the cradle; which throws, and throws with premeditation, these spiritual and angelic natures into hostile ranks, as martyrs were once hurled into the arena? Can there, then, be holy souls destined to the sacrificial altar, compelled to march to death and glory across the very ruins of their lives? Will the nightmare of gloom eternally besiege these chosen souls? Vainly they may struggle, vainly conform themselves to the world, to its foresight, to its cunning; let them grow perfect in prudence, batten up every entry, nail down every window, against the shafts of Fate; still the Demon will enter by a key-hole; some fault will arise from the very perfection of their breastplate; some superlative quality will be the germ of their damnation:

> L'aigle, pour le briser, du haut du firmament,
> Sur leur front découvert lâchera la tortue,
> Car ils doivent périr inévitablement.[1]

Their destiny is written in their very constitution; sparkling with a sinister brilliancy in their looks and in their gestures; circulating through their arteries in every globule of their blood.

A famous author of our time has written a book[2] to prove that the poet can find a happy home neither in democratic nor aristocratic society – not a whit the more in a republic than in a monarchy, absolute or limited – and who was able peremptorily to reply to him? I bring to-day a new legend to support his theory; to-day, I add a new saint to the holy army of martyrs, for I have to write the history of one of those illustrious unfortunates, over-rich, with poetry and passion, who came after so many others, to serve in this dull world the rude apprenticeship of genius among inferior souls.

A lamentable tragedy this Life of Edgar Poe! His death a horrible unravelling of the drama, where horror is besmutched with trivialities! All the documents I have studied strengthen me in the conviction that the United States was for Poe only a vast prison through which he ran, hither and thither, with the feverish agitation of a being created to breathe in a purer world – only a wild barbarous country – barbarous and gas-lit – and that his interior life, spiritual as a poet, spiritual even as a drunkard, was but one perpetual effort to escape the influence of this anti-pathetical atmosphere. There is no more pitiless dictator than that of 'Public Opinion' in democratic societies; beseech it not for charity, indulgence, nor any elasticity whatsoever, in the application of its laws to the varied and complex cases of moral life. We might say that from the impious love of liberty has been born a new tyranny of fools – which, in its insensible ferocity, resembles the idol of Juggernaut. One biographer[3] tells us gravely, and with the best possible intention in the world, that Poe, if he had willed to regulate his genius, to apply his creative faculties in a manner more appropriate to the American soil, might have become a money-making author; another[4] – an outspoken cynic this – that beautiful as Poe's genius was, it would have been better for him to have possessed only talent, since talent can pile up a banker's balance much more readily than genius; a third,[5] a friend of the poet, a man who has edited many reviews and journals, confesses that it was difficult to employ Poe, and that he was compelled to pay him less than the others, because he wrote in a style too far removed from the vulgar. How this 'savours of the shop', as Joseph de Maistre would say.

Some have even dared more, and, uniting the dullest unintelligence of his genius to the ferocity of the hypocritical trading-class, insulted him to the uttermost, – after his untimely end, rudely hectoring his poor speechless corpse; particularly Mr Rufus Griswold, who, to quote here George Graham's vengeful saying, then 'committed an immortal infamy'. Poe, feeling, perhaps, the sinister foreboding of a sudden death, had nominated Griswold and Willis as his literary executors, to set his papers in order, to write his life and to restore his memory. The first – the *pedagogue vampire* – has defamed his friend at full length in an enormous article – wearisome and crammed with hatred – which was fixed to the posthumous edition of Poe's works; are there then no regulations in America to keep the curs out of the cemeteries?[6] Mr Willis, however, has proved, on the contrary, that kindliness and respect go hand in hand with true wit, and that charity, which is ever a moral duty, is also one of the dictates of good taste.

Talk of Poe with an American – he will, perhaps, confess his genius, perhaps even show a personal pride in it; but, with that sardonic superiority which betokens your positive man, he will tell you of the poet's disordered life; of his alcoholized breath, ready to have taken light at any candle-flame; of his vagabond habits; he will reiterate that the poet was an erratic and strange being, an orbitless planet, rolling incessantly from Baltimore to New York, from New York to Philadelphia, from Philadelphia to Boston, from Boston to Baltimore, from Baltimore to Richmond; and, if deeply moved by these preludes of a grievous history, you try to make him understand that the individual was not alone blameworthy, that it must have been difficult to write or think at ease in a country where there are a million sovereigns, a country without, strictly speaking, a metropolis, and without an aristocracy, his eyes will open fiercely, and sparkling with rage, drivel of suffering patriotism will foam to his lips and America, by his mouth, will hurl curses at its old mother, Europe, and at the philosophy of ancient days.

I repeat once more my firm conviction that Edgar Poe and his country were never upon a level. The United States is a gigantic and infantine country, not unnaturally jealous of the old continent. Proud of its material development, abnormal and almost monstrous, this new comer into history has a *naive* faith in the all-powerfulness of industry, being firmly convinced, moreover, like some unfortunates among ourselves, that it will finish by devouring the devil himself. Time and money are there held in such extraordinary esteem; material activity, exaggerated almost to the proportions of a national mania, leaves room in their minds for little that is not of the earth. Poe, who came of a good race, and who, moreover, declared the great misfortune of his country to be its lack of an aristocracy, expected, as he often argued, that in a nation without aristocracy, the worship of the beautiful would but corrupt itself, lessen and disappear; who accused his fellow-citizens, in their emphatic and costly luxury, of all the symptoms of bad taste that characterize the *parvenu*; who considered Progress, the grand idea of modern times, as the ecstasy of silly idlers, and who styled the modern perfection of the human dwelling an eyesore and a rectangular abomination; – Poe, I say, was there a singularly solitary brain. Believing only in the immutable – in the eternity of nature, he enjoyed – a cruel privilege truly in a society amorous of itself – the grand common-sense of Machiavelli, who marches before the student like a column of fire across the deserts of history. What would he have written, what have thought, if he had heard the sentimental theologian, out of love for the human race, suppress hell itself; – the rag-shop philosopher propose an insurance company to put an end to wars by the subscription of a half-penny per head; the abolition of capital punishment and orthography, those two correlative follies, and a host of sick persons writing, with the ear even close to the belly, fantastic grumblings as flatulent as the element which dictated them? If you add to this impeccable vision of the True, – an actual infirmity under certain circumstances, and exquisite delicacy of taste, revolting from everything out of exact proportion, an insatiate love for the beautiful, which had assumed the power of a morbid passion, you altogether cease to be astonished that to such a man life had become a hell, that such a life speedily arrived at an untimely end – nay, you will admire his enthusiasm for bearing with it for so long a time.

[In sections 2 and 3, Baudelaire surveys Poe's life and character sympathetically. For his factual information he draws primarily on two sources: Daniel's review and Griswold's 'Memoir'. At the end of section 3, he attempts to explain Poe's addiction to drink.]

Now, it is incontestable that, like those fugitive and striking impressions – most striking in their repetition when they have been most fugitive – which sometimes follow an exterior symptom, such as the striking of a clock, a note of music, or a forgotten perfume and which are themselves followed by an event similar to the event already known, and which occupy the same place in a chain previously revealed – like those singular periodical dreams which frequent our slumbers – there exist in drunkenness not only the entanglements of dreams, but the whole series of reasonings, which have need to reproduce themselves, of the medium which has given them birth. If the reader has followed me without repugnance, he has already divined my conclusion. I believe that, in many cases, not certainly in all, the intoxication of Poe was a mnemonic means, a method of work, a method energetic and fatal, but appropriate to his passionate nature. The poet had learned to drink as a laborious author exercises himself in filling note-books. He could not resist the desire of finding again those visions, marvellous or awful – those subtle conceptions which he had met before in a preceding tempest; they were old acquaintances which imperatively attracted him, and to renew his knowledge of them, he took a road most dangerous, but most direct. The works that give us so much pleasure to-day were, in reality, the cause of his death.

IV

Of the works of this singular genius I have very little to say; the public will soon prove what it thinks of them. It would to me be difficult, but not impossible, to unravel his method, to explain his process, especially in that part of his works whose effect principally lies in a skillfully-managed analysis. I could introduce the reader into the mystery of his fabrication, paying a special attention to that portion of American genius which caused him to rejoice over a conquered difficulty, a resolved enigma, a successful effort of strength, which urged him on to delight himself with a childish and almost perverse enjoyment in the world of probabilities and conjectures, to create *canards* to which his subtle aid gave all the appearances of reality. No one can deny that Poe was a marvellous juggler; and I know that he gave his esteem especially to another portion of his works. I have a few, and very brief, important remarks to make.

It was not by his material miracles, however they may have made his renown, that he won the admiration of thinkers, but by his love of the beautiful, by his knowledge of the harmonical conditions of beauty, by his profound and plaintive poetry, carefully wrought, nevertheless, and correct and transparent as a crystal jewel – by his admirable style, pure and strange – compact as the joints of a coat of mail – complacent and minute, and the slightest turn of which served to push his reader towards the desired end – and, above all, by the quite special genius, by that unique temperament which permitted him to paint and explain, in a manner, impeccable, entrancing, terrible, the *exception* in moral order. Diderot, to take one example of a hundred, is a blood-red author; Poe is a writer of the nerves – even something more – and the best I know.

With him every entry into a subject is attractive, without violence, like a whirlwind. His solemnity surprises the mind, and keeps it on the watch. We feel at once that something grave is at stake; and slowly, little by little, a history is unfurled the interest of which rests upon some imperceptible deviation of the intellect, upon an audacious hypothesis, upon an imprudent dose of nature in the amalgam of the faculties. The reader thralled as if by vertigo, is constrained to follow the author in his entangling deductions.

No man, I repeat, has told with greater magic the *exceptions* of human life and nature, the ardours of the curiosities of convalescence, the close of seasons charged with enervating splendours, sultry weather, humid and misty, where the south wind softens and distends the nerves, like the chords of an instrument; where the eyes are filled with tears that come not from the heart; hallucination at first giving place to doubt, soon convinced and full of reasons as a book; absurdity installing itself in the intellect, and governing it with a crushing logic; hysteria usurping the place of will, a contradiction established between the nerves and the mind, and mien out of all accord expressing grief by laughter. He analyses them where they are most fugitive; he poises the imponderable, and describes in that minute and scientific manner, whose effects are terrible, all that imaginary world which floats around the nervous man, and conducts him on to evil.

The very ardour with which he threw himself into the grotesque, out of love for the grotesque, and into the horrible, out of love for the horrible, seems to verify the sincerity of his work, and the accord of the poet with the man. I have already remarked that in many men this ardour was often the result of a vast unoccupied vital energy, sometimes of a self-promoted chastity, and also of a profound back-driven sensibility. The supernatural delight that a man can experience in watching his own blood flow – sudden, violent, useless movements, loud cries thrown into the air, without any mental will – are phenomena of the same order.

Upon the heart of this literature where the air is rarified, the mind can feel that vague anguish, that fear prompt to tears, that sickness of the heart, which dwells in places vast and strange. But the admiration is stronger; and, then, art is so great! all the accessories are there thoroughly appropriate to the characters. The silent solitude of nature, the bustling agitation of the city, are all described there, nervously and fantastically. Like our Eugene Delacroix, who has elevated his art to the height of grand poetry, Edgar Poe loves to move his figures upon a ground of green or violet, where the phosphorescence of putrefaction, and the odour of the hurricane, reveal themselves. Nature inanimate, so styled, participates of the nature of living beings, and, like it, trembles with a shiver, supernatural and galvanic. Space is fathomed by opium; for opium gives a magic tinge to all the hues, and causes every noise to vibrate with the most sonorous magnificence. Sometimes glorious visions, full of light and colour, suddenly unroll themselves in its landscape; and on the furthest horizon-line we see oriental cities and palaces, mist covered, in the distance, which the sun floods with golden showers.

The characters of Poe, or rather *the* character of Poe, the man with sharpened faculties, the man with nerves relaxed, the man whose ardent and patient will bids a defiance to difficulties, whose glance is steadfastly fixed, with the rigidness of a sword, upon objects that increase the more, the more he gazes – this man is Poe himself; and his women, all luminous and sickly, dying of a thousand unknown ills, and speaking with a voice resembling music, are still himself; or, at least, by their strange aspirations, by their knowledge, by their incurable melancholy, they participate strongly in the nature of their creator. As to his ideal woman – his *Titanide*, she reveals herself under different names, scattering in his, alas! too scanty poems, portraits, or rather modes of feeling beauty, which the temperament of the author brings together, and confounds in a unity, vague but sensible, and where, more delicately, perhaps, than elsewhere, glows that insatiable passion for the beautiful which forms his greatest claim, that is to say, the essence of all his claims, to the affection and the respect of poets.

NOTES

1 Lines from Théophile Gautier's poem 'Ténèbres'.
2 Alfred de Vigny's *Stello* (1832).
3 Philip Pendleton Cooke.
4 John Daniel.
5 N.P. Willis.
6. This well-known question seems to have been taken by Baudelaire from an essay by the English critic James Hannay, which prefaced *The Poetical Works of Edgar Allan Poe* (London, 1853).

Index

The index is divided into two parts:
I. Edgar Allan Poe: Works; II. General Index

I. EDGAR ALLAN POE: WORKS

413

II. GENERAL INDEX